# WINNER TAKES ALL

# WINNER TAKES ALL

## A SEASON IN ISRAEL

## Stephen Brook

HAMISH HAMILTON · LONDON

HAMISH HAMILTON LTD

Published by the Penguin Group
27 Wrights Lane, London w8 5TZ, England
Viking Penguin Inc., 40 West 23rd Street, New York, New York 10010, USA
Penguin Books Australia Ltd, Ringwood, Victoria, Australia
Penguin Books Canada Ltd, 2801 John Street, Markham, Ontario, Canada L3R 1B4
Penguin Books (NZ) Ltd, 182–190 Wairau Road, Auckland 10, New Zealand

Penguin Books Ltd, Registered Offices: Harmondsworth, Middlesex, England

First published 1990

Copyright © Stephen Brook, 1990

The moral right of the author has been asserted

10 9 8 7 6 5 4 3 2 1

Filmset in Bembo

Printed by Clays Ltd, St Ives plc

A CIP catalogue record for this book is available from the British Library

ISBN 0-241-12635-5

*In memory of Charlene*

# CONTENTS

# ACKNOWLEDGEMENTS

Despite the frenetic pace of Israeli life, I found the people I importuned generous and helpful, and I particularly wish to thank Amnon and Daniela Ahi-Nomi, Dr Majid Al-Hajj, Yehuda Amichai, Andy and Michal Amit, Yehuda Avni, Dan Bahat, Dan Bavly, Alex and Edna Berlyne, Yaakov Boussidan, Dr David Clayman, Dr Yoel Cohen, Judge Haim Cohn, Yael Dayan, Michael Diamond, Dr Moshe Dror, Marda Dunsky, Rachamim El-Azar, Dr Reuven Feuerstein, Benny Gil, Tamar Goldschmidt, Mickey Gurdus, Eliakim Haetzni, Misbach Halabi, Yisrael Harel, Zelda Harris, George Hintlian, Gillian Hundt, Dr Raphael Israeli, Uri Kaploun, David Kroyanker, Dr Mooli Lahad, Tommy Lapid, Linda Levine, Yigal Levine, Zvi Lovenstein, Avi Marko, Yisrael Medad, Meir and Ruth Meron, Yoram Meron, Sevanah Meryn, Susanne Milner, Fay Morris, Carol Orchover, Bill Phillips, Kamal Rayan, Daniel Rossing, Gaby Rotem, Theo and Miriam Siebenberg, Debbie Siegel, Pearl Silver, Amelia Terkel, Dr Amiel Ungar, A. B. Yehoshua, Daniel Yosef, and Michael Zukerman. I also wish to thank those few individuals, mostly Israeli Arabs, who asked me not to use their names. John Levy was immensely helpful and put me in touch with many of the people who appear in the pages that follow. Malka Ben-Yosef pushed me in fruitful cultural directions, and Debbie Ben-David was extremely generous with her time and her insight, even if she never learnt how to chuck paper into a basket from behind a desk. Adele Rothman of the World Zionist Organization unflappably translated some of my more bizarre requests into practical consequences. I am also most grateful to Kibbutz Hazorea for their prolonged hospitality. Fred Worms kindly read the manuscript and saved me from errors and inaccuracies. As always, I owe much to the support and good sense of my editor, Penny Hoare, and of my wife, Maria, who tolerated uncomplainingly my prolonged absences both in Israel and behind the screen of a word processor.

**Inset map (upper left):**

LEBANON

Akko (Acre)

Mediterranean Sea

Tiberias

Nazareth

Nablus

Tel Aviv-Yafo

Petah Tikva

Ramallah

Rehovot

Jerusalem

Hebron

Dead Sea

Gaza

Beersheva

Dimona

Yeroham

Sodom

Sede Boqer

Nitzana

Wilderness of Zin

Mitzpeh Ramon

Ramon Crater

EGYPT

JORDAN

SINAI

Yotvata

Timna

Eilat

Aqaba

**Main map:**

Tyre

Metulla

Nimrod

Mas'ada

LEBANON

Kiryat Shmona

El Rom

Quneitra

Ein Zivan

Rosh Hanikra

Shomera

Shelomi

Adamit

GOLAN

Ya'ara

Me'ona

Maalot Tarshiha

Rosh Pina

Katzrin

Nahariya

Tefen

Peqiin

Hadasha

Zefat

Lohamei Hagetaot

Karmel

Capernaum

Gamla

Akko (Acre)

Araba

Tabgha

Sea of Galilee

Ramat Magshimin

Haifa

Tiberias

Ein Gev

Mount Carmel

Nazareth

Hamat Gader

Daliyat el Karmil

Yokneam

Hazorea Valley

Yizreel Valley

Afula

Mishmar Ha-Emek

Megiddo

Zikhron Yaakov

Umm el-Fahm

Beit She'an

Caesarea

Sdot Yam

The Green Line (Pre-1967 boundary)

Hadera

Mehola

Netanya

Tulkarm

Tubas

Herlia

Nablus

River Jordan

Kalkiya

Bnei Brak

Kafr Bara

Tel Aviv-Yafo

Petah Tikva

Ramat Gan

Ben Gurion Airport

JORDAN

Ofra

Rishon Lezion

Ramla

Ramallah

El Bira

Rehovot

Jericho

Ashdod

Kefar Adumim

Ma'ale Adumim

Jerusalem

Ashkelon

Bet Shemesh

Bethlehem

Kfar Etzion

Tekoa

Kiryat Gat

Hebron

Dead Sea

Gaza

Ein Gedi

Rabat

Masada

Beersheva

Tel Arad

Arad

Ein Bokek

Ramat Havar

Neve Zohar

**ISRAEL**

0  10  20  30 km

0  10  20 mile

N

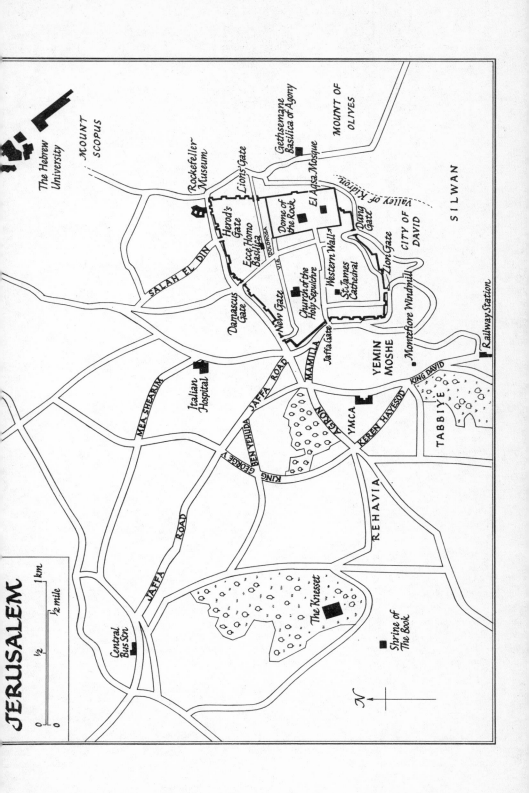

# I · NUNS AND KNIGHTS

Zionism eluded my family. Having made one wrenching transition in their lifetimes – from emotional central Europe to the reserves of England – they were, I dare say, disinclined to deracinate themselves afresh. In its purest form, Zionism holds that the fate of the Jewish people and the fulfilment of its destiny are inextricably tied to its presence in the State of Israel. To live in the diaspora and to be a Zionist are contradictory. The offspring of a family that had wandered the highways of central Europe for decades, I had no trouble accepting my status as a typical child of the diaspora. Nobody told me to feel Zionist yearnings, and I never experienced any. Despite occasional murmurings of 'You really ought to visit Israel some day', I never bothered. It was too far, I knew few people there, and my appetites and instincts were European rather than Levantine. I could live without falafel and the euphonic catastrophes of Ivrit.

No doubt a certain snobbery also underlay this disinclination. Inextricably Jewish, I nevertheless enjoyed the company of those who were not. An outsider moored alongside the multi-cabined liner of British society, I relished the absence of class-fixedness that was my lot. Feeling myself a citizen of Europe, rather than a member of a specific community or nation, I wanted the freedom to exploit that position. The prospect of immersing myself in a society almost entirely populated by other Jews held little appeal; or to be less mealy-mouthed about the whole matter, my mental picture of Israel was of a stressed and enclosed environment, a huge raucous ghetto, and every subliminal message of my upbringing had celebrated the relief of being out of the ghetto.

It was only a matter of time before my canny editor sensed a Project in this deep reluctance of mine: let me confront that unwillingness with its cause. The perversity of the idea appealed. Torn between irritation at having, after such a long disengagement, to make sense of Tel Aviv, and the challenge of writing a book about a land whose population had been doubled, it seemed, by a horde of journalists and writers far more qualified than I to understand Israel, I packed my bags.

★

For many travellers to Israel, the journey begins with a grilling by a teenage security guard at the airport. We tolerate this impertinence since we are aware of the threats Israel faces. For me the interrogation began some weeks earlier at the embassy. Although I had an appointment with the cultural attaché, the guard at the door, having checked my identification documents, insisted on asking me questions to which I could not possibly know the answer, such as 'Why do your publishers want you to write about Israel?' Our intimate chat continued for some minutes before I began to lose patience.

'I'm perfectly happy,' I said affably, 'to discuss all these matters with the cultural attaché, but I don't think I'm required to discuss my career prospects with you.'

The lanky guard smiled. 'You don't answer, I don't let you in.'

I answer.

One reason for my visit to the embassy had been to plump up my list of contacts in Israel. I produced this list to pacify the security kids at the airport, who wanted me to substantiate my claim that I was going to Israel to write a book. They seemed amazed that I had none of my own books with me, though I explained that when travelling I preferred to lug books I wanted to read rather than books I had written myself. When the security child tried to take this list off to show to her colleagues or, quite possibly, to tuck under the soft blanket of a photocopier, I objected strenuously. The list was annotated with comments such as 'Boring but helpful' or 'Pompous fool'. It took half an hour of protracted negotiation before the guards, who had been infuriatingly polite throughout, let me proceed.

I spent the night at a shabby hotel in Tel Aviv. The next morning I took the bus to Jerusalem, crossing the fertile coastal plains stitched into orchards and fields, on through the foothills overlooked by Arab villages, and up into the mountains ringing Jerusalem itself. New Jewish towns form a security necklace around the city, and gleaming housing developments with strong clear architectural lines were wrapped snowily around the commanding heights. The bus gave a hearty roar as it negotiated the last bends of the mountain highway, and plunged into the city. From the bus station I made some phone calls and found a room at one of the Christian hospices in the Old City.

Although I had maps of the city and knew where I was going, I had not yet had time to realize that geography in Jerusalem is as much political as topographical. I had to take the 27 bus to the Damascus Gate, where I would enter the Old City on foot; but I did not know that this was one of the more dangerous routes, since buses passing through Arab

East Jerusalem were frequently stoned by mischievous urchins. This particular journey was uneventful, and ended at the bus terminal a hundred yards from the gate. I asked the driver where the gate itself was and he waved vaguely, preferential treatment compared to the grunts and scowls I was usually offered by Israeli bus drivers whenever I asked for directions.

On this hot autumn morning, the street leading to the gate was an informal market, with newspaper and fruit sellers crouched on the pavements alongside their wares. Fat bunches of grapes overflowed their extemporized containers; tea vendors hunchbacked with urn and tin cups jangled through the crowds. It was perfect territory for pickpockets, but I made it without incident to the steep little plaza in front of the gate. This is the most crowded entrance to the walled city, as laden carts and human traffic negotiate the narrow twists of the lane that winds through the fortifications. When two carts meet, gridlock sets in, and the crowd must press back against the walls to let them pass.

Ten minutes later I was depositing my luggage in the cool hallway of the Ecce Homo Hospice on the Via Dolorosa itself. Although a random choice, effected by a combination of budget and ignorance, it proved a felicitous one. A lift took me up to the roof of the church to which the hospice is attached. From there, steps and walkways led to the rooms where pilgrims, mostly, were housed. The view was spectacular, with the golden Dome of the Rock outclassing the multitude of towers and minarets clustered within the walls. A bright blue sky roofed the whole scene, and in the distance, through haze, shimmered the hills of the Judean desert. One usually experiences the Old City from the ground: a maze of alleys and lanes flanked by sombre houses and the high walls of church and mosque. There is very little open space, and no such thing as a view. To see the span of the Old City, you must ascend the surrounding hills; from the Mount of Olives, one can contemplate as spectacular and moving an urban landscape as one can find anywhere in Europe or the Middle East. Now, by happy chance, I could enjoy a privileged view of the city from its very heart.

With my luggage stowed and the sweat showered off me, I set off for an unencumbered walk, making my way across the Old City along the Via Dolorosa and David Street to the Jaffa Gate. Here I left the hubbub of old Jerusalem and walked up the Jaffa Road into the commercial centre of West Jerusalem. I passed the municipal buildings, still pockmarked from the shells that hit them during the frequent battles for the city, and found myself opposite the Ministry of Tourism. In London I had been given the name of a ministry official who would, I was assured, be helpful. Although I had no appointment, I crossed the road and entered the building. It was disconcerting to find pasted to the door the following announcement:

'Due to the indifference of the management of the Ministry of Tourism to our justified and legitimate requests, we regret we cannot extend full service to our welcome guests.'

The notice offered a puzzling mixture of deference and grievance which was hard to grasp. The employees were courteous enough, and they also informed me that the official I sought was willing to see me.

Given such short notice, he told me, it was not possible to provide me with guides. I quite understand, I replied, but perhaps you could advise me about local events that it would be worth my while to attend. He thought hard, and told me I should visit the Jewish Quarter in the Old City. I told him that I was already aware of the city's major tourist attractions, and wished to be pointed in less obvious directions. He looked glumly out into the corridor and shook his head, as if to empty it conclusively of any ideas it may once have held. Since he was a deputy director of information of the ministry, I felt I deserved better than this, so I cut my losses and made a rapid and seething departure. My response might have been more temperate if I had at that stage appreciated that in Israel a civil service job is primarily a ticket to a pension, and there is no need to do excitable things such as being helpful. My official was doing no more than was expected of him: nothing.

In the afternoon I visited half a dozen hotels, seeking long-term accommodation. The cheapest and most welcoming were in East Jerusalem, but it would take further lessons in political geography, rapidly learnt, before I realized that they would not do. Although Jerusalem was reunited in 1967, there are still many ways in which the city remains divided. Modern, sprawling West Jerusalem, with its shops and pedestrian precincts, its cafés, its tall sleek hotels and leafy suburbs of low compact apartment blocks, is overwhelmingly Jewish. Before 1967 the entire Old City and the whole of East Jerusalem were under Jordanian rule and their population was Arab or Christian, sometimes both. After the reunification of the city, the ancient Jewish Quarter of the Old City was rebuilt and, as part of the security necklace around the city, some modern Jewish suburbs were built on the fringes of East Jerusalem. There are pockets of Jewish habitation in these Arab quarters, but they are very much the exception. Although the city authorities, under Mayor Teddy Kollek's enlightened leadership, have done much to unite the city culturally, politically, socially, the differences between the two halves of Jerusalem remain tangible. There is little overlap between the sophistication of Ben

Yehuda Street in West Jerusalem and the dingy cafés of the Arab village of Silwan, little more than a mile away.

The two halves of the city retain discrete infrastructures. I had arrived at the Damascus Gate at the Jewish bus station, but a hundred yards away, and unconnected, stands the Arab bus station. The two termini serve the two halves of the city. To reach the Mount of Olives, you must take the Arab bus; to visit the Knesset, you take one of the bus lines run by Egged, the Israeli national bus service. So if I were to take a spacious, comfortable, spotlessly clean room in East Jerusalem, the only way to reach downtown West Jerusalem, other than an endless succession of irregular bus rides, was by taxi or on foot. Moreover, although I was aware of the frequent strikes in the Arab quarters, I had not yet realized the extent of their impact on the life of the city.

The realization came swiftly enough when I set off in search of a meal. All the guidebooks spoke highly of the excellent food to be found in Arab restaurants, with their skewers and stuffed pigeons and trays of spicy vegetables and pans of honeyed pastries. I trudged through the often empty lanes of the Old City, occasionally saluted with the smiles and whistles of swift-footed urchins, but the Christian and Moslem quarters were silent. For the Arab city, ever since the intifada began, shuts down at lunchtime. Within minutes, streets that had been resounding to the cries of vendors and the rattle of carts are emptied of shoppers, and heavy iron shutters trundle down over the shop fronts. The Moslem Quarter, once thronged, is now traversed only by stray cats and by children practising shots at goal. Most of the Arab restaurants to which Arab and Jew alike had flocked a year earlier had now gone for good. Some days the leadership of the intifada would call a total strike, and then the shops didn't open at all and the buses didn't run. (During one of my moves from hostel to hotel, I found myself waiting for half an hour at an Arab bus stop, unaware that there was a strike that day. There were few pedestrians in this part of town, but eventually a Chasid walked by, improbably sporting an I LOVE ISRAEL badge. I asked him if there was a strike on. In an American accent he replied, 'I don't keep up with Arab bus strikes,' but immediately offered to help carry my bags. I said I would stay put for a while longer. He then asked me my name and said he would pray for me. His prayers went unanswered. No bus came.)

So I had no choice but to make the uphill hike into West Jerusalem. Here there were restaurants aplenty, but a glance at the menus posted in the windows made the heart sink. On King David Street, the Ramses Oriental restaurant offered as its first courses: Squash, Ognon, Cabbage, Wine Leaves, which could be followed with Stwed Meat. The Primavera

Italian restaurant offered specialities such as goose breast stuffed with shrimps, which seemed to lack gustatory harmony. Nor did the spelling *Pitzayola* inspire confidence. For such delicacies, the customer must pay through the nose. Israelis earn about half as much as their European counterparts, yet their restaurants are often twice as expensive. Even my cat's favourite brand of tinned food costs three times more in Israel than in England. It took me a few days, but eventually I learnt to have recourse, as most Israelis do, to street food: pizza and falafel and shwarma.

Having failed to find either long-term accommodation or an affordable meal, I returned through eerily deserted streets to the Ecce Homo. The Dutch and Canadian clerics who comprised most of its clientele had retired to bed early, and I had the rooftop to myself. I contemplated the silent towers and domes within the ancient Turkish walls, then went to bed. While waiting for sleep to slip through the night towards me, I reflected on the full day I had just experienced. Perhaps the whole assignment was an act of folly. Writing a book about Israel, it seemed, was not unlike restoring an ancient manuscript. One could fill in a few missing words, fix the punctuation, chuck in a footnote, but the text itself had long been written. We scribes, to give our redecoration of the text authenticity, would seek out the great luminaries – the novelist Amos Oz, Mayor Kollek, and a few dozen other Israelis of equal renown – who would graciously give the required interview. When I complained to the journalist Alex Berlyne that there was a circuit of celebrities which all writers about Israel were expected to follow, he sighed sympathetically: 'Yes, it's like the Stations of the Cross.'

I fell asleep. And woke, at four, to the sound of the call to prayer. For the Via Dolorosa crosses the Moslem Quarter, and the hospice is surrounded by mosques. Whether there really was a muezzin yelling from the top of a minaret I do not know, but I suspect my sleep was broken by a loudly amplified tape operated by a time switch. After twenty minutes, the wailing ceased, but by then I was wide awake.

I breakfasted with two Brazilians and a gaggle of beaming Canadian nuns. An Englishwoman working at the hospice placed her cup of tea alongside those of the nuns, and gave them a potted history of Israel, most of which she got wrong. The hospices, I came to realize, were a world apart. In East Jerusalem, the Anglicans have recreated a corner of Somerset around St George's Cathedral, and the benches of its tranquil gardens are occupied by broad-hipped English ladies with white hair reading uplifting tracts and romantic novels. Strikes, petrol bombs, stone-throwing, all these routine hazards of life in Arab Jerusalem, simply pass them by. They are visiting the Holy Land, not Israel.

After breakfast I moved to new lodgings, the St Andrew's Hospice, a cheerful place run by the Church of Scotland and its ladies. It occupies a small hilltop just the other side of the Hinnom Valley, a gully that separates the Old City from the suburbs of South Jerusalem. With the Scottish flag flapping from its robust tower, St Andrew's is a landmark. Within its walls, all is orderly, with a brisk friendliness that is firmly Scottish. The inmates were less clerical than at Ecce Homo, and pious Scots were outnumbered by German and English tourists and the occasional United Nations officer escaping for a day or two from the tormenting heat of the Sinai Desert. St Andrew's was comfortable and peaceful – no muezzins in this part of town – but too pricy for a long-term stay, so after a few days I moved into the Jerusalem hotel of my choice, the Knights Palace.

Opposite the municipal buildings on the edge of West Jerusalem lies the New Gate into the Old City, and a minute's walk through this Christian Arab quarter brings one to the stone grandeur of the Knights Palace. Located just behind the Latin Patriarchate, it was founded a century ago as a monastery or retreat house. Its broad stone-flagged corridors were lit by chandeliers, and deeply recessed doors gave entrance to rooms that were far from luxurious but tranquil and well insulated. I obtained the only room with a balcony, and this overlooked the small garden of the Patriarchate. Less than a hundred yards away were the crenellated Ottoman walls, beyond which rose the ridge on which the King David Hotel was situated. This is not an especially ancient part of the Old City. Although the streets in other parts of the city date from Crusader times or even earlier, until a century ago the Christian Quarter was a huge cereal market. This area was only developed in the late nineteenth century, when European organizations, keen to establish a presence in the Old City, bought land here.

Small groups of Belgian or Dutch tourists stopped over for three-day visits, and a backpacking couple or two made brief stops, but often I felt I was the only knight in the palace, even though the rooms were exceptionally cheap and the staff friendly. In the early afternoon a hot but bearable sun would wash over my narrow balcony, where I would bury my nose in the *Jerusalem Post* for half an hour or so. In the cool of the evening, nuns in heavy pale grey habits would emerge from their cells to water the gardens below. Across the alley, a few nondescript cubes of houses were inhabited by large and sometimes noisy Arab families. After dusk floodlights would illumine the landmarks on the horizon: the King David Hotel, Montefiore's windmill, and the tower of St Andrew's. Sounds were few but mostly congenial: the clack of footsteps in the alleys, the bark of a dog, the lustful wail of a cat, the chatter of a gardener, and, occasionally, to wreck the tranquillity, the grinding of a helicopter passing overhead.

Some months later, on returning to Jerusalem, I made my way back to the Knights Palace to reserve again that balconied room where I had been so content. But the main door was bolted shut, and entering the corridors of the hotel through a side door I found workmen wielding drills and the air full of dust. The Knights Palace had closed for good, driven out of business by the rigour of the intifada. At that moment the West Bank was in the grip of a seventy-two-hour strike; the week before, an Israeli soldier, off duty and on his way to pray at the Western Wall, had been knifed to death at the Zion Gate, one of the entrances to the Old City regarded as 'safe'. Pilgrims were still coming to Jerusalem, but not tourists. The hotel had been acquired by the Latin Patriarchate, which was remodelling the interior for its own mysterious purposes.

Rome, it has been remarked, is like a palimpsest, with fragments of its layered past peeking unexpectedly through the erasures. The same has to be true of Jerusalem, which has known the extended visitations of Jew and Roman, Crusader and Ottoman, Briton and then, making a very special return appearance, Jew. Just beyond the walls of the Old City lie the tumbled remains of King David's City and the tomb, according to legend but not to architectural history, of Absalom; within the walls are some of the holiest sites of three religions. Here are streets where Christ walked and excruciatingly died, while a few rocks away Mohammed ascended to his heaven. No one knows for sure where the Holy of Holies of the Jewish Temple was situated, but it would be no cause for amazement if the Holy of Holies and the precious Moslem site were one and the same. Jerusalem, inevitably, must be shared among religions often deficient at practising the charity they preach. Religious Jews are forbidden to approach the holy Moslem places on the Temple Mount lest they inadvertently encroach on the Holy of Holies. Moslems are hypersensitive to any archaeological exploration that comes too close to their holy sites. And the numerous Christian denominations that guard the church of the Holy Sepulchre are forever squabbling; some of the more trivial disputes are now five centuries old and no closer to resolution.

Jerusalem, jealously guarded by an excess of priests, can be tiresome as well as inspiring. Claims of piety and holiness are not reinforced by the screeching embittered tones in which such claims are often made. If I often felt inclined to lambast the self-importance of religious propagandists and sentimentalists of all the faiths with a stake in the city, I was not unmoved by Jerusalem, and the aspect that moved me most was the one to which I initially felt the greatest resistance: the rebirth of Jerusalem as a Jewish city.

When the Second Temple was destroyed by the Romans, Jerusalem lost its physical centrality to the Jewish people, and acquired instead an even more potent force as a repository of all the yearnings of a dispossessed and dispersed nation. Jews continued to live in the Holy Land up to the time of the British Mandate, yet theirs was not a significant presence, except during those medieval times when famed rabbis established synagogues and colleges in the holy cities. Throughout the nineteenth century, Jerusalem, not to mention less visited towns of the Holy Land, was notorious for its backwardness and grubbiness. Turkish rule was not especially harsh, but neither was it enlightened. Nor did the Jewish residents of Jerusalem seem too distressed by the squalor in which they lived. The growth of tourism necessitated improvements in hygiene and facilities, but still travellers returned with deeply unfavourable reports of the city.

Zionism brought a larger Jewish population to Jerusalem, but they competed then, as now, with a heady assortment of Moslems and Christians. The War of Independence in 1948 marked the end of any Jewish presence in the Old City, and the Jews retreated behind a no man's land into what is now West Jerusalem. The Six Day War reversed the situation. The Israelis annexed East Jerusalem and thus reunited the city. 67,000 Jerusalemite Arabs were embraced by their enemy. Whatever the grumblings from international bodies about the illegality of Israel's annexation – which was, of course, neither more nor less illegal than the annexation of these same acres by Jordan since 1948 – the Israelis did at least return control of the major religious sites to the appropriate religious bodies. Under Jordanian rule it had been impossible for Israeli Jews to visit the Western Wall, but now access to holy sites, of whatever religion, was granted to all.

After 1948 Jewish Jerusalem made a fairly swift adjustment to its relative confinement. A resident who has lived in the city for fifty years told me that, when the city was divided, he and many others were scarcely conscious of the division.

'All we saw was a concrete wall and sandbags. Psychologically we blocked out the Old City. If you wanted to see it you had to climb to the top of the King David Hotel. There were some gaps in the border. Mount Scopus, which is now in East Jerusalem, remained part of Israel, though until 1967 it was an island surrounded by the Jordanians. Our soldiers were sent there in armoured cars for two-week tours of duty.

Anomalies occurred because the border was drawn up according to where soldiers happened to be at a particular time.

'Before 1967 Jerusalem was a bohemian university town. The religious kept to themselves, and so did the intellectuals. It was not unlike Edinburgh, I've always imagined. Few tourists came here in those days. Jerusalem was a dead end. Once you had arrived, all you could do was turn around and go back the way you had come. It was a small provincial town, but an open one. Now it's no longer so small, and perhaps no longer so open. I remember when there were 100,000 people living here. Now there are four times that number, yet it's still provincial.'

A Danish nun, Sister Abraham, recalls the years of division as ones of confusion and complication. There were two administrations to be dealt with, and two currencies. Although Israelis were not permitted to cross into Jordan, Christians were, but only once a year and only after completing a huge amount of paperwork. 'I could spend Christmas at Bethlehem or Easter at Holy Sepulchre, but not both.'

When the Jews surveyed their former quarter in the Old City after the Six Day War, they found it in ruins. Of the almost thirty synagogues located there before 1948 none survived. Moslem religious authorities are not slow to accuse the Israelis of encroaching on their holy sites whenever archaeologists bring out their buckets and spades, but the Jordanian desecration of Jewish sites, such as the cemeteries on the Mount of Olives, between 1948 and 1967 was destructive in the extreme.[1] Since the Israelis had no intention of relinquishing the Old City after the war, they promptly decided to rebuild it. The government put together a planning team to oversee the design and execution of new construction.

Over the next few years new houses rose from the rubble. Although the rebuilt Jewish Quarter mostly respects the ancient street plan, the new houses are not built in a pastiche style, but are modern houses discreetly designed to blend in with traditional Jerusalem architecture. During the early years of the British Mandate Sir Ronald Storrs passed a bylaw stating that all new construction in the city had to be built of or faced with the dressed, natural Jerusalem stone, and this edict remains in force. Thus the new Jewish Quarter is built of the same gleaming straw-coloured stone as the rest of the city. There are some large buildings that seem, at first glance, to be out of scale – especially the new yeshivot (seminaries) – but there has always been space within the Old City for monumental as well as domestic architecture. There were fears that the revitalized quarter could become appropriated by religious Jews, but the authorities made a deliberate attempt to mix the Jewish population. However, since the restrictions of life in the Old City are less irksome to religious than secular people, many of the secular residents have moved out.

The reconstruction allowed certain amenities to be provided: squares and shops and cafés tucked into odd corners. The planning was superior to anything found in other quarters of the Old City, creating the politically hazardous impression that preference was being given to Jewish residents. The sleek elegant alleys and plazas of the Jewish Quarter are in stark contrast to the often grubby streets of the Moslem districts. The city authorities have come up with various plans for improving the quality of life in the Moslem Quarter, but they have been met with suspicion and resentment. When in the early 1970s proposals were floated to move some of the population from the desperately overcrowded Moslem Quarter to newly built modern accommodation outside the city walls, this was interpreted as an attempt to move Moslems en masse from the Old City. The improvements undertaken in the Moslem quarters have had to be piecemeal: the Damascus Gate approach was redesigned and electricity and running water were brought to many houses for the first time.

One consequence of the reconstruction of the Jewish Quarter was the discovery of archaeological remains of the first importance. If you start digging anywhere in Jerusalem or its environs, chances are that you will uncover ancient pots, the foundations of a Herodian house, Jewish candelabra, Roman weapons or Mamluk inscriptions. The planners decided to give precedence to the revelations of the past. When those laying the foundations of a huge new yeshiva discovered an entire network of Herodian palaces occupying the same site, they were required to raise the foundations of the yeshiva to leave the precious archaeological site exposed; it is now one of the major tourist attractions of the Old City. There are half a dozen such examples within the tight confines of the Jewish Quarter. Other sites could be exposed without the need for such compromises: old Byzantine streets and churches now at a subterranean level.

'I'm the Jerusalem man,' says Dan Bahat. His office at the Rockefeller Museum resembles a storeroom, packed with a few hundred boxes and crates and glass cabinets stuffed with shards and pots. Bahat, an expert on Crusader Jerusalem, is a flamboyant figure, with a large bushy moustache; his slightly supercilious manner is moderated by a carefully employed wit and charm. 'It's not easy. I have to be a diplomat as well as an archaeologist, as almost all the ancient sites here are shrines of one kind or another. Before any excavations, however minor, can proceed, I have to negotiate with patriarchs or mullahs or bishops. I accept this, as I don't want to disturb the fabric of the city any more than they do. In fact our main battle is not to persuade people to let us dig, but to stop other people from digging. We've been at it nonstop since 1967 and it's time to slow down. All excavations have to be authorized by a committee of three government ministers: for religious affairs, for culture, and for justice. It's a very wise form of control. The only problem is that the committee hasn't actually met since 1948. So I have to use my discretion, and I'm ready to take some stick when things go wrong. I often reach private agreements with the religious authorities which have to be kept secret to protect them. So being the fall guy is part of my job. Essentially, my job is to go out in the rain without getting wet.'

It's known that a tunnel runs along the northern end of the Western Wall, beyond the arcaded area that adjoins the plaza that faces the Wall. It could date from Maccabean times or even from the time of the First Temple. Bahat is convinced that if the site were to be excavated it could become the third most important tourist attraction in Jerusalem after the Temple Mount and the church of the Holy Sepulchre. But excavations begun in 1981 were opposed by the Moslem authorities fearful of giving the Jews underground access to the Temple Mount. It was, in Bahat's view, a fuss about nothing, but it put a halt to excavations, and the Moslem authorities sealed part of the tunnel with a concrete wall.

His powers are considerable. If developers want to build over or near a significant site, permission to build is given only on condition that, if appropriate, they first finance a salvage dig. Any development in Jerusalem is a risky undertaking, for if a major discovery is made, the development will either not be allowed to proceed or will have to be expensively modified. Bahat also sees his role as educational and he spends much of his time dealing with the public, responding to inquiries and running seminars. Public interest in archaeology, which constitutes a direct link with the past, is avid. A dig in London may reveal exciting Roman remains, but a dig in Jerusalem may reveal Jewish remains, psychological as well as physical evidence that the return of the Jews to the Holy Land is a return to their past. The Israeli state seal and coinage employ motifs taken from archaeological finds, welding together past and present. It is no accident that the Dead Sea Scrolls have been preserved in the *Shrine* of the Book, for, as Amos Elon has pointed out, they are regarded by many Israelis as virtual title deeds to the Land of Israel.

I asked Bahat whether there were any other great discoveries waiting to be made in Jerusalem.

'I have no doubt about it,' he replied. 'The best is yet to come. But I shan't speculate on where or what. There's an old Jewish saying that since the Temple was destroyed, the gift of prophecy has only been given to children and to the stupid.'

Bahat also failed to prophesy that a few months after we met he would be fired as Jerusalem's district archaeologist, only to resurface as archaeological adviser to the ministry of religious affairs. He has resumed work on the tunnel and the other subterranean excavations close to the Temple Mount. Soon, he hopes, the tunnel, exposing some of the most ancient foundations of this most ancient city, will be open to the public and as a national rather than as a religious site.

# 2 · SOUK AND WALL

Archaeology in Jerusalem is more than the uncovering of lost civilizations. For the links between past and present give such discoveries a special poignancy. The novelist A. B. Yehoshua has written: 'However much it is built, Jerusalem will always be marked by the memory of its destruction.'[1] In A.D. 70 the Jewish revolt against Roman rule was crushed by the troops of Emperor Titus after a long siege that ended with the destruction of the city and its Jewish Temple. Throughout the centuries that followed, no Jew has been allowed to forget this violent dispossession, and this explains the exuberant reaction of Jews, secular as well as religious, when the Old City fell into Israeli hands in 1967. After an unbelievably long wait, a rupture had been repaired, a continuity restored.

Theo Siebenberg, a Belgian businessman and ardent Zionist, had made a sufficiently large fortune by his late thirties to enable him to retire to Israel. He now lives in a spacious and luxurious house in the Old City. A slightly built and gentle man, his conversation gives little clue to the obsession that has dominated his last twenty years. He recalled for me the early days of the city's reunification.

'I remember how Jews from all the different communities came pouring into the Old City, many of them carrying scrolls and chanting and singing. I climbed up to this very spot, with its marvellous view, and said to my wife how wonderful it would be if we could live here, only a hundred metres away from the Temple Mount. Eventually the municipality decided to build 650 units in the Jewish Quarter. Just as we were being told that the list was closed, a cancellation came through, so I put my name down after all, not thinking for a moment that anything would come of it. We didn't even go and look at the site. To our surprise, we were offered it, and it turned out to be the very spot we had admired in 1967. We built this house and moved here in 1970. I knew from historical sources that this spot had been bare hillside ever since the destruction of Jerusalem. So that meant we were building our house exactly 1,900 years after its predecessor had been destroyed.'

He had wanted to excavate beneath the house, but was discouraged by the archaeological authorities; there was no reason to suppose that anything of major interest lay beneath the rubble, and the cost of excavating a hillside site was prohibitive. He went ahead anyway. To prevent landslides it proved necessary to build a retaining wall some 100 feet long, anchored to the bedrock 40 feet down. This little operation, together with the actual excavations, cost Theo Siebenberg three million dollars and took seventeen years to complete. The narrow lanes of the Old City made it impossible to use modern earth-moving equipment, so everything had to be done by hand. Buckets of earth and rubble were hauled up on pulleys, sifted, then taken out of the Old City by donkey.

He was unable to explain why he had been driven to scrabble so exhaustively beneath his house. 'I just knew I would have been miserable if I hadn't made this move to Jerusalem, and once here, digging to uncover the past was something I just had to do. The archaeologists told me I was wasting my time, but it seemed clear to me that we had to be close to if not directly above part of a Hasmonean palace.' He found a huge water cistern, probably Byzantine from the sixth century, Jewish ritual baths, ancient but disused burial chambers, and the remains of houses. The scale of the excavations, which may be visited as the Sieben-bergs have created a small museum around them, remain impressive, though the archaeologists were right in maintaining that nothing of amazing importance would be unearthed here. Siebenberg admits that his efforts, if not excessive, were, indeed, 'immense'.

'I had to hire a dozen consultants. I never knew there were so many kinds. I had one for wiring, another for acoustics, another for the foundations, and the problem was that they didn't always agree among themselves. Once I was woken in the middle of the night by a call from one of our engineers, who lived in Tel Aviv. He was so worried about the strength of a wall we had put up that he couldn't sleep. We were living right above it, and *he* couldn't sleep. Then some of our neighbours got together to obtain the rights to the areas we had excavated beneath their houses, though of course we had obtained official consent before doing so. The space was only useful for storage purposes, but they went to court anyway. We won, as the court decided that they had only bought apartments and not the title to the area beneath their houses.'

Other archaeological discoveries since 1967 have proved far more astonishing, if less heroic, than the Siebenbergs'. At the so-called Burnt House diggers found a stone inscribed with the name Bar Kathros, which is mentioned in the Babylonian Talmud as the name of a priestly family of Jerusalem; here too was found a skeletal arm reaching for a spear, emblematic of a last, thwarted protest against the Roman onslaught. Less poignant but physically more spectacular are the remains of the Herodian quarter that sprawl beneath the foundations of the Yeshiva Hakotel. A complex of ritual baths and pools is ornamented with elaborate stonework and vaulting and mosaic floors. Indeed, an adjoining group of mansions contains the earliest known mosaic floor in Jerusalem. Also found here was the first known depiction of the *menorah*, the Jewish ritual candelabrum, predating the more celebrated carving on Titus's Arch in Rome. Around the walls of the excavated rooms are vestiges of early interior decoration such as frescoes and stucco panelling. More indications of the high style of the long extinct inhabitants is given by the lovely lathe-turned stone vessels and trays and tables discovered here. Charred beams tell their own story of the violence with which this stretch of Jewish civilization came to an end. On leaving the site, it proved possible, with a little discreet peering and staring, to look into the basement classroom of a nearby yeshiva, where I saw a bearded rabbi expounding to about twenty pupils. After 1,900 muted years, the exposition of sacred texts goes on as before.

As secular families began moving to more convenient if less romantic accommodation in other parts of the city, the religious Jews consolidated their presence in the Jewish Quarter. Theo Siebenberg recalls seeing one of his neighbours, a young woman, wheeling through the district a baby that never seemed to age. When, years later, they were invited to lunch with the woman and her family, they realized that over the years she had given birth to twelve babies, keeping her pushchair constantly supplied with fresh infant. The six hundred families living in the Jewish Quarter are supplemented by yeshiva students, many from America and other diaspora countries. I had visited yeshivot in New York and London, gloomy chambers walled with shelves buckling under the weight of Talmudic folios, furnished with long tables and chairs that never matched. Although the Jewish Quarter's yeshivot are modern and smart, their occupants exhibit the same knack for creating a tatty mess. To study, to dispute, to learn, and to transmit learning, you don't need a ballroom. Inside the Shehebar Sephardi centre I watched half a dozen scraggily bearded young men in black homburgs arguing vociferously over their open books, while at the next table another student was fast asleep, his resting head barricaded by the tomes and a dozen empty glasses of tea.

Most Jews restrict their presence within the Old City to the Jewish Quarter. But not all. A number of zealots, secular as well as religious, have insisted on living within the Moslem Quarter, on the grounds that at various times over the course of the last century, Jews did inhabit it, albeit sparsely. Nevertheless, Jewish settlement here is regarded by many Jews as well as Arabs as needlessly aggressive. For it is highly unlikely that Israel will ever return reunified Jerusalem to Arab control. The Jews, therefore, are in *de facto* control of Jerusalem and there is no need to promote Jewish settlement throughout the Old City in order to press the point home.

As you walk down from the Damascus Gate into the heart of the Moslem Quarter on the way to the *souk*, you pass under a broad archway that burrows beneath a house. Adorned with a seven-foot-high *menorah* with electric lights, this is the home of Ariel Sharon, the most belligerently right-wing of government ministers. In December 1987 he organized a little house-warming party. As a result of disturbances in East Jerusalem not unrelated to Mr Sharon's imminent celebrations, no fewer than three hundred policemen patrolled the alleys around the minister's new home. Other prominent right-wingers, including the prime minister himself, Yitzhak Shamir, attended the party, signalling their approval of Sharon's pioneering attempt to 'Judaize' the Old City in defiance of the widely held view that its various neighbourhoods should be left as they are.[2]

The following day the disturbances in Arab Jerusalem worsened. Sharon sweetly declared that all he was trying to do was improve security for the handful of Jewish residents of the Moslem Quarter, something that nobody, least of all Mayor Kollek, who had been working hard to improve relations between Jew and Arab in Jerusalem, had asked of him. Moreover, the cost of improving security for Jewish visitors and residents now included an increased security provision for Sharon himself, and the *Jerusalem Post*[3] estimated the cost of guarding the minister at well over half a million dollars. Opposition politicians as well as Moslem leaders expressed their outrage over Sharon's cavalier colonization, and their indignation might have been greater had they known that Sharon, while purportedly guarding the rights of Jews in the Moslem Quarter, would never take up proper residence at his 'home', thus reducing his purchase to the status of provocative gesture.

A couple of days later there were riots in the streets of East Jerusalem; shops were shuttered, fires were set, tear gas ballooned over the streets. The intifada had begun.

Jews continued to move into the Moslem Quarter but the numbers are insignificant, no more than twenty-five families and three hundred yeshiva students. Some are religious extremists awaiting the coming of the Messiah and preparing themselves for the day of their return to the Temple Mount. Apart from Mr Sharon's *menorah*, the only outward indications of a Jewish presence are *mezuzot* on the doorposts and one or two Israeli flags flapping high above the lanes. One quiet afternoon, I took a walk through the Moslem Quarter to inspect the lovely monuments left by the Mamluks, who ruled the Holy Land after the Crusaders had gone but before the Ottomans took control. Their legacy includes some of the most graceful Islamic architecture in Israel; many beautiful fifteenth-century fountains, inscribed with flowing calligraphic inscriptions in Arabic, are slowly crumbling away in various parts of the Moslem Quarter. There is a particularly fine group of buildings close to the Iron Gate, one of the entrances to the Temple Mount, and I wandered down a dead-end alley near the gate to look at the Small Wall, a section of the retaining wall of the Mount isolated from the more celebrated Western Wall. I was approached by an Orthodox Jew in a grey suit and dark blue hat. His emergent beard wispily straggled across his chin and cheeks. Judging from his accent, he came from South Africa, and the beard from Israel.

'Do you know what you are looking at?' Patronizing words but a friendly lilt to the voice. Glancing over my shoulder at my guidebook, he patiently replaced the scholarly exposition given therein with one of his own. I did not care greatly either way. I asked him what he was doing so far from the Jewish Quarter, and he explained that many Jews were now moving back into the Moslem Quarter. The previous phase of habitation had ended after the riots here of 1936. 'Jews come here to pray on Shabbat, though no Jews live in the houses overlooking this wall. You see that top window up there that's been bricked up?' I did indeed. 'That's because there was a terrorist cell there.'

'How do you get on with the Arabs around here?' I asked.

'We live together as neighbours. Both sides wish the other weren't there, but they are, and so we have to get along as best we can.' It was candid, perhaps inadvertently so, of him to admit that the Jews who had settled in the Moslem Quarter wished that they had the place to themselves. 'In some of these courtyards you'll find Jews and Arabs living side by side, though mostly we have our own enclaves.'

When he offered to take me on a tour of the quarter, I accepted. He showed me formerly Jewish houses from which *mezuzot* had been removed, leaving diagonal indentations against the doorposts. He took me to a doorway and told me to peer through at the vaulted dome within. I was about to enter the shabby courtyard when my guide restrained me. 'That's not a good idea. This is what's left of the Reissin Synagogue, but the house is owned by an Arab family, and they are demolishing the synagogue stone by stone. Every time I come by there is less and less of it left. We should turn round here. These people are not too fond of Jews.'

The authorities, he explained, did nothing about such vandalism because they did not want to upset the status quo. My young guide left me at the foot of some steep steps that scuttled up the side of a house. There was nothing to differentiate these uneven steps from countless others in the Old City, but he urged me to climb them, then wished me good day and vanished.

The steps led to a series of little rooftop terraces linked by walkways and steps. Through unshaded windows I could see small groups of ultra-Orthodox Jews, droopy with sidelocks and black gaberdine coats. They gave me a glance but then resumed their prayers. The South African had taken me to the Kolel Galicia, a community established here in 1830, and then re-established in 1982. One of the little terraces led directly onto the roofs of the *souk*, the covered Arab markets. Once on the roofs it was easy to walk the length of the *souk*. Up here a whole other section of the Old City thrives under the rays of the Jerusalem sun. Some families have improvised a playground with swings and tyres, which children share with a dozen cats. At the far end of the *souk*, steps lead down from the roofs to the renovated alleys of the Jewish Quarter. Perched on a rooftop wall I could see the ugly tower of the Lutheran church, the domes of mosques and sepulchres, old tenements in one direction and smart butterscotch-yellow houses in the other, and pencil-thin minarets topped with Islamic crescents.

The Old City is a jumble, but it is a balanced jumble. The holiest site in Christendom coexists with sites equally precious to two other religions. Within twisting boundaries drawn up over many centuries, Armenians and Jews, Greek Orthodox and 20,000 Moslems, patriarchs and traders, urchins and pilgrims, do manage to live side by side. This crazy concatenation, this constant fancy dress party in the streets, this absurd rivalry of the supposedly spiritual, makes Jerusalem unique. So it seems all the more deplorable that men and women of influence, sheiks as well as Sharons, are willing, for the sake of a needless psychological victory, to upset the equilibrium. If Jews can oust Arabs on grounds of historical precedence, then the Greek Orthodox can oust the Jews in turn, on the basis that the Byzantines once owned the entire Old City. Far better to stop all the jockeying for position, and to continue to live side by side in a state of truce, if not of harmony. When it comes to the behaviour of the ultra-religious, one has to keep one's expectations low.

The opportunity to rebuild the former Jewish Quarter was a relatively minor aspect of the Israeli excitement at the reunification of the Old City. A far more significant liberation was the opening to Jewish prayer of the

Western Wall. These immense blocks of masonry are not a relic of the Second or any other Jewish Temple, but a massive fragment of the retaining wall of the Temple Mount. For pious Jews it is the closest approach they may make to the holy site. For twenty years it had been impossible for Israelis to approach the Wall, but after 1967 it became accessible to all. Its loss, and subsequent gain, invested the Wall with a symbolic power exceeding its religious significance. It has been co-opted by the state as a symbol of Jewish resilience. Army inductions and other ceremonies take place in front of the Wall, and in the one over-brutal planning decision of the reconstruction of the Jewish Quarter, a large plaza has been cleared facing the Wall to accommodate immense crowds, whether of tourists disgorged from coaches parked just outside the city gates or of patriotic Israelis attending a flag-flying ceremony.

By eight in the morning, long before most tourists have finished their breakfast, prayers are under way at the Wall. Regular worshippers tend to be the ultra-Orthodox, mostly Chasidim in their black coats and beards, but they do not, indeed cannot, monopolize the place. Young men in military fatigues approach the Wall briskly, swaying back and forth as they say their prayers, finding nothing incongruous about having a submachine gun slung over their shoulder. American Jews on their annual trip to Israel pay homage to the Wall even if they do not bow and pray before it. Tourists laden with the black bricks of video cameras mingle with the worshippers; they are identifiable by the stiff cardboard *kippot* (skullcaps) they have been given to wear by the guardians of the Wall. On one occasion I saw a Franciscan friar in brown robe and knotted belt and sandalled feet, and he too had a cardboard *kippa* over his tonsure. This is Jerusalem, and such sights are too common to attract attention.

But now, at breakfast time, almost all the men at the Wall are Orthodox, while on the other side of the shoulder-height partition at right angles to the Wall, a very few Orthodox women, their heads wrapped in kerchiefs, say their own prayers. If sabras have a burly vigour, sustained by a Mediterranean climate and easy access to orange juice and fattening foods, the same cannot be said for the ultra-Orthodox, who rarely see daylight. Teenage Chasidim suffer from ploughed complexions, the consequence of poor diet, constant enclosure, sexual repression, and, perhaps, a distrust of rude good health as too animal in nature. The men were *davening*, swaying back and forth, and as they did so their *payot*, sidelocks, swung wildly like the rope of a church bell out of control. Some were seated facing the Wall on simple chairs (donated by a Brooklyn family), rising whenever the liturgy required; others leaned over velvet-covered reading desks. Many men were laying *tefillin*, the small boxes containing prayers on parchment that are strapped to arm and head as part of the ritual of morning prayer. The ubiquitous black jackets and coats were slipped off the shoulder to allow sleeves to be rolled up before laying the *tefillin*; black homburgs were tipped back further than usual for the same reason. The rationale of the ritual is that the commands of the Torah, tucked into the two boxes, should influence both thought (head) and deeds (arm). Or, as the ardently outgoing Chasidic group known as the Lubavitchers like to put it, laying *tefillin* is like plugging in to the Divine mains.

I am perfectly happy to let a few dozen religious enthusiasts strap themselves into a state of worship, but I have no wish to join them. But I knew that to wander among *tefillin*-wearing Chasidim near the Wall is to invite propositions that could be hard to shake off. However, the alternative was to shrink away, intimidated before the intimidation had begun, so I strolled boldly up to the Wall, where I studied the slips of paper, on which special prayers and supplications had been scribbled, tucked between the cracks of the rough masonry. I was soon approached by an elderly Chasid.

'Two minutes!' he cried. 'Only two minutes, for *tefillin*.' His English was feeble and he spoke mostly in Yiddish, but I could follow the gist of what he was saying. I replied that I didn't want to. He was prepared for that, of course, and clutched my arm, saying repeatedly that it was a big *mitzvah*, a word that carries two meanings simultaneously: a religious obligation and a kind of brownie point earned by fulfilling that obligation. I shook my head.

'Will make you very happy, very happy.' He beamed and clutched.

'On the contrary,' I replied, beaming in turn, 'it will make *you* very happy.' This, I immediately realized, was a flawed riposte, since such a doubling of pleasure could only consolidate the *mitzvah*. I scurried off to the vaulted section adjoining the Wall, but he was waiting for me when I emerged a few minutes later. This time he had brought reinforcements in the form of a younger, taller Chasid, who piled on the verbal pressure while the old man grabbed my arm with his claw. He began with subtlety, affecting polite chitchat, where was I from, had I been to Stamford Hill, he had, and so forth. And what did I do for a living?

'I'm a writer,' I replied, hoping that this would win me respite if not respect from the People of the Book.

'Writer,' he repeated with marked scorn, since presumably the only writers he had time for were either long dead or the authors of Talmudic commentaries. 'Writer, don't be too clever. Why are you a Jew?'

Here we go, I thought, as he played his first big card: the Piling On of the Guilt.

'Because my mother was Jewish. And my father.'

'And why is your father Jewish?'

'Because his mother was Jewish.' I smiled. We could keep this up all the way back to the Patriarchs.

'No,' he declaimed. 'You are a Jew because for thousands of years we have kept *mitzvot*' – he obviously hadn't met my family – 'with nothing changing. Jews and goyim, we stay separate. You are a Jew first, then a writer. Don't be too clever. *Tefillin* takes only two minutes. If you say no, then in twenty, thirty years you will remember this day and say how foolish you were not to make this *mitzvah*.'

Yeh, yeh, but I'd kept the straps at bay for forty years and wasn't about to succumb now to a fit of ancestral sentimentality, and I began to move away. But the two practised Chasidim blocked my path. I asked them to let me pass, but they kept up a counterpoint of bilingual haranguing. I then told them that if they wouldn't leave me alone and respect my wish not to do as they wished, I would have to leave the area and they could then have the satisfaction of knowing they had forced a Jew to retreat from the Wall. Self-righteous, I know, but I was in urgent need of a torrent of words, and these carried sufficient indignation to melt a path.

On my next visit to the Wall the Chasidim were thinly represented but the Oriental Jews were there in force. It was one of the weekdays when barmitzvahs take place at the Wall. Men and boys in *tefillin* and *tallit* (prayer shawls) were parading in and out of the vaulted area where religious texts and the Scrolls of the Law are stored, while women in lacy headscarves were leaning over the partition. The women went wild with excitement as their menfolk passed back and forth, and they flung bonbons at the barmitzvah boy and ululated at almost bat-like pitch. One woman reached out her hands as if yearning to touch the scrolls, and then pressed her hands fervently to her forehead. Four or five barmitzvahs were taking place simultaneously. At one desk two men held their *tallit* aloft to provide a canopy to shield both reader and scrolls from the heat of the sun. One boy, having completed the recitation of his portion of the Torah from the scrolls, was being carried on the shoulders of a bearded relative, while his mother and aunts shrieked ecstatically from the sidelines. Other relatives viewed the occasion through whirring video cameras. Not far from the Wall, five men were seated in a row; in the centre a swarthy grey-bearded rabbi wearing a tall bowler smiled benignly. Behind the five men a rugby team of hefty Oriental Jews led the boisterous singing of traditional celebratory songs. Small boys took it in turns to crouch at the feet of the rabbi and his cohorts while they were photographed and videoed.

It was impossible not to be caught up in the infectious joyfulness of the scene. In most European or American synagogues, barmitzvahs are starchy affairs, at which the boy must perform this rite of passage into manhood by chanting his portion in front of an audience of congregants, family, and friends. The boy, especially if he is tone-deaf or stumbles nervously over his portion and has to be prompted by the rabbi standing alongside, can have a miserable time of it, while parents and relatives stifle their embarrassment beneath their smiles. Here at the Wall, the noise level was so high that the occasional error could be corrected with a shrug; the boy's recitation was egged on by father and uncles clustered behind him; his performance was being greeted with yells and whoops and ululations, not the tearful smiles of mothers breathless with relief that Jonathan hadn't done any worse than neighbouring Simon the week before. The boys here at the Wall clearly came from traditional families, casually or ardently observant, but familiar to the core with the rites and prayers of Judaism. For such boys the barmitzvah ceremony would hold no special terrors, and thus the atmosphere at the Wall was relaxed and joyful. Not even the fact that the barmitzvahs were taking place in front of an audience of camera-clicking tourists cramped their style.

On Friday afternoons, as Shabbat draws near, hundreds of Jews make their way to the Wall to greet the Sabbath. The Chasidim put away their workday garb of black gaberdine, and don long loose-fitting black or chocolate-and-caramel-striped silk coats tied at the waist with a sash. The ungainly homburgs are replaced by immense fur hats, some broad, some tall, each variation in style a clue to the sect to which the wearer belongs. White *kippot* are worn beneath their headgear in honour of the Sabbath. Close to the vaults a skinny young man, wearing a thin blue and yellow pinstripe coat, was so intent on his prayers that in the course of an hour he paused only to cough and spit. His spiritual health was clearly not shared by his body. Two Ethiopian Jews in uniform, Uzis over their shoulders, made their way to the Wall to pray for ten minutes, then left. As dusk fell, bands of youths, many in bright knit sweaters, came lurching en masse through the gates and crossed the plaza. They sang lusty Shabbat songs as they approached the Wall. These young men were modern Orthodox, which means that they were observant Jews but did not share the backward-looking ideas that led Chasidim to shun the modern world, its dress, its learning and its mores.

The Sabbath had begun. As the sun set, an autumn chill descended. I walked out of the Old City through the Dung Gate and took the road that leads back to the Hinnom Valley. As the sky darkened, the colours of the city began to change: the stone buildings lost their usual tone of the froth on cappuccino coffee, while in the near distance the boxy little houses of Silwan began to twinkle with tiny domestic lights. Not that the Wall closes down at night. It remains floodlit and there is always a sprinkling of worshippers. I went there quite late one night and sat on a chair close to the partition. It was a balmy night, and it felt peaceful alongside the heavy stones with their fissures of shadow. Near me stood a few men, motionless and rapt, their hands outstretched to touch the Wall, while from the women's section I could hear sobs, supplications. Freud, in a letter to Einstein, once referred to 'the misguided piety that makes a national religion from a piece of the wall of Herod'.[4] I sympathized with this view, but now for the first time I felt moved, as though by this inadvertent eavesdropping I was being incorporated within private acts of prayer as Jews let their thoughts and desires roam back and forth through the millennia of their history. Through the gap in the fence I could see the women moving back from the Wall, and a moment later the men did the same. Only then did I notice that they were all Japanese. There are Japanese Jews, but not many, so the probability is that they were tourists. Do Japanese tourists come to the Wall late at night and weep for the destruction of Zion? The confusion persisted as another emblem of the complexity of this passionate city. I had come here to throw some meagre light on Jerusalem, but when I left, its mysteries were both intact and compounded.

Jewish friends in Jerusalem seemed slightly puzzled, almost offended, that I chose to stay in the Old City, even though the Knights Palace was only a hundred yards from Jaffa Road. Despite all the rational explanations I gave them — it was cheap, it was quiet, I had a balcony — some of them nevertheless felt it as a slight betrayal. I shrugged off the implication: Jerusalem was one city, its propagandists were insisting, and I was determined to treat it as such. Still, dismantled frontiers leave a kind of scar tissue. It was well known that some taxi drivers refused fares to the American Colony, the loveliest hotel in the city, on any combination of the following grounds: that it was in East Jerusalem, that it was the favoured haunt of Western journalists who by reporting the intifada were damaging Israel's image, that it was patronized by PLO officials. To many Jewish Jerusalemites, habits of mind acquired or inherited from the years before 1967 persisted: the Jewish Quarter apart, the Old City was becoming increasingly alien territory, mysterious at best, hostile at worst. Since Mr Sharon's housewarming and the outbreak of the intifada, tensions had risen: there had been incidents, stabbings, muggings, and it was asking for trouble to walk through parts of the Old City, especially the remote corners of the Moslem Quarter, alone at night. Similar cautions apply to most cities, and I refused to be intimidated. Yet I never failed to jump with fright whenever an empty plastic bag rustled loudly in the evening breeze on a deserted street, for the sound replicated exactly the swish of clothing as a ruffian leaps from a dark doorway. But I learnt my way around, came to recognize and avoid the culs-de-sac, and stuck, when the streets were deserted, to the major thoroughfares.

After some weeks I thought I knew the Old City, but its delights and surprises are well concealed. One afternoon a friend took me to the Coptic Khan, one of the handful of *khans*, or hostels, in Jerusalem. This one dates from the last century, and is not of particular interest, but from the roof of a nearby building, reached up one of those anonymous staircases it is impossible to identify with certainty on an unaccompanied return visit, is the most extraordinary view of Hezekiah's Pool. One of many cisterns within the Old City, Hezekiah's Pool is one of the most ancient — dating from the time of the Second Temple — and must surely be the largest. Once a reservoir, it is now, sad to report, a rubbish dump, a deplorably unimaginative abdication of a splendid theatrical crater.

In the mornings, when the *souk* was bustling, the Moslem Quarter was irresistible. It was so full of life, so exasperating, so crammed with odours and sounds. One morning I stood on the steps leading towards the Coptic monastery and the roof of Holy Sepulchre and watched as a milling crowd in the street below gradually crushed itself to a standstill. While the tourists, revelling in the townscape, were trying to postcard it with their cameras, carts were immobilized and tea vendors were coming to a jangling halt beside them. Bedouin women built like tumuli moved in slow swathes down the lane, while children slid like wraiths between them. A man carrying trays of eggs on his head swerved and weaved until he too found himself too wedged to proceed. Greek Orthodox monks in black stoically reconciled themselves to the patient give and take that would unfasten the gridlock and allow the opposing waves of humanity to go on their way.

Within the *souks* were the spice stalls, the lanes of butchers, and the alleys of cloth merchants and gold dealers; smoke from shwarma stands perfumed the air with aromas of meat and oil. Antiquities are offered for sale, though Dan Bahat had warned me that pilferage is common at archaeological sites and that many items on sale in the city have been stolen. Others are fakes, and the certificates of authenticity flapping from items for sale in these shops were worthless. The sounds of the *souk* included those of the most bitter arguments. I once saw a stallholder, incoherent with rage, abuse an elderly Arab in a tatty beige suit who appeared to be drunk; his wrath rose to ever more improbable heights as he spat repeatedly into the face of the old man as they exchanged insults but not blows. I was once accosted, without menace, by a Bedouin woman in a brightly embroidered gown. She gabbled at me, and I understood not a word. She persisted, pointing the while at some bundles on the ground. I tried to lift the bundles onto the folded cloth on the top of her head, but they proved too heavy for me, so I enlisted the aid of a passing Arab and between us we hoisted the bulging bundles onto her head.

The Moslem and Christian quarters are overwhelmingly Arab, but trade remains trade, and alongside the piles of *keffiyeh*, the headdresses disparagingly referred to as tea towels, are stacks of knitted *kippot*, tiles painted with the legend 'Shalom Y'All' and stupid T-shirts with slogans dimly insulting to a whole range of ethnic and religious groups. 'I Got Stoned on the West Bank', accompanied with a crude drawing of a spaced-out kid, was a choice example. The *souk* flows out beyond the Damascus Gate, and wares are spread out along the shallow steps of the plaza leading up to the Nablus Road. Here you can buy a bizarre assortment of goods: Mars Bars that must have liquefied in the sun, fresh loaves wrapped in filmy pink plastic bags, newspapers, cassettes, soft drinks, clothes in varied shades of brown, and an item called Tummy Stretchers, of which there was an over-supply in Jerusalem that autumn, as hundreds of unsold boxes remained piled up in the markets. At the Arab bus station a hundred yards away, the noise was tremendous. It can't quite match the cacophony of an Indian bus station, but it comes close. Bus drivers lean on their horns to induce the drivers of the inter-urban taxi limousines known as *sheruts* to cease obstructing the exit; mounted police trot back and forth in case of trouble; a few shrivelled beggars huddle against the wall, hands out, mouths agape; moneychangers with wads of Jordanian dinars and shekels hoarsely compete with each other. And on every corner there is a falafel stand, with balls of mushed chickpea bouncing in trays of boiling fat.

The traffic around the perimeter becomes even worse on Friday mornings, when the Bedouin drive into town from all over the West Bank to attend the sheep market at the north-east corner. Flat-bed trucks wedge themselves into the small space, sheep and goats are herded into gibbering huddles, and human beings have to sidle between these various obstacles in order to pursue their negotiations. The market is too authentic to have become a true tourist attraction. Bedouin with rotted teeth yelling at each other about sheep prices exert a limited appeal to camera-wielding Europeans, especially as it is hard to avoid an occasional slither into droppings. Nor is the smell the sweetest: a bouquet of dirty wool and goat breath. I watched the conclusion of a transaction, as the happy purchaser flung bemused sheep onto the back of his truck and roared off towards the Jericho road. A lad holding a sheep in his arms yelled ineffectually after him, but it was too late, and so when the driver got back to his village with his new acquisitions, he will have found that he had been inadvertently short-changed. For many of the Bedouin at the market, business seemed an incidental part of an essentially social occasion. Men in *keffiyeh* stood around smoking and chatting, while their wives, statuesque in splendidly embroidered gowns, took up demure positions on the edges. A fat idiot boy wandered round, approaching the men from time to time with requests, I assumed, for coins or cigarettes; he was pushed away roughly and tottered through the mud to the next group.

Just inside the principal gates are the booths of the moneychangers. During my first stay in Jerusalem I achieved a businesslike rapport with a changer near the Jaffa Gate. The rates were not always that much better than at the banks, but the advantages were twofold: no bank commission, and, just as important, no hours spent queuing in an Israeli bank. Because Ibrahim knew me, we didn't have to waste time with too much preliminary haggling; we soon agreed on a fair rate, and that was that. On my second visit, I returned to Ibrahim, but he brazenly insisted on offering me a rate lower than the official one. Perhaps he didn't recognize me, but he wouldn't budge. So I walked out. Scampering feet followed me down the alley, fingers touched my shoulder, and by the time we had finished negotiating the rate had risen from 3 NIS (New Israeli Shekels) to 3.20, a significant improvement. I was in no rush that morning and told Ibrahim I might be back later. I went to the Damascus Gate, where I was offered 3.15. So I drifted back to the Jaffa Gate and entered Ibrahim's booth.

'OK, let's do business,' I said briskly. '3.20.'

Ibrahim laughed. He looked at me with pity and scorn. No way, he said. 3.20 was a preposterous rate. He'd have to close up shop forever if he so much as considered it.

'So why did you tell me an hour ago you'd give me 3.20?'

'To get you to come back to my shop.'

'But you didn't mean it?'

'No, of course not.'

So we began negotiations all over again. This time we started at 3.10, and after the usual back and forth of shrugs, dismissive laughs, shakes of the head, and moves towards the door, the rate crept up to 3.12.

'I can get 3.15 at the Damascus Gate,' I reminded him.

Ibrahim looked at me sternly. 'There were two killings today at the Damascus Gate.'

'Rubbish. I was there ten minutes ago, and if there'd been killings I'd have noticed something.'

'It was just now,' Ibrahim assured me. 'I heard it on the radio.'

By this time he knew that his ploy had not worked. We both grinned and knew we were coming down the home stretch. If I returned to the Damascus Gate, I calculated, I might well find that the 3.15 had shrunk, just like Ibrahim's 3.20, so we shook on 3.12.

His ploy was at least plausible. Had he said a stabbing or two, I might have believed him, but two killings was heavy stuff, even for the Damascus Gate. You only have to look at the clusters of Israeli soldiers patrolling the *souk* near the gate and peering down from the ramparts to know that this is a trouble-spot. One morning, walking up from the *souk* to the gate, I found the soldiers closing it. Perhaps there had been an incident, perhaps some stone-throwing on the Nablus Road. I slipped up the alleys that weave close to the wall until I reached the next gate to the east, Herod's Gate, but this too had been closed, and the crowd, mostly Arab with a sprinkling of tourists, was considerable. After a few minutes the gate was opened and, after passing through, I walked back to the Damascus Gate. Here I discovered that the crowd outside the gate had assumed there had been an incident inside the walls, which I knew not to be the case. So it never became clear why the gates had been shut. I sat on the steps of the plaza to enjoy the scene as hundreds of people from both sides of the gate surged towards each other and ground to a total halt.

There is something medieval about the juxtaposition of monumental splendour with domestic squalor. It's a common enough sight in Asia, where great gaudy temples cast their shadow over the most abject slums. In the Old City too, when one approaches the Temple Mount through the lanes of the Moslem Quarter, one has to make a sudden adjustment from the shabbiness of the district to the radiant spaciousness of the Mount. Two great mosques dominate this immense stone platform: the Dome of the Rock, and the more prosaic El-Aqsa mosque. The former is surrounded by flights of steps and airy arcades, open-air pulpits and study rooms and fountains. This is liberating after the often claustrophobic constriction of the lanes. The Moslem architects needed space in which to show off the splendour of their constructions, and they got it.

The Dome of the Rock is an octagonal structure completed in 691. It was originally faced with mosaics, but these were replaced in the sixteenth century, during the reign of Suleiman the Magnificent, with glazed tiles from Turkey. Recessed from the octagon is a similarly ornamented drum, topped with an immense cupola covered with gilded aluminium, a restoration commanded by King Hussein of Jordan. Perhaps the Turkish tiles, so vividly blue, are a trifle garish, but it is impossible to be critical of the mosque's interior, which is breathtaking both in the sheer ambition of its design and in the perfection of its execution. The drum is decorated with rich gold and green mosaics on the grandest scale, while the dome is ornamented with sinuous arabesques that diminish in size yet grow more intricate in design as they swirl up to the very top. The windows are filled with coloured glass of ravishing quality; similar windows now in the Islamic Museum within the compound show that the stone 'leading' of the windows is cut so as to tilt the entering light downwards onto the chamber below.

A rough rock of great size formed the pretext for this gorgeous outpouring of craftsmanship. It was here, says Jewish lore, that the sacrifice of Isaac almost took place, and here too stood the Holy of Holies. To Moslems, the rock is the very one from which Mohammed ascended to heaven, although the Koran does not mention Jerusalem by name, so speculation has played its part in Islamic tradition too. He certainly would have had a good view, for just as there is a marvellous view from the Mount of Olives down onto the Dome of the Rock, so the view is reciprocated from the Temple Mount. Unfortunately, the Mount of Olives ought to be renamed Mount Intercontinental in honour of the large modern hotel that sprawls across its summit. From the El-Burak steps one can take advantage of the trees planted nearby to blot out the distracting hotel, allowing the eye to linger on the olive groves, the church towers and domes, the Jewish cemeteries and the walled convent gardens. Between the El-Burak steps and the Gate of Mercy is a peaceful shady walk usually ignored by tourists, who tend to move hurriedly from mosque to mosque. On the other side of the seventh-century gate, which looks fascinating but is closed to visitors, is a large Moslem cemetery, a cunning piece of religious oneupmanship. According to Jewish tradition, the Messiah will return to Jerusalem from this direction; by carpeting the whole area with graves, the Moslems have effectively blocked off this route, and the Messiah will have to think again. I doubt that this will cause a major holdup in the schedule of the Second Coming.

The whole northern part of the Temple Mount is remarkably restful. Planted with cypress and olive trees, it offers shade to dozing Arabs. Along the northern arcades are ranges of buildings, some of which contain Islamic schools, so there is a constant sound of childish babble and fizz, refreshing after the solemnities of the mosques. At the opposite end of the compound is the El-Aqsa mosque, which is more of an everyday place of worship than the resplendent Dome of the Rock. Although badly damaged by fire a few years ago, its interior is most attractive, with rich carpets overlapping on the floor and a lovely blue and gold ceiling. An immensely long hall, it's a good place for a promenade out of the sun. Pious Moslems sit against the many pillars poring over Islamic texts, while other pious Moslems take an undisturbed nap. Because of the frequency of services, the mosque is often closed to visitors for an hour at a time, and tourists must keep out.

Seated on a stone bench not far from the entrance, I heard a guide explaining, quite correctly, as she pointed at a fountain: 'This is where men wash their hands and feet before entering the mosque.' One of her charges then asked a question, inaudible to me, to which she replied with saintly patience: 'No, these are Moslems.' A few minutes later, an American couple wearily deposited themselves on an adjoining bench. She mopped her brow, and asked her husband: 'Is this the Rock of the Dome?' 'No,' he replied testily, as they both gazed at El-Aqsa, 'this is the Dome of the Rock.'

# 3 · THE CHURCH PETULANT

Of course one should never poke fun at religion, but sometimes the temptation is too strong. Spiritual ecstasy is not my strongest suit, I admit, but I can think of few places with lower spiritual voltage than Jerusalem. It is a most wonderful city, but because of its magnificent tensions and contradictions, not on account of its alleged spirituality. Every conflict that puckers the surface of Israel – and I can think of a few hundred or so – is magnified in Jerusalem. One gets used to seeing grown men and women standing on the street screaming at each other, while no one pays the slightest attention. Riotous Moslems after Friday prayers have pelted Jews at the Wall with stones from the height of the Temple Mount; Orthodox Jews hurl chairs at non-Orthodox Jewish women holding their own services at the Wall while the Israeli police twiddle their thumbs; most of the Christian denominations represented in Jerusalem, thirty-two at the last count, are barely on speaking terms with each other.

As a child visiting Rome and as a teenager visiting the Shrine of Guadalupe in Mexico, I've seen pious women shuffling on their knees tearfully and painfully towards the object of their devotion. Now that's my idea of a pilgrim. In Jerusalem, pilgrims are people wearing identical green hats and little badges with their name and the logo of Houston Evangelical Tours Inc or some other such organization. Led by their pastor, they wander down the Via Dolorosa from station of the cross to station of the cross, pausing from time to time to mutter a prayer or sing hymns while fending off Arab postcard sellers. That archaeological research has proved that Christ's last journey must have taken place in the opposite corner of the city is an irrelevance to the pilgrims.

The terminus of their pilgrimage is the church of the Holy Sepulchre, which must be the most confusing church in Christendom. This is fitting, because the architectural chaos of the building accurately reflects the ecclesiastical chaos within and without. It was worse in the sixteenth century, when eight different groups shared the church, but the harshness of Ottoman taxation reduced their number to three. With different Christian denominations claiming exclusive guardianship of various parts of the church, partition walls were built, altars blocked, tunnels built, grottos converted. In the south aisle three arcades are slapped up against each other; pillars rise and go nowhere. Only the façade and rotunda of the church have real grandeur and a semblance of uniformity. The services of different rites are conducted simultaneously. In one Greek Orthodox section boyish acolytes assisted by laymen were chanting loudly and coarsely as priests dispensed the wafers, while a few yards away in a Catholic corner an angelic boys' choir was tweeting away.

As you enter the church it is hard not to trip over the Stone of Unction, a cracked marble slab on which the body of Christ was laid. Mount some steps, and you come to the hill of Golgotha where the crucifixion took place. Well, that's what the Empress Helena, mother of the Emperor Constantine, decided. She took a stroll here in 324 and identified, among other sites, the very spot where Christ had been buried and rose from the dead. Thus the traditional identifications are certainly ancient, and how exact they are seems of secondary importance, or indeed of no importance at all. The spot identified as the sepulchre has been a pilgrimage site since the second century, which is some kind of evidence in its favour, though far from conclusive. But the pilgrims are evidently convinced, and they are the people who count. At the Stone of Unction I watched a kneeling nun kiss the slab, run her hands over its moistened surface and rub her face. On Golgotha, pilgrims queue up to crawl under the low altar covering the spot where the Cross stood in order to kiss the silver roundel that marks the place. Beneath the rotunda there is usually a queue waiting to enter the sepulchre itself. Once inside the gloomy little tomb, there is scarcely time to marvel at it before pressure from those behind requires you to turn about and leave. Although no charge is made for visiting these holy spots, each is guarded by a priest of the appropriate denomination; I was not importuned by any of them, but other visitors clearly were. I heard an American tourist emerging from the sepulchre muttering, 'They spoil everything,' a reference to a hustling priest who had made it clear that he expected bills, not small change.

In the ecclesiastical power play that has been going on every day for about 1,500 years in Jerusalem, the Greek Orthodox are widely regarded as top dog. They certainly put on a good show at Holy Sepulchre. At four one afternoon there was a tremendous clanging of bells to announce a procession of some forty Orthodox monks. They proved to be the advance guard of the patriarch himself, an imposing, fat, white-bearded man who kept up a crisp waddle as medallions suspended from chains swung across the acreage of his chest. Following him were a hundred nuns, swathed in uncompromising black. The banging and crashing of the bells continued long after the religious swung out of the precincts on their way to the patriarchate, and so deep were the reverberations of bell and clapper that my very bones seemed to vibrate. It was a winning combination of the Grail bells from *Parsifal* and the hammerings of the Nibelungen. While all this was going on outside the church, the Franciscans were processing inside it, holding candles and censers as they chanted their way round the ambulatory, pausing at various altars and making a raid into St Helena's Chapel, even though Franciscans have no jurisdiction there.

The Orthodox and the Catholics are the big players, while at the bottom of the heap are the poor old Ethiopians. The Ethiopians' great rivals, the Copts, have managed to get their hands on an altar and about a square metre of floor within Holy Sepulchre, but the Ethiopians are confined to two chapels on two floors in an adjacent building. They have become a kind of tourist attraction. I watched a party of Italian tourists arrange themselves and their knitware along the wall of the chapel as a disconsolate grey-caftaned priest recited from an illuminated manuscript in the liturgical language of Ge'ez for their entertainment. Prompted by their tour leader, the Italians gave a rousing 'Amen' as he mumbled to a halt, and some of them were moved to drop a few shekels onto a plate.

The Ethiopians deserve better, for they have been in Jerusalem since the fourth century. They came as pilgrims and some stayed on, leading the life of ascetics. During the Middle Ages the regular infusion of fresh monks to sustain the community was diminished both by Moslem conquests in Africa that isolated the church, and by an Islamic *jihad* in 1520. Ottoman taxation of non-Moslems in Jerusalem hit the Ethiopians hard, and for 160 years they were supported financially by the Armenians. The numbers of Ethiopian monks and nuns in the city varied from a handful to about a hundred. Their centuries of abject poverty came to an end in the late nineteenth century, when the Ethiopian emperors chipped in and even contributed a new church in West Jerusalem. Outside the city there are six other settlements, including a monastery in Jericho and a house in Bethlehem occupied by a single nun. Today the Ethiopian religious community in the Holy Land numbers some seventy souls.

My only contact with the Ethiopian Church was through a nun, Sister Abraham. I had expected to meet a wizened old stick wrapped in grey, but the woman who welcomed me to her convent parlour was a stocky Danish woman in her late fifties, dressed in black with a tight-fitting white cap over her head and ears. Born as Kirsten Pedersen, she had converted to Catholicism at thirteen and had spent eleven years as a member of a closed order. While still a nun, she studied at university and, during a spell in the Holy Land, became fascinated by the Ethiopian Church. For ten years she lived in the archbishop's residence here and pursued her studies, publishing books about the community. She found research extremely difficult, as the Ethiopian Church keeps no records of baptisms or size of congregations, and its instincts are immensely secretive.

Since 1980 Sister Abraham has lived as a hermit in the garden of the Benedictine convent on the Mount of Olives. The anchorites I encountered at Walsingham in the 1960s had all gone off their heads; one of them, now dead, founded the art of streaking. Sister Abraham was, in contrast, as down to earth as it is possible to be. She joins the Benedictine nuns for Mass each morning, but takes care of all her own needs, such as food and clothing. She supports herself by teaching, and is concluding a thesis on Ethiopian exegesis. Of the fifteen tongues at her command, the Ethiopian language, Amharic, is, she told me, the most difficult. She is, characteristically, self-taught. At my request she rapidly listed the other languages she speaks: they include Latin, Greek, Hebrew, Arabic, Coptic, Syriac, Swedish, English, and Italian.

Although an extremely devout woman, she had no false respect for the institutional churches with which she has contact. She deplores their secretiveness, which stems from ignorance. Unable to understand why scholars wish to inspect certain archival materials, they find it simpler to deny permission. Moreover, interdenominational rivalry encourages them to be wary about releasing any information that could conceivably be used against them, even if it relates to events of a thousand years ago. Even the church to which she has dedicated decades of scholarly endeavour is distrustful of her. 'There are elements within the church that are very conservative, especially when it comes to education. Hardly anybody speaks English, and Ethiopian nuns are even discouraged from taking up activities such as nursing, which means they end up as kitchen slaves. There is not even an Ethiopian school here, .and the children of the community go to Israeli or Anglican schools.'

I only met this remarkable woman once, but a few months later I heard discouraging reports. Conservative forces within the Ethiopian Church were gaining the ascendancy, and she was being regarded with increasing suspicion, based, wretchedly, on envy. So instead of cherishing her, they are making her life even more difficult. Perhaps hostility towards their house scholar relieves their state of depression, for I have rarely encountered a more introverted group than the Ethiopian monks at Holy Sepulchre. I watched them at vespers, these ash-faced figures in black surplices and caps leaning on tall sticks; they chanted their rich and ancient liturgy in a breathless monotone for fifteen minutes, then filed out and returned to their cells. If they are a miserable bunch, who can blame them? The munificence of the Ethiopian emperors had ended by the mid-1970s with the deposition of Haile Selassie. Even the Syrian Orthodox, another impoverished denomination, is better off, since it has access to some funds from North America. The Ethiopians can only survive with the help of charitable contributions and ever tighter belts.

In the Middle Ages they had no fewer than four chapels in Holy Sepulchre. Now they have none, and since 1532 have lived in tiny green-doored cells on the roof of the Chapel of St Helena. Even here they have no security of tenure, since the Copts claim the space as their own and regard the Ethiopians as interlopers. This ecclesiastical dispute has been trotted through the Turkish, British, and Jordanian courts, but has never been settled, since there is no documentation on either side. This, then, is the pattern of life in Jerusalem and within the precincts of the holiest shrine in Christendom, where, if the wrong broom sweeps a chapel in Holy Sepulchre, all hell breaks loose.

The Armenians, in Jerusalem at any rate, have a happier story to tell. Armenia became Christian in 301, and founded a church in Jerusalem in the following century. Indeed, parts of the Cathedral of St James date from that period. An inventive people, they had their own alphabet by 406 and by the seventh century were using squinches – small arches at the corners of a square chamber – to support the domes of their churches, centuries before European architects thought of the device. In Jerusalem they claim to have introduced printing to the city, and an Armenian bishop doubled as the city's first photographer. Unlike the Ethiopians, the Armenians, a far larger community, sustain a whole network of institutions within the Armenian Quarter in the south-west corner of the Old City, just west of the Jewish Quarter. Most of the quarter is walled; access is guarded and the gates close at ten at night. Purposeful tourists can manage to visit the quarter, but more casual visitors are usually turned away, except from public buildings such as the cathedral and the museum. The Armenians operate two schools, one lay and the other a seminary; the languages of instruction are Armenian, English, Hebrew, and Arabic, so Armenian children grow up speaking all four. I visited the community's printing shop, where an eighty-two-year-old man has been setting type by hand for over sixty years. There are two libraries, one public, the other a manuscript library housing documents dating back a thousand years. In the public library I saw dozens of Armenian periodicals published in cities as disparate as Venice, Vienna, Paris, and Beirut, as well as journals from various parts of North America. It seemed an astonishing output for a community that numbers only seven million worldwide. As others have pointed out, there are parallels between the Armenians and the Jews. Both are small in number yet highly sophisticated; both have suffered from periods of genocide, and both have been forced into a diaspora.

The cathedral is approached across a small square hemmed in by the ancient buildings of the patriarchate. Embedded in their walls and in those of the cathedral's façade are Armenian crosses, each of a different design, which were donated by pilgrims from the twelfth to the fifteenth century. Next to the church entrance is a suspended plank that used to be beaten with a wooden hammer to call the faithful to prayer, since it was forbidden to ring church bells in the Old City until 1840. The whole cathedral is carpeted, and lit by hundreds of hanging lamps, some of which exhibit exquisite filigree work. Chapel doors are beautifully panelled with ivory, tortoise-shell, and mother of pearl. A large chapel, which formed the narthex of the cathedral until 1660, contains brightly coloured picture tiles that date from 1720 and lamps that are 200 years older. A few times I attended the main liturgy, which takes place at three on Friday afternoons. The cathedral uses a double choir, divided between two chapels; servers and choristers don pale green surplices with pink bands top and bottom, while the priests wear pixie-ish black hoods over embroidered green copes. Armenian schoolgirls in scarlet dresses sat demurely on the floor, filling the width of the nave and listening to the ceremonious liturgy, with its incessant bowing and censer-swinging and very determined chanting.

For more routine services, the community uses the twelfth-century Church of the House of Annas within the compound. When I last visited the church the piers were being stripped, revealing beneath the paint and plaster some ancient pilgrims' crosses. This church is not usually accessible to visitors, and neither is the cathedral refectory, with its 400-year-old carved stone tables. Of the eighty monks who make up the Order of St James, sixty serve in other countries, so the religious community in Jerusalem is fairly small. Their cells are reached through a maze of tiny courtyards and corridors, some enclosed, others open to the sky.

On a far grander scale is the Patriarchate Hall, built in the 1850s. Its exterior presents a neoclassical façade – a rarity in Jerusalem – forming a bridge across Armenian Quarter Road. But the interior could be a ceremonial hall anywhere in central Europe, an impression reinforced by the portraits of Kaiser Franz Josef and his wife Elisabeth, Queen Victoria,

George V, and other crowned heads. The visitors' book here begins with the flourish of Herbert Samuel in 1920, takes in the penmanship of Rudyard Kipling in 1929, and reaches its social apogee with the signature of the Queen of Belgium.

Just outside the Zion Gate, on the slopes of Mount Zion, are a number of cemeteries, including the Armenian one, where the custodian insisted on showing me round. He set off down the path rattling off information, most of which I could not follow. The words came out in no particular order. Pointing to a well, he declaimed: 'Look here down forty-three metres water.' Then we rushed over to a chapel wall: 'Here look mosaic Byzantine fourteen century very old.' I asked him questions, but received no answers, as though he were rationed in his words. Instead he raced ahead, leading me up onto the roof. 'This house of Caiaphas.' Caiaphas should have been in touch with his insurance company, for the house was in dire condition, as were many other buildings clustered at the end of the cemetery, thanks to damage inflicted by Israeli and Jordanian artillery. Many seventeenth-century tiles in the courtyard where the bishops are buried have been shattered. Our tour completed, I leant against the gate post for a minute to catch my breath before the ritual dip into the pocket.

Proud of their ancient culture, inured to suffering by the Turkish massacres of 1915 and the terrible earthquake of 1988, buoyed by their internationalism, the Armenians in Jerusalem exude confidence. As a community, they give the impression of being self-sustaining. Relations are good between Armenians and Israelis. As an Armenian friend put it, 'They leave us alone. After all, Judaism is not aggressive towards Christianity in the way that Islam can be.'

Yet there is a small blot on the escutcheon. At the entrance to the compound is a communal noticeboard, where an announcement reminds the community that a certain Armenian archbishop has been excommunicated and is, together with a few other clerics, forbidden to enter the quarter. I asked my friend why this was so. He muttered something about the archbishop having been 'too worldly'.

'Are you trying to tell me he lacked spirituality?'

'You could say that.'

After the death of the Armenian patriarch in January 1990, the expelled cleric, accompanied by his eight armed Israeli bodyguards, forced an entry into the compound while the funeral was taking place. These antics amounted to an attempted ecclesiastical coup.

In the perpetual strife between the denominations – intra-faith as well as inter-faith – it is the civil government that has to mediate whenever possible. After the Turks, the British, and the Jordanians, it is now the Israelis who are in the peculiar position of proposing a sensible arrangement when, say, nuns complain when the muezzin next door wakes them at unsocial hours, or having to determine whether it's all right for the Armenians to put a cross over the archway through which ultra-Orthodox Jews pass on their way to the Wall. For most of the disputes there is no obvious solution, certainly no legally binding solution. The Israeli official responsible for such judgements told me the best he can usually come up with is a *modus vivendi*.

'I'm happy if I can get the conflicting parties to get through today and tomorrow. I'm less concerned with eternity. I can't solve the problem between the Copts and the Ethiopians, but I can try to establish a status quo that will serve almost as well. It may not be ideal, but the parties concerned can at least live with it. Sometimes the proposed solutions are incredibly complex, specifying in the case of a divided ecclesiastical jurisdiction who will provide and sprinkle the incense, who will worship and when, and who will take care of repairs. My job is to distinguish between what both parties consider vital concerns and those matters that are merely face-saving ploys.

'Although many of the disputes sound trivial, it's important that we try to find a solution or a *modus vivendi*, because Jerusalem lives under a microscope. A minor neighbourhood dispute in the Old City can be blown up into an international incident. All the religious groups in the city also address a wider audience. They tend to see their disputes from a grandiose biblical perspective, under the influence of the holy sites among which we live. And you have to remember that there has never been a tradition of religious pluralism in the Holy Land.' All religious groups, he pointed out, occupy ambivalent positions as 'minorities and majorities. The Jews are the majority in Israel, but they also live in the Middle East and within an international community where they are a very small minority indeed. In the context of Israel, the Roman Catholics, with 25,000 adherents, are insignificant, but the authorities can never forget that the Catholics can draw on huge international resources and support when necessary.

'Every group has a kind of dual existence according to the context in which we view them, and they can adopt two ways of behaving. What I have to discern is which way is dominant in any particular situation. One afternoon some Orthodox Jews in the Old City were disturbed by a noisy Syrian Orthodox procession, and a woman emptied a bucket of water on them from a window. Some Syrian scouts retaliated by rushing into her building and wreaking havoc, and this further outraged the Jews. Now, the Jews were reacting as though the Syrians were simply continuing a long line of aggression against the Jewish people from a hostile Christian majority. So what I had to do was impress upon the Jews that the Syrians are in fact a defeated minority church. Once that was made clear, their anger moderated, as they could identify more easily with the Syrians' own sense of outrage.

'Christian Arabs too are torn, in their case between their Arab nationalism and their wider Christian communion. Christian Arabs were tolerated as *dhimmis* within Moslem societies, just as Jews were, and they established a *modus vivendi*. But when in the last century Western religious institutions came to the Holy Land, they provided moral and financial support to the indigenous Christian groups. But this also provoked a crisis of identity. They responded in different ways. Some took an assimilationist route, claiming a common heritage, which never really existed, with Moslem Arabs. Like assimilationist Jews, they often changed their names to disguise their Christian identity. Others took a more revolutionary line in the form of Arab nationalism, and the early nationalists were Christians. Nothing in this country is as simple as it appears.'

Is there no balm in Gilead? No, and precious little in Jerusalem either.

# 4 · JRSLM SCRBBL

For those who live in West Jerusalem, weeks or months may go by without direct contact with the Old City. Its complexities and absurdities have only tangential impact on the daily lives of Israeli civil servants and doctors and rabbis. Although many of them fought for the place in 1948 and 1967, they don't live there and they don't shop there. Israeli Jerusalemites, if they are reasonably well off or long established in the city, live in one of the pleasant, modest inner suburbs such as Rehavia, or in a relatively distant suburb such as Kiryat Moshe, while newcomers to the city will probably inhabit a modern apartment complex in a satellite town such as Gilo or Ramot, and commute into the city. West Jerusalem is not that large, and on the Sabbath, when there is no public transportation, I have walked from one end to the other without undue strain.

Modern Jerusalem is not a city of great architectural distinction – here, as in other Israeli cities, the major patron of architecture is the ministry of housing – yet aesthetically it is a thoroughly satisfying city, thanks to Ronald Storrs' percipient bylaw. If there are few buildings, old or new, that look wonderful, there are equally few that look ghastly. Jerusalem stone sets the lowest common denominator at a remarkably high level. Even the grandiose churches and hospitals built a century ago by national ecclesiastical bodies – Italian, French, Russian, German, Austrian – manage to blend in. In parts of what is now East and South Jerusalem there are still plenty of spacious houses built under Turkish rule, mildly Oriental in style, with thick stone walls and gardens and patios and tall shady rooms lit by arched windows, far better adapted to the Jerusalem climate than more rickety modern apartment blocks. Many of those houses have been divided up into flats or offices, for they are too large for single-family occupancy in a city that still has a housing shortage. Much of the attraction of West Jerusalem derives from its attention to local detail; on a corner that in most other cities would have been left as a pool of concrete with a litter bin, a small garden will have been planted. Improbable sculptures sprout in industrial parks; fountains splash prettily among the greenery. Around many of the more monumental buildings, such as the Knesset and the Israel Museum, are large parks, although their intersection by four-lane highways can make getting to them troublesome. Large-scale architecture of this kind, however, is not always controlled by Israelis. It's often the donors who choose the design for the buildings they are paying for. The Rothschilds, for example, provided huge sums to finance the construction of the high courts. Israeli architects objected because the Rothschilds wished to choose their own architect, and in this instance the Israelis got their way.

Jerusalem has that ineradicable dullness found in most government towns. Jerusalem is Washington to Tel Aviv's New York or, more accurately, Los Angeles. That it looks as good as it does, and works as well as it does, is due both to Sir Ronald and to the more recent efforts of Teddy Kollek. Now in his late seventies, Kollek's physical and political powers are on the wane, but he remains a major force, and, after decades in office, he has acquired a symbolic power. Although, in his prime, he would rise early each morning to inspect personally any spot where a problem had arisen, Kollek, a burly Viennese with a very gruff charm, is better known as an inspired fundraiser and publicist for the city. He still chairs the Jerusalem Foundation, a private organization that has raised almost $200 million for schemes that add either to the city's beauty or to its amenities. The Foundation has dreamt up and found sponsorship for about a thousand projects, from the most grandiose, such as new parks, to the merely practical, such as computers for school libraries. The Foundation has scattered open-air sculpture around the city, such as the two goats suspended from wires above Emek Refaim. About five sculptures are added to the streets each year. All clinics and schools sponsored by the Foundation also contain commissioned works of art, all donated.

First, the Foundation's officers dream up a project. Then they work through their fundraising offices worldwide to lay their hands on the money. Current projects include a new stadium and a science museum for children. Donors include many non-Jews, especially from Germany, and the Foundation has gone out of its way to institute joint Jewish–Arab projects, though they have not yet succeeded in finding Arab donors, which is not hard to understand. A large health centre in East Jerusalem, servicing the Arab population, has been funded by the Foundation. The most obvious emblems of the Foundation's activities are the small plaques naming parks and other amenities after the donors. Jerusalem effortlessly acts as an emotional magnet to millions: people treasure the city and wish to help sustain it. This is lucky for Jerusalem, which as a government and university city lacks major business or industrial sectors to boost the tax base.

One of Kollek's most seductive ideas was the founding of Mishkenot Sha'anim. If you stroll along the outside of the Old City from the Jaffa Gate towards the Zion Gate and look to your right, you will see the gentle ridge on the other side of the Hinnom Valley that rises from South Jerusalem up towards the King David Hotel and the business district of West Jerusalem. On the slope facing the Old City a few old terraces have been impeccably transformed into a tiny urban enclave, isolated by surrounding greenery from the rest of the city. Adjoining this enclave, Yemin Moshe, is Mishkenot Sha'anim, which resembles a double row of tall almshouses. One of Jerusalem's earliest benefactors, Sir Moses Montefiore, encouraged settlers to live outside the Old City, and these houses were constructed in the lofty Turkish style in about 1860. The upper row has been converted into a music conservatory and the lower into apartments reserved for guests of the city.

Yemin Moshe has become one of the most coveted addresses in town. Its streets are closed to traffic and the different levels of its terraces are connected by steep lanes and steps. The stone houses have been impeccably restored, and have a strange Andalucian air, since many of the windows lurk behind ornamental grilles. Flowering shrubs cascade down the walls of the houses, and iron hoops span the lanes, offering purchase to clematis and other climbing plants.

Before 1967, however, Yemin Moshe was a wreck. A Jerusalemite recalled: 'Yes, it's a lovely spot. But in those days you had bullets instead of a view, and rats the size of cats.' Yemin Moshe then overlooked the no man's land that separated Israeli and Jordanian Jersualem. After the reunification of the city, the district was restored as an artists' colony but, as usually happens to such colonies, house prices soon rose to levels that put them well beyond the reach of most artists. Many artists cashed in by selling their houses and moving elsewhere. At one of the art galleries in Yemin Moshe, I looked in on an exhibition of charming ink drawings and watercolours by Alex Singer. His brief story is unhappily typical of much Israeli experience: born near New York in 1952, he visited Jerusalem in the early 1970s, studied Russian and Jewish studies at Cornell, learnt Arabic, and emigrated to Israel in 1984. He was drafted six weeks later and in 1987 was killed during a skirmish with terrorists. Now, in this prettiest of settings, he was being gently commemorated.

Yemin Moshe, exquisite though it be, is as typical of Jerusalem as Albany is of London or Gramercy Park of New York. An increasing number of Jerusalemites live in places such as Gilo, a new housing development founded in 1972 and ranged along ridges south of the city. The bus follows the Bethlehem Road and immediately after the Gilo turn-off, if you stay on the road, you would be in the West Bank. Gilo is on the very edge of Israel, and that is no coincidence. By occupying the high ground around Jerusalem, Gilo, and a dozen other new towns like it, are designed to deter the possibility of land-based attacks on Jerusalem. If you look at the pre-1967 borders, you will see that Jerusalem occupies a spot at the end of a long wedge, and the main road here from the coast is overlooked by Arab villages. Conscious of the city's vulnerability, municipal planners have sought to minimize any possibility of attack from the West Bank. Moreover, the presence of large new Israeli towns encircling Jerusalem is also intended, though this is less a stated policy than an underlying assumption, to minimize Arab settlement around the city.

Even the apartment complexes at Gilo have a fortress-like design, each wing shading an interior courtyard of lawns and gardens and playgrounds. The concept of building structures around courtyards with elaborate gateways was borrowed from the kinds of housing developed in the last century in older Jerusalem neighbourhoods such as Mea Shearim. Most of the flats at Gilo, like their older models, have balconies and ornamental grilles. Indeed, one of the ways in which residents scrawl their signature in this austere environment is by choosing grilles that differ from those of their neighbours. Roads fan out along the ridges from the commercial sector, and although clumps of shrubbery divide the road and there has been a determined attempt at landscaping, the effect remains bleak. The shopping facilities seem sparse: there is only one post office for Gilo's 32,000 inhabitants. People came to live here because it was cheap, and though it is more costly than it used to be, accommodation remains cheaper than in Jerusalem itself. The government encourages people to move to Gilo and other satellite towns by offering subsidized mortgages.

Gilo is a new town, built from scratch. But some Jerusalem suburbs must blend with older patterns of habitation around them. At French Hill, for example, despite its romantic name, many of the blocks are grim in design, and lack balconies and patios and the other features commonplace in more recent developments. The architects managed to avoid a totally brutalist effect by employing vaguely Oriental arches and domes to harmonize with the traditional architecture of the region.

Ramot, to the north-west of Jerusalem, glories in its notoriety. This hilly suburb was much favoured by the ultra-Orthodox, with Jews in sidelocks incongruously inhabiting the idiosyncratic modern developments of its Polin area. This was built to a honeycomb design by an architect called Haecker, and over each cube of comb perches a small balcony. The trouble with Ramot is its height, facing Arab villages from one side of the ridge and Jerusalem's suburbs from the other. Not surprisingly, it was possible to see roads from Ramot, one of which was much travelled by secular Jews on the Sabbath. This met with the strong disapproval of the ultra-Orthodox of Ramot, who would gather each Saturday to heckle drivers and stone their cars. The police would arrive and quell the disturbances. One local resident told me that during the height of these troubles, her children would beg her: 'Mummy, can we go out and watch the tear gas?'

Such violent behaviour, coming from the most pious members of the community on the Sabbath, seemed incomprehensible and outrageous to peaceful Jerusalemites. One Israeli told me that when driving in this part of town on Saturdays she had two options, to risk being stoned by Arab protesters along one road, or to endure the same treatment along the other from the Orthodox Jews: 'I went for the Arab option. I was damned if I was going to live in Jerusalem and be stoned by my own people.'

The dilemma was solved with the construction of a new road sufficiently inaccessible to slings and arrows from Ramot. The ultra-Orthodox also waged a campaign against the construction of a local swimming pool, which would permit mixed bathing and all the consequent lewdness prompted by the sight of human flesh. Plans to build a modern stadium in Jerusalem were also frustrated for over a decade because the main approach road would pass within earshot of an ultra-Orthodox district, whose residents couldn't stomach the nearby presence of fun-loving, Sabbath-defying secularists. But in 1989 the objections were overcome and the stadium, financed by the Clore Foundation, will at long last be built.

From northern Jerusalem a new road leads to the popular new town of Ma'aleh Adumim, eight miles from the municipality of Jerusalem. Like Gilo, Ma'aleh Adumim is still expanding. The housing trickles onto the lovely bleak rolling hills that ripple towards Jericho and the Dead Sea. The town edges the Judean desert and the climate is more harsh than in Jerusalem. When the town was landscaped, research was undertaken to determine which plants would thrive best in the inhospitable climate. Now the town is full of greenery, and rose bushes bloom blood-red along the roads. The housing is more varied than in older satellite towns: there are Gilo-like apartment blocks around courtyards, cottages (which in Israeli usage means you have your own front door, a garden, and a balcony that can't be overlooked, although there may be three dwellings contained within the cottage), and villas, which are detached houses. The villa area is less methodical, less obviously planned, and there is more liberty of design. Purchasers of plots here can import their own architects, as long as the design conforms to certain regulations. The overall effect of the new town is less uniform than in the older developments; the benevolent but sometimes heavy hand of the master planner is less evident. Yet although out here in the desert there is an abundance of space, it is surprising to see how close the houses are to one another. It's as though, despite the inaccessibility of Ma'aleh Adumim, those who live here need all the reassurance they can get.

It is the recent immigrants who often move to these modern suburbs. Har Nof, indeed, is almost exclusively populated by Orthodox American Jews, who occupy large apartment complexes that rise above cliffs strewn with detritus: rubble, oil drums, old piping, piles of sand and obsolete concrete mixers. A more varied development is East Talpiot, once a barren and hilly area just off the Bethlehem road and now a neat district of small white blocks. Near the community centre stands a large Alexander Calder cow, and local kids like to tug at its movable parts. Until 1973, when the rate of immigration began to slow down, this was one of the favourite destinations of newcomers from Russia, Ethiopia and South America. The district does have one splendid amenity: the Hass Promenade, where you can stroll for a few hundred yards in either direction, pausing for coffee and cakes periodically while enjoying superb views onto the Old City and the Mount of Olives. In 1989 an extension, the Sherover Promenade, leading all the way into Abu Tor, was completed.

That such views of Jerusalem are still as thrilling as they are is no accident. Protracted battles between property developers and municipal planners were waged through the mid-1970s, and luckily for Jerusalem, the developers lost. In what is today the Liberty Bell Garden just a few hundred yards from the Jaffa Gate, developers proposed to erect two 500-bedroom hotels and towers up to eighteen storeys high. After three years of debate, the municipality, which had initially been wavering on the issue, eventually required the developers to modify their plans. New hotels have risen along the ridge from Yemin Moshe to the downtown area, but the towers are much lower, the designs less brutal. The Jerusalem skyline has not been preserved intact, for that would be impossible, but the more gross intrusions and manipulations have been avoided. It is said that it was the construction of the ugly Sheraton Plaza Hotel that persuaded Teddy Kollek to keep any new hotels well away from the Old City.

Respect for the existing city and its architectural traditions is not the only factor that planners and builders have had to take into account. The architects of the satellite towns failed to define unambiguously those parts of the apartment complexes that were the responsibility of individual flat-owners and those areas that were public responsibility. There were Holy

Sepulchre-like arguments about who cleaned what and who maintained what. Moreover, the thoughtful provision of play areas within courtyards led inevitably to noise levels that other residents found irksome. Designers of blocks intended for ultra-Orthodox occupation had to ensure that flats were divided so as to provide as many bedrooms as possible, since families of ten or twelve children were not uncommon. Double kitchen sinks were required for the maintenance of dietary laws, and balconies had to be left open to the sky so that residents could construct the outdoor shelter known as a *succa* during the festival of Succoth (Tabernacles).

About one third of the Jewish population of Jerusalem is ultra-Orthodox, and although they tend to live among their co-enthusiasts, their presence influences the life of the city. Jerusalem, in short, is very quiet. The city takes its pleasures decorously. Discos, for instance, are thin on the ground. On Friday afternoons the entire city grinds to a halt. Two or three hours before the Sabbath begins, buses are snuggled up tight in their garages. All but a handful of restaurants and cinemas have rolled down the shutters. The city has gone into a deep sleep. For the visitor, the alternatives are acquiescent torpor or to follow the sybaritic Jerusalemites as they speed down the highway to Tel Aviv. One Shabbat I attended the Great Synagogue, a grandiose building, large enough to accommodate different styles of service simultaneously. In the main synagogue a muted congregation idled through a diffuse and stately service, while at the Beit Hamidrash (study house) downstairs frenzied prayer was being offered in the expressionist style of the very Orthodox. Jerusalem's neighbourhoods are dotted with synagogues to suit all tastes, and the Great Synagogue, paid for largely by the Wolfson family, has never captured the hearts of Jerusalemites, though its social cachet appeals to the smart set and to tourists. Then I wandered down the road to the Conservative synagogue, a congregation with mostly American adherents, who conduct parts of the service in English. Here the service is on traditional lines, with modifications, but the sexes are not separated, as in Orthodox synagogues. This morning the synagogue was packed, as the congregation was feting one of its stalwarts who was celebrating her seventy-fifth birthday.

Religion out of the way, I crossed the road to the Sheraton Plaza at noon, together with dozens of other worshippers. In the lounges sat smartly dressed women in bright shallow hats. The men were in hats or *kippot*, though I saw one man in a *kippa* using the public telephone in the lobby. I was scandalized by his disrespect for the laws of the Sabbath and threw cocktail olives at him, but he fought me off. There were even a few Chasidim seated there, gossiping and sipping a cool drink. *Tallit* bags were slung onto the coffee tables. Since Orthodox Jews may not handle money or write on the Sabbath, I wondered how the Chasidim would settle their bill, but didn't have the patience to wait and find out. The ingenuity of the Orthodox in finding ways to obey the letter of the law while denying its spirit is inexhaustible. Emerging from the hotel early in the afternoon, I encountered on King George Street about fifty women dressed in black, holding up placards demanding an end to Israeli occupation of the territories. These Women in Black (*Nashim Beshachor*) demonstrate here in silence every Saturday afternoon. Alongside them five elderly men were mounting a counter-demonstration with such placards as: BLACK WIDOWS ARE ARAFAT'S BEST FRIENDS.

When the Sabbath ends on Saturday evening, downtown Jerusalem reawakes. Pizza stalls reopen, and hundreds of people, mostly teenagers but also Orthodox families and middle-aged couples, stroll towards Ben Yehuda, a pedestrian mall lined with shops and cafés. Those who can't find a seat outside a café perch instead on the benches that encircle the trees along the mall. Vast wedges of chocolate cake are consumed; portions in Israel are large to compensate for the lack of quality. Cones jammed with blue ice cream are another popular choice. Amateur musicians take up their positions: a pair of guitarists strumming a Beatles number, a zither player zithering quietly for his own amusement, and at the bottom of the street a saxophonist improbably honking out 'Auld Lang Syne'. Israelis are modest drinkers, sipping at beer or at wines doctored so as to resemble fruit juice, and public drunkenness is rare.

So what else does one do for kicks in Jerusalem? Well, if it's Tuesday evening I can recommend the Jerusalem Scrabble Club, or Jrslm Scrbbl Clb as it likes to call itself, which meets upstairs at the YMCA. The room is filled with fifty players and any overflow spills over into the corridors. The club was founded by ex-Montrealer Sam Orbaum, a bouncy balding gnomish man in his mid-thirties, a copy writer for the *Jerusalem Post* and the numero uno Scrabble player in Israel. There is no formal membership of the club: you just turn up and engage a partner. When I walked in the door the room was tense with concentration, but there were outbreaks of jollity and outrage, depending on the progress of the games. I could identify Sam easily: he was the man playing two games simultaneously, while a pair nearby were playing Clock Scrabble. Some of the bags in which tiles are concealed are embroidered with their owners' names – perhaps they double as *tallit* bags on Shabbat. Scrabble dictionaries were scattered about the tables. Sometimes special contests are held, to find the best K-word or the best word derived from Yiddish or Hebrew. At the end of the evening Sam collects and tabulates the scores of each game. After five years, he has declared, 11,925,405 points have been accumulated by some thousand players.

On Sam's two boards I found the words ZOOID, XI, TOQUET, JUN, BO, BAX, and the minimalist AA. In case it's not clear, Scrabble at the club is played only in English, although many players have Romanian or French as their native language. Sam was trailing one of his opponents badly when I sat down to observe the game, but I was warned by other spectators not to write him off quite yet: 'It's like drowning a kitten. It's not over till the last gurgle.' But Sam did lose one of his games. When it was over I pointed languidly to the word WIERDOS on the board and declared: 'I'm afraid this game is invalid. There is a spelling error on the board.'

'Yes,' said Sam, 'we know that.'

On Monday evenings, also at the hospitable YMCA, you can have a go at folk dancing, if you must. I observed the proceedings from the doorway. There were about thirty people, mostly women, lined up in rows. Loudspeakers transmitted the massed choir music so beloved of Israelis. The 'dancers' would take a few paces forwards, hop back two, and then perhaps give a sideways kick or some other foot flourish, and conclude the sequence with some handclaps. An energetic snub-nosed redhead was letting rip with a full disco squirm, and very fetching she looked too, but folk dancing this was not. But, come to think of it, what folk? Jews have traditions of Chasidic dancing, but folk dancing? That's peasant stuff, and there are no Jewish peasants. Nor do Israeli folk sing lustily in English to the Motown rhythms which were now issuing from the speakers. Most of the dancers were Swabian matrons, not Israelis at all, and were plodding about to the strains of what could have been music from the least popular radio station in Düsseldorf, while underwriting ideologically the virtues of wholemeal and unshaven armpits. I left the folk to it, and went out for a beer.

When these entertainments begin to pall, try the home-grown pageants laid on by local people. Excellent performances are always to be seen at the Jewish market at Mahane Yehuda halfway up the Jaffa Road. This is mostly a food market, though you can also buy kitschy paintings of your favourite rabbis. Rubbery sausages as pink as flesh and marbled with unspeakables are piled up behind glass. Cooked meats and sausages, drying out at the edges, turn brown on the counters, making them look even more inedible than they did in the first place. At the butchers' stalls, frozen joints are popular, as are chicken parts and organs, and breaded cutlets that resemble ship's biscuits. There are glossy olives and matt pickles; dates, nuts, raisins, sultanas large and small. The market fills a couple of half-covered alleys; naked light bulbs over the stalls cast a harsh light onto the produce below. At election time this is where the politicians come with photographers in tow in search of the ethnic vote. Most of the stallholders are Oriental Jews, and their allegiance is divided among Likud and the various religious parties. The Labour Party, which is perceived as numbingly middle-class, exerts little pull around here. In 1988 Shas, the Sephardi Orthodox party, had a particularly striking poster, which went down a treat at Mahane Yehuda. Soldiers kept an eye on the proceedings and monitored the shouting matches between aspiring politicians and their outspoken critics behind the olive tubs. In Israeli politics, the market traders fulfil the same kind of role as Manhattan taxi drivers and Dutch herring sellers, always ready with an earthy quip and a trenchant opinion.

At the lower end of Jaffa Road is the main post office, which I got to know well, after queuing regularly at its international telephone exchange. I marvelled at the pair of ill-tempered women behind the counter, directing traffic to the booths and taking our money. If they exuded constant exasperation, I soon understood why, for the women required polyglot skills. No two people in any queue spoke the same language, and a morning's transactions were conducted in a babble of Yemeni Arabic, Marin County American, Spanish, Midi *patois*, and, once in a while, rasping Hebrew. One morning I was taking a parcel to the post office and crossed the road, straight into the holsters of two policewomen, who in Israel suffer for their art by being compelled to wear daft blue and white caps that poke up above their hairdos. I swiftly recalled something that Alex Berlyne had said to me: 'Israelis have no respect for authority. In any discussion, "no" is the opening position in negotiations. People in authority will bend the rules in certain circumstances, so it's worth having an argument. But it makes life tiring.'

Now I had the opportunity to put the theory to the test. One of the cops addressed me in Ivrit. I replied in English. She asked me, in deep-throated English, why I was crossing the road? I resisted the temptation to say, Because I want to get to the other side, and replied instead that as there was no traffic I decided to cross.

'Why did you cross at a red light?'

'Well, as I said, there were no cars about, so I thought it was OK to cross.' A lie, I confess.

'You are Israeli?'

'English.' Avoiding 'British', with its links to the unpopular Mandate.

'Your passport.'

A little bluffing was necessary, as I didn't have it with me. 'I'll have to take my clothes off if you want to see my passport.'

She furrowed her brows, not grasping the connection. Again: 'Your passport.'

I whisked my shirt out from the confines of my trousers, loosened my belt, and grasped the clasp of my money belt. The cop realized I would have to disrobe further in order to extract my documents, which would have caused a riot among the modest ultra-Orthodox Jews all around us. She gave up and waved me on with what I believe is known as a caution. I regarded this as a successful case of absorption into the Israeli way of life, for I had not been cowed by officialdom but had stood my ground. And what's the point of having a Jewish state if you're not allowed to jay-walk in it? Officialdom, however, was waiting for me at the post office, where I wanted to send some books home. The packages were unsealed and checked by the clerk; all was in order. But he refused to take the package until he had seen my passport. It was the rule, he said, though he pleasantly admitted he had no idea why I had to identify myself in order to send half a dozen books to myself. Since I didn't have my passport with me, I had to waste half the day by returning to the hotel and retrieving it.

In the evenings I sought culture. The Cinematheque, founded in 1981, has been a great success. The Jerusalem Foundation provided the structure, and other foundations most of the funding. In addition to screening up to four films each day in two auditoria, the Cinematheque maintains a library, an archive of 9,000 films, runs film history classes for adults, welcomes gangs of schoolchildren, and hosts film premieres. While I was in Jerusalem, the Cinematheque had organized a programme to supplement a psychotherapists' conference on incest. Which films, I long wondered, were selected? Now that the Cinematheque is allowed to open on Friday and Saturday nights, it has become a social centre, especially on Fridays at ten, when teenagers come in droves to see the latest videos. Given the size of the country, the Israeli film industry is reasonably well developed. There have been annual film festivals since 1983, and between ten and twenty feature films, at varying levels of artistic merit, are produced each year.

The Cinematheque is a godsend for secular residents, but as far as tourists are concerned the major cultural attraction of Jerusalem is the stately, sumptuous Shrine of the Book at the Israel Museum. An icon of female sexual symbolism, the structure that houses the Book – the Dead Sea Scrolls – is breast-shaped and entered through a long tunnel. The scrolls are too fragile to be displayed, so we must make do with facsimiles of six of them, immaculately displayed in glass cabinets that encircle the white chamber. The scrolls provide a wealth of information about Jewish culture two thousand years ago, reminding visitors both of the continuity of that culture (the ancient *tallit* on display doesn't look all that different from those worn today by religious Jews at prayer) and of the primacy of the word, the text, the code. The Israel Museum itself has a wealth of archaeological and ethnographic and religious art collections, as well as paintings from the impressionist and surrealist movements, but for me the most precious item on display was the recently unearthed minute and wonderfully shapely ivory pomegranate, a relic from Solomon's Temple of the eighth century B.C. Displayed alongside it was a scroll from the seventh century B.C. with the words of the priestly benediction (Numbers VI: 24–26), and thus the oldest extant version of that precious text. Within the grounds of the museum is the stylish sculpture garden designed by Isamu Noguchi: beautifully proportioned billowing dunes of gravel fringed by olive trees, a Japanese conception employing Levantine materials.

There's a less publicized slice of Jerusalem life to be savoured up on Mount Scopus at the Hadassah Hospital. When it comes to matters of life and death, political and tribal differences are thrust to one side. Because many Israeli-trained doctors prefer to work in the United States, most of the doctors here are Arabs or immigrants from countries such as Britain and Australia. Along the corridors near the maternity wards stroll Moslem women from the West Bank or from Arab countries with less admirable medical facilities; swathed in cloth from head to toe, their light brown faces rendered moonlike by all this bandaging, they have the discreet cinnamon sexiness of young nuns. Glowering over the telephone installed in the corridor was a heavily bearded Orthodox Jew waving a cigarette as he made an anxious call. Strict Moslems and Orthodox Jews do have this in common: they make a lot of babies. Even from the lobby I could hear the yells from the nursery behind the swing doors, where the newborn are lined up swaddled within their cots. In the lounge are Birth Albums, recording the vigils of expectant families, their joy in the outcome registered in scrawls of thanksgiving and comic drawings.

Mount Scopus is in East Jerusalem and so is the Mount of Olives. Getting there can be an instructive journey. Walk to the Arab bus station near the Damascus Gate and find the 75 bus. If there are two or three lined up, all pointing in a different direction, board the one with the motor running and noxious fumes pouring out of the exhaust. Arab buses are shabbier than their Israeli counterparts. Nobody pays any attention to the No Smoking signs, least of all the drivers. Almost all the passengers are Arabs, plus, *de rigueur*, two Scandinavian backpackers doing their best not to look bemused. One morning I was seated quietly in the bus waiting for the driver to flick his cigarette out of the window and grind the gears before departure, when there was a sudden commotion around the platforms. Arab boys jumped onto the bus shouting and pointing; Moslem women in white headscarves dove into the ladies' lavatory; fruit sellers gathered up their crates and ran for it. I assumed that this panic was in response to some act of violence, but this did not appear to be so. Yet the panic did not subside, and some passengers urged the driver to pull out of the bus station, while others begged him to open the doors so they could flee on foot. A minute later the shouting had died down, the crowds and the pedlars were returning to the platforms, and everything seemed normal once more. I asked a fellow passenger to tell me what was going on. He replied: 'Police come. Make trouble.' But I had seen neither police nor trouble.

The bus pulls out and rumbles up steep streets to the ridge of the Mount of Olives. On the left are the shallow terraces of the Jerusalem Centre for Near East Studies, an outpost of Brigham Young University. Since this is a Mormon institution, there was a tremendous fuss when it became known that Brigham Young were planning this branch office on a site overlooking the Old City. There were fears, not altogether groundless, that the Mormons would start waving their Book at pilgrims and Jews alike, and there were also objections to the architectural design. Eventually, the objections were overcome, and if the clean-cut young men from Salt Lake City are slipping tracts through Jewish letterboxes, nobody ever mentioned the menace to me. The bus grinds along the top of the ridge, passing monasteries and hospitals, and ends its journey among a small group of shops. From here a lane leads down a slope to the walled Benedictine convent where I met Sister Abraham, and then swoops up to what was until late 1988 the Hotel Intercontinental. It was a wonderful hotel: air-conditioned, with comfortable benches on which to sit and read undisturbed, and a public telephone in working order. Best of all, it had no guests, though I occasionally saw a United Nations van in the car park. It didn't seem to have any staff either. When I returned in the spring of 1989 the hotel had changed its name under new management and was still just as empty.

A dozy camel under the care of a squad of Arab lads is parked in the little plaza beneath the hotel, from where there is a celebrated view of the Old City and West Jerusalem. Bus tours come up here and pictures are taken. Presumably, some of the tourists hire the camel for a brief trot. An Israeli police jeep often idles nearby, and the cops seem on friendly terms with the Arab trinket sellers and camel guardians. From the plaza, a very steep lane leads down the hillside, passing the immense Jewish cemeteries, which date from the fifteenth century. Some of the graves have been restored in recent years; others still suffer from the vandalism that characterized the years of Jordanian custodianship, when two-thirds of the Jewish graves were destroyed. After a few paces, you are in Christian territory. A gate leads to the striking Dominus Flevit church, built in 1954 with a dome that resembles a tear, or a breast as depicted by Allen Jones. A few yards further down is the exotic Russian church of Mary Magdalene, built by Czar Alexander III in traditional style, with seven golden onion-shaped domes. At the foot of the hill is the Garden of Gethsemane, small and cramped and filled with ancient and wizened olive trees. This tranquil little garden, too domesticated for one to imagine easily the agonies that may have taken place here, is adjoined by one of the ugliest churches in Jerusalem, or anywhere. Many nations contributed to the construction of this aptly named Church of the Agony, and it shows. Its gloom was enlivened during one of my visits by American pilgrims who held each other's clammy hands as they prayed, then reached out their arms palms upwards as they waited for blessings to drop, and then gave each other the kiss of peace close to the spot where Judas gave Christ the kiss of betrayal.

Just in front of the church is the Jericho road, flowing down the Kidron valley from East Jerusalem. Alongside this road is a sunken plaza that leads to the fine Crusader Church of the Assumption. From the portal, forty-eight steps plunge down an aisleless tunnel to the transepts below. Some feeble light is provided in this subterranean chamber by flickering candles and countless lamps, mostly unlit, suspended by chains from enamel eggs. In this spot, the Virgin Mary was supposedly buried, so there is the usual scattering of unsavoury priests loitering about and trying to persuade visitors to light a candle. I like this church; it has an appealing creepiness, as one never knows when a black-cloaked cleric with warts on his hand is going to leap out from a darkened chapel. The tomb of Mary is lovingly swamped with flowers and icons, paintings and embroideries, and is less claustrophobic than her son's sepulchre a mile away.

Across the Jericho road a lane passes through olive groves to the tomb of Absalom, an eerie and mysterious monument. A square structure, hewn from the solid rock and faced with eroded pilasters, the tomb is topped with a conical roof that resembles a bathroom plunger. Like so many ancient buildings in Jerusalem, it offends against the Trades Descriptions Act. Since it dates from the first century B.C., it could not possibly commemorate the son of King David after whom it is named. Never mind, it's a splendid structure, quite unlike anything else in Jerusalem. There is usually an Arab boy in attendance who will take a shekel or two off you and give you in exchange a paragraph of information which can also be found in the guidebook tucked under your arm.

This little tour is big on Biblical Associations and I always enjoyed it, especially as it is all downhill. The only drawback is that the tomb of Absalom is relatively isolated. No buses run anywhere near it, and you have the harsh choice of retracing your steps – upwards, and very steeply – to the Mount of Olives, or of toiling in the opposite direction through the Moslem cemeteries to St Stephen's Gate on the eastern side of the Old City, from where it is a mere twenty minutes on foot, up a shallow but steady incline, to the Jaffa Gate. I never minded these long hikes back to base in Jerusalem. The buildings become familiar but one can't tire of them, and few cities in the world can match Jerusalem for the diversity of cultures packed within it. The fancy dress party never ends, and even the tourists are invited.

# 5 · A FULL HEART

I had been intrigued by all that I heard about Reuven Feuerstein. A Romanian-born Israeli now in his late sixties, he had established a formidable reputation as an educational psychologist by developing techniques that allowed him to salvage, intellectually and hence emotionally, children that others had abandoned as ineducable. For Feuerstein, intelligence may be God-given but it is not quantifiable on arrival. He dismisses IQ tests because they assume intelligence is doled out in fixed measures, whereas in his view intelligence can be acquired and cognitive deficiencies remedied. According to Feuerstein, trained mediators can, with the help of exercises – in his jargon, 'an instrumental enrichment program' – teach children who are considered stupid or retarded to broaden their cognitive abilities, to make connections with the world around them that will eventually help them to make sense of that world and manipulate it. The tests he has devised are primarily directed at helping the child to group and organize material.

I found Dr Feuerstein in his shabby office in the Jerusalem headquarters of the Hadassah Wizo Canada Research Institute. When I was ushered in, I found him busily conferring with colleagues. Nonetheless he waved me in, and told me to pull up a chair and listen in. Feuerstein's working day is fluid rather than structured; one appointment flows into the next, and visitors must tap into his flow when the opportunity presents itself. Our first conversation was snatched and bitty, yet he never ignored my presence, and each time he had dealt with a problem he would turn to me and explain what had just taken place.

One social worker at the institute was unsure whether a child, Yigal, should remain in their care. Dr Feuerstein thought not, but the social worker expressed considerable doubts. Feuerstein prevailed, and said that Yigal should be placed with a family in the near future. The social worker reminded him that Yigal's behaviour was erratic, even belligerent. Feuerstein conceded that the decision was a hard one to make: 'This will not be easy on the family he is placed with. They will not be punished in the next world, but in this one.' Dr Feuerstein is given to such oracular pronouncements. With his stocky build, white beard, and a black beret that never leaves the back of his large head, he would have made a tremendous rabbi. Indeed, in Feuerstein religious belief and public conviction seem intimately connected. It is as though he only reluctantly admits the possibility of a beneficent creator giving life while condemning the living to an inadequate mastery of their environment. There are few children so closed to the world that they cannot be taught to increase their power-giving connection with it. In his view, seeming unintelligence is often, though not always, no more than unrealized potential.

He invited me to remain by his side as he interviewed three boys. The first was thirteen, a North African. He had been placed in a home for retarded children, yet it was clear that despite certain problems of grasp and execution the boy was in no real sense retarded. Feuerstein instructed that the boy should be placed with Youth Aliyah, an organization with which Feuerstein has worked for decades. The second boy, a charming eight-year-old with huge mongoose eyes, was wheeled in, then lifted by his mother into a chair alongside the psychologist. The boy smiled beautifully, but could only respond to questions with gestures that were not easily elucidated.

Feuerstein dipped into his pocket and fished out a piece of toffee, wrapped in bright paper. Holding it out, he encouraged the boy to grasp it, but no sooner did the lad do so, than Feuerstein flicked the sweet into his own palm, which he clenched. At first the boy found this amusing, but soon grew frustrated with finding the toffee first within his grasp and then a second later out of his reach. He then used his other hand to pry the sweet loose from his tormentor's hand. Feuerstein allowed him to succeed, and the boy exploited his gain by popping the toffee into his mouth.

Feuerstein turned to me: 'I taunted him because I want him to co-ordinate his movements, and I want him to persevere at the task. And, as you see, eventually he used his second hand. That's good. By using toffee as the bait, he may have broken teeth but he will have a full heart.'

The third boy, Danny, was sixteen, born in Venezuela, unable to read or write or speak. He communicated with falsetto squeals. Yet his disposition seemed gentle, even affectionate. Feuerstein turned to me again: 'These kids have been written off. This boy here has been taught nothing in his sixteen years. I want to change their destiny.' Grandiloquent stuff, but Feuerstein has an impressive record of success. He continued his examination of Danny by leading him through one of the tests he has devised. This one had to do with placing a part within a whole, a concept

Danny grasped not at all initially, but, after ten minutes, a veil slowly lifted. But it would take months of perseverance, on the part of Danny and his mediators, before whatever potential cognitive skills he possessed would be released from the shell within which they had been bound throughout his life.

Feuerstein's own formidable intelligence is as creative as the forces he seeks to release in others. He has trained children afflicted with Down's Syndrome to care for elderly people. 'In this way,' he observed, 'everybody wins.'

Reuven Feuerstein invited me to spend Friday evening with his family. They live in the suburb of Kiryat Moshe, to which I walked from the Old City because I had no choice. I allowed plenty of time, dawdling along the way by the entrance to the Mahane Yehuda market on Agrippa Street. Traffic along the surrounding roads had come to a halt; cars misparked while their drivers loaded up with provisions for Shabbat. Meanwhile the stallholders were beginning to dismantle their display tables. Further up the road, outside the Belz yeshiva, little boys in stiff boxy caps were playing and chattering while their fathers removed from the back seats of their parked cars the large brown boxes containing their fur hats.

It took me well over an hour to reach the Feuerstein house, and the warmth of the afternoon left me parched and inert. Mrs Feuerstein revived me with coffee and cake. Two of her sons, now in their twenties, were staying for the weekend, as was a nephew from Switzerland and a friend of the same age, a yeshiva student. This was an Orthodox household, but with none of the fiery oneupmanship of the ultra-religious. The Feuerstein boys had all been to yeshiva, but had also served in the army. The conversation was breezy and fragmented as the various members of the family wandered from room to room or flopped into armchairs with a magazine for a few minutes before recalling some errand not yet completed.

At four-thirty the Sabbath candles were lit, and then Reuven and I set off for synagogue. It was a slow walk, for he runs out of breath easily, but it allowed him to point out the physiognomy of the neighbourhood. The synagogue was a modern building, with a congregation to match, a modern Orthodox collection of academics and businessmen, including a fair proportion of left-wingers. Almost to a man, they wore the badge of the modern Orthodox: a knitted white *kippa* with blue edges. The courtyard was filled with family groups, gossiping men, and clusters of pretty girls biding their time before entering the building and climbing to the gallery. Reuven darted into the synagogue hall, made a swift circuit, then darted out again, followed by a small group he had recruited along the way.

Standing in the courtyard, he thrust a prayerbook into my hand, turned his back to me, and faced the synagogue doors as he began to recite prayers, backed up by his band of recruits. He later explained that since this week was the anniversary of his mother's death, he had to honour the occasion by reciting the *maariv* prayers in synagogue that afternoon. But we had arrived too late and prayers had already begun. Undeterred, Feuerstein had rounded up a *minyan* (the minimum number of ten males required before a service can be held) and conducted his alternative service in the yard. When he had finished we entered the synagogue hall and took our places. Small boys rushed to his side as he lowered himself into his pew, for every child in Kiryat Moshe knows Reuven has an inexhaustible supply of toffees. With his deft palming and unpalming, with a vanish and a clench, he postponed the moment of gratification until the giggles of amusement were suppressed by grimaces of frustration, at which point he would allow the sweet to be snatched from his grasp.

After the service, we emerged into the courtyard, where families, divided by gender throughout the service, were being reunited. The sense of haven that Israel has provided to those such as Feuerstein, who were hounded from their homes and fortunate enough to survive their persecutions and wanderings, became palpable. In this gently Orthodox suburb, the Jew is truly at home. There is no need to glance over one's shoulder on slipping out into the street, nor need *kippot* be concealed under hats. On Friday night in Jerusalem, the Jew is at his ease; for many it is as though they can scarcely believe that after two thousand years of dispersal it is possible to find themselves so free of fear.

During the service too, the air of relaxation was all-pervasive, and the convivial hubbub of prayer was laced with mere gossip and blather. Reform Jews, who have adopted a liturgical structure – readings, hymns, sermons, organ wash – modelled on church services, look askance at the lack of decorum in Orthodox synagogues. Yet I have always relished the very familiarity of the Orthodox service, the notion that in the course of a long, discursive service it's perfectly acceptable to switch off for a few moments, to greet friends or take a stroll or peek at the wavecaps of millinery up in the ladies' gallery.

Reuven, however, discerning my reluctance to participate in the service, had been ill at ease. As we walked back to his house, he explained: 'I had a strange feeling in *shul* this evening. There was a lot of noise, talking, during the service. Usually I don't mind that. My social needs are expressed horizontally as well as vertically – it's good to be able to talk to someone you haven't seen in ages, just for a minute. I felt strange because you were with me as a guest. I felt embarrassed on your behalf, but not on God's. And I couldn't understand why. Then I understood. God is not a guest. People have tried to improve our behaviour in *shul*, and some people said we should keep the children out during the service. I said: If the children go, I'm going with them, and that was the end of that.'

At the house there were cries of 'Shabbat Shalom' and kisses as we stepped across the threshold. While we were at the synagogue, other guests had arrived. The artist Yaakov Boussidan and his American-born girlfriend joined us, and Mrs Feuerstein's old stooped mother sat beside her daughter. The young men slung prayerbooks no larger than a pocket transistor radio around the table and launched us into a round of prayers and chants, harmonized by Mrs Feuerstein. Kiddush was recited, and the entire family, Reuven included, approached the grandmother, who placed her hands on their heads as they bowed or knelt in front of her while she recited her blessing on them. Reuven then presided over the ceremonies of the Sabbath eve, the salting of the bread, the blessings over the bread, and its circulation around the table; soon there followed a bewildering variety of dishes, heavy fare such as quiche and gefilte fish, rice and bouquets of salad.

It was not difficult to discern the strength that Jews draw from the Sabbath. It may or may not be an occasion for great piety, but gathering *en famille* on the same evening each week gives structure not only to the routines of work and rest, but allows the most subtle connections between religious faith, family cohesion, the hedonistic pleasures of the table, the satisfactions of repetition, and the obligations to history and memory. Of course this is true of diaspora Jews as of Israeli Jews, yet it seemed obvious that celebrating the Sabbath in the Land of Israel was fitting in a way no comparable celebration in the diaspora could be. The inscriptions on ancient stones in Jerusalem, the precious Temple relics displayed in the Israel Museum, the everyday language of the streets, and the ancient liturgy of Jewish prayer were part of a continuum, and one did not have to be devout to experience it.

Dr Feuerstein stresses the importance of such ceremonies and celebrations to the survival of Judaism. 'Jewish culture is the strongest paradigm of mediation, though there are of course other cultures, such as the American Indians, who have a comparable mediation. In the Jewish tradition the need to transmit the culture is so strong that the process of transmission becomes more important than its content. Not that the content of *mitzvot* is nonsensical, but the process is equally important. In Judaism there is a strong emphasis on "you shall tell", "you shall describe", "you shall answer the question". The whole Passover night is a method of posing a set of questions that will then give place to a set of answers. By the incomprehensibility of certain customs, such as dipping two times or drinking four cups of wine, you force the children present to ask the questions.'

Jewish law, he continued, is transmitted in an oral and a written tradition, and it was forbidden to write down the oral tradition. The whole point of its remaining oral was to encourage a creative response to it, by adding and embroidering. 'Leave it open, let people interpret it in whatever way they do. A written tradition cannot be changed, but with an oral tradition everything is possible. It's not a science of what has happened but of what can happen or could have happened.'

The buzz of intellectual activity around the Feuersteins' table on Friday night illustrated this perfectly. The presence of opinionated young men, and their even more opinionated father, not to mention the thoughtful utterances of Yaakov Boussidan and the occasionally disconnected humming and chanting of Reuven's wife, gave an operatic quality to the evening. Reuven teased me by seeking my opinion on the truly awful wine he had poured into my cup; he sought my opinion repeatedly on many topics, misinterpreting my attentive silence as unease. One moment Reuven would be speaking about a conference he had attended in Dublin, and the next he would slide into lovely Chasidic melodies, most of which petered away into cadences of 'loi-la-loi-la-loi'. He sang a sad Yiddish song he had learnt as a child in Romania, and then told us how he had come across the identical melody, only with an altered rhythm which he illustrated, as an Andalucian song. We speculated as to how this could be so. Then, in more rabbinical mood, he spoke of the difference between God's commands to Noah and those to Abraham, and pondered the need for equilibrium in our lives. His son Aharon drew analogies from Greek mythology and, yeshiva-trained, quoted verbatim other instances from Genesis. There was talk about the passage of angels to earth, and of instances when the journey was made in reverse. No notion expressed around the table was dismissed, however preposterous. On first utterance, each idea was regarded as a connection made, a leap of argument, even if subsequent examination led one to conclude that it was nonsense. Intellect, as well as emotion, was accorded the highest value.

Talk, inevitably, drifted towards the topic of the intifada. Reuven intervened, characteristically, with a tale about the Baal Shem Tov, the founder of the Chasidic movement. The upshot of the story was that when the Baal Shem Tov was about to slaughter animals for the community, his tears, not a whetstone, would moisten the knife. 'It's the same with us. We recognize necessity, but we take no pleasure from the terrible things that we must do. There is no rejoicing in Israel when Palestinians are shot.'

My evening with the Feuersteins made me curious to see how Shabbat was greeted in other Jerusalem households. A few weeks later I was invited to spend Friday evening with Amos and Shulamith in the Old City. We had never met before, and the arrangements were made through a mutual acquaintance. They occupied a characterless flat in the rebuilt Jewish Quarter. I arrived just after four o'clock. Shulamith opened the door, clearly flustered by the last-minute rush to complete her culinary preparations before the Sabbath began and all work had to cease. Her husband had just left for the Ben Zakkai synagogue and I was welcome to join him. She dispatched one of her small daughters to show me the way. In silence my little guide led the way through the alleys to the synagogue, one of four restored Sephardi synagogues clustered together in the Old City. On arrival I recognized Amos: he was the rather surly man who had tried to turn me away from the same synagogue when I tried to visit it a few days earlier. I had not been wearing a *kippa*. I had improvised a head covering with my handkerchief and, with a weary shrug, he had let me in. If he recognized me on my reappearance, he didn't let on.

From the start we had difficulty communicating. An Iraqi by birth, Amos spoke very little English. So he introduced me to other members of the congregation, a businessman and a Brooklynite of Syrian origin who told me, 'I'm now living in Jerusalem, *baruch ha-shem*' – praise be to God. On learning that I was a writer, my hosts lost their customary deference towards the literary profession and became defensive. Amos wanted to know whether I was for or against Israel, and the businessman said he hoped I would find some positive things to say. Not for the last time were Israelis assuming that all British writers are hostile newspapermen. There were only about twelve men in the synagogue when the service began, most of them yeshiva students in dark blue suits with homburg hats tilted back over high foreheads. The service was led by Rav Medina, an imposing grey-bearded figure wearing a long black coat; he had a fine voice, but recited the liturgy at breakneck speed. The Orthodox tend not to linger over their prayers, possibly because they have to get through so many of them each day. Pepper and salt were added to the service by two small boys, who didn't miss a trick and whose shrill trebles rose clear above the mature male rumbles of the rest of us.

After the service, I walked back to the flat with Amos the silent. The man was obviously weary and looked as though he had a migraine, so I didn't press him with small talk or heavy questions. Back at the flat, I realized why he was so worn out. He and Shulamith have nine children, and although only three were present, they made a fantastic amount of noise. Their eldest daughter, now in her late twenties, lives in Los Angeles. Three other children were away on military service. Shulamith, who grew up in Morocco, spoke French, and that is how we conversed.

Before the meal, the children led the singing. Kiddush was recited, and I sipped the only wine I would taste that evening. Blessings were recited over grapes (symbolizing the fruit of the vine), over salads (fruit of the earth), and a small piece of fish (fruit of the sea). The Sabbath loaf was blessed, dismembered, dipped in salt, and passed around. Shulamith, beaming, entered from the kitchen carrying a platter of fish and delicious chickpeas. I assumed this was the main course and ate copiously, urged on by the family. I felt a lurch of dismay when some minutes later she produced a tureen filled with soup and vegetables, and a mound of chicken. For dessert there was fruit. Between each course there were more songs, led by Yaakov, a boy with a strong voice who couldn't carry a tune – not that this bothered him – and his pretty sister Anat, a surly girl of about nine with a fine voice, and the tiny one, aged three or thereabouts, who joined in as best she could. The tiny also treated me to an American-Jewish song, presumably of Los Angeles origin, taught her by her eldest sister. Its chorus had words along the lines of 'Here in my head, deep in my heart, deep in my toes', all lisped in a strong Israeli accent, with r's like avalanches. Her brother and sister moved on to other songs, but tiny persisted with the American one, in my honour. Amos, desperation in his drooping eyes, occasionally tried to lower the volume, but the kids were in control, and he slumped back in his chair. Additional diversion was provided by a grandmother, who was agreeably senile; she walked into walls and muttered to herself and had to be reined back in when she got out of line.

Shulamith, unlike her zonked husband, was aware that the evening had been fairly disastrous. A large, motherly woman, she urged me to return another evening when her older, English-speaking children would be around. She had done her best to explain to me the various ceremonies of the evening, and I warmed to her. After dinner Amos threw himself onto a sofa with a religious book – there didn't seem to be any other kind on the shelves – and made no further acknowledgement of my presence. I couldn't help thinking that he might have been more sociable if he could devise a way to keep his rowdy little children in control. It wasn't merely the decibel level that irked me; it was that the racket precluded the possibility of any conversation. The only quiet moment during the entire evening occurred when the meal was over and the family sank into silent prayer. There was no attempt to detain me, and with the meal over I left speedily.

# 6 · TORAH, TORAH, TORAH!

Both the Feuersteins and Amos's family were Orthodox, but not ultra-Orthodox, and the distinction is an important one. The so-called modern Orthodox, like these two families, obey Jewish law and tradition, but live in the modern world; they were probably Zionist in the broadest sense and eager to make their contribution to the Jewish state, including military service. The ultra-Orthodox – or *haredim* as they are known in Israel – think very differently. They too, of course, obey Jewish laws, and with a fervour that strikes other religious Jews as verging on the fanatical. Menfolk are required to study their religion throughout their lives, even though this throws the primary responsibility for earning an income and bringing up eight or twelve children on their exhausted wives. Modern Orthodox wear modern clothing; *haredi* men wear black. Modern Orthodox cover their heads with knitted *kippot*; *haredim* wear large black hats over black *kippot*, and *haredi* married women either shave their heads or keep their hair concealed beneath snoods or scarves. Modern Orthodox go to university and watch television; *haredim* study only at their own yeshivot and eschew such intrusions of the world as newspapers (other than their own) and television. Crucially, in Israel, many, though by no means all, *haredim* are deeply opposed to Zionism, and express that opposition by refusing to pay taxes or perform military service.

Many Israelis kept telling me I was paying too much attention to the *haredim*, whom they consider tiresome but insignificant. They can certainly be tiresome, but they are profoundly significant both because they command respect as repositories of Jewish law and tradition and because they question the very foundations of the Jewish state. They may only constitute 10 per cent of Israel's Jewish population [1] but six years ago they made up 27 per cent of the Jewish population of Jerusalem. Because of their high birthrate, that proportion is now estimated to be one third. Within the next ten years the non-*haredi* Jewish population of the capital could be outnumbered by the largely non- or anti-Zionist *haredi* and Arab populations.[2] Moreover, the *haredim* have their own political parties which, thanks to Israel's parliamentary system, wield power out of all proportion to their electoral support.

Casual observers view the *haredim* as monolithic, but they are deeply fragmented, and from time to time violence breaks out between different sects. Nevertheless their bonds are greater than their divisions. They share similar values, although some are more extreme than others in their observances, more passionate in their rejection of the temporal world. Each sect is led by a *Rebbe*, who has often inherited the role, and many of the disputes among the ultra-Orthodox arise from personal conflicts between their leaders. The power of the *Rebbe* is immense; he is consulted by his followers on all important matters relating to their lives. Marriages, new jobs, surgical operations, voting – all are heavily influenced by the omniscient *Rebbes*. Some are accorded the status of living saints, so perfect is their virtue, so fervent the devotion they inspire.

Chasidim constitute one of the most important and visible groups among the ultra-Orthodox. Chasidism was founded in the eighteenth century in present-day Poland and the Ukraine as a reaction against what was perceived as excessive scholasticism. The Jewish tradition of intense study was all very well, argued the first Chasidim, but had an air of exclusivity that struck many ordinary Jews as remote. Closeness to God could be attained not only by constant study of holy texts, but by the act of prayer, and prayer was open to all, regardless of background or education. Chasidism was democratic in its appeal, if autocratic in its structure. It made great inroads in eastern Europe throughout the nineteenth century, leaving its ideological opponents, the *mitnagdim*, in retreat.

One of the innovations of Chasidism was the exaltation of the *Rebbe*, whose primary role was as an intermediary between his followers and God. Chasidic *Rebbes* were known as *tzaddikim*, holy men, saints, and their powers could be inherited. Thus Chasidic dynasties were founded that are still in existence. *Mitnagdim* were profoundly suspicious of the personality cult that seemed to accompany the Chasidic movement, and their fears had, and still have, much foundation.

The Holocaust came close to destroying Chasidism, based as it was in eastern Europe. The various Chasidic sects – Belz, Lubavitch, Ger, Vishnitz – take their names from the towns where they were once based, towns that before the Second World War were great centres of Jewish learning and culture. The handful of survivors settled in Jerusalem or Brooklyn or Stamford Hill and, against all the odds, maintained their way of life more or less intact. One of the emotional consequences of the Holocaust was a return to Orthodoxy by many Jews, some of whom were deeply attracted to the undeniable authenticity of the ultra-Orthodox sects. One of the sects, the Lubavitch movement – based in New York but with branches throughout the Jewish world by the 1960s – engaged in aggressive missionary activity, not among Gentiles, but among Jews. It sought to demolish the notion that Chasidism had become a refuge for nonagenarian Polish rabbis; all were welcome to join, even the most secularized of Jews. Their numbers grew. The *Rebbes* discouraged birth control and preached the virtues of large families. Some declared that they were seeking to undo Hitler's work, to replenish Jewish stock.

Two Chasidic sects are very powerful in Jerusalem: the Ger and the Belz. The *haredi* district of Tel Aviv, Bnei Brak, is a stronghold of the Vishnitzers. Some Chasidic groups, such as the anti-Zionist Satmar Chasidim who originated in Hungary, remain Brooklyn-based and have little influence in Israel. The Lubavitchers – also known as Chabadniks – acquired increased power in Israel after the unprecedented intervention in the 1988 general election of their charismatic *Rebbe*, who has never set foot in Israel. The Breslau Chasidim buck the whole trend by operating without a *Rebbe* ever since their founder died in the early nineteenth century. The Belzers claim to have 25,000 families within their fold, although in Jerusalem they are outnumbered by the Gerer Chasidim. The Belzers are also well represented in Bnei Brak and other Israeli cities, as well as in North America. All hell broke loose when the Belzer *Rebbe* announced that he was setting up an organization to monitor the standards of kashrut, the Jewish dietary laws. Kashrut supervision ensures that animals are slaughtered according to Jewish law, and that no non-kosher traces, however minuscule, make their way into food and drink intended for consumption by Orthodox Jews. The extreme *haredi* group known as the Eda Haredit in Jerusalem had long enjoyed something close to a monopoly when it came to kashrut supervision, and great strife followed between the two organizations and their followers. Kashrut supervision is not simply an act of religious policing; its services must be paid for, and thus an economic argument entered into the disputes. The Edas enjoy a slight edge because of their very extremism. If a slab of meat has the Eda seal of approval, then other Orthodox Jews reflect: 'If it's good enough for them, then it's good enough for me.'

The Belzers run all manner of social welfare institutions and about eighteen schools and yeshivot, whose graduates are advised on their careers by the *Rebbe* himself. The Belzers have had many uneasy moments. One *Rebbe* only narrowly survived the Holocaust by being smuggled out of Nazi Europe disguised as a Hungarian general. His fifty grandchildren all perished, and the leadership of the court after his death fell to his nephew, the present *Rebbe*, after a lacuna of ten years. (When a *Rebbe* dies and there is no obvious successor, the elders of his court get together to sort things out. Family members are given priority, but are not always suitable for the mantle and other candidates have to be approached.) At first the young *Rebbe* failed to produce an heir, but eventually, after eleven years of marriage, a son was born. The rejoicing among the Chasidim was intense. The child was carefully reared, and rigorously instructed in the faith; by the time of his barmitzvah in October 1988 it was clear that he had the makings of a *Rebbe*.

The skilled eye can identify which sect a Chasid belongs to. Their antique costume permits many variations. Chasidic garb has become a badge of the tribe, a semiotic code, and also a mark of perversity, since it is hard to imagine any clothing less suited to the baking Jerusalem climate than the heavy costume of the *haredim*. The Belzers tuck their trousers into ankle socks, some inches higher than the tucking-in point favoured by the Gerrers. The black hats of the Belzers are distinguishable from those worn by the Vishnitzers only by the side on which the bow is tied. The Gerrers' weekday hat is uncreased but has a turned-up rim. On Shabbat and festivals the Belzers wear a narrow *schtreimel* (fur hat), but the Gerrers prefer the tall, dervish-style fur *spodik*. There are also variations in *payot*. The Gerrers, when absent from Jerusalem, tie them together over the top of their head and conceal them under their hat. *Mitnagdim* routinely conceal their sidelocks behind their ears. *Payot* swinging from the sides of the head is a sure sign of an approaching Chasid. Well, not quite, for the Lubavitchers, who wear black but skip the *schtreimel* and the knickerbockers, also tend to dispense with *payot*. All Jerusalem male Chasidim have beards, whereas I have encountered clean-shaven adherents of Chasidic sects in north London. There are many other indicators of affiliation: some Chasidim wear a *tallit* over their shirt, others do not; the Toldot Aharon group favour stripey coats.

The *mitnagdim*, who distrust the very notion of the *tzaddik*, stimulate group identification by different means. Since they venerate scholarship and study, their social centre is the yeshiva, and heads of yeshivot wield great influence. The *mitnagdim* flourished in Lithuania, especially in Vilna, and the movement is still associated with that country. One of the most celebrated Lithuanian rabbis, Avraham Karelitz, known as the Hazon Ish, initiated the movement of his adherents from Jerusalem to Bnei Brak, where his successors now run yeshivot. Of these the most notable is Eliezer Schach, head of the Ponivezh yeshiva and of his own political party, Degel Hatorah. He provides good copy with his regular denunciations of the Lubavitcher *Rebbe*, whom he detests.

Another group of *haredim* is known as the Yerushalmim, the descendants of ultra-Orthodox families that have lived in Jerusalem for generations. These hold within their ranks both Chasidim and *mitnagdim*. Some of the Yerushalmim, notably the Neturei Karta and Toldot Aharon, are thoroughgoing anti-Zionists. Toldot Aharon adherents are identified by their stripey coats, which earn them the sobriquet of the Zebra Squad, and from their habit of burning down bus stops that carry advertisements that offend their sense of modesty. Their umbrella organization is the Eda Haredit, which routinely issues *cherem*, denunciations and boycotts of religious opponents. In 1988 they drew up the *cherem* against a leader of Neturei Karta who had dared to question the anti-Zionist commitment of the Eda, and the head of the Satmar Chasidim, Rabbi Moshe Teitelbaum. Gripping stuff, with much the same fascination, and the same unimportance, as the infighting among Trotskyite splinter groups.

Almost all these *haredim* are Ashkenazim, descendants of German and East European and Russian Jewry. But there is also a tradition of piety and religious observance among Sephardim, the Mediterranean and Oriental Jews. Ultra-Orthodox Sephardim match the Ashkenazi *haredim* in the intensity of their observance, but the cultural tradition is entirely different. Ashkenazi culture is Yiddish-based, and many Chasidic and other *haredi* groups spurn the modern world. Both these traditions are alien to the more worldly Sephardim. Thus ultra-Orthodox Sephardim have their own synagogues and yeshivot, many of them in the Old City. Nor should one overlook the born-again *haredim*, known as *baalei teshuvah*, many of whom have joined the crusading Lubavitchers. Some of the extreme sects are very wary of these born-again Jews, not because they question their motives, but because those *baalei teshuvah* from non-Orthodox or secular backgrounds may be the descendants of people whose Jewish identity is questionable, because of improper conversions or other lapses.

On Shabbat, police barriers block the roads that lead into Mea Shearim and other *haredi* districts that have spread throughout north Jerusalem. The somnolence of Jerusalem on Shabbat is not without a powerful appeal. On this one day of the week families in their finery can stroll down the middle of roads that on every other day bristle with traffic. City noises – not only the roar of buses and screech of cars, but the hammerings and squealings of building construction and the whirrings and bangings siphoning out from countless workshops – are stilled. On a Saturday afternoon, the Chasidim in their silk coats and broad fur hats and white stockings pace grandly through their districts, accompanied by their wives, equally resplendent in tightly buttoned, all-encasing, occasionally well-fashioned clothes. They walk slowly, for there is all the time in the world on Shabbat, and the men clasp their hands behind their backs. Groups of teenage girls also wander the quiet streets; they wear long-sleeved pastel-shaded dresses that often look a size or two too large, and white stockings to conceal their legs.

The windows of the houses and apartment blocks are open, and it is astonishing how many rooms contain immense bookcases laden with religious folios and other texts. There is the sound of singing from some houses, where men have gathered to celebrate the Sabbath in less formal ways than the prayers of the morning. I sheltered from the sun on a bus stop bench and scribbled a few notes. A Chasid walking by murmured 'Shabbos', since I was contravening Jewish law by writing on the Sabbath, but he left it at that. Two youths laughed at me as they passed; they probably thought I must be waiting for a bus, unaware that no buses run on Shabbat. On the wall of a house opposite were political posters which I was unable to translate, so I stopped two young men who were strolling by and asked them whether they spoke English. They did indeed, since they were Americans spending a year at yeshiva in Jerusalem before returning to college in Miami. Although their Hebrew was so feeble that they were unable to translate the slogans on the wall, they were glad to talk, and didn't respond, as some *haredim* do when addressed, like frightened rabbits.

In Mea Shearim itself, the war of the posters is at its most intense. This was election time, and posters and banners were even more abundant than usual, praising and denouncing the innumerable political and religious factions within the *haredi* community. Printed notices in English, directed at tourists, 'warned' women that they should be discreetly dressed, with long sleeves and skirts below the knees. In some alleys notices discouraged mixed groups, and another sign requested men not to walk here bare-headed. To stroll down Mea Shearim is to tiptoe through a minefield of prohibitions, fearful lest a skinny youth dressed in eighteenth-century Polish garb should come leaping out of a doorway to berate you for a dress code violation. It is not sufficient for a *haredi* to pursue purest Orthodoxy; it is also necessary, it would appear, to upbraid those who fall short of your own exacting standards. Even violence, such as the stoning of cars, becomes justifiable as an act of religious self-defence. For the Orthodox Jew believes we are responsible for the shortcomings of our brethren, and thus it is our duty to keep them in line. Ultra-Orthodoxy is puzzled by the notion of tolerance, which it can only regard as indefensible slackness.

From Mea Shearim itself, lanes lead into courtyards known as *batim*. These were built to house ultra-Orthodox immigrants in the nineteenth century, and were usually named – Batei Ungarn, Batei Warsaw – after the settlers' places of origin. Here too are the stern notices: JEWISH DAUGHTERS! THE TORAH OBLIGATES YOU TO DRESS WITH MODESTY. WE DO NOT TOLERATE PEOPLE PASSING THROUGH OUR STREETS IMMODESTLY DRESSED.

The scale of the *batei* is domestic, with sagging washing lines and old women in headscarves gossiping in the corners while pale little boys like stick insects in peaked caps and sidelocks dart from house to house. This system of courtyard development was devised for reasons of security. Mea Shearim was founded in the 1870s. Since the district was outside the Old City, it was prone to attack from brigands, and gates guarded the area at night. Mea Shearim was not designed as an ultra-Orthodox enclave, but became increasingly extremist in the early decades of this century. With the absence of traffic and television aerials and other indicators of twentieth-century technology, the *batim*, and the life lived within their walls, have remained unaltered for a hundred years. They are self-sufficient fortresses of Orthodoxy, and it is no accident that the name of one of the most extreme *haredi* groups, the aggressively anti-Zionist Neturei Karta, means 'Guardians of the City'. Their hysterical style is captured by a bilingual poster I found on a wall near the Mea Shearim market: ZIONISTS ARE NOT JEWS BUT DIPLOMATIC TERRORISTS.

On weekdays in the *haredi* districts the yeshivot are the centre of activity. Here, and in the smart modern yeshivot of the Old City, young men may spend up to ten hours a day poring over the Talmud and other Jewish texts. The Torah as given to Moses on Mount Sinai is accepted as revealed truth, but that truth must be teased from the text by commentary and interpretation. Students usually study in pairs under a system called *havruta*, arguing between themselves or in small groups. There will also be more formal sessions when a rabbi will listen to and correct the students' interpretations. Morals are pointed, lessons learnt, conflicts exposed and resolved; the method of education is less an imbibing of knowledge than a development of mental and argumentative powers, only directed towards religious ends. The students, resident at the yeshiva, establish bonds both with their fellow students and with the often charismatic rabbis. Prayer and study become interrelated; social life and Talmudic exposition overlap. Many yeshiva graduates continue their studies in a *kolel*, a kind of yeshiva for married men. It is perfectly acceptable – indeed a paradigm of religious devotion – to attend the *kolel* for the rest of your life if you have an aptitude for such intensive study.

There is nothing new about yeshivot. The system was commonplace in eastern Europe. What is new is their ubiquity. Before the Second World

War it was estimated that at any one time in Europe there were no more than 12,000 yeshiva students. In modern Israel, with a Jewish population half that of pre-Holocaust eastern Europe, there are some 60,000 students at 370 yeshivot, including some 13,600 *kolel* students.[3] One might expect that such an extraordinary renaissance of Jewish learning would lead to an explosion of scholarship, but this appears not to have been the case. The yeshiva encourages scholasticism but not research, profound learning but not fresh interpretation. Modern scholarship – biological, astronomical, psychological – is rarely admitted into the yeshivot, and the students are kept in woeful ignorance of the intellectually turbulent world around them. There are Orthodox rabbis such as Adin Steinsalz and David Hartman whose learning and sophistication command respect in international academic circles, but they are very much the exception. Their celebrity makes them suspect within the very circles they ornament. In 1989 Rabbi Steinsalz, who won the Israel prize for his Talmudic commentaries, published some pamphlets on characters in the Bible, and promptly incurred the wrath of the Eda Haredit and of Rabbi Eliezer Schach. Steinsalz had offended by implying that the Oral Law was not handed down to Moses on Mount Sinai at the same time as the Written Law. Steinsalz promptly issued a recantation, and ultra-Orthodoxy and fundamentalism again became inseparably linked.

To make intellectual progress, one must be free to question, and the yeshiva student may question only within the strictest of parameters. You may question whether Rabbi Akiva put the right gloss on a certain text, but you may not challenge principles regarded as fundamental and inviolate. The final arbiter of truth is the authoritarian figure of the *rosh yeshiva*, who heads the institution. For students such as the youths from Miami and Reuven Feuerstein's sons, a passage at yeshiva is complementary to their basic education, not a substitute for it. The same cannot be said of those from *haredi* backgrounds who acquire matchless skills at Talmudic exegesis but remain wholly ignorant of their co-religionists Freud and Einstein. The yeshiva system is psychologically reinforcing, and thus a breeding ground for fanaticism and wilful incomprehension. The system also seeks to protect young *haredi* men from contamination by the outside world: if you never have to work, you need never leave the confines of the community.

The *haredi* community is not a rich one, for within each family there are so many mouths to feed. True, *haredim* don't have to save up for a sports car or a beach holiday in Greece, but, like the rest of us, they need shelter and food. With so many able-bodied males closeted away in yeshivot and *kolelim*, the earning power within the community is diminished.

Many yeshivot could not survive without the generosity of donors from the diaspora, where religious Jews are repeatedly told what a great *mitzvah* it is to sponsor study in the Land of Israel. Some Chasidic communities in North America are extremely prosperous, and their adherents are only too happy to support *haredi* institutions in Israel. The Reichman brothers of Toronto, Chasidic Jews and property developers, are said to have donated $100 million to such institutions during 1988.[4]

For the moment the burgeoning *haredi* community may be able to get by with the help of such handouts, but it is an insecure foundation. Yet it is hard to see how the community can become self-supporting. Many of the men contribute nothing to the economic health of the community. Those men who do earn a living often do so within the community, making *tefillin* or writing Torah scrolls, jobs that require enormous diligence but earn scant financial rewards. Others, according to Abraham Rabinovitch, become smugglers and black marketeers: 'It need not take you out of the *haredi* neighbourhood, or even the yeshiva; it leaves much time for study; it can be profitably pursued even without formal education; and, not least, it undermines the Zionist economy.'[5]

Some of their wives do work, but the jobs open to them are limited: many teach at the community's schools, though increasing numbers must seek work outside the community. Some families take national insurance from the state which they hold in contempt. Moreover, living in districts where every neighbour is a soul-mate, sharing to the letter religious, political, and ethical values, families can depend on intense mutual support. Women look after their neighbours' children whose mother has just given birth to her umpteenth child; financial calamities are averted with the help of friends, who know you will do the same for them. This is all very splendid, but it doesn't solve basic problems, such as where are we going to *put* Shmuel, our twelfth child? Despite a level of overcrowding most civilized societies would regard as intolerable, instances of crime – at least within the community – are negligible, and alcoholism and drug-taking are almost nonexistent.

The *haredi* community might well have collapsed long ago had it not been for the heartwarming support given to their institutions by the State of Israel. This is achieved by the blackmail from which few governmental systems dependent on proportional representation can be entirely free. The *haredim* are highly organized politically. When the Lubavitcher *Rebbe* tells his thousands of followers in Israel to vote Agudat Yisrael, they do so. When Eliezer Schach tells the *mitnagdim* to vote for Degel Hatorah, few will disobey. Nor are the ultra-Orthodox parties solely dependent on *haredi* support. The Sephardi ultra-Orthodox, tired of being patronized by the Ashkenazim, broke away to form their own party some years ago. This party, Shas, has won considerable support from traditional Sephardim who may be far from Orthodox, but find its values closer to their own than those of, say, Likud.

For decades Israeli governments have been dependent for their very existence on the support of the religious parties. With the major parties neck and neck in many recent elections, the leaders of the religious parties are in a position to negotiate aggressively with the mainstream leaders in order to pry loose as many concessions as possible in exchange for their support. These concessions invariably include increased funding for the yeshivot. Thus institutions that prevent fit young men from making any contribution to the economy or army, that often preach hostility to the very notion of the State of Israel, are underwritten by the despised national government. In 1986 yeshivot received $40 million directly from the government, and the figure is constantly rising. In some cases up to half the running costs of yeshivot is met by the government. It is, one must admit, a neat trick.

Another concession is the exemption of yeshiva students from military service. For this Israelis must blame David Ben-Gurion, their first prime minister, who in the early 1950s made a deal with the *mitnagdim*'s leading sage, Rabbi Maimon, whereby draft-age yeshiva students could defer their military service. In those days there were no more than 450 such students, and the concession was relatively trivial. Today, it liberates 19,000 from military service, though it is fair to add that many yeshiva students, especially among the modern Orthodox, do not make use of this deferment.

So, while yeshiva lads are either arguing strenuously with each other about conflicting commentaries on weights and measures, other Israeli men not only submit to military service for three years (women serve for one year less), but until late middle age must also spend up to sixty days each year on reserve duty. As I drove about the country, I often gave lifts to hitch-hiking soldiers, of whom there are hundreds on any highway at any one time. Some of them grumbled about the nuisance of reserve duty, but none of them actually complained, since the whole country — *haredim* excepted — acknowledges Israel's need to maintain constant military readiness. There is considerable resentment among secular Israelis at the refusal of the ultra-Orthodox to shoulder this burden of citizenship, but rather less than one might have supposed. Perhaps Israelis have become reconciled to this idiosyncratic consequence of their political system.

The *haredi* justification for such privileges is that intensive study of Jewish law and lore are essential to the spiritual survival of the Jewish people. Throughout Jewish history, it is argued, scholars have been granted privileges. Even during the forty-year wanderings of the Israelites in the desert, the priestly Levites were exempt from military service. Yeshiva students are thus presented as a precious national resource that must not be endangered or distracted. The system is open to flagrant abuse, as yeshiva students prolong their 'studies' indefinitely so that the deferment can also continue indefinitely. In general the austere Lithuanian yeshivot are more rigorous in discouraging such freeloading than their Chasidic counterparts. There are honourable exceptions, including the students of the Hesder movement, which was established by the socialist Zionist youth movement B'nei Akiva. There are only a few thousand students in Hesder yeshivot, but they all combine military service with their study. If the Hesder students can do it, so can the rest of them.

Some *haredi* groups have made their distaste for the Israeli state so plain that in the unlikely event that any of their number volunteered for military service, they would be rejected as a security risk, and quite rightly. But there is no serious danger of that happening. For alongside the ideological reasons for refusing to serve, there is good old *haredi* paranoia, the fear of exposing its young men and women to ideas hostile to ultra-Orthodox values. Nor are they referring only to moral corruption, in the form of sexual attraction. Most *haredi* men, even more than their womenfolk, are woefully uneducated except in the most narrow religious sense. Access to secular ideas and to the realities of daily life in the Middle East could be deeply subversive of their values.

Were the ultra-Orthodox parties not so thoroughly fragmented, their influence would be even more baleful than it already is. On the local level they can make a powerful impact, especially in Jerusalem, where they have fought protracted if losing battles against the rights of the non-Orthodox to drive their cars, swim in their pools, go to see a film on Friday night, or listen to the radio in their homes on Saturday afternoons. In Bnei Brak masked *haredim* have taken to beating up courting couples.[6] At the national level, they lobby, so far unsuccessfully, for amending the Law of Return so as to discriminate against converts to Reform Judaism wishing to emigrate to Israel. And, as we have seen, they have acquired for themselves a most bountiful gravy train.

There are more reasonable voices among the Orthodox, though one must strain hard to hear them. During the 1988 election campaign, Meimad, a religious party with a vaguely centrist programme founded by Rabbi Amital, the head of a huge yeshiva at Gush Etzion, took to the hustings. I went to one of their meetings, which was addressed by a thoughtful ex-Bostonian called Avraham Stein. He was no *haredi* but he lived on a religious kibbutz, and considered his religious observance as central to his life. He was missing his hands, lost during the Yom Kippur War. He did attack the secular left in Israel for keeping young Israelis ignorant of their Jewish cultural heritage, but he also attacked the religious right for its growing extremism and zealotry. In a veiled attack on the Lubavitch movement, which has done little to dampen rumours that its aged *Rebbe* could just possibly be the Messiah, he criticized religious groups that hinted that the coming of the Messiah was imminent. He also attacked the attempts of the religious right to put their beliefs on the statute book by lobbying for unenforceable legislation to prohibit, say, the raising of pigs or the selling of *chometz* (leavened bread) during the Passover period. You cannot, he argued, legislate to bring about greater spirituality. Amending the Law of Return, he insisted, was a sledge-hammer designed to crack a nut, since the numbers of American Reform and Conservative Jews seeking to come to Israel these days was negligible anyway. 'For this we have to tear the nation apart?' He talked sensibly, was utterly reasonable, and Meimad did not win a single seat in the Knesset.

Among secular Israelis, especially in Jerusalem where the exposure to *haredim* is greatest, the response towards them varies. Some see them simply as a nuisance. As long as they stayed within their ghettoes they could be regarded as harmless eccentrics, but now they were settling in districts that were secular or mixed. Districts such as Mea Shearim and Geula, exclusively *haredi*, had become too small to contain the expanding ultra-Orthodox population, swollen by a high birthrate and immigration. Once *haredim* have moved into predominantly secular districts, the pressure mounts. One Shabbat the residents are using their cars as they've always done; a week later, a campaign has begun to close the street to traffic. Sometimes this campaign, projected as an attempt to stop the desecration of Shabbat, has taken the form of slashing the tyres of offending cars. Secular Jews who live on the fringes of *haredi* districts have found their apartments firebombed if they refuse to knuckle under to *haredi* norms.[7] There is grudging acceptance among secular Israelis that in some carefully defined areas, notably marriage and death, the state has recognized religious law as binding. This is not because of theocratic leanings, but so as to avoid clashes in such fundamental matters between civil and religious authorities. Even the most atheistic Israeli, on breathing his last, may not be cremated – this is contrary to Jewish law – nor buried without religious rites. On the Sabbath in some towns, no telegrams are delivered, no escalators are in operation, no public transportation functions. Secular Israelis have learnt to live with all that, but many of them want no further encroachments by the Orthodox. They have no wish to see Israel transformed, step by step, into a theocracy.

There is dismay in secular circles when, as happens quite frequently, *haredi* rabbis explain appalling disasters by citing, for example, the failure of many Jews to ensure their *mezuzot* are correctly scripted. A Jerusalem newspaper printed the following advertisement in February 1989:

'On November 23, 1987, Judge Ayala Procaccia ruled that it was *illegal* for the municipality of Jerusalem to close commercial establishments on Shabbat. God's response was swift. 72 hours later a terrorist on a handglider [*sic*] penetrated Israel's air defenses and attacked an army base killing Israeli soldiers.'

A thoroughly secular Jerusalemite, who cited some other instances to me, added: 'This is a measure of their lack of any sense of reality. It was the kind of explanation that might have been perfectly suitable within his own community, the kind of thing you murmur over the fence to your neighbour. But the rabbi made the mistake of offering the same explanation to a nation of disbelieving Israelis. And we were appalled.'

When in March 1989 *haredi* worshippers at the Western Wall exploded with rage at non-Orthodox women who were conducting their own service at the site — a practice which is certainly nontraditional but not, most rabbis agree, contrary to Jewish law — the implications were rich indeed. Many Israelis saw this as yet another attempt by *haredim* to appropriate something, in this case an historical artefact and emblem, that belongs to all Israelis. They were treating the Wall as their private domain. Nor was the irony lost on most Israelis that it was the non-*haredi* population that had liberated the Wall in 1967 while the ultra-Orthodox had sat in their ghetto and twiddled their thumbs.

Not all secular Israelis feel this impatience with the ultra-Orthodox. One acquaintance felt that the malign influence of the *haredim* has been exaggerated. 'It's true that sometimes the Orthodox try to impose their values on the rest of us. But that's partly because of the belief that each Jew is responsible for every other Jew, and that leads the more Orthodox to try to correct the behaviour of the rest. And there are positive things about the *haredi* way of life. I wouldn't want to change places with one of their women, but I do know that the women are treated with respect and honour, which is more than can be said for Israeli women in a more secular environment.'

Most secular Israelis concede that Jewish identity is inevitably tied to the vigorous survival of the Jewish religion; since they themselves cannot ensure that religious survival, they are reluctant to criticize those to whom that survival is entrusted. But as the Reform Rabbi Dow Marmur has remarked: 'Secular Israelis have a need, so it seems, to maintain religious institutions which will keep the faith on their behalf but, at the same time, by the extremist nature of these institutions, make sure that the majority of Israelis have nothing to do with them. In this way the dominant religion of the Jewish state has become institutionalized vicarious Judaism.'[8]

Some intellectuals, such as Amos Oz, resist the notion that their identity is rooted in a religion: 'Religion is a central element in the Jewish civilization, perhaps even its origin, but that civilization cannot be represented as nothing more than religion ... [Nobody] can tell me, in whatever terms, that it's a package deal and I should take it or leave it. It is my right to separate the wheat from the chaff.'[9]

Yet the greatest threat to *haredi* life and values comes less from secular opposition than from within. Economic life within the community is stagnant. Poverty is widespread. Without the generosity of donors from diaspora countries and government subsidies, their way of life could be doomed. There is no guarantee, in a volatile society, that subsidy and blackmail will continue undiminished forever. If *haredim* are forced to earn their keep, they can do so only with a far greater measure of secular education than they permit at present. To survive in the modern world, they must mix in the modern world; and once they compromise their self-imposed isolation, psychological as well as physical, their survival as a powerful subgroup within Israeli society could also be threatened. At present they are a protected species, but they must be aware that many species protected a few decades ago are now extinct.

To inspect *haredi* anti–Zionism at its purest, I was advised to contact Moishe Hirsch, the self-styled minister of the Neturei Karta group with a passion for publicity, especially in the form of American television cameras — but nobody knew where he lived. A well-connected friend tried phoning an Orthodox friend of hers. 'Do you have a number for Moishe Hirsch? Oh, that's too bad. No, I haven't had a Mars Bar all day. Hey, why don't you just shut up? Bye, Marty.'

'What was that all about?'

'Marty's always trying to save my soul. That's why he was going on and on about my passion for Mars Bars.'

'They're kosher, aren't they?'

'Close enough, but some religious authorities are dubious about the milk used, as the factory didn't have somebody checking every ten minutes to see that there were no pigs standing in the milk.'

The closest I could get to an address for Hirsch was an instruction to walk into Mea Shearim and look for the posters declaring 'I Do Not Take Part in Israeli Elections' that adorn his home. The trouble is that such posters are ubiquitous in Mea Shearim. I entered the heart of the district and asked for Hirsch's whereabouts. In the market everybody knew his name, but few seemed to know where I would find him. I went round in circles for half an hour until by chance I encountered one of his neighbours.

'Do you know where I could find Moishe Hirsch?'

'There.' He pointed to a small stone house in a courtyard, then turned away in disgust. 'Hirsch not a *yehud* [Jew]. Hirsch a Palestinian.' A remark that remained murky until after I had spoken to the gentleman in question. At that moment I saw a slight figure with a wispy white beard and thin white moustache leaving the house. It was Hirsch. He made a great song and dance about how difficult it would be to find time to see me, but eventually agreed to meet me the following day at the American Colony Hotel.

I arrived early, and a few minutes later saw Hirsch crossing the street towards the hotel in his heavy black coat and shallow black hat. We sat in the flower-filled courtyard of the hotel, but he declined any refreshment. Beneath his coat he wore a white shirt, and over the shirt a *tallit*; if the heat of the day bothered him, he didn't let it show. An American by birth, he has lived in Jerusalem since 1955. Neturei Karta is a loose organization with no formal membership; it has its own yeshivot but is also represented within other organizations, and overlaps with anti-Zionist Chasidic sects such as Satmar. It never became clear what Hirsch's exact status within Neturei Karta was, for the movement has disowned him from time to time. Not that it mattered, since he represented to perfection the serene anti-Zionist view.

'Zionism is nationalistic, claiming a land and a language devoid of divinity. Zionism is an infringement of the principles of our faith, which are that this land is given to Jews on the condition that they adhere to God's will. When we failed to do so two thousand years ago, God took the land back. In time God will send the Messiah to redeem the land and we will return. But the Zionists don't see it that way. They have decided they don't like exile, so they'll just take the land back. That's why the Jewish state is a sacrilege. It's just cashing in on the holy nature of Israel. Zionists use the Wall and Masada for their ceremonies, but it's just a form of exploitation.'

'I understand your theological objections, but if it weren't for the Jewish state, you probably wouldn't be here now, would you?'

'Maybe, maybe not. Jews have lived in Jerusalem for centuries. There's no reason why they shouldn't have continued to do so.'

'How come the state tolerates you in its midst?'

'The establishment recognizes Neturei Karta's right to our point of view, our faith. We don't vote, we don't pay taxes, we won't accept state funding for our schools, we won't use their language, in fact we dissociate ourselves as much as we can from the state and its institutions. We still have to breathe occupied air and drink the municipality's water, of course. What we say is this. We have to adhere to the will of God. We have been put on earth to nourish our souls for eternity. We see ourselves as Palestinian Jews, and most of us were here before the Israelis. In fact we have requested the United Nations to give us refugee status and passports, since our land has been taken from beneath us. We are subjects of Israel against our will. *Haredim* came here as individuals, not on waves of Zionist *aliyah*.'

Hirsch had a faint smile on his lips as he spoke. Nothing ruffled his sense of certainty. He did not harangue me, he had an answer for everything.

'Aren't you being insensitive to the special circumstances that afflicted European Jewry after the war?'

Then he lost me, launching into a dissertation on how Hungarian Jews had connived with the Nazis. The upshot of the argument was unsavoury: that the Holocaust was the Jews' own fault. Nor did he have any sympathy for more recent victims of Arab discrimination in the Middle East who have come in their thousands to start a new life in Israel. 'Zionism is nothing but lust and expansionism. Jews have lived in Moslem countries for centuries. Then the Zionists deliberately caused friction in those countries as a way of getting the Jews to come to Israel. They came from Morocco and Yemen, and had to abandon their Jewish culture that was thousands of years old.'

'Don't you accept that there is such a thing as Arab nationalism, and that Jews who had once lived in relative freedom in Moslem countries found they could no longer do so?'

'Yes, I do, but it was Zionism that caused Arab nationalism.'

I suggested that Neturei Karta were about forty years too late in their campaign. In response Hirsch cited scripture to show that after another forty years there would be a major change in Israel. When I asked him to be more specific, he shrugged and said he had no powers of prophecy.

'How about a prediction instead?'

'Well, I would guess that the present State of Israel won't continue as it is.'

'If you are so bitterly opposed to every aspect of the Zionist state, why don't you leave it? You could return to New York, couldn't you?'

'Many Neturei Karta supporters have done just that, because some of our rabbis feel that Zionism poses a physical and spiritual threat to us in Israel. But we don't interfere with secular Israel. We simply have nothing to do with it, not even with the religious parties. We're opposed to strife between the *haredim* and the secular, but at the same time we're opposed to the desecration of our religion. We don't support the religious parties because the more kosher the State of Israel becomes, the more misleading it becomes. Fortunately we are a growing movement, and the Zionist brainwashing is losing its effect. We're trying to educate people, to persuade them of the rightness of our cause. The deeds of all Jews affect the whole nation, so we need to teach our fellow Jews.'

Hirsch and his cohorts are not content with seeking to undermine the ideological foundations of Zionism. That is a legitimate exercise, though not surprisingly an unpopular one in Israel. More importantly, Neturei Karta has undertaken political initiatives in support of the Palestinian cause. Hirsch had recently written an article for the Palestinian newspaper *Al-Fajr* arguing that the intifada is divinely inspired. He told me smugly: 'Some of the Arab leaders are our best friends.' The geopolitical goal of Neturei Karta is to persuade Mea Shearim to secede from the Israeli state and attach itself politically to any future Palestinian state or Palestinian-Jordanian federation. Like-minded *haredim* from other parts of Israel would then presumably move to this enclave in order to fulfil their anti-Zionist mission. This would be feasible, Hirsch argues, if Jerusalem were to become a dual capital. 'We have had contacts with the Palestinian National Council, not directly, but from abroad. I have had contact with Arafat and proposed to him that he appoint someone from Neturei Karta as a minister for Jewish affairs in any Palestinian regime, and he has agreed to do so.'

Hirsch's supreme self-assurance was beginning to irritate me. When he told me, with some satisfaction, that he had often been arrested by the Israeli authorities, I could not help muttering that I wasn't surprised. His activities would be close to treasonous if they were not so ludicrous. I brought the interview to an end, and accompanied him across the rubble-strewn waste land that separates East Jerusalem from the *haredi* districts. As we walked, I asked him why there was so much violence within his community. He denied that this was the case, though he conceded that there had been one or two incidents, the work of a very few hotheads. No sooner had he offered this explanation than, seemingly from nowhere, two youths wearing *tallit* rushed up to us, knocking the hat and *kippa* from Hirsch's head. They jostled him, shouting 'Traitor!' in Yiddish, and then ran off. Hirsch was not hurt, but he was clearly embarrassed by the emanation of the very phenomenon he had just dismissed. He stood in the road, staring at his assailants as they retreated. 'Just as I thought,' he said to me with dignity, 'those were some of the hotheads I was mentioning to you. I recognize those boys.' He was probably trying to save face, and I let him do so. To attack an old man and rough him up is inexcusable, but I can't say I felt sorry for him.

# 7 · AMONG THE PATRIARCHS

'O little town of Bethle —' Stop right there. There's nothing little about Bethlehem. Having walked on a hot afternoon from Rachel's Tomb on the edge of town to the Church of the Nativity, I speak from experience. Bethlehem sprawls along the ridges and down the slopes. Even more than Jerusalem it gives the impression of being the Holy Land headquarters of the Christian orders. The road into town winds past missions, orphanages and hospitals on the hillsides, while at road level hundreds of scarcely distinguishable souvenir shops sell crucifixes, olive wood nativity scenes and other junk.

From the small terrace where the Jerusalem buses stop there is a fine view onto the rolling barren hills, pale brown and buff in colour, with the half-hearted green of irregular olive groves splattered among them. It's a very different landscape from the cultivated foothills between the coast and Jerusalem. Here the fields are small, the soil coarse and stony. Arab houses — all variations on the cube — are dotted about at random like thrown dice. Donkeys carry crops from field to market. Methods and patterns of cultivation haven't changed much, I imagine, since ancient times, and this landscape perfectly fits the stereotypical notion of 'biblical'. Less desolate and dramatic than the Judean desert around Ma'aleh Adumim, its domestic scale matches biblical notions of toilers in vineyards and wells and reaping and sowing.

Manger Square, on the other hand, has no such echoes, despite its proximity to Jesus's birthplace. That is because Manger Square is a car park. Coaches laden with pilgrims attempt to turn corners that won't be turned, and car drivers look on in despair as the buses block the road. If you clamber over the parked cars to the centre of the square you will see a fountain. It is dry. Along the sides of the square are a heavily fortified police station flying the Israeli flag, a mosque, a handful of restaurants and souvenir shops, and the Church of the Nativity. The famous church is entered through a stone door no more than five feet high. By this door is posted a list of rules, signed by the Civil Administration of Judea and

Samaria, as the authorities would like us to refer to the West Bank. It informs us that neither animals nor arms may be taken inside the church. The interior is stately, with double aisles marked off by Corinthian columns, and sections of a lovely mosaic floor exposed beneath the present floor level. The church is not in a particularly good state of repair; the transepts have stains on the walls, and bad pictures on crumpled canvas hang crookedly from the heights.

Sweaty pilgrims are put into appropriately spiritual mood with the help of taped Christmas carols dribbling into the nave through grilles near the altar steps. Entering the crypt, I approached the tiny grotto of the nativity. Hung with dozens of brass lamps, it resembled a shop in the *souk* more than a place of worship. It was, of course, the gifted Empress Helena who identified the spot where the actual birth took place. A much larger section of the crypt, now blocked off by a wall, is under the custodial care of the Franciscans, and you must approach it from the modern church that the Franciscans have built adjoining the ancient one. Down in this crypt were two dozen Hungarians, who found their exit blocked by a party of descending Spanish tourists. For a few minutes nobody moved, and while they were sorting themselves out, I explored the various chambers carved from the rock. St Jerome had installed himself in one of these cells when translating the Bible into Latin, but there is not a great deal to see here, other than walls, a ceiling and a floor.

On a subsequent visit to the church with my wife, a model of piety, we encountered in the crypt of the nativity a group of British Catholics piping 'Away in a manger'. My wife dabbed the tears from her eyes as I tugged her gently to the steps leading up into the chancel. Here she spotted the usual grubby Orthodox priest, and chose this moment to stage a scene in the very poorest taste. Clutching my arm and pushing me towards the bemused priest, who was happily picking his nose, she addressed the cleric: 'Father, Father, this man is a Jew and he wants to convert.' A brief but violent episode ensued as I fought off my wife and ran for the door, but I was blocked by the massed ranks from Inspirational Tours of Houston, and she almost succeeded in hauling me back in. To punish her, I made her visit the Milk Grotto, a couple of hundred yards from the church. This shrine is notable for its many tacky representations of the Virgin breast-feeding. Here, it is said, the young mother produced a surplus when nursing the infant Jesus; as he cried over spilt milk, the liquid turned the stone of the grotto to chalk. Little bits of chalk may now be purchased for a handsome sum from the Franciscan stewards, who assure us that a reverent visit from nursing mothers will aid their lactation.

Despite the to-ing and fro-ing of pilgrims and their coaches, all is not well at Bethlehem. The effect of the intifada and the endless strikes is particularly noticeable precisely because it is, or was, a prosperous town. Although Bethlehem is only about five miles from Jerusalem, many Jewish Jerusalemites have convinced themselves and their visiting friends that the town is no longer safe to visit. Parked cars bearing sandy yellow Israeli licence plates, instead of deep blue West Bank plates, have had their windows broken – even hire cars rented by tourists. You only have to glance at the ranks of souvenir shops to realize that the town is geared to a level of tourist trade far greater than the modest traffic found today. Traders grown used to constant invasions of tourists now have to contend with a mere trickle. Relations between Arab merchants and Jewish tour operators and other entrepreneurs have become discreet at best, as it bécame imprudent for shopkeepers to appear to be too pally with the Israelis.

I never quite understood the purpose of the Arab strikes, which seemed to have the effect of scoring own goals. They did inflict damage on the Israeli economy – some $666 million in 1988, according to the government's own figures – but the main brunt was borne by the economies of the Occupied Territories. The long-term economic impact of the strikes may continue to be hurtful, but their psychological impact has waned. After all, who in Haifa or Ashdod gives a damn if the buses aren't running to Hebron or if the shops in Nablus are shut all day? Walk through the Old City or through Bethlehem on a strike-bound day and you will see that many Arab shop-fronts are shuttered but not padlocked. Behind the steel rollers some kind of commerce is still being pursued, and tourists are discreetly ushered into shops to inspect the merchandise. Nor do the strike organizers prevent Arabs employed by Israelis from working. It is only the Arab sector that shuts down.

One of the managers at the Knights Palace was a gentle, literate man with whom I would talk whenever possible. When I asked him to explain the purpose of the strikes, he would only say, 'To make an impression.' He agreed that they hurt Arabs more than Jews, murmuring that 'there are many sacrifices.' He would never give me a point of view. Other Arabs in Jerusalem with whom I discussed the matter were equally noncommittal, talking loosely about the need for Arab and Jew to live together. Majid Al-Hajj, a lecturer in sociology at Haifa University, described the strikes as a consciousness-raising effort that seeks in some mysterious way to alter the social and class structure within Palestinian society. Maybe, but for all that the economies of the Occupied Territories, despite links with Jordan, remain strongly dependent on Israel. There are, to give one example, no more than 3,500 cows in the whole of the Territories, so for dairy products the Palestinians are almost totally reliant on Israel. Efforts are being made to bolster the economic independence of the Territories, but resources are sparse and the strikes themselves mean that belts must be tightened still further.

The Israelis repeatedly point out that the standard of living of the Palestinians has increased by leaps and bounds under their administration, especially in comparison with economic progress under Jordanian rule between 1948 and 1967. The statistics are impressive – the numbers of Palestinians with cars, with television sets, and all the other indicators of upward mobility – but, as the Palestinians remark, irrelevant. Their goals are, in the first instance, nationalistic and political rather than economic. During my stay in Jerusalem, I sought to gain access to some West Bank towns to see for myself. There was nothing to prevent me taking a bus ride to any town I wished, but I had no contacts there. When a friend suggested I latch onto a medical team in the Territories, that struck me as a splendid idea. The only problem was obtaining permission from the army. This took weeks of phone calls, but eventually permission was granted.

Early one morning I went to the Hyatt Hotel to meet a young woman called Dalia. The Israelis were perturbed by a few outbreaks of polio, and a programme had been launched to vaccinate the entire population, including the Palestinian population of the Territories. Dalia headed one of these medical teams. We travelled in a van prominently marked with the Red Crescent, the Middle Eastern version of the Red Cross, and emblazoned with other signs intended to deter stone-throwers. We drove first to Ramallah, a large Arab town north of Jerusalem. Here we stopped at the Public Health Division offices. While Dalia was occupied here, I talked to the director of the office. He confirmed that there had been an improvement in the standard of health care since 1967, although it could be difficult to administer because of the fluctuating population. There was so much movement in and out of the Territories that nobody knew for sure what the population was. The official figure was about 900,000, but he thought it was at least one million. Many Palestinians have medical insurance, though it is not compulsory, and many people prefer to consult expensive private doctors rather than visit the many clinics in the towns and villages. Up to the age of three all medical treatment is free. So too was the polio vaccination, and already half the population had been treated.

We went first to the nearby El-Bira clinic, where townspeople were being vaccinated by a white-clad Moslem nurse, and to a school temporarily transformed into an adult vaccination centre. Shortly after the intifada began, the 1,194 schools in the Occupied Territories, as well as the five accredited universities, were closed by the Israelis on the grounds that they had become breeding grounds for political dissent. Since many of the stone-throwers were school-age children, it was hard to see how instability was lessened by allowing 319,000 children to roam the streets. When UNRWA, the United Nations Relief and Works Agency that supervises the refugee camps in the Territories, tried in March 1989 to set up informal teaching sessions to keep the kids occupied, they were refused permission to do so by the Israeli authorities.[1] In July 1989, most West Bank schools were at last reopened.

Having inspected the school, we set off on a longer journey that took us through a more hilly landscape to the village of Beit Iksa. Its rocky slopes were strewn with old cars, rusty cans, plastic bottles, old tyres, empty cartons. The soil was too stony to be easily cultivated, but there were a few olive groves and the remains of some run-down terraces. Herds of sheep and goats belonging to Bedouin encamped nearby grazed on the thin soil. The programme of vaccination had only just begun that morning at the Beit Iksa clinic, which had been established by the Jordanians, although there was no electricity until 1988. Even now, the irregularity of the electricity supply thwarts the clinic's regular operation. Inside, there were posters warning about the danger of exposing food to flies, and reminding villagers of the importance of washing hands and vegetables before eating. The most common problems in villages such as Beit Iksa were food poisoning and typhoid, especially among the Bedouin. There had been no diphtheria since 1974 and no polio for five years.

We visited a small Bedouin encampment not far from Beit Hanina. Conditions were primitive, with sackcloth-covered tents supported on poles and pegs, but organized with the usual Bedouin meticulousness. Stacks of mattresses and bedding were neatly piled within the tent, and near the entrance a fire was smouldering. A baby snoozed in a sackcloth hammock, which was being gently rocked by a little boy. A travelling medical team had just arrived — by taxi, as there were insufficient vans for all the teams — and was vaccinating the family. The Bedouin family greeted us warmly and the visit was a protracted one. I had lost my sense of direction by now and had no idea where we were, but then I noticed a cluster of modern buildings along the top of a ridge. It turned out to be Ramot, the northern suburb of Jerusalem. Between the tent and the apartment block lay no more than a mile of stony hillside, but it was as though the deepest of chasms separated the cultures on either side.

Driving back to Ramallah, the doctor accompanying us admitted that the intifada had made life more difficult for medical workers. Army roadblocks and other impediments slowed down communications. Dalia was less diplomatic. She was fed up with being at the receiving end of stonings from refugee camps as she drove her teams around the Territories. Her impression was that many West Bank Palestinians wanted normal life to resume once again and longed for an end to strikes and disruptions. In her view, the strikes continued because the disaffected Arab population had been intimidated. And the solution? She thought stronger government would be helpful. Her impatience was also mirrored by official policy. Although serious medical cases among Palestinians had often been referred to Hadassah Hospital, their numbers were decreasing steadily. The justification for admitting fewer Palestinian patients, including children, was financial. Ironically, taxes on West Bank Arabs have increased since the intifada began in order to help pay for its suppression, and many Palestinians responded by withholding payment. The Israelis therefore felt it was appropriate to reduce the level of costly services such as hospital care in Jerusalem.[2]

The more questions I asked, the more I read, the more the contradictions went haring off in different directions. Statistics showed significant improvements in living standards and municipal services on the West Bank; doctors working there could discern no such amelioration. Israeli hospitals were continuing to treat large numbers of Palestinians despite the intifada; Israeli hospitals were now cutting back on such treatments. The Palestinians did not relish the strikes that had become a regular feature of their lives, but tolerated them because they would contribute to achieving their political aims; the Palestinians were tiring of the strikes, but were afraid to say so. Who was answering honestly, and who diplomatically? How could one tell when answers were being tailored to suit the expectations of the questioner? 'It's all relative,' people would murmur, but nowhere had I encountered such an explosion of relativity as in Israel. The ice was always thin. Staircases that led upwards turned into steps that led downwards. Truth loomed large or receded dimly in response to factors, including my own presence, that I could not gauge accurately. An experienced observer, I would use my eyes, but had no way to assess what I was seeing. Responses, whether positive or negative, became emotional ones, since there seemed no way for the intellect to operate clearly, dispassionately. In Israel you grow used to clutching your head in confusion.

My next excursion to the West Bank was achieved by the method referred to earlier: boarding a bus and buying a ticket. I decided to visit

Hebron, a large town some twenty miles south of Jerusalem, as a student of architecture. Within the town stands a fortress founded by King Herod, and within its walls are the tombs of the Jewish patriarchs and their wives, tombs that are shrines to Moslems and Jews alike. I was the only non-Arab on the bus, and most of the passengers wore traditional dress: the men in long robes and the women with their heads wrapped in spotless white kerchiefs. An elderly Arab of great dignity boarded the bus. His long black robe had been skilfully patched, though the frayed fur lining betrayed its age. While the bus idled at the terminal, small kids rushed up and down peddling small trays of chewing gum.

The road to Rachel's Tomb, the turn-off for Bethlehem, is essentially ribbon development, although close to the road there are some fine villas and monasteries from Ottoman days. Beyond Rachel's Tomb, the land is more sparsely inhabited; there are signs of determined attempts to cultivate what must be an ungiving soil. Most of the stone terracing on the hillsides has long been abandoned. In the gullies and wadis, untrained vines trail along the ground. Every few miles Jewish settlements peer down from hilltops. They are easily identifiable, both by the guard posts at the entrances, and by their red-roofed villas, so different in style from the boxy Arab houses.

It was Saturday lunchtime when the bus pulled into Hebron, and the town was already closing up for the day. Only a few market stalls and falafel stands remained open. Hebron is as dilapidated as the bulky ten-year-old cars parked in the streets and inappropriately adorned with foreign car badges: A for Austria, D for Deutschland, F for France. Battered lorries churn up the dust, and caked sludge drops from their mudguards onto the streets. The speediest vehicles are the open jeeps in which helmeted Israeli soldiers buzzed through the town. I realized I was an object of mild curiosity as I walked through the streets, so I slung a camera over my shoulder to indicate that I was a tourist. Tension was acute in Hebron between Arab resident and Jewish settler, and I had no wish to be falsely identified as a settler taking a solo hike as an act of bravado.

A sign to the Jewish cemetery pointed up a steep lane, which I took. The cemetery is an ancient one, and I was keen to see it. But soon the road forked, and although I sought directions from local residents, no one spoke English. I walked on for a hundred yards, but then felt isolated and uneasy, and turned back. I continued along the main road, passing the entrance to the heavily guarded Jewish settlement in the town centre.

There had been a synagogue here since the sixteenth century, when it had been founded by Jews fleeing from Spanish persecution. In 1929 the building was burnt and looted during rioting, and although about 300 Jewish residents were rescued by Arab friends and neighbours, fifty-nine were slaughtered. Under Jordanian rule, the synagogue was razed and replaced by public lavatories. (This is an ancient tradition in the Holy Land. When the Crusaders captured Jerusalem, they adapted the El-Aqsa mosque for the same purpose.) After 1967 the Israeli government did not respond to requests to rebuild the synagogue, and settlers took matters into their own hands. Rabbi Levinger, one of the ideologues at the forefront of the movement pressing for Jewish settlements in the Territories, headed a group of twenty-five families that rebuilt the synagogue with the help of the Hebron Fund, an American 'charity'. They now live in houses close to their place of worship. Some of those houses were bought from their Arab owners, others acquired by intimidation.[3]

Of the many Jewish settlements in the Territories, Levinger's tiny ghetto is surely the most provocative. Jewish villages on the West Bank are either in isolated strategic positions or on the outskirts of existing Arab towns and villages. Only in Hebron is the settlement in the heart of an Arab town. Whatever historical justification Rabbi Levinger and his acolytes may have for their wilful choice, they have presented the Israeli authorities with a security migraine, and Hebron, on the three occasions I visited the town, has always been stiff with soldiers. Violence between the two communities has become depressingly commonplace. Levinger may have history on his side, but he has exacerbated an already delicate situation. A month before my first visit to Hebron, Levinger had been at the receiving end of Arab stones, whereupon the rabbi took out his gun and fired into the air. The stone-throwers were unimpressed, so he fired into a shop, killing its owner and wounding a customer. In April 1989 the rabbi was charged with manslaughter.

The mighty walls of Herod's fortress rise up on the far side of a small park, adjoining a small district of ruined old houses. There are a number of entrances to the fortress, all guarded by Israeli soldiers. It comes as a surprise to discover that the interior is now a mosque, and that the tombs of the patriarchs are within that mosque, since Moslems also revere the patriarchs. The tombs of Isaac and Rebecca are massive and tall, shaped like Nissen huts and covered with heavy embroidered cloths. They lie snugly within red and white marble huts with green cloth-covered roofs. Around the tombs, on lakes of carpet, some Moslem worshippers were reclining and reading their newspapers. Chambers leading off from the courtyard within the fortress have been converted into synagogues, though Arabic inscriptions on metal bands across the entrance doors remind one again of the uneasy sharing. Here are the tombs of Abraham and Sarah, Jacob and Leah, of similar design to those of Isaac and Rebecca, but placed behind grilles rather than enclosed within huts. Some Jewish teenagers were out in the courtyard receiving a brief lecture, and after they left the fortress a soldier entered the little synagogue and searched it.

The synagogue is an innovation, as Jews used to be barred from worshipping at the tombs. One of the most vocal of the Jewish settlers, Eliakim Haetzni, who lives in Kiryat Arba just outside Hebron, gave me his version of recent events. 'At the second holiest shrine outside Jerusalem, we Jews could only pray seven steps outside. As for the rest, Islam said no, nyet, you can't enter. Abraham had two sons, Isaac and Ishmael. Ishmael wouldn't let Isaac in. So, Moshe Dayan allowed Jews to enter the building – but only as tourists. And we said, What is this? We want to pray here. He said no. We clashed with the Israeli army and fought the Israeli authorities for ten years for the right to pray here and have a synagogue here. People were brought before military courts, were sent to jail, and we succeeded. Now there is a synagogue inside, and this is the only place in the world which is both a synagogue and a mosque. When Isaac wins a war he doesn't send Ishmael seven steps outside, but at least we should have equal rights. We had to force the Israeli government to do this, and this gave us some bad press. Thank God.'

All the same, they have to walk here with armed escorts. I saw two Jews wrapped in long white *tallit* wandering up the slope to the fortress. Their voices were raised and I was not surprised to hear a Brooklyn twang as they argued about liturgical matters. I asked the soldiers at the entrance whether many tourists came to visit the tombs. They laughed. 'This is a dangerous place, and now it's more dangerous. Like the Wild West.' (For years many Israelis have referred to Judea and Samaria as 'the Wild West Bank'.) His companion added, 'We have Yiddishe Rambos,' and he didn't sound sympathetic.

'Is it safe for me to wander around Hebron?'

'No.'

'Even with my camera, so people can see I'm a tourist?'

'You may look like a tourist, but an Israeli tourist.'

I shrugged, and they laughed. I set off back down the slopes to the market and the road that led back to the bus station. Behind me came a group of some thirty young men, all in knitted *kippot*, most of them wearing white shirts and blue slacks. Every third man had an Uzi machine gun slung over his shoulder. When I turned and photographed them, they did not respond favourably, and some of them ran towards me shaking their fingers. I let them pass me, as I felt far less safe in the midst of a platoon of settlers than I did on my own. They disappeared into Levinger's compound. I couldn't wait to get out of Hebron – not because I felt in any danger, but because I was depressed by so much aggression around me.

A day later I would read in the newspaper that 'a bottle of acid was thrown at Jewish youths returning from prayers at the Cave of the Patriarchs, and two were slightly hurt'. Levinger and his disciples wanted to prove that Jews could, after a gap of fifty years, rebuild Jewish life in a shabby Arab town. They had done so, but at a terrible price. To live besieged in a stance of enervating and continuous defiance is a pyrrhic victory indeed.

My first encounter with a Jewish settlement on the West Bank was accidental. At loose ends one morning, I was strolling near the bus station when I encountered Yaakov Boussidan, the artist I had met *chez* Feuerstein. He was on his way to a silkscreen workshop in Ofra, the oldest settlement north of Jerusalem, to supervise work on prints that would form part of an immense new book on Jerusalem. He suggested I come along.

The bus took us through the northern suburbs and El-Bira, the Arab town where I had visited the clinic. This whole stretch of road up to Ramallah is built up, with new houses dotted at random along the slopes. Many of these houses are large and luxurious villas with iron gates, roof terraces and coloured glass in the picture windows. Although the basic design is blockish, there are attempts at ornament in the form of strange hat-like roofs perched over turrets, and bands of pink stone add colour to the off-white exteriors. This surge of lavish construction seemed surprising, given the perilous state of the local economy. Yaakov explained that many Palestinians had taken a leaf out of the Zionists' book, and had become adept at raising money outside the country. Moreover, many Palestinians had found employment in Gulf states and then returned to the Territories, having amassed a pot of money. Israelis are content to live in apartments, but self-respecting Arabs like to own their houses. The Israelis are fond of savings schemes and the stock market; Palestinians prefer to invest in land and buildings. Hence the rash of building, largely unregulated, on the fringes of Jerusalem. El-Bira is a university town, and relatively prosperous, though Yaakov said it wasn't that long ago that he recalled seeing impoverished huts where handsome villas now stood.

Most Arab construction is unplanned. You have a plot of land and you wish to build a house? Easy. You assemble your materials and a gang of workers and set to work. Some of these houses are built in a matter of days. Nobody worries unduly if at first the new building is not connected to existing infrastructure such as electricity or sewage. Although some of the lots are fenced in, very few have gardens, and the majority of houses, new and old, sit grandly in a sea of rubble. The clannishness of Arab life is suited to living in detached houses rather than in the planned communities favoured by Israelis. An Ottoman bylaw still on the statute books prohibits the authorities from demolishing a building that has been erected overnight. Occasionally those who violate the building codes are brought before the courts and fined, but the problem is so widespread that most illegal building goes unchecked. It is further complicated by the fact that records of ownership are usually patchy, confused, outdated or non-existent. The obvious thing to do would be to combine the small parcels owned by different individuals, and then redivide them so as to provide space for roads and schools and planned infrastructure, while leaving each individual owner with the same amount of land, even though it might be differently shaped. The Israelis contacted the *mukhtars* to explain this concept of reparcelization, but without success, if only because the *mukhtars* themselves tended to own most of the land and had most to lose, as they saw it, from the scheme.

One of the most curious features of contemporary Arab domestic architecture is the passion for placing miniature Eiffel Towers on top of their houses. Some of these metal contraptions are forty feet high. Indeed, the towers are the most visible of Arab status symbols, and the taller the radio mast, for that is what the fretwork of metal disguises, the richer and grander the proprietor. The architectural historian David Kroyanker told me that the Eiffel Towers date back to the times of the British Mandate; they were modelled on the RKO advertisements and thus became a symbol of Western progress and affluence. Nowadays the towers are mass-produced and you can order one in any size you can afford.

Ofra presents a bewildering contrast. With its neat houses, each with solar panels jutting from the red roofs, winding up the curving lanes, the settlement could have transplanted from a Midwestern suburb. True, some of the landscaping is half-hearted, but the semi-arid soil is not easily cultivated. Uniform globe lamps light the streets, and there are meticulous street signs on each corner. There is no indication of the inconveniences that have become routine to the Ofrans: erratic water and electricity supplies in particular. Small adventure playgrounds are abundant, and as I walked through Ofra on a warm autumn afternoon it seemed that the entire population was seven years old. At the foot of the slope on which the houses are built are the few institutional buildings: the general store, some workshops, the school, and the administrative buildings. At the very top of the small hill is a large airy building, constructed from lovely rough-hewn marble, that resembles the Knesset in design: the synagogue.

At the silkscreen studio, Yaakov introduced me to its owner, a small courteous man who is the son of a former Yemeni Chief Rabbi. On the walls of his office a photograph showed his grandfather wrapped in voluminous *tallit* and surrounded by some twenty children, including dark-eyed little girls in lavish Yemeni head-dresses; one of those little boys was now showing me the photograph. In thirty years he has moved from an essentially medieval world to the sophistication of modern Israel. The quality of his workmanship is high, but it needs to be to compensate for the very high prices that such studios must charge. Raw materials, such as handmade paper and ink, stagger into the country burdened with 300 per cent duty. Fortunately labour is relatively cheap; one of the press operators here was a former computer designer from Boston who had settled here as an act of idealism. In common with other enterprises at Ofra, the workshop employs no Arabs. Since Arab labour is very cheap, the settlement does not wish to be accused of exploitative colonial-style behaviour. The same policy is common at most kibbutzim too. The only exception is in building construction; even the most idealistic settlements and kibbutzim find themselves obliged to use Arab labour.

I spent half an hour chatting to the man guarding the entrance to Ofra. The settlers take it in turn to guard the town and others are detailed for night duty. The guard seemed keen to give me the impression that Ofra was little more than an ordinary village, its 170 families workers on the ground rather than ideologues. Many of them commuted into Jerusalem as though Ofra were just any old dormitory suburb. True, most of them support Tehiya or the National Religious Party, both far on the right of the political spectrum, but that didn't mean that Ofra was packed with fanatics. I didn't realize it at the time, but the man I was talking to was Yisrael Harel, one of the leaders of the settlers' movement, a moderate in comparison with some other leaders. The community he described seemed hard to recognize as the home of some members of the Jewish Underground who had planned to blow up the Temple Mount and of men who, in May 1989, conducted violent attacks on the nearby Arab village of Bitnin.

I asked Yaakov how he would characterize the Ofrans. He replied: 'Orthodox, and very fine people, and nervous as hell.'

If Yisrael Harel gave little away about Ofra, he proved helpful in putting me in touch with other Jewish settlers on the West Bank. I arranged to visit Tekoa, a community of ninety families not far from the ancient fortress of Herodion. I took the bus one morning, and at Rachel's Tomb an army jeep whizzed out from a checkpoint and blazed a trail for us through Bethlehem. Jewish Jerusalemites looked aghast when I mentioned my occasional travels on Arab buses, but they are far safer than Israeli ones: Palestinian urchins don't stone their own buses. Most dangerous of all are settlers' private cars. Drivers carry spare tubeless tyres, as at night nails are sometimes strewn across the roads. Damage from rocks and petrol bombs to private cars is, however, paid for by the government.

The escort proved ineffectual. Just after we turned onto the Herodion road, we heard the sharp bangs as rocks hit the side of the vehicle. The bus I had been riding back to Jerusalem from Ofra had also been stoned, but mildly. This time the assault was generous in volume and potentially hazardous. I sat back and watched as large stones came sailing over the rooftops. One shattered the window in the row behind me; another thumped onto the roof. There was mayhem, briefly, as the passengers, who included several armed soldiers, argued noisily with the driver. Should they stop and attempt to pursue the assailants, or should they ignore the episode and drive on? It seemed to me that the argument was academic by now; the stone-throwing youths had long dispersed and were probably back in their homes.

Tekoa was founded in 1975 under the Labour government as a para-military settlement, since the site is of strategic importance. In 1977, when Begin became prime minister, Tekoa was one of twelve original settlements to be 'civilianized'. The early settlers were Soviet immigrants, and conditions were primitive. Not all the founding families stayed, and the population dwindled until 1979, when a gradual expansion began.

Set on high ground, Tekoa has impressive views of the hills of Bethlehem and Gilo and, in the other direction, towards the Dead Sea and Jordan; on clear days the airport at Amman is visible. Because of its exposed position, the settlement is often buffeted by winds strong enough to bring down power lines. In the evening, when I waited twenty minutes for the bus back to Jerusalem, they were cold enough to chill me to the bone. As at Ofra, the houses here are based on standardized modules, so that although not uniform in appearance, they have a family resemblance. As families grow, their houses expand with them. Some have acquired an air of pretension in the form of stone facings and garden gates.

Some settlements accept newcomers on a first come, first served basis, but Tekoa is more like a kibbutz or moshav, in that the community as a whole makes decisions. After a preliminary interview, prospective settlers spend a weekend at Tekoa. They are told how communal living has its ups and downs, and the Tekoans take pains not to paint too rosy a picture of settlement life. Some Tekoans are religious and others secular, and newcomers have to be happy with that mixture, which is atypical of West Bank settlements. The next step is an interview with a committee of the Jewish Agency, including a psychologist; the community usually accepts the committee's recommendation, although it has the power to ignore it. The next stage is for the new family to join Tekoa on a trial basis. After a year, the community votes on whether to accept the newcomers as permanent members.

I asked Dr Amiel Ungar, an American-born political science lecturer at Bar-Ilan University, whether he and his fellow Tekoans had ever voted against allowing trial members to remain. 'Only on three occasions, and always for very sound reasons,' he replied. 'They were clearly obnoxious.' During the trial period they live in temporary housing, or rent houses which they can later purchase. Building lots are very cheap, about $5,000 in 1989, and mortgages heavily subsidized. On the other hand, new settlers are reminded that in exchange for the financial bargain there are responsibilities, such as contributing twenty working days each year to security duties. Like most settlements, Tekoa has a high immigrant population; about one third are 'Anglo-Saxons'.

The settlement is about 40 per cent self-sufficient, but many Tekoans commute to Jerusalem. 'The founders of Israel,' Ungar told me, 'set up kibbutzim and moshavim on the basis of self-sufficiency. Everybody knows this is no longer possible, and the Jewish Agency can't provide for more than 20 per cent of the economic infrastructure. For instance, there is no point in continuing agricultural expansion. The last thing Israel needs are more tomato mountains or reserves of frozen eggs.'

Tekoa has developed its own enterprises, including a mushroom farm, a jewellery workshop, vineyards, and a dairy for the production of sheep's milk. Mordechai Lavi, a Soviet immigrant, has founded a small educational software factory, employing eight people. It was intended to develop the nearby ruins of Herodion, a fortress built by Herod on a mountaintop from which he removed the summit, but the intifada put a stop to that scheme. Social amenities include a school, with only the first two grades at present, a day care centre, and a clinic, at which Dr Ungar's British-born wife is the nurse. Older children either board elsewhere, with relatives or friends, or commute to Jerusalem or the larger settlement of Gush Etzion. Water and electricity supplies are identical to those provided to surrounding Arab villages, so there has been no disruption or sabotage. Communications with Israel are by radio telephone, so there are no lines or cables for belligerent Palestinians to cut. Despite the generous terms on which housing is made available to settlers in the Territories, some families with an overdose of children have difficulties making ends meet. I was shown a hut filled with old clothes, to which indigent members of the community may help themselves.

Tekoa rules itself on the Town Meeting system, though the settlement's affairs are administered by a governing board that meets weekly. Its five members are elected for two-year terms. An acceptance committee processes applications for membership. Despite this apparatus of self-government, Tekoa, like all settlements, must bend to the will of the Israeli military government, which controls movement within the Territories.

When I arrived I noticed that there was no fence around the settlement. I was surprised by such apparent slackness on the West Bank; the army too has urged the Tekoans to build a fence, but they refuse. Dr Ungar explained: 'We maintain day watches and night watches, we have guards at the school and at the community centre, and we have regular drills. We don't fool ourselves into thinking there is such a thing as perfect security. There have been infiltrations, orchards uprooted. But we don't want to live in a ghetto, nor do we want our members to develop a false sense of security. Nobody underestimates the risks involved, and most people keep arms in their houses. We've only had one fatality, in 1982, when David Rosenfeld was stabbed near Herodion. He was unarmed and was murdered by Arabs from Zatara who were undergoing an initiation rite for Fatah. After David's murder, we discussed how we should respond to his death, and we decided to set up a second settlement which we named after him.' Some thirty families live at El David, and, according to Ungar, they are a resilient bunch, even though they lack proper housing and amenities.

'Despite David's death, until the intifada began, our relations with the

Arabs round here were good. I'd give rides to Arabs I saw on the road, they used to come to our infirmary, things like that. Now the man I used to give rides to turns his back when he sees my car. I understand why. If he's too friendly towards us, he might get a visit in the middle of the night from some of his friends and never be seen again.'

Dr Ungar took me to meet Daniel Yosef, a British-born member who has been at Tekoa for three years and is now the settlement's chairman. A neat, trimly bearded, reticent man, he works for the World Union of Jewish Students. I asked them whether, given the diversity of the membership, there was general ideological agreement at Tekoa. 'Everyone asks that . . .' said Ungar, but that didn't seem to make it easier to answer. 'There's an ideological commitment to living in this part of the world, to Eretz Yisrael. Politically, the party that received the largest vote in 1988 was Tehiya. Likud, NRP, Moledet, also attracted votes, and even the left-wing parties picked up a few.' Yet to the horror of most Tekoans, the town's rabbi, Menahem Froman, had a meeting in September 1989 with, of all people, the prominent PLO supporter Faisal Husseini. According to Rabbi Froman, they discussed philosophy.

I asked them what would happen if one day the West Bank ceased to be under Israeli control? They waffled. It all depended, they said, on the provisions made for their own security, which was not news to me. Any agreement, they said, would have to include the following element of reciprocity: If almost a million Arabs could live within Israeli borders, then the Jewish settlers in the Territories should also be entitled to stay.

'We came here,' said Dr Ungar, 'knowing that there was no insurance to cover our future. We came because of the links we feel here with Jewish history. But of course we want to stay – we don't want to live out of suitcases any longer. We recognize the possibility that this land could cease to be part of Eretz Yisrael, but we have to live as though it's not going to happen. I've seen other supposedly irresistible forces of history evaporate after a few years. We've learnt to live with periods of despondency. Remember that in the 1920s and 1930s the smart money was opposed to quitting Europe for Palestine.'

Daniel nodded. 'People just get on with their lives. What you're talking about is only a distant possibility. We simply don't foresee a situation where you won't have a Jewish Tekoa. And that means a secure Tekoa, not a besieged one. For Judea to be *Judenrein* is simply unthinkable. My view is that if the so-called peace parties won an election and we were voted out of here, there could be a breakdown of government. We feel there's enough room for everyone to live in Eretz Yisrael. The Arabs have got to recognize the Jewish connection with the land, and that Jews have just the same inalienable rights that they are claiming. Do Arabs anywhere recognize Jewish legitimacy? But the intifada hasn't cowed us. Nobody has moved out of Tekoa as a consequence. The truth is that Israel wants peace, and though everyone laughs at this idea, it is true and it will come to be.'

Amiel Ungar chuckled gently. 'I'm more pessimistic than Daniel. I don't have such high regard for enlightened Western opinion. I think it's a distinct possibility that people will continue to buy Arafat's line. But it's all right. We're used to hardship. One per cent of Israel's population died in 1948. Look how Sharansky suffered. The Ethiopians perished in enormous numbers on their journey by foot to Israel. We Jews still have a streak of romanticism. We're being subjected to the same test as previous generations of Jews, and it's our obligation to stand up to it. Nobody envisaged Tekoa as a quality-of-life settlement. In a way we are more discomfited by our fellow Israelis than by the Arabs. Dealing with our compatriots is the big psychological challenge.'

I was interested that Ungar should have used the word 'romance', as I suspected that the very riskiness of the enterprise constituted part of its appeal. When I put this to them, Daniel replied: 'Jewish history and destiny are one big romance. I don't want to give the impression that people enjoy their journey back here from Jerusalem every evening, but our pride in Tekoa is not unlinked to romance, to being out on the front line. I feel strongly that if we weren't out here in Judea, what's happening all around us, the intifada, would be happening in Tel Aviv. Our being here distances that terror. Not everyone appreciates that. Most Israelis aren't exposed to the issue of the settlements. Very few have the curiosity to see for themselves the West Bank and what we have achieved. It's no longer trendy, as it used to be, to idealize rural communities.'

'We're a sort of Israeli counterculture,' Amiel Ungar elaborated. 'The flashy arbiters of taste live in Tel Aviv. In their eyes, the settlements are going against the grain. But, as we see it, living in the settlements offered us an escape from bureaucracy. People out here feel strongly individual, much more so than is possible in standardized city apartments.'

'It's true of the kids too,' added Daniel. 'They have a tremendous sense of freedom, great self-confidence, and no fear. Of course that changes somewhat as they grow older. The older kids travel more, and are more aware of the dangers. But they develop a kind of patriotic loyalty to the community even to the point of being unsympathetic to the rights of the Arabs. These kids don't have a historical context into which they can put all this. If someone hits them, they hit back, and hard.'

Amiel looked anxious, as though I might be getting the wrong impression from Daniel's paean to tough kids. 'We don't see that much aggression. Sure, some kids put rocks in their briefcases to throw back if trouble arises. But I have to admit there has been a hardening of attitudes, among adults too. If it's a case of us or them, it's normal for people to favour "us".'

For Amiel and Daniel, the reasons for coming to Tekoa were essentially ideological. Here they live on the front line, direct descendants of the wandering Children of Israel and now pioneers of Eretz Yisrael, forging the future with solar heating panels on their houses and good jobs on the safe side of the Green Line. The best of both worlds.

For Daniel's next-door neighbours, motivation was undisguised: it was economic. Yosef grew up in Turkey and emigrated to Israel in 1967; his wife was Moroccan and had only been in Israel for five years. Yosef and I had no common language, so I spoke to his wife while he retreated into their bedroom to watch television. They had been living in Jerusalem, which they found expensive and far from ideal for their two small children. They still commute to Jerusalem to work, but the kids can stay at Tekoa, mingling safely with the hundred other children here. 'They're happy, they can play in the street, and it's a job just to get them back into the house.' As for her own safety, as a West Bank commuter, she shrugged it off. 'When we were living in Jerusalem, Yosef's bus to work was stoned every day. Listen. The intifada is everywhere. The intifada only stiffens our determination to be here, to show we're not defeated. As a Moroccan, I like community life. I like the way people drop in, as you've just done. That kind of thing is difficult in cities. And Jerusalem is so expensive. You can manage if you have parents to support you, but it's hard for a young couple like us with no family in Israel.'

It was dark by the time I caught the bus back to Jerusalem. We were followed by an army jeep, its searchlights beaming white and hard onto the roadside houses and shrubbery. As we roared along, silhouetted heads peered out from the windows of Arab houses, backlit by fluorescent strips along the ceiling. This journey was uneventful, but it was always a relief to be out of the West Bank. The tension there was palpable, though the bland domesticity of many of the settlements was, intentionally or otherwise, liable to lull one into a misplaced sense of normalcy. Yet I always returned with an overwhelming sense that something is profoundly wrong out there, as though the Territories were an atrophied limb attached to an otherwise vigorous body. The status quo, under persistent challenge from the intifada, seemed unacceptable. These were the months before Prime Minister Shamir came up with his 'peace plan' in 1989, and there was nothing in his rhetoric or that of his ministers to suggest that

Likud had the resolve, let alone the imagination, to solve this problem. A year later the situation remained, despite diplomatic flutters, unchanged. There were plans to deal with the intifada, there were tactics of containment, but no strategy to address its causes. The leaders of the intifada, having lived among the Israelis for some twenty years or more, understood very well the moral susceptibilities of their masters. By using no firearms and resorting instead to stones and occasional petrol bombs, the Palestinians forced the Israelis to respond more violently than the provocation warranted. So by December 1989 535 Palestinians, some of them children and teenagers, had been killed by retaliating troops. Only eight Israeli soldiers had been killed. The genius of the intifada was to force the Israelis into acting like a neo-colonial power, compelled to use violence to crack down on dissent.

It was not always thus. During the early years of the occupation, control was in the hands of the military government under Moshe Dayan. The sensitivity to Arab feelings that so exasperated Eliakim Haetzni was typical of Dayan's rule, which left in place the various social and administrative structures established or maintained by the Jordanian government. There was no attempt, for instance, to introduce Israeli law or currency into the West Bank. The early settlements were established in the Territories under the aegis of the military authorities for security reasons, not because of any ideological commitment to 'Greater Israel'. By 1977 there were thirty-two such settlements, but the benign face of Israeli occupation gradually darkened. After the Yom Kippur War of 1973, some Israelis felt that their plight would have been even more perilous had it not been for the West Bank acting as a buffer of sorts between Arab armies and Jewish centres of population. In the mid-1970s municipal elections led to the rise at local level of pro-PLO officials, a state of affairs that Israeli governments found increasingly intolerable. When Likud came to power, attitudes hardened, and the settlers grew more confident, more ideological, more ambitious. Israeli hostility towards dealing with the PLO, although well-founded in purely historical terms, became increasingly implausible in view of the fact that the PLO commanded overwhelming support in the Territories.

While the political situation deteriorated, the Territories prospered. On the West Bank the gross national product between 1968 and 1980 increased on average by a remarkable rate of 12 per cent annually. Salaries increased just as dramatically, giving many Palestinians a purchasing power greater than anything they had known under Jordanian rule. Yet far from leading to a growing feeling of gratitude towards the Israelis, the tangible benefits of the occupation, such as better and more widespread education, only increased the Palestinians' opposition to living under Israeli rule. The intifada has been a propaganda triumph, but at the cost of undoing much of the good work undertaken by the Israelis: universities are closed, movement is heavily restricted, daily harassment has become a routine hazard, and civil rights are disregarded when expedient. The situation is particularly appalling in the Gaza Strip, where the Arabs, unlike the Jordanian citizens of the West Bank, are stateless. Crucial identity cards are issued only after the most stringent bureaucratic procedures to establish that the applicant owes no taxes; Gazan vehicles cannot leave the Strip to take people to work or make deliveries of agricultural produce unless tax payments are up to date. Drivers who fail the test have to leave their vehicles at the checkpoint at a cost of NIS 30 per day until the back taxes have been paid. Israeli Arabs who had friends in Gaza would tell me horrific stories of ill treatment by Israeli border police and soldiers, but I had no way of verifying them.

The intifada has also led to a revival of Jewish 'underground' activities that most Israelis hoped they had seen the last of earlier in the decade. In 1980 some fanatical settlers attacked Arab targets, most notoriously by car-bombing two Arab mayors; there were also plans – thwarted, we can be thankful, since the consequences would have been horrific – to blow up the Dome of the Rock. By the mid-1980s these self-righteous, often murderous Jewish 'underground' activists had either been arrested or dwindled in numbers and effectiveness. Unfortunately some right-wing politicians remain only too eager to treat Jewish terrorists as heroes. The men convicted of bomb attacks on the West Bank mayors and of murdering three students in Hebron's Islamic College were sentenced to life imprisonment in 1985. In 1989, after dogged lobbying, Israel's President Chaim Herzog reduced their sentence to ten years, and with time off for good behaviour, these killers will be released a mere five years after entering prison. Moreover, they are spending the latter part of their sentence not even in a prison but in a yeshiva under conditions comparable to mild house arrest. Another Jewish terrorist, David Ben-Shimon, serving a life sentence for a rocket attack on an Arab bus in 1984 that killed one man and wounded ten others, was actually invited to lunch at the Knesset in the summer of 1989 by two Shas MKs while he was 'on leave' – whatever that may be – from his prison. There are no pressure groups urging the release of Arabs convicted of terrorist offences, of course, and there is something unusually shaming about justice so unevenly applied.

Lawlessness is reappearing in the Occupied Territories. The underground group called the Sicarii is using violence not only against Arab targets but against Jews whom they consider insufficiently hawkish. Settlers' militias are commonplace, and so are attacks on Arab villages, all in the name of self-defence. The settlers argue that the IDF (Israel Defence Forces) is no longer able or willing to protect them, so they must undertake the task themselves. While the penalties for Arabs who take the law into their own hands are understandably draconian – you can get a year behind bars for stone-throwing and ten for petrol-bombing – violence perpetrated by settlers, including many fatal shootings of Arabs since the intifada began, is largely ignored by the authorities, except in the most extreme cases such as Rabbi Levinger's shooting spree in Hebron.

The ideologues made their first organized appearance in 1974, when a few hundred enthusiasts, most of whom belonged to the National Religious Party, founded Gush Emunim (Bloc of the Faithful) under the mentorship of Rabbi Zvi Yehuda Kook. Rabbi Kook argued that unless the Jews retained sovereignty over the entire Promised Land, the coming of the messianic age would be delayed.[1] The Gush Emunim doctrine was simple enough: Jewish lands (as defined by them) belong to the Jewish people, who are thus entitled to take possession of them. Existing Palestinian settlement of those same lands should not be regarded as an impediment. Eliezer Melamed, rabbi of the religious settlement of Bracha, expresses views representative of the Gush Emunim line:

'The Arabs here have no right to the land. The land belongs to the Jewish nation. That is my morality. It is for the nation to decide whether the Arabs will continue to work the land. I don't speak of taking the land by force. But nations have a right to expropriate . . . I am prepared to give Arabs respect and good conditions as individuals, but not as a nation . . . What the Jewish nation has learned from the intifada is that coexistence is impossible.'[2]

When Gush Emunim was founded, the Labour Party governed Israel, but when Likud came to power in 1977 the political climate changed. Settlements were founded in areas close to centres of Arab population, a move certain to exacerbate tension. In eight years Likud spent a billion dollars on sixty new settlements. The government acquired land by confiscating unregistered or uncultivated areas, though unscrupulous Israeli brokers engaged in fraudulent transactions to persuade Arab landowners to part with their properties. After Likud was joined by Labour in a coalition government in 1984, investment in new settlements was almost halved.

Gush Emunim is now in a state of abeyance. It has been largely superseded by Tehiya, a political party that espouses the same ideology, but plays down the religious element. Many of the Gush Emunim leaders joined Tehiya; among the party's demands is the annexation of the Occupied Territories, a move that even Yitzhak Shamir, with his stated refusal to give up an inch of 'Greater Israel', has not officially contemplated. Tehiya, unlike the National Religious Party, receives no more than 20 per cent of its support from Orthodox Jews. Its representation in the Knesset is slight but useful, since its former leader, Professor Yuval Ne'eman, headed the ministerial settlements committee that was instrumental in establishing many new settlements.

Many of Tehiya's leading lights are Americans, including their highly articulate parliamentary adviser, Yisrael Medad. Some 20 per cent of the settlers are Anglo-Saxons, a high percentage in relation to their scanty representation in Israel as a whole. Medad explained: 'It isn't really surprising that many Anglo-Saxons are drawn to the settlements. Settlement is akin to pioneer Zionism. Many of those who came on *aliyah* want something more exciting out of living in Israel than sitting in a café in Tel Aviv.'

This accords perfectly with the romanticism of some of the Tekoa settlers I had met. Amiel Ungar and Daniel Yosef had been mild in their zeal, however deep their commitment, but to hear the true voice of settler fanaticism, one must listen to Gush leaders such as Daniella Weiss, with her rantings about establishing a Greater Israel that would be governed under Jewish religious law, while those tiresome Moslem mosques on the Temple Mount would be replaced with a rebuilt Jewish Temple. Or to Tehiya MK Geula Cohen, associated many years ago with the Stern Gang, who believes the best solution to the intifada is to deport Arabs.

I visited Yisrael Medad at the Knesset building a few days before the 1988 elections. At the security gate, I was intrigued to discover my name listed on the computer, which printed out a pass for me. I walked across the huge plaza to the imposing but ugly Knesset building itself. From the plaza it's impossible to see the lower floors of the building, so it squats flatly, a blockish horizontal mass depressed further by overhanging concrete eaves. Its beige-red stone is less creamy, less silky than the off-white Jerusalem stone, and the vertical windows are like arrow-slits. The MKs have individual cubbyholes on the lower floors, while on the top floor are the offices from which the fifteen parliamentary factions conduct their intrigues.

Medad is tall and lanky, with curly grey hair and a full beard unevenly flecked with white. I found him personable in the easy-to-like American style, open and without formality. As Tehiya's ideologist he was earnest but not without humour. Born in New York to a moderately Orthodox family, he attended yeshiva. After training in Israel, he returned to New

York to lead the local branch of Betar, a right-wing Zionist youth movement based on the ideas of Jabotinsky. In 1970 he came to Israel and joined Begin's Herut party, but after the Camp David agreement he and Geula Cohen broke with Begin and formed Tehiya. By 1984 Tehiya had won five seats and was the third strongest party in the Knesset, although factionalism has diminished their numbers since then.

Although Tehiya is associated with its principal plank of 'keeping the land of Israel', Medad was at pains to stress that it is not a one-policy party. They are pressing for longer school hours with more instruction in Jewish and Zionist studies, and Medad is perturbed by certain cultural trends: 'Anybody is free to write, for example, a play attacking Israeli actions in Judea and Samaria. But I don't see why a government-sponsored theatre or arts festival should put it on. It's not the job of the state to seek out people who attack it.'

Like politicians on the left, Medad attacked the Likud policy, as it then was, of autonomy, which he described as 'a corridor leading to a Palestinian state'. Instead, Tehiya wants to create 'facts on the ground': public buildings and roads in Judea and Samaria. There are 80,000 settlers there now; he would like to see the infrastructure put in place to accommodate up to 200,000. Tehiya also favours annexation. According to Medad, no parliamentary approval is required for this; Israel already has the right to annex the Territories. I asked him how the Palestinians would respond to annexation. Some, he replied, would admit that after sixty years they had lost their fight. They would continue to till their soil and send their children to school, recalling that Israeli Arabs are the most prosperous Arabs in the Middle East. 'Israeli Arabs don't get their hands chopped off.' A small minority might pursue terrorist activities, but unsuccessfully. Gradually the Arabs would be admitted to Israeli citizenship. Medad feels that as long as the world argues that there should be a Palestinian state, trouble is sure to continue, since this stimulates the Arabs to exert pressure on Israel. But once annexation has taken place, that pressure will be deflated. He was unconcerned about world opinion in response to annexation. Since the United States recognizes that Israel is its only dependable ally in the region, he argued, that reliance would be unaffected by annexation.

Despite the passionate sense of mission of the settlers, their presence seems remarkably impermanent. The early kibbutzniks, active during the British Mandate, had a genuine commitment to the land. German and Polish students turned themselves into farmers, and reclaimed the land. No such process is taking place on the West Bank, and it's probably just as well. As Dr Ungar readily admitted, even at a fairly successful settlement such as Tekoa, the level of self-sufficiency was only 30 per cent. Many settlements are little more than dormitory towns that happen to be located in the Occupied Territories. Israel doesn't need any more farmers, since it scarcely knows what to do with the existing ones.

Thus Yisrael Medad's analogy with the kibbutz movement is far from exact. The settlements are being founded to make a political point; what matters to the movement's leaders is the political equivalent of the theatre manager's bums on seats – the quality of the play matters less than his ability to fill the theatre; for the settlers' leaders it is more important to have families installed in the more remote reaches of Greater Israel than to fret over their economic vitality and independence. The dominant Likud faction in the 1988–90 coalition government requested that NIS 80 million be spent on eight new settlements, but Shimon Peres, who as finance minister had more important things to worry about, told them to get lost. As always happens in such cases, a compromise was reached.

Yet the whole issue seems increasingly irrelevant. Whether a few more settlements are established no longer seems important. If and when an Israeli peace plan actually gets to the stage of negotiating over the future of the Occupied Territories, it seems unlikely that the presence of Jewish settlements will prove an insuperable obstacle. When Israel concluded its peace agreement with Egypt, the Jewish settlements in the Sinai Desert had to be abandoned, and this was achieved without too much hysteria. The same may well happen again.

# 9 · QUID PRO QUO

Never phone an Israeli family at nine in the evening. They will be watching the television news. Israelis are obsessed by news. British long-distance bus drivers turn down the radio when a news summary interrupts their diet of Wham. Israeli drivers turn up the sound whenever news bulletins are broadcast, and then turn it down a few decibels when the Moroccan caterwauling resumes. This appetite for news is unsurprising, not only because of the precarious international situation in which Israel has been continuously enmeshed, but because domestic politics are volatile and crisis-laden. Within an hour, a cabinet minister could have denounced a colleague, a coalition could have collapsed or, as happened in the spring of 1989, Rabbi Eliezer Schach might have voiced his opinion that the Lubavitcher *Rebbe* probably wasn't a genuine Jew.

An acquaintance in Jerusalem was an acute observer of the Israeli scene, so whenever we talked I would quiz him. After a few hours, his wife would gaze forlornly at us and plead for a change of subject. He would acquiesce: 'We all find this exhausting, this incessant political chatter, but we can't help it, we do it all the time. On Friday evenings we get together with our friends, quite late, after the news of course, and we argue about how we can achieve peace. We all shout at each other, even though we more or less agree. The people on the other side of the divide, the right-wingers, we don't discuss politics with them at all — we have no common ground. And this goes on till four in the morning. Of course, we never listen to what anyone else is saying, as we've heard each other's views many times before. In Israel everything is political. Voter turnout at elections is about 80 per cent. Everybody watches the news. Israeli politics are continuous, and every part of our lives is connected to it.' Another friend explained this obsession as follows: 'Israelis are political because politics controls the whole system in which we live. Because resources are limited, there's a ceaseless battle between factions and parties over who gets what.'

In Israel even the media are politicized, and some newspapers have direct links with political parties; the better ones happen to be slightly left of centre. The newspaper of record, *Ha-aretz*, is owned by but independent of the American publishing house Schocken; it sees its role as being in opposition to the government of the day. The *Jerusalem Post* has more influence than its modest circulation of 25,000 (double for the weekend edition) would suggest. This is because it is the only significant Israeli newspaper that those of us who don't speak Ivrit can understand. Slightly left of centre and occasionally prim, it publishes features and articles from all parts of the political spectrum. After the Canadian conglomerate Hollinger Inc. acquired control of the *Post*, its editorial independence appeared to have been undermined. The editor, Erwin Frenkel, resigned because of alleged interference by the *Post*'s publisher, Yehuda Levy, and took many leading journalists with him. Whether Levy and the new editor, N. D. Gross, will alter the tone and character of the newspaper, only time will tell.

The two most popular Israeli newspapers, *Ma-ariv* and *Yediot Aharonot*, are just to the right of centre. Both are supposed to be afternoon newspapers, but so intense is the rivalry between them that both appear in the morning. There is no major newspaper of the right; it's as though Israelis somehow expect journalists to be liberal or left-wing. A more recently established paper is *Hadashot*, part of the *Ha-aretz* stable; it has the appearance of a popular newspaper but occasionally publishes items that leave the military censors deeply unhappy. David Angel of the Jewish Agency told me he had heard of a leader writer who writes for two newspapers, expressing opposing views in each. Even if the story isn't true, in Israel it at least sounds plausible.

Because much coverage of Israeli affairs by foreign media has been unflattering or critical, the foreign press is regarded as hostile. Yitzhak Rabin, when questioned about unsympathetic coverage of his 'iron fist' policies during the intifada, replied that Jews love to be loved, but that the government couldn't abandon its policies simply because the foreign media didn't care for them. Yet the Israelis, like their supporters among diaspora Jewry, are obsessed with what they see as media bias. A hostile leader in, say, the *New York Times*, becomes a news story in Israel. The former journalist Amnon Ahi-Nomi assessed the Israeli attitude for me: 'It's not that Israelis are resentful of criticism from the outside world. It's that they no longer hear it. All Israelis despise the United Nations, and share the feeling that the world is against us. Alternatively they label critics as antisemites, even though most Israelis have never encountered antisemites, apart from Jewish ones.'

Despite their sensitivity to criticism from outside, Israelis do not expect their own press to be servile. After the slaughter at the Sabra and Shatila camps in Lebanon, the newspapers pursued the question of who was responsible for the killings, even though at that time most Israelis still supported the war in Lebanon.

According to Dr Yoel Cohen, a media-scrutinizing research fellow at Bar-Ilan University, there is relatively little government interference in broadcasting except for television news, even though the government appoints the director general of the Broadcasting Authority. Cohen's main criticism of Israeli news coverage is that so little time is devoted to foreign stories. When General Zia of Pakistan was killed in a plane crash, no Israeli newspaper made it the lead story. Only on Saturday nights is there any extended international coverage. The main explanation is that the Broadcasting Authority simply can't afford to keep a battery of foreign correspondents posted around the world.

Dr Cohen explained that press censorship was established by the British and has remained more or less unaltered ever since, though it has decreased in its extent. The censor is appointed by the ministry of defence. There have been only two in the last forty years, and the present censor is Yitzhak Shani, who, according to Dr Cohen, keeps punctiliously to the letter of the law. 'In fact, when an attempt was made to replace him with someone less scrupulous, it was the media who came to his defence.' There are seventy categories of material that can't be published, such as information about Israel's nuclear research, but no restrictions on Israeli newspapers reprinting material published abroad. Consequently, when Israeli journalists have a story that they can't use, they tip off their friends in the foreign press so that they can then copy the story once it has appeared abroad.

There is also a suspicion that stories are sometimes suppressed because they are embarrassing rather than because they pose any threat to security. When Mordechai Vanunu, accused of leaking information about Israel's nuclear capability, revealed on the palm of his hand that he had been kidnapped by Mossad, the Israeli secret service, the press could use neither the story nor the photograph, although neither endangered national security. In December 1988, during the crucial meeting of the Palestine National Council in Algiers, Uri Porat, director general of the Broadcasting Authority, told news editors to keep coverage of the event to the minimum and not to screen scenes of jubilation, for fear that such scenes could prove contagious in the Territories.[1]

There are also reports of brazen forms of news control and manipulation, including radio jamming, selective leaking and the repellent practice of disguising security men as journalists, which further imperils the already sufficiently dangerous profession of news-gathering.[2] Sometimes even political humour has been subject to censorship. The satirist Meir Shalev once produced a mock interview with Herzl, using only Herzl's own texts, but had two-thirds of it gutted by the head of the Broadcasting Authority, supposedly on the grounds that the words of the founder of Zionism were potentially subversive.[3] In December 1989 the Authority banned the playing of songs by two leading Israeli popular singers because the lyrics referred to the government's handling of the intifada. Although the decision was later rescinded, it showed both a pettiness and an authoritarianism more reminiscent of old-style East European political systems than of a modern democracy.

The intifada has brought further restrictions on the press, especially photographers. Local military commanders have the discretionary power to ban the media from their districts, a tempting power to abuse since military commanders can't help viewing pressmen as a nuisance. Nevertheless, experienced journalists, Israeli and foreign, maintain a useful network of contacts within the Territories. It is the Arab press that bears the brunt of the Israeli censor's powers, although the Israeli authorities claim that despite all the restrictions, Arab newspapers in the Territories enjoy more freedom than in any other Arab country except Lebanon.[4]

Despite censorship and other restrictions, there are many aspects of the Israeli media that other democracies should regard with envy. In Britain, the contents of cabinet meetings are a closely guarded secret; in Israel the agenda for such meetings is published in advance, so that at least the public knows which matters are under discussion. Israeli politicians don't know the meaning of confidentiality, and ministers routinely leak cabinet proceedings to the media when it's in their political interest to do so. Nor are public figures afraid of public discussion. When the IDF Chief of Staff Dan Shomron made a speech in which he observed that the only solution to the intifada had to be political rather than military, the prime minister took grave exception. But at least the issue was openly discussed, as it should have been, and would not have been in many other countries.

Two days before the election I was shopping in a Jerusalem supermarket when I overheard two American women arguing in the next aisle. The first was yelling: 'I have lived here for years, day in, day out, and I know what I'm talking about.' The second woman tried to butt in but was interrupted by the first, who repeated herself, then added: 'It's just like the blacks and the whites in the States, exactly the same. Believe me, I live here and I know.' Replied the second: 'Your problem is that you haven't been listening to a word I've been saying.'

The row fizzled out, and I never discovered what had prompted it. But it's entirely characteristic of Israeli life that a political spat can suddenly break out between two strangers in a supermarket. If the snarling had been in Ivrit, no doubt all the other shoppers would have joined in too.

The Israeli political system is the purest of democracies: proportional representation. Any idiot can campaign on the stupidest platform and if he or she can convince enough voters nationwide, the reward is a seat in the Knesset. The proliferation of small parties in Israel provokes a constant shifting of ground as this group forms a temporary alliance with that faction while stabbing a third group in the back – until next month, when positions are reversed. Social democratic Labour and the right-wing Likud remain the two largest parties, followed by a dozen or so small parties. A party only needs five or six Knesset seats out of a total of 120 to find itself the third largest political force in the country. Elections take place every four years and there is no second chamber. After decades of coalitions and the deals that underwrite them, ideological differences between the parties become blurred. They evolve into interest groups, with access to jobs and influence, rather than vehicles for political ideas.

From the earliest days of Jewish settlement in Palestine, political parties actively encouraged emigration to Israel and looked after, and thus secured the political allegiance of, the new arrivals. Political parties had their own kibbutzim, their own banks and trade unions, their own newspapers and schools, their own housing schemes and medical insurance. Even football teams are associated with different parties. Since the establishment of the state, such all-inclusive political control has diminished, but even today banks, newspapers and medical insurance schemes remain affiliated to various parties, especially those on the left. A major political battle has been shaping up for years for control of Histadrut, the huge labour organization that has long been a fiefdom of the Labour Party but is now increasingly factionalized. Likud had its eye on Histadrut, and on the influence and patronage that control of the organization would give the party, but Labour's grip was confirmed in the Histadrut elections of November 1989. Histadrut, which controls 40 per cent of the Israeli economy, embraces various trade unions, a nationwide compulsory health insurance scheme known as Kupat Holim Clalit, banks and both heavy and light industries; even the hostel where I stayed in Beersheva was part of the Histadrut empire. A friend observed: 'Histadrut is supposed to look after the interests of the workers, but it's also the largest employer in the country. That's daft.'

The proportional representation system ensures that the broadest possible spectrum of political opinion is represented in the Knesset. Since no single party has ever won a simple majority of seats in the Knesset, a succession of coalitions has ruled Israel since its foundation. The major drawbacks of the system are twofold. First, the percentage of votes that any party needs to secure election is so low that single-issue parties (better conditions for Yemeni babysitters, free holidays for veterans, more frequent buses on the Tel Aviv–Haifa run) sometimes win a seat or two, prompting a confusion of function between pressure group and political party. Secondly, there are no constituencies, and thus no MK is responsible directly to the electorate. The aim of the ambitious politician is not to win the support of voters, but to secure a safe slot on the party list. Once he has done that, he can spend the entire election campaign abusing the voters because he knows he will be elected anyway. Meanwhile the poor old citizen with a legitimate grievance is in trouble, since no MK has any political incentive to come to his or her aid.

The system also gives rise to the professionalization of politics. Once you have secured your power base on a party list, it is difficult to be dislodged. Cut off from an electorate that has no function other than to trot to the polls every four years and confirm your party-given right to a Knesset seat, you can wheel and deal to your heart's content. Because your tenure depends on the party rather than the electorate, you will be careful not to rock the boat. Pursue a line that is out of step with the party's leadership and you may, like the veteran Labour politician Abba Eban in 1988, find yourself dropped from the list and booted out of parliamentary politics. The only thing for disaffected politicians to do is to form a new party. Thus Geula Cohen, disillusioned with Likud after Camp David, marched off to form Tehiya; and a few years later the Tehiya MK Rafael Eitan, disillusioned with Tehiya, stomped off to form Tsomet.

With so intricate a network of alliance and patronage between unions and parties, partners within coalitions, and local mayors with independent political machines, Israeli politics offer a favourable climate for corruption. Yet most Israelis with whom I discussed the matter thought that, apart from individual cases that crop up in any political system dependent on donations, their politics were by and large free of organized corruption. The following view is typical: 'Local politics works on the old boy network, on wheeling and dealing, but that's not to say it's corrupt. It's the same in organizations such as the Jewish Agency. In Israel there's a high level of political engagement on the part of ordinary people, which is healthy for democracy. But there's too much of it. Everybody is a politician, everybody has a view, and people tolerate an amazingly high level of connivance among their politicians. In the 1988 election candidates ran up huge expenses that some of them found difficult to pay off, so after the election the MKs passed a bill to ensure that their expenses were all covered. It was outrageous, but people here just accept it. One of the commonest expressions we have is, "That's the way it is." They shrug it off. No one takes responsibility for their actions.' A day after I heard this view, I read that the Knesset had just reversed legislation passed by the previous Knesset forbidding MKs from holding outside jobs while serving in the Knesset. The *Jerusalem Post* fumed at this self-serving volte-face, but its rage had no impact. It rarely does.

For years the Labour Party could assume that, in alliance with various coalition partners, it was the natural party of government. Menachem Begin brought that assumption to an end in 1977. Labour had become associated both with the perilous Yom Kippur War of 1973, as well as with vested interests such as Histadrut and the kibbutzim. While broadly socialist in ideology, it had become remote from the working class it supposedly represented, in particular the Sephardi proletariat from North African countries. It seemed to be trying to be all things to all people. Likud pursued the 'Oriental' voters assiduously and the strategy paid off. The stubbornly elitist image of Labour probably means that its position as the dominant force in Israeli politics has now been ceded, for the immediate future, to Likud.

Yitzhak Shamir may score zero as an international statesman, but he is an astute domestic politician. After the 1988 election when the coalition with Labour was reformed, he promoted many younger Likudniks, while Labour's failure to do the same on a comparable scale confirmed the impression that it was a party of the past. Israeli leaders have never excelled at stepping down gracefully to make way for a younger genera- tion. A non-Jewish Jerusalemite believed that Labour was nearing the end of the political road: 'Western-style intellectuals are more and more in the minority. I can't see any way in which Labour can regain its former power. It's been reasonably successful at attracting some of the Sephardi vote in recent years, but I suspect that as soon as the Sephardim realize they're on a sinking ship, they'll jump off fast, into the arms of Likud or Shas. The majority of Israelis no longer share the humanistic, socialist values of the European immigrants who formed the backbone of the Labour Party. It's sad, but the party is becoming an anachronism.'

The other great shift within Israeli politics has been the growing power of the religious parties. There is nothing new about religious parties in Israel. Labour governments were sustained in office by coalitions with the National Religious Party, which in those days was pragmatic and Zionist. Indeed, Ben-Gurion deliberately included the NRP in his cabinets to ensure that it remained within the Zionist consensus. Today the NRP is scarcely distinguishable from Tehiya in its views on the Occupied Territories and 'Greater Israel'.

After a while the religious parties learnt to exploit their position of power to wrest concessions and funding for their institutions from the government. By the late 1980s some two-thirds of religious MKs represent anti-Zionist *haredi* parties solely concerned with pressuring the government, any government, to hand over more money for yeshivot and to introduce divisive legislation such as amending the Law of Return. In the 1988 election, charismatic rabbis promised their followers blessings upon their house if they would toe the party line. The former Sephardi Chief Rabbi, Ovadia Yosef, who likes to dress in a kind of hussar's uniform, whizzed about in a helicopter showering blessings on all who would vote for Shas, the Sephardi Orthodox party; while the Lubavitcher *Rebbe*, from his Brooklyn stronghold, did much the same in support of Agudat Yisrael. The erudite judge Haim Cohn told me that in his view the religious parties regard the state as no more than a cow that they can milk. Like many other educated Israelis, he deeply resents the fact that ultra-Orthodox demands for ever larger sums for their yeshivot are made at the expense of national institutions such as universities.

The NRP backs the Likud's hard-line policy towards the Occupied Territories, but not all the *haredi* parties share that view. In the summer of 1989 Rabbi Yosef of Shas, in a moment of enlightenment, said – to President Mubarak of Egypt, no less – that religious law does justify territorial compromise, on the principle of *pikuah nefesh* (the saving of lives). This statement, however, contradicted a ruling issued by the Chief Rabbinate of Israel in 1979, stating that there was a 'severe prohibition against transferring ownership of any of the holy and promised lands of Eretz Yisroel to foreigners'. For good measure, they added that *pikuah nefesh* gave no reason to override this prohibition. After Rabbi Yosef's statement, the Chief Rabbinate mustered its forces again and reiterated its declaration that the Torah forbids territorial concessions.[5]

Although it's dispiriting when clerics adopt hawkish positions during their uninvited interventions in politics, it's hard to remain depressed when witnessing the sheer theatricality of Israeli election campaigns. In February 1989, during the battle for the post of mayor of Beit She'an, two Likud candidates were pitted against each other. One of them, Jackie Levy, was the son of David Levy, a right-wing Likud minister with a powerful personal following among Sephardim; the other, the 'official' Likud candidate, rejoiced in the name of Shlomo Ben-Lulu.

David Levy attended an election rally in support of his boy, and spoke as follows: 'They call me a mafia chief. They portray me as a sheriff who threatens all of you here. They called me Don Corleone, but I managed to overcome all this because I have your love. And that love of yours is the dearest thing of my life.' Tear-jerking stuff, but not out of character for the ebullient Levy. Meanwhile, at a rally for Mr Ben-Lulu, the starchy Likud foreign minister Moshe Arens was addressing the audience in the following terms: 'I support Ben-Lulu not just because I admire his skills, not just because we are both engineers' – I'm not making this up – 'not just because I love him' – this is quoted verbatim from the *Jerusalem Post* of March 28 – 'and I do love him.' To be fair to Mr Arens, his remarks may have gained something in the translation, since the Ivrit word for 'love' and 'like' are the same, though it ought to be clear from the context which nuance was intended.

Well, Mr Arens's love did the trick, because Ben-Lulu won, declaring: 'We fought against evil people. We fought against the Levy family headed by the Byzantine ruler David.' Outside David Levy's house, people gathered and wept, while in distant Beit She'an, Ben-Lulu's followers roamed the streets chanting, 'Shlomo, King of Israel – David Levy, go to hell.'[6] If this is how candidates from the *same* party behave towards each other, you can imagine the tone of political discourse between different parties.

Israeli politics are equally diverting at cabinet level, especially since nobody sneezes during a cabinet meeting without it being reported in the press. Everything is leaked as a matter of course. In March 1989 the Knesset finance committee met to approve the budget for 1989–90. Its basic provisions had been agreed in advance as part of the coalition agreement between Labour and Likud. The parties had agreed to spend NIS 35 million on infrastructure and new settlements in the Territories, and to increase the cash handout to the ultra-Orthodox from NIS 30 to 40 million. In return, Labour could expect NIS 88 million for Kupat Holim Clalit and funds to help bail out the ailing kibbutzim. Meanwhile the *haredim* were hoping to extort further sums for its 'educational' institutions in exchange for their support for the kibbutzim.[7]

In the days that followed, the ultra-Orthodox parties seemed to be doing rather well. Their handout had been increased to NIS 47 million, in the form of a blank cheque, since there were to be no controls over how that money was to be spent by the institutions. Shimon Peres, as finance minister and sugar daddy of the kibbutzim, was happy to accept this deal. That's the way Israeli politics has always been conducted: I'll let you raid the Treasury, if you'll let me do the same. Unfortunately for Peres, the younger members of his party – who had been treating their leader, with his unfortunate knack of losing too many elections in a row, with increasing disrespect – these obstreperous Labour MKs, outraged by the extortion, blocked the deal. The *Jerusalem Post* sighed: 'Even though the religious bloc did not receive what it views as its rightful slice of the budget cake this week, it will eventually get it anyway. That is the wisdom of the present system.'[8] They were right. A few days later the cabinet agreed to introduce special legislation to transfer 'general reserve' funds to three ministries which would then hand those funds over to 'institutions to be named by the Orthodox parties'. Game, set, and match.[9]

Such machinations are not unique to Israeli politics. What is striking about them is the openness with which they are reported. Israel's open politics may also be an additional benefit of proportional representation; all discussions at ministerial level involve members of different parties, some of whom will have much to gain by judicious leaking.

Ben-Gurion was probably the most respected leader Israel ever had, yet he never attracted more than 38.2 per cent of the vote, which he attained in 1959.[10] Respect for authority does not come naturally to Israelis. In most European countries, it is unwise to argue with a policeman who accuses you of some misdemeanour. In Israel, the automatic reaction of an apprehended citizen is to protest innocence loudly and vigorously. If he is obviously guilty, he will respond by pointing out that the circumstances are such that no charges should be pressed. To any rule, the Israeli will always claim that he is an exception. This is the individualist reflection of the larger political truth that Jews have difficulty grasping the notion of consensus. The consequences may be chaotic, but one cannot help respecting such reluctance to hand over power to officialdom.

A 'National Unity' coalition government ruled Israel from 1984 to 1990, with sometimes farcical consequences. By prior arrangement, Shamir and Peres swopped jobs halfway through the parliamentary term, and at times were clearly working at cross-purposes. By 1988 many Israelis were fervently hoping that the November elections would give either Likud or Labour a sufficient edge to allow it to form a more ideologically coherent government, with clearly defined political strategies. At the start of the elections, there were no fewer than twenty-seven parties. Some, such as the Movement for Discharged Soldiers or the Yemenite Association of Israel, could be discounted as single-issue parties. There were the parties of the left: Labour, Mapam, and the Citizens' Rights Movement (Ratz). In the political centre were Shinui (the Centre Movement) and the moderate religious party Meimad. On the right were Likud and the more extremist parties such as Tehiya, Tsomet, and Moledet. The religious parties were the National Religious Party (NRP), Agudat Yisrael, Shas, and the 'Lithuanian'-dominated Degel Hatorah. On the far left stood the Democratic Front for Peace and Equality (Hadash), a communist party that had long been a political vehicle for Israeli Arabs, together with Rakah. Other Arab parties included the Arab Democratic Party and the Progressive List for Peace.

Mapam was prepared to trade territories for peace, and would negotiate to that end with any Palestinian organization prepared to recognize Israel and renounce terrorism; Mapam also advocates the separation of religion and state. Labour was pinning its foreign policy on an international peace conference that Shamir would never permit to take place. Ratz's programme did not differ substantially from that of Mapam, but envisaged an interim stage in the peace process akin to the nebulous 'autonomy' proposed by Likud. Among the parties of the right, Likud, like Labour, opposed the religious parties' demand that the Law of Return should be amended, but was more likely than Labour to bend to pressure on this issue.

Tsomet, founded the previous year by the former chief of staff in Lebanon in 1982, Rafel Eitan, declared that the Occupied Territories were not to be negotiated away, and that Israeli law should be applied to them; in religious matters the party was more easy-going. Moledet argued that Palestinians living in the Occupied Territories should be offered 'voluntary transfer', a euphemism for throwing them out. Tehiya's programme resembled Tsomet's, and included extending Israeli sovereignty to the Territories; the party opposed any separation of religion and state. The NRP also favoured extending Israeli sovereignty to the Territories and opposed uprooting any settlements; it argued for amending the Law of Return, and wanted support for its own schools to counter the vast sums siphoned off to *haredi* institutions, and aid for its kibbutzim and United Mizrachi bank.

Shas was prepared to contemplate trading land for peace; in religious matters, it wished to apply Jewish law as the judicial system of the state, but seemed less exercised by the Law of Return. Agudat took a hard line on the Territories, argued for the adoption of Jewish law as the law of the state and favoured amending the Law of Return, a favourite hobbyhorse of the absentee Lubavitcher *Rebbe*. Degel Hatorah was the most dovish of the *haredi* parties. Hadash recognized the PLO as the sole legitimate representative of the Palestinian people and favoured withdrawal from the Territories to the June 1967 lines; it argued for a separation of religion and state. The Arab Democratic Party, essentially a one-man faction, adopted a similar line in foreign affairs and argued for a stronger role for Israeli Arabs in state institutions. The Progressive List for Peace favoured an independent Palestinian state alongside Israel.

One other party running for the Knesset in 1988 was Kach, founded and led by the rabidly nationalistic New York rabbi Meir Kahane. However, about two weeks before the election the Israeli Supreme Court disqualified Kach on the grounds that its programme was racist and thus violated Israeli law. Few, other than Kahane's supporters, regretted this ruling, though it was greeted with disquiet in some quarters. Meimad, the only religious party to have lobbied for Kach's disqualification, argued that Kach is openly anti-democratic, and that the state has every right to ban political organizations that vow to subvert its democratic foundations. Others argued that, however deplorable Kahane's policies may be, the state has no right to prevent citizens, however misguided, from voting for them. No sooner had the court ruled than we had the interesting spectacle of the other right-wing parties doing their best to mop up Kach's support, which was estimated to be considerable. Shamir stepped up his warnings against Palestinians who employed firearms in the course of their uprising. Moledet let its mask of euphemism slip, and altered its main policy of 'voluntary transfer' to 'transfer'. Shas leaders stressed their more nationalistic views in an attempt to attract Kach votes.[11]

The party programmes tended to accentuate simple issues with which voters could identify. This allowed them to avoid discussing the one issue that casts its shadow over all others: the Israeli economy. Despite widespread acceptance, in both major parties, of the need to dismantle an over-centralized economic structure, bureaucratic restrictions and other controls still hamper the development of the private sector. Likud began the process of economic reform, but it has not been easy to challenge the powerful vested interests, notably Histadrut. Israelis don't fret about the economy because money, while in short supply, doesn't seem to preoccupy them. Money, in Israel, does not determine status. Everybody wants a good standard of living, of course, but the rich are not held in any special esteem. 'There's an old joke,' says Tommy Lapid, a Tel Aviv journalist, 'that Israelis earn, say, NIS 2,000, spend NIS 3,000, and live from the difference. We do live well, and we have the safety net of welfare to save people from destitution. So people spend. People want a good life, and above all they want to be able to travel abroad, but they don't need money for status. Israel is a meritocracy. The prestigious occupations are those of professor, general, artist, doctor, writer, judge, and they're not closed to you because of your birth or social background. Businessmen are not looked up to in the way they are in the United States.'

Travel abroad certainly seems to be an Israeli fixation. About 20 per cent of Israelis travel abroad every year, in spite of a travel tax of $150 every time they leave the country. How Israelis finance their travels is something of a mystery as salaries are very low. A teacher earns about $500 per month, a nurse or policeman a little more, a professor or doctor $1,000. Many items such as clothing and any goods that have to be imported are far more expensive than in Europe or America. To live reasonably well and drive a car you need to earn at least $1,500 per month. Living on overdrafts is an accepted way of life. 'I'm in minus!' is a well-known Israeli lament. Even people on fixed salaries don't always get paid. In July 1989 the municipality of Beersheva ran out of money and its 400 employees had to go without their wages for a month.

It's hard to assess the true state of the Israeli economy. On the one hand this small country has built up a sophisticated trading network with those nations that do not embargo its products. Israelis have a keen eye for gaps in the market – winter vegetables are an obvious example, but diamonds and foodstuffs also generate huge sums – and are adept at filling them. As in the case of Switzerland, it's a triumph of skill over resources. Despite fluctuating trade deficits, Israel's ability to generate revenue from judicious exports seems soundly based.

That's the good news. But on the other hand, the universities are broke, 'free' education has to be subsidized by parents, and vested interests such as the trade unions and an exceedingly bloated civil service resist reform. Israel has no oil or coal of its own, which is one reason why solar energy is so important; potash and some other chemicals extracted from the Dead Sea are among the few minerals found in the country. Electricity consumption often exceeds supply, and power cuts are frequent, a major hindrance in a technologically sophisticated society. The agricultural sector is bankrupt: kibbutzim and moshavim are being bailed out by the government at enormous cost, and the 8,000 private farmers are heavily in debt. Inflation and unemployment are both rising. Finance minister Shimon Peres pledged to reduce inflation to single-figure levels by the end of 1989, but the inflation rate for the year rose to 20.7 per cent and the unemployment rate to about 9 per cent. Industrial growth was negligible, lower in 1989 than at any time since 1982. Purchasing power was gradually dwindling. About 40 per cent of the national budget is spent on servicing and repayment of debts. Taxes are among the highest in the world. The intifada continues to hamper the growth of the economy, as the number of Arabs working within the Israeli economy dropped by over 30 per cent. Tourism has decreased. Bankruptcies are common: about 2,000 companies went under in a single year. And what, one should ask, would the situation be like without the United States' annual contribution of $3 billion?

The traditional explanation for Israel's economic problems has been its defence budget, which soaks up about one third of the total national budget of $24 billion. Yet too often this excuse disguises the poor performance of other sectors of the economy. Other reasons include the failure to reform the country's institutions, overmanning, and high subsidies for unprofitable enterprises. Israel is still dishing out the subsidies, for fear of alienating the volatile workforce and of increasing further the rate of unemployment. Even the policy of giving generous grants to development towns has its dangers, as cowboy entrepreneurs move in to take advantage of the subsidies, then fold their tents when the subsidies are eventually reduced and set off for the next town that has become the cynosure of the ministry planners. Emigration also affects the economy. Israel has superb institutes for higher education, but the brilliantly qualified engineers and scientists who emerge from them often fail to find work in Israel and leave for the United States or Canada, where they are well paid for their skills and have greater opportunities for research as well as for promotion. All kinds of figures are bandied about which are impossible to check, but I heard that 1,500 Israeli computer engineers work in greater Boston alone.

The slices of the financial pie are cut to different sizes. Peres's February 1989 budget pledged more resources for the infrastructure and for research and development. To pay for all that, there would be increased charges for education, health, and national insurance, and government hospitals would be privatized. There would be staff cuts in the civil service, and subsidies for public transport and frozen poultry would be eliminated. Those were the proposals – before the horse-trading. The plan to introduce competition into the public transport system was soon ditched. The cabinet gave priority to the hand-outs to favourite institutions – the yeshivot, the West Bank settlements – and to bail-outs for the kibbutzim and the huge Histadrut subsidiary, Koor. Peres is much criticized for his apparent willingness to lend an ear to any organization or group in financial difficulties. To pay for all these special, and possibly deserving, pleas, Peres must indulge in financial juggling in order to keep the government's deficit under control. His next budget proposed cuts in social insurance payments and agricultural subsidies, and the ending of free schooling. Since the ministers of defence, agriculture, education, and health were all from the Labour Party, Mr Peres, as usual, had a battle on his hands in 1990, since a majority of the cabinet announced their opposition to the budget.

However, not everybody is gloomy about the economic prospects. The leading Tel Aviv accountant Dan Bavly told me: 'We have to accept that our economy is still very volatile. In 1987 and 1988 it was clearly depressed, with some stagnation, but we may be turning the corner. The intifada has been terribly debilitating. There's been a drop in the Arab labour force and in Arab consumption. Tourism and exports have dropped, though tourism is now beginning to revive. In 1989 these factors haven't changed but other indicators are more favourable. We're beginning to think about 1992 in Europe, and the possibilities for greater international trade contacts. We have two main strengths: a preferred trading relationship with the EEC, and a free trade agreement with the United States. If we could only learn to exploit this situation, we could in time become a bridge between the EEC and the United States. We're excellent at marketing our products, though many people will claim otherwise, and that's especially remarkable when you remember that 80 per cent of our markets are more than 1,500 miles from our ports.

'We're still paying a belated price for the runaway inflation from 1978 to 1985, when it rose to 400 per cent. The inflation encouraged entrepreneurs to neglect their capital. When inflation slowed down, entrepreneurs and farmers failed to count their shekels. They had grown used to manipulating inflation, and when inflation ended they had a bumpy landing. And of course unemployment is a serious problem. It's hard for us to absorb the new labour force emerging from the army and the universities. And we have to do something about this, as we're already seeing plenty of migration from the development towns in the Negev and the Galilee to the big cities. We need to renew our investment in Israel itself, which we've been neglecting for about twenty years. We need private capital both from Israel and from abroad, but we can only persuade Israelis to renew their investment here if there's a turn-around in the economy. We're moving in the right direction, but we won't make much progress until the intifada ends and until we increase political stability and have more free enterprise.'

The need for more free enterprise is echoed by, among others, the industrialist Stef Wertheimer. A school dropout at thirteen, he runs Iscar, a company that manufactures hard metal tools and engine blades. He argues forcefully against the confrontational style of Israeli politics, with powerful unions pitted against employers, and government-sponsored enterprises, such as Koor, riddled with political appointments and overmanning. Wertheimer believes government handouts to prop up collapsing industries encourage people to think that efficient management isn't really necessary. He favours selling off the various Histadrut enterprises, and he would do the same with the kibbutzim, rather than see them sustained by the government and the banks, on the condition that the purchasers would keep them in operation. His most radical suggestion is that the Israelis should dispense with American foreign aid and learn to stand on their own feet, however great the hardships initially. 'What we have today for a government,' he wrote in 1987, and little has changed, 'is twenty-five ministers engaged principally in the distribution of funds provided by the American taxpayers.'[12]

There is clearly widespread dissatisfaction with the way the economy is handled, especially in rural Israel, where the decline of the agricultural sector has been devastating. Dr Moshe Dror, an educationalist in the Negev, finds the management of the economy wrong-headed: 'We're fucking up the land, industrializing it when everybody in other countries is getting out of industry. We did the same thing with agriculture, going into it in a big way just as everyone else was pulling out.'

Nor is there any shortage of conflicting advice. Some argue that interest rates are far too high. Boaz, a farmer in the Galilee, told me: 'The government blames the banks, and the banks blame the government, and both the government and the banks say that people are spending too much. But we pay very high taxes and national insurance, and what we get in return is poor services.' Despite the grumbling, and the hardship in the countryside, Israelis refuse to get too excited by these economic problems. As long as the overdraft is manageable, as long as the car has four tyres, and as long as a regular wage is paid, they are reasonably content. They pay their bills, eventually, and they take their pleasures. Nobody believes in letting such a trivial matter as money get in the way of enjoying life, which in this beleaguered country is too precious not to be relished to the full.

# 10 · THE VOODOO FACTOR

Elections prompt rallies and meetings, and I went to as many as possible during the 1988 campaign. One of the first I attended was to be addressed by six politicians, each from a different party. The chairman had difficulty remembering which speaker belonged to which party, but with twenty-seven parties to choose from the slip was not just forgivable but scarcely avoidable.

First we heard from Moshe Amirav of centrist Shinui. Amirav spent twenty years in Likud, but committed the unpardonable sin of speaking to Palestinian leaders, some of whom were PLO members. He urged pragmatism rather than ideology, but it was hard to derive much substance from his speech, which reflected his personal dream of 'Greater Israel' but also his willingness to give up some of his dreams in order to achieve peace; the Palestinians, whose rights of self-determination he recognized, would have to do the same.

Ratz's Benny Temkin took a higher moral line. The occupation of the Territories must end and so must the accompanying denial of human rights. What's at stake, he argued, was not the survival of Israel but the survival of democratic pluralistic society in Israel. If democracy is denied to some of the people, then in effect it's denied to all. He opposed religious coercion of all kinds, and also attacked Labour for using the demographic argument in its campaign. This argument states that if the Territories remain under Israeli control, then within two decades Arabs will out-number Jews in the Jewish state. This argument, Temkin was suggesting, was a subtle form of racism, preying on people's fear of Arabs.

Likud was represented by an urbane lawyer and MK, Uriel Linn. He coolly stated the Likud approach to achieving a peaceful settlement. The government must build on existing agreements, such as UN Resolution 242 of 22 November 1967, which calls for the withdrawal of Israeli armed forces from territories occupied in the recent conflict; the termination of all belligerency; and respect for the sovereignty of every state in the area.

Any treaty, Linn argued, must be negotiated directly with the Arab states, a dig at Labour's proposals for an international conference involving superpowers. The argument was essentially historicist, and not for the last time was an audience left puzzled by Likud's newfound passion for Resolution 242 and for the Camp David agreement, which its leaders had hitherto actively opposed. Unlike some of the other speakers, Linn touched on economic issues, reminding the audience of the huge loans serviced by the government and that Israel was only half as productive as a medium-sized European country. Spending must be reduced and the economy freed from government controls.

Avraham Burg spoke for Labour. He has had politics in his blood from birth, as his father, Dr Yosef Burg, was for forty years a National Religious Party MK and cabinet minister. Burg junior had studied in a yeshiva, and was thus well equipped to trade biblical quips with ultra-Orthodox opponents. He began by deriding the small parties as 'sputnik' parties, and said that it was only worth debating with the 'sun', Likud. For him the crucial question was: Under what circumstances would Likud agree to give up territory? Which is the real Likud position: surrender nothing or observe the Camp David agreement? Even within Likud, he observed, there was no consensus; some ministers favoured Shamir's notion of autonomy for the Territories, others were annexationists. 'Shamir's only initiative in two years has been to say no.'

Burg said that the intifada broke out because the Palestinians had come to the conclusion that the Israeli government was not interested in working towards a political solution. He deplored what he described as the 'bisexual coalition' of the National Unity government, a marriage not of love but of necessity. Labour's plan was to work for an interim agreement that will give peace for five or ten years and provide a basis for a final settlement. When a questioner from the audience asserted that there was a *halachic* justification (that is, a justification according to Jewish law) for keeping the Territories, Burg was scornful. *Halacha*, he said, had nothing to do with it. Quoting chapter and verse, he denounced the unholy alliance between religiosity and territoriality within the Israeli body politic.

Uriel Linn, responding to Burg's taunts about whether any circumstances existed in which Likud would give up territory for peace, said it would be a grave mistake for the government to spell out the details. This argument, which we were to hear repeatedly from Likud spokesmen, reminded me of Richard Nixon's 'secret plan' for ending the war in Vietnam, which he couldn't describe for fear of jinxing it.

The Meimad viewpoint was put by Avraham Stein, who castigated the left for its ideology, which did not identify with Eretz Yisrael, 'which is ours by right, religiously, historically, ethically, morally'. This sounded like NRP talk, until he qualified it by saying there is a need to forgo something which is ours for a higher value, namely, peace. The left, he accused, undermines Zionism by favouring a give-away that would invite the next war by placing Israel in an inferior tactical position. However, the pessimism of the radical right also invited the next war; thus he argued in favour of territorial compromise. To give up Nablus and Hebron, he argued, is to cut off a hand to save a life. Stein then took a leaf from Likud's book of diplomacy by saying that it was impolitic to be too specific, as that wrecks your bargaining position.

I could sympathize with Burg's dismissal of the minor parties. Their programmes smacked of a make-it-up-as-you-go-along politics; their discourse rarely rose above the level of bar-room chat. Few policies were thought through, and this was as true of Labour and Likud as of the piddling parties. The extremist parties repelled because of their dogmatism, and the mainstream parties irritated with their waffle. They have to waffle, of course, because of the electoral system. In the great bargaining sessions that take place after any election and before the formation of the ruling coalition, there is bound to be give and take. The less specific any party is about its policies, the easier it is to twist and wriggle and renege without being accused of some terrible betrayal of principle. Everybody knows that election promises are worthless because nobody knows until the election is over whether the party giving the promise will be in a position to deliver the goods.

In December 1988 Natan Sharansky, the most eloquent of the former Soviet refuseniks, gave his post mortem on the election process: 'The ease with which all the candidates seemed to discard their election promises was disheartening. Even before the count was finished the religious parties declared that "all the options were open", and that they were waiting for the highest bidder; the Citizens' Rights Movement demonstrated a willingness to abandon its stand against religious legislation; Labour has indicated it could relinquish its most cherished principle and central element of its platform – the international conference – and the Likud was willing to antagonize world Jewry and change the Law of Return.'[1] All perfectly true, but Israelis with longer experience of their political system would shrug off the observation, murmuring: so what else is new?

I decided to inspect the unacceptable face of Israeli politics by attending a Kach rally. Margaret Thatcher, after eleven years in power, is said to be bashful about the term 'Thatcherism', but Rabbi Kahane has no such modesty. His English-language election meeting, held the day after the Supreme Court disqualified Kach from participation in the election, was

THE VOODOO FACTOR · 125

entitled, hysterically, 'The War Against Kahaneism'. The audience was overwhelmingly American, mostly college students. A fat boy, evidently a Kahane groupie, urged me to buy the rabbi's books, but I'd already handed over enough money to Kach just to gain admittance. He yelled to us all: 'Yesterday was the lowest day in the history of Israel, the day they banned a Jewish party and allowed an Arab one to run. I felt like sitting *shiva*.'

Kahane always denies he is racist, but many of his supporters certainly are, and the following remarks from the woman seated behind me were typical: 'The Arabs own everything, they have the Temple Mount, everyone's afraid of them. It's just like the blacks in America.' One of Kahane's aides, Barbara Ginsburg, waved the flag of paranoia: Kach was banned, she told us, because polls were showing Kach running in third place, which would have guaranteed the party a role in the next government.

When Kahane arrived, he briefly acknowledged the cheers, strode to the front, and launched into his speech with the minimum of preliminaries. He spoke without notes. He was of slighter build than I had imagined from photographs, the aggression residing in the voice and the cocky posture rather than in the bulk of the man. He was not devoid of wit and charm, though both were vitiated by streaks of self-aggrandisement and sheer nastiness. He began by saying that the court decision, while appearing to be a defeat, was a victory in Jewish terms. 'Our victory was that we did not change a single word, a single letter, in our platform in order to win in the court.' He was unrepentant, for the battle he was engaged in was to determine whether Israel would be a Jewish state or 'a paler carbon copy'. Opprobrium was not new to him. He had been arrested sixty-two times and, as an MK, had been barred from appearing on radio and television and in schools. He and his supporters had experienced physical violence at rallies – though most accounts suggest that much of the violence is provided by Kach supporters.

The court decision, he told us, 'is their greatest defeat, because it's based on fear. I raise the most painful issues imaginable, from which they flee in panic because they cannot face them. These issues go to the very heart of what a Jew is, what a Jewish state is, what is Zionism, what is democracy. I raise the issue of Zionism versus democracy. My seven-year-old grand-child knows that they are incompatible. What is Zionism if not a movement for a Jewish state? And what does a Jewish state mean if not a state in which Jews will always be sovereign and control the state and never allow anyone else by any means to be a majority in the country? Having lived for two thousand years as a minority, enjoying such minority benefits as crusades, inquisitions, pogroms, and Auschwitz, we decided that we'd had quite enough and decided to be the majority. And always the majority. That's called Zionism.'

Or that's what Kahane calls Zionism. With that premise, he can proceed with his scare-mongering. 'So the contradiction arises: do the Arabs have the right to be the majority in this country, yes or no? They can't answer that. These people are too terrified to deal with the issue, and when someone does raise it, in their horror of having to choose between democracy and Zionism, they shut that person's mouth.' The terrible dilemma Kahane presents is no dilemma at all, unless Israel annexes the Territories, in which case it adds two million Arabs to the population, as Labour's demographic argument warned. If one excludes the Arabs of the Territories, then the Jews are already in an overwhelming majority – some 81.5 per cent – in the State of Israel, and Kahane's fears become an irrelevance.

Kahane, who is no mean orator, exploited the demographic argument. 'You think that Arabs are fools? An Arab is sitting in Nazareth, a citizen of Israel, and he hears Peres say, "We must compromise otherwise there'll be too many Arabs." You can imagine how well that goes over with him. He just loves that kind of talk. The truth is that no one has greater contempt for Arabs than liberals and leftists. Is there one person in this room who thinks he can buy an Arab's national pride by giving him an indoor toilet? You don't buy a person's national pride with electricity. An Arab is not interested in living standards, he wants to live in his own country, and Jews that can't grasp that haven't got the slightest amount of national self-pride. That's why they don't understand Arabs. That's why I do, and they understand me.'

So far so good, for this analysis of Arab discontent, although simplistic, is accurate enough. But there is a sting in the tail: 'It's because I respect them and know you can't fool them that I want to throw them out of here. The Arabs want to take this country from us. They truly believe it is their country. Why can't we get that into our heads? They sincerely believe that we are thieves. What is so difficult to understand? And they want to drive us out of here. They're not interested in the West Bank. They're not interested in East Jerusalem. What was bothering them when they had East Jerusalem and they went to war? Could it be that they wanted West Jerusalem?' Then one of those rhetorical flourishes that make Kahane such an arresting speaker: 'I just toss it out as a wild guess.' He continued: 'They want the entire country – and I understand that. The Arab may say he accepts Israel because it exists, but his dream is to make it Palestine, and if you were Arabs you would also want the same thing.

THE VOODOO FACTOR · 127

'So the question arises: what do we do? The Arab birthrate here is staggering. We pay them national insurance for every single child until the age of eighteen, because we are not normal. Normal people don't subsidize their own suicide. The Arabs have babies and the Jews have abortions. There's no *aliyah* today. People say *aliyah*'s the answer – for someone else. Nobody's coming to Israel. On the contrary, half this country would like to leave. Thank God for American quotas on immigration, otherwise half of Israel would be driving taxis in New York City. That's the bankruptcy of Zionism.' (Kahane was speaking, of course, before the unexpected increase in *aliyah* by Russian Jews in 1990.)

'I don't hate Arabs. I love Jews. I wish the Arabs well – but elsewhere. They have twenty-two countries – God bless them. We have only one, and it's ours, all of it. It's nothing to be ashamed of. I want an exchange of populations. We took in 800,000 Jews from Arab countries. Now it's time to complete the exchange. Don't let anyone ask: what if Jordan doesn't want them? I don't want them either, and I'm stronger than they are. That's called self-preservation. Believe me, under a prime minister called Kahane, they will move. If I had been prime minister since last December, we would not have had 326 Arabs killed. We would not have had soldiers having to beat up Arabs. That's insanity. Not one Arab would have been killed! Not one Arab would have *been* here. I don't want to kill Arabs, and I don't want them to kill us, because our lives count more than their lives.'

Is Kahane, as his enemies maintain, a racist? The answer, transparently, is yes. Kahane, who has no pretensions to moderation, does expose the cant that marbles the mainstream parties: 'The intifada will never come to an end. The PLO represents the Palestinians and don't kid yourself: if they had free elections tomorrow, the PLO would win 85 per cent. Of course this is so! And the intifada will spread into Israel. There isn't a day or night that Jewish buses aren't stoned in this city. Jews are afraid. This is how we live? This is the dream of two thousand years?'

This is typical of Kahane, this shift from analysis to scare-mongering. He was equally adept at deflating the humbug of the far right. He began by mocking those advocating a policy of 'voluntary transfer'. 'Of course, why didn't I think of that? I'll ask every Arab tomorrow, and they'll all say yes. What a fraud it is!' So how will Kahane himself deal with the Arabs of Israel? Well, if he ever becomes prime minister, he says with relish, half of them would immediately head for the border. Arabs would be offered compensation for their property, and if they refused to accept it, they'd be chucked out anyway. 'I mean it and they know that I mean it. You are leaving, with or without money – they'll take the money.

People may protest, but that's okay, we'll survive that. The last people the Arabs will want to start a war with is Kahane – with nuclear weapons.'

Kahane's dreamy swagger, his delight in his own thuggishness, clearly appeals to those who yearn for 'strong leadership'; he reinforces that need by terrifying his listeners, insisting that the enemy is within: 'People only speak about the Arabs of the Territories, when every child knows that the Arabs of Israel are infinitely more dangerous, because they are voters, they are citizens, they're educated, they're intellectuals. The revolution doesn't come from the numb and the dumb. The revolution always comes from the intellectuals.'

Kahane not only wants to throw the Arabs out of Israel, but he wants to turn Israel into his version of a truly Jewish state. 'There is a basic contradiction between Judaism and certain basic Western values. I cannot believe that the court compared my condemnation of intermarriage with the Nuremberg laws. That is so obscene, and that one of the judges wears a *yarmulke*, that is outrageous. In Judaism of course intermarriage is banned. This isn't a Kahane law. The things I've written may not go down well with an assimilated Jew – but it's Judaism. And in Judaism no non-Jew is allowed national rights. Judaism is not Thomas Jefferson or Burke or Voltaire.

'You can take it or leave it: I prefer an honest atheist to a fraudulent rabbi. There's nothing special about being Jewish except one thing, and that is Judaism. We stood at Mount Sinai and we received a Torah from God. We received truth. If you don't believe that, fine. But then stop saying you're proud of being a Jew. What are you proud of? Jewish ethics? What makes ethics Jewish? You think Christians can't be ethical? Everybody's ethical – ask them. Secular Zionism in this country is bankrupt. They can't keep their kids Jewish. The kids are more honest than their parents. You ask a kid here what he is, and he'll say, "I'm an Israeli." That's an identity? An Arab can be an Israeli, a Druze can be an Israeli, a Chinaman can be an Israeli. An identity is: I'm a Jew who lives in Eretz Yisrael.'

Many in the audience wanted Kahane's advice: how should they vote now that Kach had been disqualified? He asked his supporters to hand in blank ballots. The election results, he predicted, would be striking: Likud would lose two-thirds of its strength (nothing of the kind happened). His deepest regret seemed to be that he couldn't use his latest ploy, that of promising that the Arab village that gave Kach the largest number of votes would be offered visas to the United States – as though such visas were in Kahane's personal gift. Indeed, the disqualification only seemed to reinforce his braggadocio: 'What the courts did was make me the most popular Jew in Israel. Don't think Israel is represented in the kibbutzim or among the newspaper people hanging around in the King David bar. Go into the neighbourhoods, the development towns – that's Israel. That's where 60 per cent of the Jews of Israel live. That's where Kahane is king.'

After the election Kach dropped from sight. Only after the terrible incident when an embittered Palestinian forced a bus into a ravine in July 1989, killing sixteen passengers, did Kahane's supporters re-emerge from their swamp, staging anti-Arab demonstrations and stoning Arab cars and behaving with precisely the violence and hatred that Kahane has always disclaimed.

For comic relief I attended a political meeting entitled 'Inner Perspectives of the Current Elections'. The speaker was Rabbi Yitzhak Ginsburgh, and the venue was the Central Hotel. None of my friends knew of Rabbi Ginsburgh. If I wanted to find out who was running the meeting, they said, I had to find out who owned the hotel, but such research was beyond me. The meeting was held in one of those ghastly Israeli basement halls, stridently lit with fluorescent tubes, scattered with metal frame chairs of maximum discomfort; the walls were veneered with mirrors and a variety of decorative coverings: golden aluminium strips, purple velvetex, hospital-green door frames, linen with spangles, fake pine panelling. Within five seconds I knew who was sponsoring the meeting, as a video screen dwelt adoringly on the pixie-like features of the Lubavitcher *Rebbe*. A cheerleader introduced the proceedings, which would begin with an enthralling new video of the latest *farbrengen* (Chasidic gathering) at Lubavitch headquarters at Crown Heights.

The video screen turned yellow, then emitted white flashes; not an example of the *Rebbe*'s supernatural powers, but a technical fault. The cheerleader pressed some buttons and introduced another cassette, showing the *Rebbe* arriving at a kind of Chasidic garden party in a huge Oldsmobile and clambering eagerly up to a lectern to address the faithful for a few hours. Meanwhile industrious little habadniks entered the hall, lugging six-foot screens to construct a *mechitzah* that would separate the sexes and prevent winking. Since the screens also blocked the video, we never heard the *Rebbe*'s peroration. I couldn't sense much erotic tingling in the air that night: Chasidic men are scrawny or pot-bellied, while their womenfolk are invariably of an ample size. Sex objects they were not, but you can never be too careful, especially if you've had to make love through a blanket for twenty years of married life. In such circumstances even a glimpse of lobe beneath a headscarf could bring on a pounding of the blood.

Enter Ginsburgh, middle-aged, with a long grey beard. He spoke in American-English, but was clearly neither. He began by hailing the *Rebbe*'s intervention in Israeli politics; he had declared his support for Agudat in response to attempts by Rabbi Schach to cast out the Lubavitchers. The *Rebbe*'s intervention had to be a source of joy, even though it was prompted by the deceit and lies so typical of politics. Torah teaches that a new light shall appear over Zion – the greater the surprise, the more joyful we should be. Truth has entered the place of deceit. All this I could follow, if yawnfully, but then the rabbi lost me. He introduced the kabbalistic notion of the *tzimtzum*, which means creating a space for reality to fill. What is happening, he told us, is an important stage in our arousal to await the messiah. *Mitnagdim* (boo) interpret *tzimtzum* literally, since for them the only source of truth and access to God was through Torah. Chasidim, however, interpret it by saying that God is present even when not apparent. God's force was hiding from us and not showing His real face until He chooses to rectify the world at some preordained moment – and wasn't that much the same as the *Rebbe*, who had been concealing his political hand until now? The new face, the *Rebbe*, was here all the time but we didn't notice it till it appeared. Neat, eh?

Taking a more mournful tone, Ginsburgh told us how our generation lacks leaders to take us to the Messiah. The reason for this is that *mitnagdim* still hold sway. *Mitnagdim* believe the world is for real, whereas Chasidim, with their less literal interpretation of *tzimtzum*, believe that such things are only half real or not real at all. Chasidim find God in everything, including an apparent vacuum, as in a game of hide and seek. The Chasidic relation to the world is different, as is the role of the leader. Even in Agudat there is no real leadership. But the *Rebbe*'s inspiration will change all that, and in Ginsburgh's own words 'the lion is prouncing (sic) out and will consume lies into truth.'

This unique insight into the inner perspectives of the election had now been going on for ninety minutes. I was deeply absorbed, but a good many of the audience were fast asleep. I tiptoed away as the rabbi droned on.

I went to one more election meeting, a Likud rally at the Hilton. This attracted a large crowd, even if half of it consisted of Likud campaign workers rather than voters seeking enlightenment. A tape played the mindless Likud campaign ditty over and over, perhaps thirty times, providing the best of reasons not to vote for Likud. While waiting for the star attraction, Moshe Arens, we were warmed up by a brutish South African. Any immigrant who believes in Western values and the free economy, he told us, had to support Likud. He noted that many of his South African friends were now tempted to vote for Tehiya (which tells us quite a lot about Tehiya), but he urged us to 'rally to the flag', as though Likud had acquired exclusive rights to the Star of David.

Arens, a dapper undemonstrative figure, arrived and began his speech. Politicians, he admitted, were inclined to 'hyperbowl' (sic), but these were the most important Israeli elections ever. Labour had moved to the left. The Progressive List for Peace and Rakah were competing for the votes of PLO supporters among discontented Israeli Arabs, and neither party had Israel's best interests at heart. The Middle East, as he likes to remind American audiences, is not the same as the Middle West. Israel must be strong economically if it is to be strong militarily, politically, socially. Israel's slack productivity cannot be attributed solely to high defence expenditure. The management of the economy is at fault. We have a Bolshevik economy, centralized and opposed to market forces. No industrial organization stands on its own feet; all are subsidized by the taxpayers. The bosses of these organizations are political appointees and their decisions are political. The Koor scandal − referring to a large Israeli Histadrut-owned conglomerate in desperate financial straits − had exposed the failure of the system. Only Likud can change the system.

Since Likud had no clear policy concerning the Territories or peace negotiations with the Arab states, Mr Arens had to resort to heavy waffle when broaching these matters. He indulged in crude non sequiturs such as: 'There are those who say that the whole of Eretz Yisrael is too big for us. Well, they're too small for Eretz Yisrael.' Curiously, even though the meeting was packed with Likud supporters, the response to his speech was lukewarm. As one young woman pointed out, Arens had told us why we shouldn't vote for Labour, not why we should support Likud instead.

Arens radiated mediocrity, but it was hard to be impressed by any major Israeli politicians, although some of the younger ones, such as Binyamin Netanyahu and Avraham Burg, were obviously intelligent and articulate. Peres could be schoolmasterish and dour; if he possessed any lightness of touch, it didn't come across in the translation. Sharon's thuggishness was repellent. Rabin, as the man responsible for dealing with the intifada, had depressed many Labour supporters with his 'iron fist' approach that had left hundreds of Palestinians dead, while the intifada continued unabated. As for Shamir, he could win awards as the most rebarbative of Western political leaders. He radiated lack of distinction. His legendary pig-headedness, derived from the harsh experiences of his youth, seemed poor equipment to deal with the complexities of the late 1980s. His very lack of imagination took on a heroic quality, so dogged was his ordinariness, so complete his contempt for anybody in Israeli politics who actually had ideas in their head. He reminded me of the kind of shopkeeper who refuses to take back the rancid milk he has just sold you; small-mindedness was elevated in him to a political virtue. Indeed, the fact that he is so unremarkable is precisely what endears him to half the electorate. Like Begin before him, he is a little old eastern European Jew, the grandfather in the *shtetl*. That he is now prime minister of Israel proves that the Cossacks and Nazis didn't have it all their own way. The success of Begin and Shamir shows you don't have to be Einstein to be a celebrated Jew. By all accounts a masterly party organizer, Shamir had managed, through skill and will, to dominate the coalition in which he was supposedly an equal partner, and would do so again after the election.

Nobody could accuse this crabby old man of giving himself airs. Nobody could accuse him of impracticality, since he had no policies. Everybody knew that 'autonomy' was a non-starter. Eventually, in response to heavy breathing from the Americans during his trip to Washington in the spring of 1989, Shamir produced a peace plan so vague that it never became clear whether, for example, the Arabs of East Jerusalem would participate in the proposed elections in the Territories. After months of inconclusive debate over the plan, Shamir allowed it to be demolished by his right wing in the form of David Levy and Ariel Sharon, thus sending the whole process back to square one and imperilling the future of the coalition. A cartoon in the *Jerusalem Post* showed the diminutive Shamir holding up his arms in triumph – only they were padlocked and the gargantuan figure of Sharon was walking off the edge of the picture holding the key.

On election night, English-language coverage was provided at the Hyatt Hotel. Within seven minutes of the polls closing, the first computer projections of the results were flashing through. They proved remarkably accurate. The two main parties were neck and neck. Tehiya did less well than expected, with only three seats, but the equally unsavoury Moledet and Tsomet picked up two each. The surprise of the evening was the strong showing of the ultra-Orthodox parties, especially Shas. On television Shas's Rabbi Peretz was oozing with satisfaction at the prospect of being a power broker in the negotiations that were bound to follow. A welcome feature of Israeli election coverage was that during the gaps between results and interviews, there were satirical sketches, such as the one by Tuvia Tzifir impersonating two tubby rabbinical figures doing a song and dance routine about how they were going to screw the government. The ultra-Orthodox politicians are always a good target for satirists, since *haredim* aren't supposed to be watching television in the first place, and thus are in no position to complain.

When Arens told the Hilton rally that this was the most important Israeli election ever, he was not being especially contentious. The severity of the intifada, the economic plight of the country's major institutions, the mauling Israel's image had suffered internationally – all this had to be reversed by the new government. Yet as the results flickered onto the screen, it was curious to reflect that the final outcome would be largely dependent on Rabbi Peretz's negotiations with the two main parties.

The next morning, as I chatted to my Israeli friends, I found them in a state of deep depression. One told me she had wept as the results came through. An arts administrator said she feared that the influence of the religious parties could lead to greater censorship and political control of the arts (the opposite happened). Another friend contemptuously referred to the *haredi* leaders as 'Khomeinis' and derided their 'voodoo hocuspocus'. Certainly the Lubavitcher *Rebbe* and the *tzimtzum* had cleaned up and the ailing Agudat Yisrael was experiencing a new lease of life. One perspicacious Israeli said that the only consolation was the prospect that the very success of the religious parties might go to their heads and lead them to make demands so excessive that not even the power-hungry Likud leaders could agree to them, since the majority of Likud supporters are not religious. Nor was it likely that Likud would team up with extreme right-wing parties, whose demands were equally unacceptable to mainstream Likud supporters.

Cynical but astute Israelis thought the best possible result would be a new coalition which would be formed with the primary aim of reforming the electoral system so as to increase the thresholds at which small parties could claim Knesset seats. This would lead to more stable governments and coalitions, and lessen the influence of the extremist parties. Israel, after weeks of negotiation, got the new coalition, but didn't get the electoral reform. When the next election takes place the yeshiva students whom all Israeli taxpayers are subsidizing so heavily will again abandon their studies for weeks at a time to campaign for the *haredi* candidates who will keep the gravy train rolling along.

Shamir opted for a renewed coalition with despised Labour rather than make politically costly deals with the minor parties. Moreover, by including major Labour politicians within the government, he in effect neutralized them for eighteen months. Labour was more likely to take a dovish stance in opposition than it could do from within the government, especially with a former prime minister, Yitzhak Rabin, in the crucial post of defence minister. Shamir's strategy was remarkably successful, and after the municipal elections of 1989, in which Labour performed dismally, his hold over Israeli politics was powerful indeed.

'I don't like this card,' said the kibbutznik. 'It gives the wrong impression.'
I could see what he meant. The greetings card showed children splashing
about in an Olympic-sized swimming pool under blue skies. A lovely
scene, but not the first image that leaps to mind when one thinks of a
kibbutz. Yet those poster images of tanned kibbutzniks marching through
the fields with hoes slung over their shoulders now seem over-simplistic.
Kibbutzniks are Israel's foremost agriculturalists – but the kibbutzim have
evolved into more complex societies than their portrayal as idyllic rural
communes suggests.

The luxurious swimming pool at Kibbutz Hazorea, about fifteen miles
south of Haifa, has become a slight embarrassment, since it highlights the
relative success of the community. Hazorea, through a combination of
diligence, good fortune, and shrewd investment, has prospered and its
members enjoy a good standard of living and a rich cultural life. Other
kibbutzim, especially those in more remote parts of the country, are in
decline thanks to a mixture of mismanagement and sheer bad luck. The
successful kibbutzim must therefore tighten their belts out of a kind of
solidarity with less fortunate kibbutzniks, and employing images of
swimming pools is not the most tactful way of going about it.

Hazorea was founded in 1936 by German immigrants. One of the
largest kibbutzim, it now has 500 members and a population, including
the many children, of about a thousand souls. Hazorea remains an
agricultural settlement, with its herds and orchards and cotton fields, but
most of its energies are directed at various industrial enterprises, for this
was one of the first kibbutzim to opt for industrialization. Its furniture
factory is today less profitable than the plastics factory, Plastopil, which
employs seventy-five members. Established in 1963, Plastopil operates
around the clock, producing such items as photodegradable plastics for
agricultural use, and 70 per cent of all Israel's milk sachets. (Unfortunately,
Israel's milk marketing board is switching to cartons, which is bad luck
for Hazorea.) Hazorea also operates a Quality Control Centre, testing

products and the calibration of hi-tech instruments. A fish farm, breeding ornamental fish for export, generates more revenue, but agriculture is no longer a money-spinner. Milk production is restricted because of quotas; nor is cotton especially profitable, but much of Hazorea's land is only suitable for this crop.

Plastopil has difficulty exploiting its own success. It is staffed entirely by members of the kibbutz, as a matter of principle, but this also acts as a constraint on growth. The dilemma is symptomatic: when entrepreneurial vigour clashes with communal ideals, the latter take precedence. Such brutal notions as cost-efficiency often take second place to ideological considerations. Not only does the kibbutz refuse to employ outside labour – since this would introduce a two-tier system of members and non-members, of those with a stake in the future of the community and those with a purely economic connection to it – but it is reluctant to take harsh decisions. When it was proposed that the kibbutz close the furniture factory, for sound economic reasons, the argument was lost on the grounds that eighteen jobs would be lost. Social considerations won the day, which is humane but not necessarily in the long-term interest of the kibbutz.

Hazorea's economic success is evident at first glance. The main buildings are arranged around a large lawn: an enormous block containing the dining room and social centre and offices adjoins a large and well-equipped theatre. On the far side of the lawn is the infirmary and, half concealed behind trees, the children's houses. The dairy sheds and factories are lined up along the main road from Megiddo to Yokne'am, concealed from the residential parts of the kibbutz. The houses are built on the slopes of some steep hills that mark the western edge of the Jezreel Valley. Paths meander through the woods, linking the different residential areas. Most of the houses are simple bungalows, but there are also some more modern two-storey structures. Bridges straddle the rivulet that trickles through the kibbutz, and discreetly gouged out of a far corner of the land is the splendid pool. I asked Meir Meron, one of the surviving founders of Hazorea, whether it had been difficult to construct the living quarters without clearing the woods. He laughed, and told me that when the first settlers arrived here the hillsides had been bare. Every scrap of vegetation, all those tall pines and flowering shrubs, had been planted. He showed me early photographs of the heath and scrub that had been Hazorea in the 1930s. And in those days most of the now fertile Jezreel Valley was a malarial swamp.

To survive, Hazorea must grow, but not too much. It will absorb two new families each year. The children of present members are, of course, encouraged to stay on the kibbutz and become full members in their own right, but the community is not hostile to outsiders. It was often said to me that newcomers sometimes became more committed than those who, as it were, inherited their membership. Outsiders made a conscious choice and a considered commitment. But bringing in outsiders is risky, for once a kibbutz has accepted a new member or family, it is almost impossible to get rid of them. Even if no new families were admitted, strangers would still attain membership. For every child of the kibbutz who marries a non-kibbutznik brings in an outside partner. Difficulties can arise when a couple gets divorced and the imported partner remarries, since the kibbutz cannot veto a choice of spouse but must accept individuals who may have no strong personal connection with it.

Hazorea remains faithful to the original traditions of the kibbutz movement, at least those of the left-wing Artzi group of which it is a member. There are about 275 kibbutzim in Israel, with a population of about 135,000; over half the kibbutzim are loosely affiliated to the Labour Party through the United Kibbutz Movement, while some seventy-five or so other Artzi kibbutzim are linked to Mapam, which stands to the left of Labour. There are also about a dozen religious kibbutzim. The founding of the movement was a triumph of will over proclivity, for Jews are not usually thought of as good team members, nor as enthusiasts for manual labour. The collectivist movement was born of the realization by Zionists such as the Russian A. D. Gordon that Jewish settlement in the Holy Land could never be more than sporadic if no firm economic base were established. The very first kibbutz was founded near the Sea of Galilee in 1909. The movement put socialism at the service of Jewish nationalism. Communal living made it possible to develop such matters as training and housing efficiently and rapidly. Kibbutz members earn no wages and have no individual wealth, though in recent years some kibbutzniks have bent the rules by building up nest eggs with the help of relatives who live abroad. Members must place their labour at the disposal of the kibbutz, and submit to the will of the majority in the form of elected committees. In return, the kibbutz undertakes to care for its members from cradle to grave, offering complete security.

The kibbutz instils a sense of group identification so powerful that kibbutzniks have long been regarded, and not without hostility in some quarters, as elitist. Kibbutzniks were well aware of the contribution they were making to the economic success of the youthful state, and the sophistication of the movement meant that intellectual and cultural concerns were never neglected; there was no conflict between toiling in the fields all day and discussing Marxist theory or modern poetry around the dinner tables. Although on average about 4 per cent of the Israeli population is composed of kibbutzniks – and the figure has never risen above 8 per cent – their influence on civic life has been immense. During the War of Independence, the Palmach, a militia formed by the rural kibbutzim, played a crucial role. One third of the young state's first constituent assembly in 1948 was composed of kibbutzniks. For the first twenty years of Israel's existence, a third of all cabinet ministers were kibbutzniks. The number of kibbutznik officers in the IDF is six times greater than their proportion of the population would lead one to expect,[1] and during the Six Day War, one quarter of the casualties were kibbutzniks.[2] By suppressing individual desires for the benefit of the community, kibbutz members were expressing an exalted view of Zionism that made them obvious candidates for high office in the civil and diplomatic service, in the army, and in politics. Even Israelis who had no wish to live on a kibbutz raised their hats to those who did, though attitudes have become more ambivalent in recent years.

The kibbutz system is sufficiently supple to allow its members, when duty calls, to leave the community for extended periods of public service. David Ben-Gurion, when he retired from politics, chose to spend his last years on a kibbutz in the Negev desert. About 70 per cent of kibbutz members who have left the community to work as soldiers or diplomats or administrators return to their kibbutz on retirement.[3] There they resume a way of living that is distinctly modest. The largest house at Hazorea consists of no more than a bedroom, a living room, and a kitchen and bathroom. Since children never live with their parents, there is no need for additional accommodation. Often a bedroom must double as a study. Instead of receiving wages for your labour, you are awarded points, which you may use to buy goods at the kibbutz shop; you may also accumulate points to be exchanged for holidays abroad or luxury items. For food and lodging, of course, there is no charge. Mountainous quantities of fruit and grains and eggs and yoghurt are consumed each morning at the cafeteria dining room to lay the foundations for a hard day's work.

One member of Hazorea told me: 'Not everybody can get along with the kibbutz system. All essential items are available for the asking, but some people are still uncomfortable with having to ask for things, even though they are entitled to them. Of course, we're lucky here. Nobody goes short. But I know some kibbutzim where each family can only have six eggs per week. And people who have worked on their kibbutz all their lives are beginning to worry that when they get old, instead of having the kind of security they've been promised, they may get thrown out instead.'

Things have not yet come to such a pass at Hazorea, which generously honours its obligations to its members. Should a member become physically or mentally ill and unable to work any longer, he or she will be looked after and given the finest medical treatment. Members who become handicapped or terminally ill are accommodated in luxurious sheltered housing in the very centre of the kibbutz, a symbolic reassurance that even those who are no longer productive remain central to the community rather than expelled to the margins. Members are even entitled to bring their parents to live on the kibbutz: they will be required to purchase their house here (if one is available, and there is usually a waiting list), and they must pay a small sum for its upkeep and contribute to compulsory health insurance.

Ageing kibbutzniks experience no loss of status in the community. It is hard to stroll along the paths at Hazorea without being clipped by an eighty-year-old crone whizzing by on a golf cart. In the dining room the elderly expertly manoeuvre wheeled trolleys to convey trays of food to their favourite tables. They are a gritty lot, these ageing founders. A rejection of good manners and civility as the formal veneer obscuring the corruption of bourgeois values was part of the kibbutz mystique. These old-timers haven't mellowed with the years. Hazorea sprawls, and I would occasionally have to ask for directions. The old-timers tended to give me a grunt and a nod at best, however smooth my courtesies. When members in the secretariat or the post office appear gruff and unhelpful, it is because they are not used to giving explanations. On a kibbutz you are supposed to work things out for yourself. If you're a visitor and thus unfamiliar with the system, that is your tough luck. Like most large kibbutzim, Hazorea runs an *ulpan*, where would-be immigrants can learn Ivrit while participating, to a limited extent, in kibbutz life. I later encountered some graduates of the Hazorea *ulpan* who praised the facilities at the kibbutz, but complained of the coldness they encountered. Months went by before any of them were invited to the home of a kibbutz member.

I was more fortunate, especially in my next-door neighbour Dafna, a warm-hearted ex-Glaswegian, and her Israeli husband. She affected a cynicism that was only skin deep, as in her insistence that she found her children unbearable most of the time. I would visit her for the pleasure of hearing Ivrit spoken with a Glaswegian accent. She spent her mornings supervising the workroom established for older members who can no longer work in the fields or factories. They come here for four hours in the morning, have lunch together, are given some physiotherapy, and then return on their golf carts to their houses. When I walked in, I nearly tripped over an old lady in a wheelchair who had fallen asleep over her loom. Dafna waved me over and, handing me a mug of coffee, explained how her charges kept themselves occupied: 'They do embroidery and weaving. That man over there puts plastic covers on books.' I looked in his direction and saw that he was otherwise occupied. Dafna shrugged. 'He also reads the newspaper.' The fact that these old people are occupied is more important than the nature of that occupation. It's a way of getting them out of their houses, of allowing them to feel that, however great their frailty, they can still contribute to the kibbutz that is their home.

Hazorea makes its one concession to social decorum on Friday nights. Like most kibbutzim, Hazorea is defiantly secular, and there is no synagogue. Nevertheless Jewish customs are maintained, even though in secularized form. On Fridays the children bake the traditional *challa* bread and bring it to their parents. Friday is also the one night when families make a special effort to be together, to dress up, and to eat with the rest of the community in the dining room in the midst of tablecloths and candles and small cups of wine. Tanned women with a dab of makeup on their faces sit next to young men and women in uniform who look like their siblings but turn out to be their children. The major Jewish festivals are also celebrated, especially Purim, when children are encouraged to run riot. During Passover, there is a huge *seder* dinner, but the traditional Passover liturgy, the Haggadah, has been rewritten to bring it into line with socialist Zionism.

On Shabbat many Hazoreans take long walks or picnic on the wooded slopes above the kibbutz. For a couple of weeks each spring, the bosk a few miles east of the kibbutz is renowned for its springtime display of pink Persian cyclamen. I joined one Hazorean family on an outing to this dazzling spot, but unfortunately at least five hundred other nature-loving Israelis had had the same idea. There was even a mobile snack bar parked nearby. The remainder of the population was at Mount Gilboa paying similar homage to the black irises that flourish there.

Although each kibbutz is independent, it also belongs to a larger organization, such as the Artzi group, which offers a central structure that can provide certain services, notably cultural ones, to individual kibbutzim. Cultural activities tend to be a mixture of locally organized events and programmes made available by the central body at an advantageous price. The central organization sometimes lays on a kind of huge audition to which the cultural committees of individual kibbutzim are invited; from the acts presented, the committees can choose and book events that would be appreciated by their kibbutz. This system works well for large kibbutzim with substantial cultural budgets, but smaller communities often have to team up in order to be able to afford visiting artists or groups or lecturers.

Hazorea is fortunate in having its own museum, which houses a permanent collection of Oriental art and provides hanging space for touring exhibitions. During my stay, there was a remarkable display of photographs by Ilan Wolff, who uses not a camera but a metal drum with a tiny pinhole pricked in the side. The curvature of the drum distorts the image, but Wolff cleverly and subtly controls the distortion to give alarming but diverting effects, such as an Eiffel Tower on a bent base and a Flatiron Building in Manhattan about to topple over. (It is sadly typical of much artistic life in Israel that Wolff now lives in Paris.) Hazorea has its museum, and other kibbutzim have their folklore choirs or modern dance troupes or publications. According to Amos Elon, the movement publishes some 200 periodicals – scientific, literary, political, agricultural – in addition to newssheets for each kibbutz.[4]

My first week at Hazorea was 'intifada week', and a whole series of events had been laid on to focus the members' minds on the uprising. The Palestinian leader Faisal Husseini was supposed to come and speak, but he had been summoned abroad at the last minute. Journalists came to lecture, and some members participated in a Peace Now visit to the West Bank. The celebrated film *The Battle of Algiers* was shown, with its uncomfortable parallels with the intifada. Hazorea has its own video channel, which records meetings and lectures that not all members may have been able to attend. One evening I watched part of a lengthy discussion among kibbutz members who were serving in the IDF on the problems of performing military service in the Territories.

On a lighter note, one of the children's houses announced that it would be giving a concert after dinner; the programme would focus on the work and inspiration of Mozart. The ten-year-olds wore jeans and track suits – no party frocks for performers on a kibbutz. Dominating the stage were two portraits of the composer based on the wrappers of the famous chocolates that bear his name. The draughtsmanship was not the most exacting I have seen, and poor Mozart looked as though he had just been exhumed. The first item showed Mozart to be the composer of weird unearthly sounds, such as those generated by six recorders all playing at cross-purposes. Ayal, the boy who had invited me to attend the concert, took a back seat on stage throughout the performance, banging his finger-cymbals absentmindedly as he stared dreamily into the distance. A little girl played the flute, rather well, while her grandmother accompanied her on the piano. Next the kids formed a massed choir and sang the alphabet, an item that left me completely baffled. We were then treated to two songs, and the audience joined in. Ayal's mother, Michal, assured me they were by Mozart, but I had never encountered them before.

Mozart, I also discovered, was the composer of 'Ba Ba Black Sheep', which was performed by three girls with mandolins and two girls with flutes. After that a child was let loose on a set of drums and made an astonishing amount of noise: an early jazz composition, no doubt, by Wolfgang Amadeus. A girls' chorus sang Papageno's opening aria from *The Magic Flute*, and threw in references to Purim, reminding their parents of the imminence of the festival. A piano duet followed, and a girls' recorder ensemble with cello ostinato accompaniment. Three boys and three girls in cobbled-together eighteenth-century costume danced and giggled their way through the minuet from Act 3 of *Figaro*. They were terrible: bowing and scraping and courtly graces don't come naturally to kibbutzniks. Despite the comic moments, it was striking that a bunch of ten-year-olds could put on such a varied musical performance at all.

Of course a kibbutz is pure heaven for a child. Soon after birth, a baby kibbutznik leaves home, and takes its bags to the baby house. Six weeks after the birth the mother resumes her job for half a day, leaving ample time to spend with her new child. Each day from four until eight the babies, and children, transfer operations to their parents' house, and babies may, until the age of six months, opt to spend the night with their parents. Until the baby is eighteen months old, the mother is entitled to come to the baby house each morning to wake her infant. The babies live in groups of six, with two nurses for each group. The houses are adapted for infantile life, with miniature furniture and play areas both indoors and outdoors. The kibbutz virtue of self-reliance is inculcated from an early age, and it is not unusual to find a two-year-old making its own way to its parents' house at four in the afternoon. At night, after the mothers have tucked in their babes and said good night, the houses are guarded by two members on night duty on a rota basis. Highly sensitive microphones relay any sounds of distress or disturbance to the guards, who will then check that everything is all right.

In addition to basic education, the kids at Hazorea are given supplementary education in such subjects as literature, art, and English. I watched one exercise in which children were given the core of a famous painting by Van Gogh or Degas and told to fill in the edges of the picture in the same style. The aim of this kind of exercise, I was told, is to develop independence in the children while requiring them to relate to and share with other people. There are few conventional toys in the children's houses. Teachers use scraps to instil such concepts as colour, texture, and size. Music is used, not only for the aesthetic pleasure it brings, but to teach notions such as fast and slow, loud and soft. Outdated machinery and equipment are not discarded by the kibbutz, but handed over to the children. By playing with, say, old tractors, the children are encouraged to construct an imaginary world that imitates the real world they will later inhabit.

There has been much criticism of this separation of child from parent, but I could see much to recommend it. The children almost certainly receive much more personal attention than they would get in the course of a conventional upbringing. Ayal's mother Michal, herself a child of the kibbutz whose own four children were all raised here too, maintains that parental influence remains the dominant factor in a child's upbringing, even though the children never sleep at home. Children only grow closer to their nurse than to their mother when the mother is particularly cold or unresponsive to her own children. Just as Hazorea refuses to hire outside labour (with the exception of Arab construction workers provided by the Artzi organization), so the children's houses do not employ outside nurses, although other kibbutzim have done so. At Hazorea, according to Michal, they feel that the children derive an important sense of connection with the community by having as their nurses women who are as much part of their permanent environment as their parents.

At the age of twelve or thirteen, the Hazorea children go to a high school they share with three other kibbutzim at Kibbutz Mishmar Ha-Emek, three miles down the Megiddo road. The 350 children live in groups of thirty, which can be separated according to sex, or mixed. Michal recalls that during her schooldays girls and boys would take showers together without any self-consciousness, though she doubts that this still goes on. The students live four to a room and express their personalities in the limited space available. Over one bed I saw an earnest United Nations poster, while the bed opposite was watched over by the angelic features of Samantha Fox. The girls' rooms are immediately identifiable by the cuddly toys and plastic make-up kits on the bedside tables. By living and studying in the same building, the school tries to minimize the distinction between study and the rest of the time spent at school.

In the evenings the children must supervise each other. This is less a matter of principle than of expediency. Most of the teachers are kibbutz members, who want to spend their evenings at home or watching movies in the auditorium, not keeping kids out of trouble. Some outside teachers are employed, but the children give them a hard time, and are disinclined to accord them the same familiarity and respect that they give to teachers who, as fellow kibbutzniks, have been known to them since infancy. During weekends and school holidays, the children move from the school into houses on their kibbutzim, which they share with each other. The lack of supervision has led to problems such as minor house-breaking, attributed to boredom rather than to latent criminality. Such problems are dealt with not by harsh disciplinary codes but by discussion. One Hazorean told me: 'The kibbutz operates according to a set of norms. Problems arise when people decide they aren't going to play by those rules. But we don't want to police our kids, and we prefer to appeal to their consciences. Only with serious matters such as drugs do we take a hard line, and call in the police.'

A kibbutz school also differs from other Israeli schools in its incorporation of labour. There are classes from seven until noon, but after lunch all the children must work. Some return to their kibbutz to work on the farm; others remain at the school, to work in, say, the library or on the school farm. At fifteen, children are required to spend one day a week working in preparation for professional life on the kibbutz. Michal's eldest daughter Anat took me to see the fish farm, where she works most afternoons. Fish farms have been successful enterprises for many kibbutzim, since most ornamental fish come from the United States or the Orient, whereas Israel is far closer to the lucrative European markets. This farm now exports a million dollars' worth of live fish each year. The fish are dispatched in double plastic bags – manufactured, or course, at Plastopil – and given a dose of oxygen that will keep the fish alive for three days, sufficient time for air freight to convey them to their destinations. The great risk in fish farming of this kind is disease, and many farms have been wiped out by virus infections. At Hazorea new species are kept in isolation for two years to ensure they are free of disease before breeding begins.

Blending education and labour is not only a matter of ideology. Anat's grandparents, Ruth and Meir Meron, recalled the terrible days of October 1973, when they, along with the rest of the country, were taken by surprise as war broke out. Soldiers and reservists donned their uniforms and made for their barracks, and over the next few days news trickled back to Hazorea and every other settlement in Israel as casualties mounted. On a single day two Hazorea members were killed in combat. But in their absence it was the children who took over the running of much of the kibbutz. Trained from an early age to operate equipment and familiar with the routines of the workplaces, they were able to minimize the economic impact when hundreds of able-bodied men and women left overnight for the battle zones.

When I visited the school, the entire student body was involved in a two–day session devoted to an examination of how the arts reflect society. Painters, dancers, photographers, and other artists descended on the school to work with the students on this ambitious project. Kibbutz schools, unlike most ordinary state schools, have the flexibility to organize such sessions. The previous year comparable projects had examined forty years of Israeli history and the Arab problem.

Meir Meron, for many years the school's headmaster, told me that one aim of kibbutz education is, of course, to induce the students to remain within the movement. He also believes that kibbutz education offers a broader perspective and generally more liberal approach than do the state schools, which have a more nationalistic stance. The kibbutz encourages pupils to study by themselves, viewing teachers as guides rather than as instructors. Debate and discussion are encouraged. About 80 per cent of male graduates pursue further education — the figure is lower for girls — and they do well at university. Their free-ranging education may have given them less factual knowledge than their counterparts from more conventional schools, says Meron, but their analytic gifts and intellectual self-reliance tend to be greater.

Conscious efforts are made to develop good relations with the large Arab population of northern Israel. The school begins teaching Arabic in the sixth year. Meetings are arranged between the students and Arab children of like age, but these are not always successful. This has more to do with style than hostility. Children of the kibbutz are no more adept at getting on with the few students at the school who do not live on a kibbutz. Non-kibbutznik children live in their own house, for differences between the two sets of children are so strong that it is difficult for them to live or even work together, though they share meals and sports activities. The outsiders usually come from troubled backgrounds or broken homes, which explains why they are boarding at this school; they tend to have a lower academic standard than the kibbutzniks and receive special coaching. Meir Meron admits that kibbutznik children can be snobbish and know their own worth, although he denies that the school system encourages an elitist view. It remains true, as many have observed, that kibbutzniks are happiest in the company of other kibbutzniks — and not only during their schooldays. Because kibbutz life is so homogeneous, it can be difficult for the children to connect with other people from other backgrounds. A kibbutz, after all, is a completely self-contained community. With only a few cars at the disposal of a thousand souls, opportunities to leave the community are scarce; it would be almost unheard of for a member to walk a mile down the road to Yokne'am to do some shopping. Whenever I was driving from Hazorea to Tel Aviv or Haifa, I would notify the office, and at the appointed hour I would find a few Hazoreans waiting by my car for a lift.

Kibbutz life and education generate an astonishing degree of self-reliance among the children. They are often obstreperous, but rarely shy. Brought up in the continuous company of their peers rather than by parents who act as figures of authority, they grow up with no false respect for adults. This can be disconcerting for adults accustomed to the deference shown by children from more traditional societies, but it is also refreshing to find yourself on equal terms with a six-year-old. While admirable in principle, however, such an absence of hierarchy can strain the nerves. Kibbutz houses are small, and when the children tear in for a few hours in the late afternoon, the noise can be terrific: three kids screaming at each other, the television bleating in a corner, the kettle whistling, the splattering of the shower, the phone ringing, and adults trying to make their voices heard. But then no one confuses a kibbutz with a monastery.

In the 1980s just over half the children of members were opting to stay at Hazorea as members in their own right. This rate of retention is some indication of the quality of the kibbutz; but children are delaying for increasingly lengthy periods the moment when they make that final decision to stay or go. The previous generation made up their minds immediately after military service. Nowadays the young people prefer to work and travel for a few years after military service, and may not make up their minds until they are about thirty, by which time the kibbutz has lost some of their most productive years. Even after they have become members, they are often reluctant to participate in the running of the kibbutz by taking their turn on some of the forty-one committees and accepting other administrative roles. On a small kibbutz, such lack of continuity can pose a grave problem. To have a static structure with constant overheads and at the same time a shrinking population is enough to give any manager a severe headache.

# 12 · WHICH WAY TO TUBAS?

All Israelis are politically minded, and kibbutzniks more so than most. Although Hazorea is affiliated to Mapam, about a quarter of the members voted for other parties in 1988. Some disapproved of Mapam's decision to stand independently of the Labour Party, with which it had been allied, and voted for Labour instead. The left is as prone to factionalism in Israel as anywhere else. A political observer remarked to me that 'in the 1950s fifteen kibbutzim split in two when Stalin's misdeeds began to come to light. They divided not over how to run their kibbutzim, but over Stalin. I'm glad to say that even in these troubled times, such splits that can tear families apart appear to be a thing of the past. But we are undoubtedly a very ideological society. Jews have always had an ideological culture. That's why we came into conflict with the Romans, who had a civic culture, while we were killing each other over such matters as the existence of the afterlife.'

During Hazorea's 'intifada week' in March 1989, the pressure group Peace Now proposed that convoys of private cars and coaches from all over Israel should cross into the West Bank with the simple purpose of meeting Palestinians in their villages and exchanging ideas with them for an hour or two before returning across the Green Line. Hazorea was invited to participate, and I signed up. The evening before the convoy rolled, radio reports hinted that the army would not allow the vehicles to enter the Territories. We set off anyway, about thirty of us, *ulpan* students and volunteers as well as kibbutzniks. I was surprised at the small turnout from Hazorea, but assumed that many members either felt the exercise would be futile or preferred to spend Shabbat in less strenuous fashion.

At Mishmar Ha-Emek we teamed up with other kibbutz groups, filling two buses as well as a few private cars. We were instructed not to wear our Peace Now badges until well inside the Territories, for fear of provoking arguments with unsympathetic Israelis en route. Confrontation was the last thing the organizers wanted, and spokesmen had been designated to negotiate with the army patrols we would certainly encounter. Our destination was still secret but was rumoured to be a refugee camp near Nablus, which is about as deep into the West Bank as you can get.

We drove towards Beit She'an, where the epic electoral battle between Jackie Levy and Shlomo Ben-Lulu was taking place, and passed the awesome jail stuck on its own in the middle of the valley. We continued down the Jordan Valley road, passing fruit stands and poorly tended Arab fields. We had entered the Territories, and near Mehola were stopped at an army checkpoint. The road had been blocked with a hinged metal contraption from which sharp nails protruded upwards. It seemed unlikely that we would be allowed to proceed, but apparently the army was still awaiting instructions. Shortly before noon we were astonished to learn that permission had been granted for us to continue. We affixed our lapel badges and stuck posters in the windows of the buses and cars so as to identify us as Peace Now supporters, not as Israeli settlers on a rampage.

We turned off onto mountain roads, passing Bedouin camps and an army base. The usually barren hills of Samaria were pale green with the approach of spring, and speckled with poppies. Here and there a field as dry as rubble had been ploughed or planted, but the cultivation was scant. I asked a Hazorean why Arab fields gave the appearance of being poorly tended, whereas the fields belonging to kibbutzim were impeccably maintained and irrigated. 'That's because Arab farms are family smallholdings. They're too small for mechanization to be profitable, whereas on kibbutzim the reverse is true. But nowadays many mechanized Israeli farms have become unprofitable because of high overheads, while the Arab farms still support, modestly, the families who own and work them.'

We passed through a wretched village of dilapidated single-storey houses. It was clear that we were not unexpected, and that welcoming delegations had turned out in every village to wish us well. Women in long robes, with small children clutching their hands, stood by the roadside, waving and giving us the peace sign. A boy jolted by on a donkey, which sported between its ears a Peace Now sticker. At Tubas we came to a halt. We had been supposed to continue a few miles to El Fara, but the army ordered us to go no further. That didn't matter, since Tubas was a sizeable place with about 13,000 inhabitants and there was no shortage of people to talk to. At the foot of the town was a kind of square, and here some hundred or more Arabs were awaiting our arrival. We mingled among them. One young man spoke excellent English, perfected during three years at Glasgow University, where he had gained a doctorate in genetics. He was a teacher here, but because the schools were still closed he was unable to work; nor was it permitted to hold informal classes in people's homes. He was just about able to survive on the half-pay he was receiving. The intifada had meant that the economic situation was fairly grave in Tubas, but many of the townspeople were involved in farming, and there was no shortage of food. In towns such as Nablus the problems were greater, and made worse by the frequent curfews. Instead, Tubas suffered from a shortage of services. There was no hospital here; women in labour and those taken ill suddenly had to drive to Nablus, a forty-minute journey at best along mediocre roads, and considerably longer if, as often happened, army roadblocks were in operation. The Arabs, he said, resented paying taxes and getting nothing in return, though he neglected to mention that many Palestinians were no longer paying taxes.

As we were talking, some townspeople standing in the little square began yelling something about the PLO. There was a good deal of laughter at this. Normally such shouts would have been regarded as provocative and might have attracted the unwelcome attention of Israeli soldiers, but the Palestinians, emboldened by the presence of Israeli civilians, knew the army were unlikely to intervene. There were also shouts of 'Say Yes to Peace' and a chorus of 'We Shall Overcome'. I asked the geneticist whether there was much harassment from the army. He replied: 'It is constant. Just yesterday I was stopped and lined up against a wall for fifteen minutes. For no reason. ID checks are a way of life here. There are about a hundred soldiers stationed near Tubas, and they often patrol the alleys and the *souk*.' But there is little tension between the town and the Jewish settlement some four miles away, largely because the settlers keep to themselves. Nevertheless, he told me, there was anger in the town, for seven youngsters had been killed since the intifada began. He was not very hopeful about the future, but said that there was no going back to the situation that prevailed before the intifada; the solution probably lay in some kind of federation with Jordan, where he and many other Palestinians had relatives.

Those of us who spoke English had a more successful time of it than those who only spoke Ivrit, for few of the townspeople spoke Hebrew, and even fewer of the Israelis spoke Arabic. This didn't seem to stand in the way of a remarkable rapport between the townspeople and the visitors, some of whom were invited into houses and plied with soft drinks and coffee. After about half an hour, an officer with a megaphone asked us to return to our vehicles, but no one paid much attention. We were enjoying the novelty of speaking across what is usually perceived as an abyss of fear and suspicion. One of the Peace Now leaders began to address us from the top of the square in hectoring tones, and helmeted soldiers moved in to drag him from the rock on which he was standing. There was no great indignation at this rough treatment, as it was obvious that the Israeli was deliberately pushing his luck. He was later released by the soldiers and told brusquely to return to his coach. A Hazorean woman asked the soldiers standing near us not to take it out on the townspeople after we had left.

'Don't worry,' the soldiers replied, 'we're not angry with them. We're angry with you for coming here. What are you doing here?'

I followed the woman as she approached some of the Arab women, who were standing well back from the square. She quizzed them efficiently about their place within the community. They were free to do as they please, they reassured her, but the kibbutznik reminded them that their brothers and husbands had told them not to join the menfolk gathered in the square. We do participate in the intifada, insisted the women, but the kibbutznik peremptorily told them that if and when the Palestinians achieved some kind of independence she suspected that the women would be sent back to their kitchens.

Listening to the radio during the return journey, we learnt that the other convoys had been turned back at the Green Line by the IDF. A few activists had abandoned their vehicles and proceeded on foot to a rendezvous with a group of Palestinians. No mention was made of the success of our convoy. In retrospect the whole exercise seemed a non-event – after all, we had done no more than drive for a few hours to talk freely to some Palestinians. Yet in the context of Israeli life, so trivial an accomplishment had required intense organization and a large measure of luck. The army had used its might to defeat not a revolution or an assault, but a conversation.

The next day the prime minister dismissed Peace Now as 'a marginal element that can't influence anything' – in which case one wonders why he had taken the trouble to attack it. For good measure, he accused it of sabotaging Israel's struggle for security, 'for our very existence'.[1] Tehiya's Geula Cohen, equally predictably, spat with fury: 'Peace Now is a fifth column. It encourages the enemy. It split the nation during the Lebanon war, and today it encourages the intifada to spill more blood. It will be responsible for a civil war here which will threaten the country.'[2]

It's a strange state of affairs. A few thousand men and women talk to a few thousand men and women on the other side of an invisible frontier, and for their pains are depicted as enemies of society. Naive we may have been, but malevolent we were not. As is so often the case in Israeli political discourse, the subtexts are more complex. For Shamir was not only castigating those he saw as seeking to undermine the status quo of hostility and occupation, but reassuring the Israeli right wing that he was, deep down, every bit as tough as they were. Denunciations of the peace camp portray it as little more than a band of starry-eyed left-wingers. Nothing could be further from the truth. For instance, a group known as the Council for Peace and Security, which argues for the evacuation of most of the Occupied Territories, includes thirty reserve major generals, eighty brigadier generals, a former head of military intelligence, and a former head of the civil administration of the West Bank.[3]

The next day the kibbutzniks had to return to their own domestic problems. For the entire movement is in deep trouble. Perhaps the wonder is that it succeeded at its rare combination of utopianism and practical achievement for as long as it did. How many collectivist movements elsewhere have survived for half as long? Of course they would not have been so successful had they not enjoyed mainstream political support. They were never regarded, as were the hippie communes of North America, as freakish indulgences. Indeed, it was the kibbutzim that staffed a disproportionately high sector of the Israeli establishment. As pioneers of agricultural technology, they were responsible not only for much of the country's prosperity, but for its enlightened and progressive image. Even today, they generate almost 10 per cent of Israel's gross national product. Agriculture, however, is no longer as important as it used to be, and consequently the role of the kibbutzim has diminished.

Quite apart from the economic problems, there are the social quandaries. Hazorea remains faithful to the original ideals of kibbutz life, but many other kibbutzim are more pragmatic. Communal child-rearing has been abandoned by some, for the simple reason that mothers wanted to have their children living with them in their home. Michal, a Hazorean born and bred, deplores those who place their selfish wishes ahead of the communal ideals of the movement, but she also recognizes that within the next ten years even Hazorea's children's houses will disappear. If the community can afford it, extensions will be built to parents' houses so that children can sleep at home. Where children sleep may seem a trivial matter, but it reflects the struggle between individualism and collectivism that threatens the whole movement.

Sometimes success can breed its own problems. A well-known depilatory, Epilady, is the brainchild of Kibbutz Hagroshim, and the product is exported to fifty countries, generating an annual turnover of $130 million. But you can't run an operation like that without managers. On a kibbutz, managerial positions are supposed to be rotated among the members to avoid the evolution of a managerial class. But of course it's simply impractical to keep changing your managers. Hagroshim has contracted out work to nine other kibbutzim, and while this can be a godsend to neighbouring kibbutzim that have fallen on hard times, such a policy can also undermine the movement's ethic. Meir Meron observes: 'Those who work for us should live with us. Some kibbutzim have accepted wage labour, but this creates a two-tier system, since workers can never enjoy the status of kibbutzniks and participate in running the enterprises. Naturally, we support the unions and Histadrut, but because of our structure we can't give promotion opportunities to non-members.'

The overriding problem of the entire movement is one of heavy debt. It was shrewd of many kibbutzim to diversify their modes of production, blending agriculture and industry. But such shifts required heavy invest-ment. Some kibbutzim, inexperienced in running industrial enterprises, invested unwisely or managed poorly. Others were simply unlucky, as soaring interest rates gobbled up their profits. The total debt incurred by kibbutzim is estimated to be just under NIS 7 billion. This poses two problems: how to rid the movement of its debt and place it once again on a sound financial footing, and the degree to which fortunate kibbutzim should bail out those that are floundering. The first problem was being solved, thanks to the felicitous presence of Shimon Peres at the Treasury. The second problem is contributing to divisiveness within the movement.

A manager at Hazorea put the dilemma this way: 'Hazorea is well run. Many of our founders came from Germany, so we received a large amount of reparations money after the war, and that certainly helped. But we invested it well, and we're doing all right. But one of our neighbours is close to bankruptcy. What do we do? The general feeling seems to be that we're prepared to be generous in supporting the less successful kibbutzim, but not to the extent of suffering ourselves, especially as most of the failures stem from mismanagement. It's not always the fault of individual kibbutzim. They took advice from the economics departments of the movement's organizations, and sometimes that advice was poor. We're advising other kibbutzim on how to put their affairs in order. The trouble is that Israelis always think they know better and they're slow to learn from the mistakes of others. When they make a mess of things, it's always someone else's fault. Attitudes are going to have to change.'

Nor are kibbutzim immune from the vagaries of the marketplace. One of the most successful of kibbutzim, Netzer Sereni, is now in deep trouble. Its principal products were trucks and other military equipment, much of which ended up in pre-revolutionary Iran. That market has now vanished. Kibbutz Urim has a thriving farm and a successful factory producing sleeping bags and quilts. But with debt requiring annual disbursements of NIS 4 million in interest alone, the future is bleak. The Urim kibbutzniks can tighten their belts to the last notch, but the burden of debt will remain.

Despite the crucial role the movement played in the development, economic and social, of the state, many Israelis are disinclined to take a sentimental view of its present plight. The following remarks by the economics editor of the *Jerusalem Post* expresses the hard-line view: 'The kibbutzim made hay while the sun shone for years, raising their standards of living and speculating with their excess money on the stock exchange . . . The government should save the kibbutzim only on a limited basis. They should be forced to sell part of their industry, ask for partners for the rest of their industry and farming enterprises, and even think of merging kibbutzim.' [4]

But Mr Peres decided to look after his own, and in March 1989 a deal was worked out. Ailing kibbutzim must increase their productivity and lower their consumption, and members are being encouraged to seek jobs outside the kibbutz in order to bring in some cash. Kibbutzim in areas popular with tourists are being urged to open guest houses. About NIS 1 billion of the debt will be written off by the banks, and NIS 3.3 billion will be rescheduled. Reducing both the standard of living and new investment by 5 per cent will gradually reduce the burdens, while at the same time the government will invest a further NIS 650 million. Some assets will be sold, such as urban property, which will raise a further NIS 750 million. The kibbutz movement as a whole will not be allowed to perish. Quite apart from the widespread dismay that would be felt in Israel were the movement to collapse, it should be remembered that two-thirds of the kibbutzim are located in areas, especially border areas, where most of their critics would not dream of living. Their very location helps to maintain Israel's security. Were the kibbutzim and moshavim to vanish, the result would be a virtual depopulation of the border areas.

Not surprisingly, founders such as Meir Meron view with sadness the recent history of the movement to which they devoted their lives. When I asked him how the kibbutzim have changed over the years, he replied: 'The principles on which they were based still exist but they don't direct behaviour to the same extent as before. Nowadays the style of life, of clothing, of interests, are much the same as in the rest of Israeli society. You used to be able to recognize a kibbutznik in the street – not just by clothing, but by general bearing. The goal of the kibbutz system is to form another society, to set an example. Perhaps the sense of the difference, of the value of the system has diminished, and there are now more doubts about the rightness of our path. It's inevitable that as the influence of the left diminishes in Israel, our pessimism grows. We used to play an important role in many governments, but this too has diminished. And our economic base has changed. There are great differences between purely agricultural and half-agricultural kibbutzim. The development may have been necessary, but it alters the quality of life. Agricultural work can be repetitive, but it's in the open air and subject to the seasons. Factory work is often numbing, and gives less scope to individuals. What I notice is that kibbutzim have become much more materialistic. The political discussions that are a regular feature of kibbutz life now attract mostly older members. Our younger members have less involvement in political ideas. But there are also positive developments, at least at Hazorea, where we are bigger and stronger than before.'

Adamit, a kibbutz with only seventy members up on the Lebanese border, has none of the institutionalized atmosphere of Hazorea. It lies at the end of a long steep road that zigzags up into the mountains. For some reason the roads of Upper Galilee have become death traps for local wildlife. It is impossible to drive for five miles without encountering the corpses not only of domestic animals, but of sheep, foxes, and even cows, their limbs stiffly extended in *rigor mortis*. In February this evidence of slaughter was already shaded by trees that glittered with pale pink blossoms. From the top of the road to Adamit there are spectacular views over Galilee, and north across a deep wadi into the equally beautiful hills of south Lebanon. When I arrived, I wandered towards the children's houses, which were packed with boisterous toddlers. I introduced myself to one of the teachers, Irit, whose principal occupation seemed to be tying children's shoelaces. She showed me Adamit's prize exhibit: a shell partially embedded in a copse at the centre of the kibbutz. Its arrival was a freak occurrence, and security has not been a major problem here since the shelling in 1982.

Adamit was founded in 1970 by American immigrants, who for some years acted at cross-purposes. Some had come from other kibbutzim; others were immigrants with romantic expectations. United neither by ideology nor political purpose, the new kibbutz floundered for many years. Some members left, disconcerted by the social conflict or weary of living on a mountaintop a mile from Lebanon. Adamit in its early years resembled an American hippie commune airlifted into the Middle East. Just after the Yom Kippur War, membership shrank to thirty-five.

Gradually the numbers were replenished. The founders' children began to grow up and take their places within the community.

Adamit's farm is down in the valley, where they grow citrus fruits, avocados, corn, and sunflowers, and raise chickens. A reasonably profitable factory manufactures pipe flanges. Bracha, an American woman who has been at Adamit since 1973, expresses doubts similar to those voiced by Meir Meron: 'We started the factory in response to pressure from the Likud government to spread our investments. But in a factory you share the work to a lesser extent than you do in the fields. You have managers, you have no choice, and that's contrary to kibbutz ideology. I'm a farmer and I can't help being sad that agriculture has declined here. The factories soak up more and more people, and that's depriving agriculture of expertise, which in turn accelerates the decline. We're having to cover our bed with a quilt that's too small to fit.'

Not all the members work at Adamit; some are employed at other kibbutzim. They employ some outside labour – a nurse, a motor mechanic – but no Arab workers. All jobs rotate after three years, and members are having to take on responsibilities at a younger age than formerly. One year they elected as secretary somebody who had only been at Adamit for two years. A small kibbutz such as this cannot afford, nor has the facilities to mount, the kind of cultural programme the Hazoreans take for granted, but there's a movie once a week and joint activities with neighbouring kibbutzim. Performers are still brought up the mountain to entertain the members, though it would probably be cheaper to hire a bus and take the kibbutzniks down to Haifa for the evening. A bus connects Adamit with the coastal town of Nahariya, and members can sign up for one of the community's cars for personal use in the evenings.

In 1988 Adamit took a step that many at Hazorea still shudder to contemplate: children are now allowed to spend the night with their parents. Bracha had opposed the change: 'It reflects a shift from a group-oriented ideology. What happens is that as members grow older, they become more concerned with their personal needs.' Once children begin to spend more time at home, their parents quite naturally stay at home too, which diminishes the social life of the community. Many social activities have been scrapped, and travel has become more restricted. Bracha told me she has had no new furniture for fifteen years. The future remains uncertain. The membership is more varied than in the past, with roughly a third each of North Americans, South Americans, and Israelis, together with a sprinkling of Italians and Swiss. Membership has remained stable, despite the departure of a number of families a few years ago.

Why had they left? 'For a variety of reasons,' said Bracha, cagily.

'Some were disenchanted with the way of life here, some with Israel itself. Others felt that this was their last chance to make a major change in their lives before entering middle age. Those of us who are staying on have our dissatisfactions too. Some of the younger single members are unhappy because of the shrinking social life. It's a real struggle. And of course we worry about the whole situation in Israel. Sometimes we feel we could be living in South Africa for all the support we feel for the government. So there are times when I'm very unhappy about what's going on. But I shan't leave Israel.'

'Beautiful but dead' was how one Israeli – from Tel Aviv, naturally – described Haifa. Compared with Tel Aviv, all Israeli towns seem dead, certainly after eleven at night. Still, he had a point. Haifa is one of those cities it must be delightful to inhabit, but where visitors find little to do. Laid out on terraces across the precipitous slopes of Mount Carmel, Haifa is a city of views. You step out onto the terraces of the houses or the balconies of tall apartment blocks, and gasp as you see the curve of the bay leading north to Akko and Nahariya, a thin line of white and gray demarcating the blue of the riviera. Crammed between sea and mountains, Haifa has a Mediterranean elan, placid, cheerful, relaxed, even elegant. One is pleasantly aware of the mix of cultures. The most famous monuments in the city are not even Jewish: the Bahai shrine with its golden dome, set among lovely formal gardens, lush and semi-tropical, and, at the other end of the mountain, the Carmelite monastery, lofty and domed.

The Galilee, Haifa's hinterland, has 60 per cent of Israel's Arab population, and the Arabs of Haifa live in a state of reasonable harmony with the Jewish population. Beit Hagefen is a cultural centre expressly designed to bring Jews and Arabs together, although some observers say that these days it has little influence over the life of the city. As a stratified town, with layers of habitation at various heights along the ledges of the mountain, Haifa encourages the tendency to hide oneself away from the rougher corners of the city, such as the scruffy port area, redeemed for me by the glorious aromas emanating from the Arab bakeries. Less attractive odours waft from the factories and oil refineries and concrete works on Haifa's outskirts. Climatic inversions result in noxious air pollution, made to a highly sulphurous recipe, that sometimes climbs the mountain and invades the richest suburbs. Because the refineries were granted a kind of extraterritoriality in the 1930s, it has proved very difficult to regulate their industrial misdemeanours.

Tucked into one corner of the mountain is the Technion, Israel's leading technical institute. Founded in 1924, it now has twenty faculties, many of which have close ties with the industrial and military establishments. Sometimes departments expand in response to pressure from the government for more computer technicians or electrical engineers. The top faculties include computer science; aeronautical, industrial, mechanical and electrical engineering; and medicine. Research is strong in such fields as laser technology, fibre optics, medical technology, and weaponry. At a small industrial park adjoining the campus, new hi-tech companies can lease space in order to work closely with researchers at the Technion. The smallness of the country means that the Technion has tremendous educational influence: 70 per cent of Israel's architects are trained here. I hope its professors weren't responsible for the unadventurous design of the campus, a sprawl of concrete blocks uncompromising in their functionalism.

Competition among students to gain admission is intense, and the Technion can afford to be choosy in selecting its 6,000 undergraduates and 2,500 graduate students. M.Sc. students are given scholarships in exchange for teaching or laboratory work, so it's tempting to stay on if you can't find a satisfactory job after gaining your B.Sc. The fees cover only 10 per cent of the Technion's annual budget of $100 million. Until 1982, government funds covered 75 per cent of the budget, but funding dropped steadily, until by July 1989 the money ran out. All plans for expansion of its research facilities became dependent on private donations, mostly from the diaspora. A Swiss resident, Bruce Rappaport, who ran into a spot of difficulty in 1988 when he was implicated in an alleged attempt to bribe Shimon Peres,[1] has given millions of dollars to the Technion. 'Friends of the Technion' in many countries raise funds, and the same method is used to support most Israeli institutes of higher education, as well as museums and orchestras.

This contribution is crucial, since the Israeli government spends no more than $15 million annually funding basic research. The $3 billion Israel receives each year from the United States government does not include the many millions more donated by individuals to support specific institutions. The Americans alone raise $25 million annually for the Technion. A special visitors' centre at the Technion welcomes Americans in particular, offering them a film show narrated by Kirk Douglas, as well as various exhibits. The centre is named after Jack Lemmon, not because he paid for it, but because it's a good public relations move.

A peculiar condition of higher education in Israel is that attendance at courses is likely to be interrupted by spells of military service. Israeli men not only spend three years in the army after finishing high school, but

subsequently devote up to sixty days each year to reserve duty. When the
call to duty coincides with examination periods, the disruption can be
acute. The Technion alleviates this to some extent by amassing a large
video library, so that students who have missed classes can catch up on
their own. Courses take about four years to complete, with a further four
years for a doctoral degree. On graduation, D.Sc.s often cannot find jobs
in Israeli universities, so they continue their studies in the United States,
from which they may or may not return. Rarely is the traffic two-way.
There are few foreign students at the Technion, since all instruction is in
Ivrit. Even immigrant professors offered jobs here must, eventually, learn
enough Hebrew to teach. Moreover, salaries at Israeli universities cannot
compete with those offered by their American or European counterparts.

The student body includes about 400 Arabs and sixty Druze. Technion
administrators deny that relatively low Arab enrolment is a symptom of
discrimination; most Arabs, they say, live in villages, from where it is
more difficult to qualify for higher education than it would be from more
sophisticated urban schools. The same, they say, applies to Jews. Once
admitted, Arabs may apply to join any faculty they wish – in theory.
Everybody knows that Israeli aircraft companies, concerned about security
and industrial espionage, will never employ an Arab engineer, and many
qualified Arabs find that 'security' is often used as an excuse for not hiring
them.[2] So Arab students, perfectly sensibly, don't bother to apply to
faculties that will give them an education they can't use.

The other university in town, Haifa University, has the better site,
right on top of Mount Carmel. With its unlovely twenty-nine-storey
tower block placed next to flat shallow buildings, it resembles – in
conception if not in sheen – the United Nations headquarters. This is not
surprising, as Oscar Niemeier designed them both. The university is
essentially a liberal arts institution, specialising in education, psychology,
and social work. Only 42 per cent of the funding comes from the Israeli
government; 30 per cent is provided by the 6,000 students and 4,500
external diploma students, and the remainder is raised, of course, by the
Friends of Haifa University.

The arts are represented here by a museum and a slide library devoted
to art and architecture. Rummaging through the 100,000 slides, I found
that the box marked KITSCH was unexpectedly empty. The campus's
Hecht Museum has the somewhat nationalistic theme of 'the story of the
people of Israel in the land of Israel'. Its collection includes a lovely
Canaanite cosmetics box depicting a duck or swan with its neck arching
down over its back, and fine mosaics of a menorah taken from a sixth-
century B.C. synagogue at Beit She'an. And for good measure Mr Hecht,

who was paying a visit to his own gallery when I was there, has thrown in his collection of impressionists and post-impressionists. Distributed throughout the public interiors of the campus is a collection of paintings by Jewish artists who died in the Holocaust.

Haifa University, unlike the Technion, does not attempt to educate an elite, but provides university facilities for the whole of northern Israel. About 18 per cent of the student body is Arab. Haifa University, according to an Arab faculty member, Dr Majid Al-Hajj, is the only place in Israel where Jews and Arabs are equal in educational terms. Arab students are given special help with Hebrew if they need it, and the university does not shy away from exposing the students to the troublesome issues of their coexistence. Soon after my visit a special study day was devoted to the problems of the Arab municipalities. But the paths of Arab and Jew are likely to diverge after graduation. The possibilities open to Arab graduates are far more limited, and most become teachers or social workers. The university is proud of the fact that there are more Arabs on the faculty than in all other Israeli universities combined, but as they themselves will admit, that's not saying much. Of the 5,000 university lecturers in Israel, only ten are Arab, excluding the faculties of the West Bank universities closed since the intifada.

The most conspicuous Arab community in the Haifa region is the Druze, who inhabit the villages on the heights south of Mount Carmel. Israel's 75,000 Druze inhabitants occupy a curious position within the national mosaic. Although Arabs, they do not regard themselves as Palestinians. They are neither Moslem nor Christian, but practise a highly secretive religion that broke away from the mainstream of Islam in the eleventh century.

There are Druze communities throughout this part of the Middle East, in Lebanon and Syria as well as Israel. Mountain warriors by tradition, the physical isolation of Druze villages has helped them to maintain their own cultural identity. Despite their warlike reputation, they tend to accept the mores of their host nations, just as Jews do in diaspora countries. The Druze have no quarrel with the Israelis, who have a deliberate policy of rewarding them for their compliance. In February 1989, for instance, the Druze of the Golan Heights were granted new benefits, including visits to relatives in nearby Syria. Unlike the overwhelming majority of Palestinian Arabs, Israeli Druze serve in the army and the border police, where they perform with zeal some of the tougher assignments, which does little to endear them to the Palestinians.

I arranged to see a Druze writer in Daliyat el Karmil, and from Yokne'am I took the road that heads across the mountains to Haifa, passing through the Druze villages. The road twists through a landscape of rolling stony shrubland, dotted with scrub oak and carob, glistening during those early spring days with yellow and scarlet flowers. Arriving in Daliyat, I parked my car close to the centre of town and asked for the house of Misbach Halabi. Druze women in deep blue robes and white shawls covering the lower part of their faces and shoulders strolled about, and outside the place of worship priests wearing red-roofed white turbans sat talking to their friends. Brightly coloured rugs flopped over the balconies of the simple houses. At first I was directed to the house of a different Mr Halabi. To reach the right Mr Halabi's house, I had to follow a path darkened by the corpse of a cat.

I was greeted at the door by three men – which was my host? – and ushered into a large pine-panelled room with sofas pushed against three of the walls, a common enough arrangement in Arab homes. One wall was covered with a blown-up full-colour photograph of what looked like a Bermudan beach, and on another wall there was a curious photomontage of Druze religious leaders. Halabi himself was about fifty, plump and fleshy, and very apologetic about his English. He suggested I direct my questions to one of the other men, who spoke excellent English and whose name appeared to be Natur. In the meantime Halabi shuffled off to make coffee. Halabi, I learnt from his friends, is the author of four books about the Druze, runs the workers' council in Daliyat and is active in Histadrut. Natur identified himself as the editor of a Druze magazine, and had ambitious plans for a new Arabic encyclopedia.

Daliyat is anything but the isolated mountain village it appears to be. Although its inhabitants used to live off the land, few do so now. About 200 families are involved in local trade and commerce, including construction companies that send teams to work all over Israel. Other villagers commute to Haifa or Netanya. When I asked about the religion, I drew a blank. Natur said that only about a quarter of the Druze were actually religious, and in order to know anything about the mysteries of the faith you have to be an active participant. That in turn means renouncing tobacco and television, restrictions that younger Druze in particular find irksome. Yet the religion, however inscrutable, helps to keep the community together. 'For a thousand years,' said Natur, 'the Druze have been attacked by Christians and Muslims, and our religion gives us strength and brotherhood.' Their moral standards are high, he told me; there is little criminality in the form of rape and theft, and women enjoy equality with men, though they are less well educated.

I took this glowing report with some scepticism. Others had told me how ill educated many of the Druze are, that very few Druze attend university. When Natur told me that hardly anybody marries outside the community, the claim, which may well be true, reminded me of similar assertions by Orthodox communities. The Druze are certainly tightly knit, but I doubted whether they were quite as free from feudalism and complex structures of authority as Natur was suggesting.

Unlike the Palestinian Arabs, the Druze did not flee in 1948. 'We can live with any regime,' says Natur, 'as long as it leaves us alone. We are strong politically, and we're not afraid of the Moslems. If they are becoming more fundamentalist, that is not our problem, any more than what happens on the West Bank is our problem. That's why many Druze serve in the army. The only thing that would disturb us would be if we were asked to fight against Druze in Lebanon or Syria.'

Their politics don't differ greatly from those of any other Israeli group. 'Labour governments treated our politicians well and included them in their administrations. We had some influence under Labour, and received benefits. Today there is support for a number of different parties, including Likud, though the mayor here is a Ratz supporter.' Whereas the Palestinians operated through their own political parties, and thus minimized their influence on national politics, the Druze were sensibly opportunistic, and hardly a week goes by without Jewish politicians commending their loyalty.

A coastal road links Haifa with Akko, carving its way through urban sprawl that it has doubtless helped to create. This agglomeration of factories, housing estates, military bases, supermarkets, garages, and children's playgrounds, all lining the edges of an untraversible highway, resembles the outskirts of Naples in its chaotic ugliness. It is as though cool, lofty, mountain-clinging Haifa has made a suburb of a city, and cast out all the grim, polluting, land-scarring elements onto the flatter land to the north and south.

The coastal highway skirts away from Akko itself; known to the Crusaders as Acre, it has retained some character as an Arab town. The Arab section lies within the old walls, close to the former harbours. The rest of the town is blandly Jewish, though some handsome stone houses with tall pointed windows, relics of the Ottoman past, lend it scattered distinction. But if the Jewish town is a hodgepodge, the old Arab quarter is coherent, with its mosques and minarets and caravanserais, its lanes and alleys, tightly organized yet far less claustrophobic than the dark narrow streets of the Old City of Jerusalem. The large arcaded courtyard of the Khan El-Umdan is far more of a public space than anything you will find in Moslem Jerusalem, with the obvious exception of the Temple Mount.

The monuments of Akko date from Crusader and Ottoman times, and many of the most handsome were built by Ahmed Jezzar Pasha, the Turkish governor of the city in the late eighteenth century.

Although Akko is a tourist attraction, it still retains a pleasantly run-down air. Abandoned buildings used as rubbish dumps provide hostels for dozens of grubby cats, a dingy façade disguises a smart restaurant, air-conditioned and with picture windows looking out to sea across the ancient harbours. Cheeky Arab boys keep an eye on the souvenir stands and play football in the alleys. Large-hipped women, some in long embroidered robes, others in Western dress, tour the market stalls and stubbornly negotiate the heavy traffic that clogs the lanes to which vehicles have access.

Some of the Jewish residents have their eye on ancient Akko and would like the Arabs to move inland. Indeed, one of the main talking points of the 1989 municipal elections here was whether the deputy mayor, David Bar-Lev, was indeed proposing the wholesale expulsion — he used the euphemism of 'transfer' — of the Arabs of Akko. The drift away has, in any case, begun, and many Arabs have been lured to suburban communities where they live among themselves. The process was given an unsavoury boost when in 1983 the chief rabbi of Akko ruled that Jewish law forbade Jews from living in the same areas as Arabs, and thus vice versa, a remarkably self-serving application of religious law.

Other relics of Ahmed Jezzar Pasha's architectural legacy can be seen further up the coastal road. A large aqueduct lopes across the plain, straddling the fields where local kibbutzim cultivate bananas and avocados. A few miles inland, up in the hills of Galilee, apples and pears are more likely to be grown. Unfortunately they are less profitable than the coastal crops, which is another reason why many of the inland kibbutzim and moshavim are in financial difficulties. The road passes the modern resort of Nahariya and ends, for all practical purposes, at the border town of Rosh Hanikra. This is a dramatic spot, for the road dashes up onto high cliffs, and from the border café there are lovely views back down the coast to Mount Carmel.

The border itself is predictably intimidating, with its gates and radio masts, its rotating scanners and unhidden cameras. This is a popular spot for excursions, as a cable car descends to grottoes beneath the cliff. I gobbled some ice cream at the café, while out on the terrace a group of burly United Nations soldiers from Norway admired three pretty Israeli women in military uniform. There was only a trickle of traffic, almost all UN cars and trucks, coming across the border. Israelis like to remark with raised eyebrows that the only people driving around Israel in new

Mercedes saloons are UN functionaries. UN officials can get advantageous tax breaks if while in Israel they buy expensive cars and keep them abroad for a year before returning home, where they can sell them for a handsome profit.

Halfway between Haifa and the border is the kibbutz called Lohamei Hagetaot. Hazorea has its art museum, but Lohamei Hagetaot has a Holocaust Museum. It is hard to overestimate the centrality of the Holocaust to the Israeli state of mind. Had there been no Holocaust, indeed, it is probable that the State of Israel would not have come into existence at all. The near destruction of European Jewry made it almost impossible to deny the Jewish claim to their own homeland, despite the attempts by successive British governments to renege on Balfour's undertakings of 1917. After the war many camp and ghetto survivors eventually made their way to Palestine, where they entered Israeli society at all levels: they were to be found in yeshivot, in kibbutzim, in small shops; some adjusted, some remained bitter, and their collective experience infused Israeli life with its poignancy.

The Holocaust has left a psychological legacy that may not always be healthy, but it is entirely understandable. At its crudest it takes the strident form of 'Never again!' The belligerency of Meir Kahane and his followers feeds off and exploits this fundamental sense, which most Jews share, that they should and must defend themselves against threats to their survival. It explains, in part, the abrasiveness of the Israelis. The history of the Jews, visible on the ground in Israel, is a tale of repeated persecution and dispersal. Now that the Jews have their homeland it is not surprising that they intend to maintain their identity and guarantee their future by every means at their disposal. If that entails, among other consequences, keeping the country in a state of permanent military alert, so be it. If that means developing their own arms industry because hypocritical European nations refuse to sell arms to the Israelis, so be it. If that means ferocious retaliation in response to terrorist attacks, so be it.

The Jews, and this is not an exclusively Israeli attitude, will not be led to the lip of oblivion ever again. So it is no wonder that when demagogic Arab leaders spoke of driving the Jews into the sea, the rhetoric sent a very special chill racing down the Jewish spine. Other enemies of the Jews made similar promises in the past, and tried to keep them. The post-Holocaust generations will defend themselves, whatever the cost, because they know from the most bitter experience than no one else will. Some Israelis wish to put all that terrible history behind them, so that the nation will no longer be conditioned by the past, hampered by guilt and dejection. Yet even the rejection of such conditioning is itself a form of conditioning. Jews cannot shake off the past, however shaming some of it may seem, because Jewish self-awareness is indistinguishable from that history.

Yet it is all more complex than it seems. For mixed with the belligerence is the shame. There is no pride in having been brought to the brink of destruction, no joy in the vanishing of the tremulous sweetness of the ghettoized eastern European way of life (even though, ironically, many early Zionists came to Palestine in order to flee from a world they found claustrophobic and stifling). Thus Israeli responses to the Holocaust have a strange double-edged quality that is less commonly encountered in the diaspora. Nearly fifty years after the event, plays such as Joshua Sobol's *Ghetto* and other works by writers too young to have had direct experience of the events, explore such painful issues as the degree of collaboration that existed between oppressed and oppressor. They remind one that even the condition of victim is streaked through with the most acute moral dilemmas. One Israeli from eastern Europe told me: 'There's no getting away from the fact that Israel was built on the ashes of six million. Rightly or wrongly, that's what most Israelis believe, that statehood was only granted because of the Holocaust. But we always twin the Holocaust with the Resistance. It redeems our honour and gives us a sense of identification, assuring us that we won't be annihilated without a fight. The Masada complex is about ensuring that a Holocaust never happens again, that we'll never again be enslaved. Unfortunately we're becoming frightened by these negative symbols.'

What I think he meant by that last remark is that there is a danger in founding a nation on the longing for survival, for mere existence is meaningless unless the values that give the Jewish people their distinction also survive. If, as many believe, the price for survival is an ever greater brutalization of the population, then doubts arise as to whether the cost may in the long run prove excessive.

In the Jerusalem forest, Yad Vashem, a great memorial to those who died in the Holocaust, has been constructed. Gardens framing powerful sculptures on the theme of the extermination of European Jewry surround a complex of buildings that include an archive, a museum, various galleries, and a Hall of Names in which detailed files identify millions of individuals who perished in the death camps. An avenue is planted with trees, each in tribute to a gentile who risked his or her life to save some Jews from death. One cannot fault Yad Vashem. It is dignified, impeccably planned, and painstakingly avoids sensationalism. And yet, and yet. Seated on a bench near the entrance to the museum, I would watch the parties of visitors recently disgorged from their buses as they slowly tramped up the path. They had the apprehensive look of all tourist parties making their way to Yet Another Sight. Shoulders slump under the weight of cameras. Coiffures become unruly in the heat. Shoes pinch. The tourists come from all over the world, more non-Jews than Jews, for Yad Vashem is very much part of the tourist itinerary. It is a dangerous celebrity.

My misgivings grew as I went to the Hall of Names to see whether the names of my relatives who died in the camps were on file. I stood behind an old woman as she made similar inquiries, reading names from a faded notebook. She fidgeted while the man behind the counter searched through his microfilms. Behind us were small groups of tourists, not obtrusive, but present all the same. What for the old lady and me was still part of our reality, unfinished business, was for them memorialized, institutionalized, locked into the past. Our pain, made distant by the passage of time and regeneration, was the subject of their irreproachably respectful visit.

The other aspect of Yad Vashem, and of most current commemorations of the Holocaust, that troubles me is the designation of those who perished as 'martyrs'. This is a misreading of history, a public relations slickness to gloss over the fact that the Jews who died had no choice in the matter. Martyrs choose death rather than surrender their principles, renounce their beliefs; their death is not accidental. My grandmother, who was dragged from Prague to a ghetto in Poland, and from the ghetto into oblivion, was no martyr. She was a victim. There was nothing heroic about being done to death in the Nazi murder factory, however much courage many individuals showed during their last minutes. To martyrize the dead diminishes the horror of what occurred.

My misgivings became even more jagged at Kibbutz Lohamei Hagetaot. Here the museum fills a large square building which resembles a miniaturized Knesset. Much of the exhibit is devoted to prewar Jewish Vilna, showing the cultural and intellectual vitality of the town, and to the nearby *shtetl* of Olkieniki. Although there were exhibits chronicling the rise of Nazism and of anti-Jewish atrocities – how could there not be? – the strength of the exhibit lay in its celebration of the vigour of the now vanished East European Jewish culture rather than an obsessive retelling of the awful tale of the Holocaust. The exhibit devoted to the camps themselves was confined to the basement. As I descended the steps, I heard a voice raised high in indignation. Standing around a model of an extermination camp stood an American man in his twenties, declaiming from a book and gesturing with his hands, to an audience of twenty teenagers. He was reading from a description of the arrival of Jews at

Auschwitz – probably Elie Wiesel's autobiographical account – and pointing as he read to various buildings or chimneys referred to in the text. He threw every ounce of emotion he possessed into his declamation. It was a performance. The teenagers looked subdued, but I couldn't tell if they were moved or embarrassed.

Truth needs no megaphones. Being gassed doesn't become more horrible and pitiful by being described *fortissimo*. Here, at its worst, was the cult of the Holocaust. I do not become more deserving of attention or pity or respect because my forebears suffered so grievously, yet the teacher was somehow trying to crawl within the heroic aura of martyrdom. The children standing around the model were all Jewish: they were not, I am sure, unfamiliar with what he was telling them. To pile on the horror with such theatricality achieved nothing. The only response when gazing at models of death camps, at the wallets the Nazis made from Torah scrolls, or at photographs of piles of clothing shed before the fatal showers, is an urgently reflective silence. To rant in such surroundings is an unforgivable sentimentality, couching Jewish suffering in a morass of morbid self-indulgence.

In Amos Oz's story 'Late Love' the narrator is obsessed by antisemitism, and convinced that the Russians are still out to destroy the Jews. He says: 'I know it personally, from the inside. From the year '19.' He personifies the paranoia still rife in modern Israel, as, more cynically, did Menachem Begin, who wore the Holocaust like a badge as though to deny others the right to criticize. 'We Jews have been through so much – how dare anyone tell us what we may or may not do!' – this sentiment ran manipulatively through so many of his public pronouncements. The rantings of Meir Kahane play on the same paranoid feelings. Yet one would have hoped, after over forty years of independence, that Israelis would have attained sufficient psychological security to keep that particular card held close to the chest.

I prefer to take as a model of how to respond to the Holocaust the story, not atypical of those who survived, told to me by an elderly Israeli. He grew up in Vilna, and when the Germans occupied Lithuania he became a partisan in the woods and successfully evaded arrest. Towards the end of the war he made his way first to Romania, then to Italy, and to Germany. From Germany he went to Czechoslovakia, then back to Italy, from where he eventually caught a boat to Palestine. As an illegal immigrant, he was arrested and jailed for some months. He fought in the War of Independence and again during the Six Day War in 1967. To his own disbelief, he found himself fighting once again, but this time alongside his son, in 1973. Today he is involved with fundraising for Israel in the diaspora. For him the legacy of his experience is a conviction that anything can be achieved if you want it badly enough; however severe the obstacles, there are ways to overcome them. You need luck too, of course, but first of all you need will.

His is a positive transformation of the hardships he suffered. After hearing his story, and others like it, one does indeed feel constrained from voicing criticism. In these accounts there is no self-pity, no sentimentality, which makes it all the harder to take issue with those who have repeatedly put their lives on the line. The respect one gives such people is gladly offered but cannot, as the loud young man in the basement museum seemed to believe, be claimed as a right.

# 14 · WATER ON STONE

To find a landscape in the Galilee sufficiently timeless to look biblical, I had to travel inland. The terrain is varied, with flat farmland overlooked by Arab villages on the flanks of hills, and further north, towards Lebanon, a wilder landscape, more dramatic, more lonely. Here two peoples, Arab and Jewish, exist side by side, with their different cultures, different styles of housing, different methods of farming. One day I drove along the narrow road linking the two remote Jewish villages of Yadofet and Hararit along the high ridge of the Asamon Mountains. To the north the view was of red-soiled slopes planted with olive groves, immediately identifiable as Arab cultivation. To the south stretched the plain of Bik'at Beit Netofa, bisected by the Kinneret-Negev Conduit, which was built in the 1950s to carry water south from the Sea of Galilee, or Lake Kinneret, as the Israelis call it. On either side of the conduit were large fertile fields, with strips of photodegradable plastic shielding the crops. I left the ridge road and descended to the Arab village of Araba, where I got thoroughly lost in its rutted lanes, to the mild amusement of the Friday lunchtime crowds strolling about.

Eventually I reached Nazareth, a town that is architecturally blank but redeemed by its up-and-down site. There is nearly always a traffic jam stretching for miles through this major road junction of a town, even at times of the year when pilgrims and other tourists are scarce. Nazareth is the largest Arab town in Israel, with the exception of East Jerusalem, and half the population is Christian. The main church, the Basilica of the Annunciation, is a chilling concrete job enclosing some ancient remains and assembled mosaics. It has all the architectural charm of a bus garage, and its sole feature of interest is that, like the Convent of St Francis at Assisi, it is built on two levels. I was standing in the lower church trying to squeeze a little pleasure from this uninspiring design, when I heard the happy strummings of a guitar, followed by voices lifted in song: 'Jesus promised life to all.' Some teenagers had gathered in the crypt, and plunged into gloom by the architecture, had burst into song to revive their spirits. The hymn was the musical equivalent of a smile button, Christianity with blond hair and freckles. My own, purely aesthetic, tastes in this particular religion run to masochistic Easter processions and austere Romanesque naves, so this evangelical attempt to make me feel good made me twitch with irritation.

I fled to the upper level, which is decorated with large mosaic murals, mostly garish and crude, contributed by Christian communities from all over the world. I was charmed by a pretty if ethnologically suspect Japanese Madonna and Child in kimonos. But Cameroon won hands down, with a brick-red, black and white number, highly stylized, with two glove-puppet figures (Madonna and Child? Jesus and God the Father?) rising above a crowd of women carrying baskets on their heads. While I was admiring this lively but perplexing mural, a band of Spanish pilgrims complete with bishop turned up, so I left them to their devotions and visited the nearby church of St Joseph, also a modern structure but traditional in design. This too is built over a grotto and a baptismal font with a remarkable resemblance to a *mikveh*. The grotto is said to be the site of Joseph's workshop. I don't question the story for a moment, but I can't help wondering why Jesus and his family always inhabited grottoes.

I swopped a Christian shrine for a Jewish one when I travelled on to Tiberias. Nazareth is twenty miles east of Haifa, and Tiberias a further twenty in the same direction. The road passes through farmland and eucalyptus groves, and the sunshine bounces off the bare and stony hillsides. The first glimpse of the Sea of Galilee is particularly lovely, as one hits the top of a crest and sees the dark blue water cupped within its rounded shoreline, and beyond it the hazy sun-washed Golan Heights. The road plunges down to the town, crouched 700 feet below sea level. Like most Israeli towns, it seems untouched by such concepts as town planning. Large modern hotels stand cheek by jowl with the ruins of fortifications, jutting walls of Crusader castles that go nowhere, shacks that turn out to be grilled meat restaurants, dusty shopping streets, and small plazas. Yet Tiberias is a pleasant breezy town, accommodating both pious *haredim* seeking spiritual kinship with the Jewish sages buried here, and tourists in shorts who stroll through the town working their tongues around cornets of soft ice cream. I took a walk along the lakefront, but found my attention drawn less by the lapping waters than by the large ill-kempt Jewish cemetery that rises up behind a neat little marina. Beside one of the tombs, piled high with stones and pebbles as a mark of respect, two black-coated Sephardi Jews, swarthy and heavily bearded, were swaying in prayer. Previous worshippers had tucked countless scraps of prayer-scrawled paper between the stones.

Not far from the town centre is the tomb of Maimonides, the great Jewish sage, doctor, and theologian who, after an active life in Cordoba and Cairo, was buried here in 1204. Tiberias, after the destruction of the Second Temple, became a major centre of Jewish learning, and a version of the Talmud was completed here. In the Middle Ages the town stagnated, and 150 years ago it was almost destroyed by an earthquake. The tombs, not only of Maimonides but of Rabbi Akiva and Rabbi Meir, survived. The tomb of Maimonides is approached up a flight of shallow steps flanked by seven black marble lozenge-shaped piers to which brass wings are attached. At the base of the piers, which represent the numinous mystical concepts of the *zefirot*, are stone troughs and basins through which water, intended to flow, did not. For this overblown symbolism we must thank the 'architect' Arieh Rachamimov. Near the entrance to the unroofed enclosure where the tomb stands, a woman was selling medallions and other religious knick-knacks. Some women in *sheitels* were deep in prayer, but the tranquil mood was soon disturbed by a party of youthful American *haredim*. The young men wore navy blue suits and homburg hats a few sizes too large. There are two tombs in the enclosure, one of beige marble, and a more ancient-looking one behind it, hewn from white stone, and the Americans weren't sure which one they should direct their prayers towards. The bewigged women were pressing lips against the beige one, which provided a clue. The prayers were perfunctory, as the Americans devoted far more time to buzzing away with their video cameras.

From Tiberias I drove towards Tabgha at the north end of the Sea of Galilee to visit the church built over the spot where Christ induced the loaves and fishes to multiply. The Byzantine church built here in about 480 was destroyed in the seventh century after the Moslem conquest. The remains were excavated in 1932 and the new church built in 1980 in a neo-Byzantine style. The architects used a lovely flesh-toned stone and produced a design of great dignity and simplicity. The elegant mosaic floors, portraying birds and flowers, blend ancient and modern craftsmanship.

Continuing north from the lake, the road begins to climb up to sea level and beyond. After passing the Mount of Beatitudes, I came to a place called Vered Hagalil, which happens to be a dude ranch. Individual cottages, at some distance from the neighing stalls of the horses, are placed among lush gardens overlooking the lake. Tucked among flowering cactus and shrubs, and voiced over with the sound of chattering birds, Vered Hagalil must be one of the most tranquil spots in the Galilee. The owner, Yehuda Avni, had time to sit down with me over a cup of coffee, and told me how he had come to establish a dude ranch in the Galilee.

'I'm convalescing, so I'm allowed to talk,' he began, and he talked. He had grown up in Chicago and after emigrating to Israel he joined a kibbutz in the Negev before helping to set up a new moshav, where he remained for nine years. He ran a profitable farm and enjoyed the kind of life the moshav offered, but didn't always go along with the decisions the community made. So he reflected: he liked farming, people, horses, and Israel, and the only way to combine those interests was to start a dude ranch. It was hard to find a suitable property: most land is leased from the state, and its collectivist bias makes private estates rare. Eventually he found these forty acres, grew roses to make some money, then built stables, acquired more horses, and began organizing two-day trail rides. At the same time he was clearing the land and planting trees. Next he opened the restaurant, and built a few cottages for overnight guests. By 1967 the operation was in full swing. He can accommodate eighteen families, and there are twenty horses for them to ride. Not all the guests want to ride; others are more interested in hiking or archaeology or hunting, and Avni can help them all to pursue those interests. There is plenty of game in the Galilee, in the form of wild boar, partridge, quail, and deer, and fishing too. When devising the trails, Avni followed old cattle paths, some of which, he is convinced, are thousands of years old; he also makes use of old Roman roads as well as more recent fire breaks and access roads in the woods. Some groups stay out in the hills for up to five days, sleeping at kibbutzim or Druze or Bedouin villages. The less adventurous can take one-day trails that bring them back to the ranch each night.

The climate around the lake is mild in winter, which is why it is such a popular resort, but the mountainous Galilee can be freezing. Because of the overall gentleness of the climate, many flats are unheated, so when the temperature does drop below freezing you really feel it. Even in March I felt chilled to the bone in another holy city of the Galilee, Zefat, also known as Safed. Three thousand feet up in the mountains, the town is built on three ridges, each of which seems to be exposed to a different gale. Zefat was settled by Sephardi Jews after their expulsion from Spain. Like Tiberias a thousand years earlier, Zefat became a centre of Jewish learning, especially of the more mystical, kabbalistic variety. Unfortunately the one-way system of Zefat is almost as complex as the kabbalistic system of textual interpretation. The first time I attempted to visit the town I got hopelessly lost. I managed to visit every grubby housing estate and hospital, following roads that all came to a dead end, often with a drop of a few hundred feet into a ravine as formidable as any Mexican *barranca*. Near the town centre, there are no signs in any language other than Hebrew. On my second attempt I took a map with me and did slightly better, managing to park the car no more than half a mile from what I judged from a cluster of stone domes to be the old quarter of Zefat. I walked to the artists' quarter close to the old synagogues, but it was early afternoon and everything was closed up. A howling wind was whipping across the mountains and I was not inclined to linger. The artists' quarter lacked artists, the synagogues worshippers. The streets the guidebooks called quaint struck me, in my chilled and unsympathetic condition, as merely dingy.

The likes of Rabbi Joseph Caro, who wrote a major compilation of Jewish law, the *Shulchan Aruch*, which is still widely used today, no longer dwell at Zefat, and most of the Jews I saw looked suspiciously like Lubavitcher Chasidim, patrolling the empty streets with loudspeaker vans, urging – this was election time, as usual – the populace to vote for the neolithic candidate of their choice.

Leaving Zefat I picked up a hitch-hiking soldier. He slumped in the front passenger seat, a gloriously unkempt figure, an Israeli McAuslan. He was returning to Netanya, and this was his usual method of getting home from army service.

'It's a long way from Netanya to Zefat. When do you set off each morning?'

He yawned. 'Depends when I wake up. About seven, usually.'

'What's your job?'

'Same as what I do in the army. I'm an electrician. I also drive a truck.'

It was clearly not an arduous life. Military service, especially reserve duty, has become part of the daily routine for Israelis, albeit one which upsets civilian hierarchies. On reserve duty it would not be considered unusual if a taxi driver were the commanding officer of a university professor. Amos Elon has written that Israel 'is very far from being a military society . . . There is no deliberate attempt to break the will of recruits. It is a citizen army, and the gap between officers and men is minimal. There are few privileges of rank. The Israeli military code bluntly states that officers have no privileges whatsoever, only duties.'[1]

An Israeli journalist told me: 'Ours is a no nonsense army, unlike any other army. We don't have parades and all those trappings. The IDF even has an office whose function is to keep outsiders off their back if war breaks out. They don't want romantic amateurs from Chicago in the army, however well-meaning. After all, we don't have a problem with draft evasion. It's easy enough to get out of military service – you can get religion or ask a psychiatrist to give you a certificate – but the stigma is huge. Even people in the peace movement accept that peace can only be sustained if Israel is and remains well defended. So to skip military service is seen as the moral equivalent of pushing an old lady down the stairs.'

It is because of the ubiquity of military service that the failure of most Israeli Arabs, other than the Druze and some Bedouin, to serve in the army is viewed with such derision, even though everybody knows that most Moslem Arabs volunteering for military service would be routinely rejected on security grounds.

The laid-back electrician sprawled down the passenger seat gave the impression that reserve duty was not a demanding chore, but it is a disruptive one, especially to self-employed men and also to employers who have to take on more staff to cover for absent reservists. And of course there are occasions, in Israel all too frequent occasions, when armies must fight. Reservists can be called up at virtually no notice. All it takes is a phone call. 'This means,' a friend in Jerusalem told me, 'that what happens in and to the army concerns everyone in the country. Last night some soldiers were killed in Lebanon, so everyone gets on the phone because we all know at least one person that is on duty up there. I phoned a friend last night and we chatted about some new clothes we'd both bought that day. Then she said: "Fuck the dress. He's okay." She knew why I'd phoned.' If you're an Israeli, you learn to live with anxiety.

Soldiers are required by law to disobey any order that is manifestly illegal. There is not even shame attached to a reluctance to serve in the West Bank, where most soldiers loathe being sent. This is why the army has to rotate spells of duty in the Territories. The journalist told me: 'The few who refuse to serve there are usually reservists or soldiers who've already had experience of the West Bank. They can't be called shirkers. They just find themselves doing things they hate to do and that shocks them.' A kibbutznik at Hazorea told me: 'On reserve duty I once had to guard the West Bank settlement of Kiryat Arba. That really pissed me off. If people want to live in Hebron, that's their business. But why the IDF should have to guard them I don't understand.'

In Israel, any identification of the army with right-wing attitudes would be false. Many former generals are politically on the left. There is a high turnover among senior officers, and once they are out of uniform they are free to protest about what they have been asked to do, and they exercise that freedom. In recent years some politicians have blamed the army for its failure to bring the intifada to an end, but the generals, quite rightly, insist that the intifada is first and foremost a political problem. It is quite common for a general to retire from the IDF in his forties and take up a new career. Most officers do not regard the army as a profession.

All immigrants under the age of forty-five must undergo basic training and accept reserve duty. This usually has social benefits too, for in the egalitarian environment of the army, immigrants can gain a broader picture of the Israeli life they are in the process of joining. Women serve for two years in the army, but are exempt from reserve duty. A Jerusalem friend told me: 'Women can have a difficult time in Israeli society. We're told to be tough, we serve in the army and work just as a man does – but we're also told to be sexy, not to be too successful. If you're talented, you're not supposed to be too good-looking. We're always receiving ambivalent messages.'

I picked up dozens of soldiers, male and female, in my travels, for I hoped they would be a valuable source of information. So they would have been, for they were a mixed bunch indeed; only the moment they clambered into the car they all, without exception, fell fast asleep.

One morning Avi Marko, a social worker based in Karmiel, a new town that is booming in the otherwise economically depressed Upper Galilee, invited me to join him on his rounds. For him the challenge of the Galilee was in trying to persuade professional people to come and live there. Other than the beauty of its landscape, it seems to have little to offer. Public transportation is poor; the winters can be harsh, the cultural provisions negligible. Moreover, security remains an anxiety.

'This is the one border which terrorists are able to infiltrate,' Avi told me. 'There have been many attempted crossings, and rocket attacks, too. Schoolchildren were massacred in Maalot in 1974, and just a few months ago a rocket fell in the Arab quarter of the town. People forget that when the rockets land in the Galilee, they're as likely to kill or wound Arabs as Jews. The amazing thing is that relations between the two peoples are as good as they are. It's the old story. Arabs feel they lack rights, but Jews feel that Arabs lack obligations. But the two sides co-operate – they have no choice.'

In the weeks following my visit, there were two failed infiltration attempts by members of the Democratic Front for the Liberation of Palestine. I asked Avi if the intifada had spread into the Galilee.

'There have been a few incidents of rock-throwing, but in general the answer is no. The Arabs know that if it were to spread, there would be a local response from the Jews. They also know the government would crush any uprising within Israel itself. But even without the intifada, it would remain difficult to get Israelis to come and live in the north. They don't even come to visit. Apart from the coastal resorts there are only a few hotels and kibbutz guesthouses in the Galilee. That means even domestic tourism is just about nonexistent, even though Israelis love hiking and nature trails and the terrain up here is ideal for that.'

We passed Peqiin, an Arab village overlooked by a Jewish moshav. The village has an ancient synagogue that, according to Avi, has been cared for by the same family since biblical times. Unfortunately the only members left are an elderly woman and her unmarried daughter, so the family is likely to die out.

We stopped at Tefen, an industrial park on the outskirts of Kfar Havradim. Tefen is a bold attempt to pretend that the Galilee has as much to offer the entrepreneur and manufacturer as the coastal areas around Tel Aviv. The brainchild of industrialist Stef Wertheimer, Tefen was built by the government but influenced by Wertheimer's ideas, which stressed aesthetic and atmospheric elements as well as planning and design. The buildings are spacious colour-coded units spread out along the slopes. Not all the buildings are occupied, and if the whole sprawling complex, with its landscaping and outdoor sculpture garden, has the look of a showcase, that is exactly what it is. Tefen is an adjunct of Wertheimer's vision, which is to ensure that Israel comes of age as a small industrial nation. For decades Israelis have grown used to government subsidies and contributions from the diaspora. It's time, according to Wertheimer, for Israel to stand on its own feet, even if that means hardship in the short term. To that end he has established nine-month courses at Tefen for entrepreneurs, and has flown over business school professors from Harvard and MIT to teach them.

Tefen has no greater booster than American-born Elaine Levitt, who runs an employment agency here. Realizing that she had in me a captive audience, she began with a pep talk about the Galilee, how one feels closer to Israel even though one is living on its fringes. This is wishful thinking: the heart of Israel, if there is such a place, is probably to be found in Ramla or Kiryat Gat, the dreary towns just inland from Tel Aviv, where aspirations as well as demography are as close to average as one can get in this jumbled-up country. When her paean had run its course I tried to elicit more information about the Tefen experiment.

'We've had,' she began, 'various stages of settlement in the Galilee, beginning with kibbutzim and moshavim, and then development towns such as Maalot. Yet nothing seemed to happen. We brought Moroccan tradespeople here twenty or thirty years ago, and taught them how to become farmers. Now their children are the leaders of the various communities in the Galilee and they know the future lies in industry as well as in agriculture. What Tefen is trying to offer is factories and workshops producing goods for the domestic market – scanners, cutting tools, electronics, plastics. I have to admit that not everything sticks. Some people came here, didn't make it, and have left.'

To persuade businessmen to come here, all manner of inducements have been offered: subsidized building costs, tax rebates, foundation grants for hi-tech industries. Organizations such as ORT have helped to train unskilled young men and women to become, for example, machine operators. There have been complaints that Tefen is exploiting a pool of cheap labour in the Galilee, but Mrs Levitt denies that this is so, though she admits that there was one factory here that had a bad reputation for paying rock-bottom wages. There is idealism at work at Tefen as well as hard-headedness, but it is by no means certain that the experiment will succeed. As we bounced out of Kfar Havradim in Avi's car, he said despondently: 'Which industrialist would want to try to run an efficient operation out here over mountain roads that are so poorly maintained? The idealism is splendid, but where's the infrastructure to back it up?'

There is more idealism in evidence at the nearby development town of Maalot, which shares its municipal administration with the neighbouring Arab town of Tarshiha. Under an arrangement unique in Israel, the municipality has a Jewish mayor and an Arab deputy mayor. Elaine Levitt, who lives in Maalot, remarked: 'The two communities may not love each other, but they respect each other.'

Another Galilee community where Jews and Arabs coexist is Moshav Ya'ara, the only mixed settlement in all of Israel. Here 245 Jews live alongside seventy Bedouin Arabs. The moshav was established by Yemenites in 1950 until they were replaced by Moroccan Jews. Because both these North African groups spoke Arabic, they were able to communicate easily with local Bedouin Arabs, who had been pro-Jewish even before the establishment of the state. Yet the Bedouin are not fully integrated into the community. They send their children to the moshav's Orthodox kindergarten, but there is no intermarriage. Nor do the Bedouin have any say in the running of the moshav; in return they neither pay taxes to the moshav nor participate in guard duty. Such exemption is not a privilege, for the moshav never wanted the Arabs to enjoy equal rights, as that would mean they would be competing for the same resources.

Other towns of Upper Galilee have greater problems than Maalot. Shelomi has the appearance of a walled fortress. Avi told me that the town had been blighted by its particularly unruly youths, many of whom were drug addicts. 'It's not that surprising when you think of what towns like this have been through. It was hell here in 1982. Rockets fell every day. People in the rest of Israel tend to forget how bad things were. It's hard to find work, and salaries are lousy.'

Close to the border we came to Shomera, a community consisting of an army post, a moshav and a school, attractively located among pine woods and hills. A few miles further on we passed a roadside memorial to two soldiers killed by terrorists in 1972, one of many such memorials in the border area. For a while the road followed the border fence, which is touch-sensitive. A New Yorker living in the area told me: 'There's a lot of fear on the moshav where I'm living. We can tell there's something happening in Lebanon: we hear booms, we see the helicopters, the lines of tanks, the flares at night. A lot of this isn't publicized, but it's not quiet round here, and everybody knows that terrorists are trying to get across the border. Some people are constantly nervous, others accept it.'

Avi noted: 'One thing all Israelis agree on, and that is that we need the security zone in Lebanon. If it didn't exist, the skirmishing that's going on constantly in southern Lebanon would be happening here in the Galilee. About that at least we have a national consensus.'

A week later I visited another part of the Galilee, the thumb that protrudes northwards from the Sea of Galilee through the fertile river plain of the Jordan. The main town up here is Kiryat Shmona. In 1981 the town was shelled constantly for twelve days, and 80 per cent of the population fled. Terrorist raids have claimed eighteen lives. It was in response to the 1981 bombardment that a British-trained psychologist, Dr Mooli Lahad, established the Community Stress Prevention Centre here. Dr Lahad points out that the stress is constant, but until recently people did not know how to recognize or cope with it. Teachers, for example, had not been trained in how to deal with the extreme anxiety often felt by their pupils. Every school in this part of the country had bomb shelters, and, rather than construct additional classrooms, many schools now hold some classes underground; this gives a degree of abnormality to the experience of learning that needs to be understood by those teaching under such conditions. The aim of the centre's programmes is not simply to help victims of stress, but to give the local population the tools and skills they need to cope with a continuously stressful life as well as with specific emergencies. Crisis centres, says Dr Lahad, are common, but their preventative programme is unique.

By now, some 1,200 teachers have attended courses, as well as doctors and nurses. An emergency team has been set up to rush to the scenes of disasters such as earthquakes and car crashes. 'The ideas we are putting into practice aren't new,' Dr Lahad told me, 'but they used to be applied only to specific cases such as rescue teams or patients before major surgery. The problem in the Galilee is that we can't predict who is likely to be subjected to abnormal stress. What we have done is to recruit helpers who live within the community and can assess who will need professional help when the going gets rough. People have different ways of coping with anxiety. Some do it through emotion, others through religious belief, or social skills, or imagination and improvisation. What we're trying to do is increase the flexibility of response. The previous experience of stress also plays a part. So does the person who happens to be with you at a time of crisis. We've found that a continuous level of stress acts like water on stone: it makes a gradual impact even though the stone is the stronger material.

'Personal crisis changes the belief that yesterday produces tomorrow. There's a loss of predictability. Crisis disrupts the mental structures that allow you to live your life. In Israel, many people used to cope with their stress by giving meaning to it, but today people have more doubts about the reasons for their anxiety. Zionist idealism isn't as strong as it once was. If you want, you can interpret this lessening of conviction in a positive way, as a sign of maturity, a willingness to entertain the possibility that right isn't always on our side.'

Stress, in Dr Lahad's view, contributes to many well-known features of Israeli life. 'People who don't deal with their stress become irritable or even violent. That's one possible explanation for the large number of road accidents here. People grow careless about life and test their vulnerability. Israeli drivers are usually skilful and improvise well, yet they're aggressive and sometimes reckless. The road becomes a miniature battlefield. These days it's compulsory to have air conditioning in cars. The idea is that by keeping cool, literally cool, you will be less tense. How can people not be tense when we are on a permanent military alert?

'Stress is also a major factor in emigration. If you can't find meaning in your experiences, your hardships, why hang about? Israelis travel so much in order to clear their heads. People need the outlet, which is why I believe the government is wrong to tax air travel. Taking a trip gets Israelis away from such things as listening to the news compulsively every hour. When we made peace with Sadat, huge numbers of Israelis flowed into Egypt. It was the only place we could get to easily. It was the same with the West Bank after 1967. Everyone went to look at what was on the other side of the border. We live surrounded by barriers, and up here in the north people feel hemmed in by the borders.

'But you must remember that the fences also keep people out.'

On the eastern shore of the Sea of Galilee the hills rise up to the Golan Heights, formerly Syrian territory but since 1967 under Israeli control. Unlike the West Bank and Gaza, the Golan has since 1981 been subject to

Israeli law, which some regard as tantamount to annexation, though international law does not recognize Israeli sovereignty over the Golan. Yet the Golan is calm, and even the intifada has had very little impact here. The Heights are of immense strategic importance, as Israelis living in kibbutzim such as Ein Gev on the shore of the lake have long known to their cost. For years Ein Gev was shelled by Syrian outposts on the Heights, but by June 1967 the Israelis had had enough. Having vanquished, among others, the Syrians, the Israelis encouraged the establishment of kibbutzim and moshavim on the Heights, but these communities found themselves unprepared when war broke out again in 1973. On this occasion it took far longer for the Israelis to drive back the Syrians. As in the Galilee, the Jewish settlements were intended to supplement the purely military presence of the Israelis in the region.

The Golan still looks like a war zone. With its high moorlands and exposed plains, the whole area is far more bleak than the Galilee. Consulting a map by the side of the road, I found myself under observation by a sparrow hawk, and a minute later a large marten crossed my path. There are, it seems, more cattle than human beings, and the scattered settlements are fenced around with reels of barbed wire. Driving along the pitted roads that traverse the Heights, one passes numerous army camps, with tanks and other armoured vehicles lined up in neat rows. Nor is it uncommon to see a tank transporter grinding along the narrow roads, or military jeeps travelling at insane speeds with their long antennae bent back by the wind. Bright yellow signs warn travellers not to leave the road, for huge Syrian minefields have yet to be cleared. The Golan is a great place for a hike, but you are likely to return without your legs.

Up here you don't find the alternation of Jewish and Arab villages of the Galilee. The 9,000 Jews of the Golan – the numbers have gradually been declining – live either on kibbutzim and moshavim or in the new 'capital' of Katzrin, and they are outnumbered by 16,000 Druze. The Druze villages here seem very different to those south of Haifa. At Masada, not to be confused with the fortress that overlooks the Dead Sea, the houses are built on terraces from roughly hewn basalt; the dark stone is intimidating, the wild landscape equally so. A few miles from the village are the finest extant ruins of a Crusader castle in Israel, Nimrod's Castle, stretched along a high spur with the snow-topped peak of Mount Hermon as its backdrop.

The Israelis and the Syrians watch each other across the heavily fortified border. An intimidating Israeli communications centre, masts and dishes twitching in the air, rises in place of fire and ash on top of an extinct volcano. A local kibbutznik told me, 'From there they can read the small ads of a newspaper being read in a café in Damascus.'

In the crater of the volcano, the kibbutz of Ein Zivan has planted a large apple orchard. Although the decision to do so was probably prompted by sound agricultural considerations, I couldn't help regarding this peculiar plantation as a satisfying instance of Israeli *chutzpah*. Israeli viticulturalists are also convinced that the Golan, with its long cool growing season, is the best locality in Israel for the cultivation of grapes for wine. In the small industrial park at Katzrin is the Golan winery, which produces Israel's best wines. Not that the competition is very impressive. Most Israeli wines come from grapes grown near the coastal plain: overripe and lacking in acidity and indifferently vinified, they produce wines that are often prematurely oxidized and incapable of ageing. Because Israelis tend to know little about wine – the only affordable imported wine comes from Romania or South Africa and is almost as nasty as the native product – the majority of the population must believe that the tired jammy liquids bottled by Carmel and Monfort and others are the best that can be hoped for.

The Golan winery is proving them wrong. Its grapes are grown at heights of up to 1,200 metres, often by Golan kibbutzim, and ultra-modern vinification ensures that the wine is fresh rather than exhausted when it is bottled. Unfortunately the wine is expensive, both because costly materials such as French oak barrels have to be imported and because of the complications required in order to ensure that the wine is kosher. The vines may not be harvested until four seasons have passed, and the vineyards must lie fallow every seventh year. From pressing the grapes to bottling the finished wine, all work must be performed by religious Jews under rabbinical supervision. No women may work on any stages of winemaking until the wine has been bottled. Only religious Jews may touch the hoses or tanks or draw samples from barrels. The current winemaker, Jim Klein, like his predecessors a Californian by birth and training, is Jewish but not Orthodox, and if he wants to taste the wine during any part of the vinification process, he must ask a worker to draw off a sample for him. The bottling room is also operated by Orthodox Jews. Klein may enter the room but must not touch anything. Should he or a non-Orthodox visitor do so, the entire batch of wine would be regarded as non-kosher.

Bizarre though such working practices may appear, they are only half as weird as the conditions in which the grapes are grown. I visited the vineyards at Ein Zivan, a kibbutz facing the abandoned and ruined Syrian town of Quneitra. A fierce and cold wind was battering the slopes, and the climate seemed propitious neither for man nor for grape. The border forms the edge of the kibbutz. Deep anti-tank trenches, filled with water, threaten to drown any invading Syrian tanks. Piles of boulders are stacked along the roadside, forming a barricade broken only by the width of the carriageway. Should an attack commence, the local Israeli commanders can detonate charges that would cause the boulders to block the road.

In the shallow valley below Ein Zivan is the United Nations station, with its neat white boxy buildings. The remains of the tree-lined roads and solid houses of Quneitra are easily made out, and in the distance are the contours of New Quneitra, its replacement behind current Syrian lines. Those who inhabit the settlements overlooking the frontier are encouraged to see that the Syrians have begun planting orchards not far from the border. This they tentatively interpret as a pacific sign, though nobody lets their guard down as a result. There is also said to be reasonably good rapport between the Israeli and Syrian troops as they face each other across the no man's land, despite the state of enmity that exists between the two countries and the huge Syrian arms build-up in recent years. Israeli reserve soldiers report that when they peer across the border through their binoculars, they can see their Syrian counterparts doing exactly the same.

Since 1975, when three students were killed in a terrorist raid on Ramat Magshimim, the Syrian government has made it very clear that it will not permit terrorist infiltrations across the border. This does not defuse the widespread anxiety voiced by Golan settlers that another Syrian attack is by no means unlikely, and that the outcome of yet another war would be even less predictable than it was in 1973. The inhabitants of Ein Zivan recall how in 1973 they were warned of the likelihood of Syrian attack. Two hours later, as buses were arriving to evacuate the settlement, the Syrians bombed the kibbutz. Everybody dashed for the shelters. When the raid was over, the settlers left Ein Zivan, and for many months the kibbutz was occupied by the Syrians. Even after the war ended, shelling continued. It became so much a part of the way of life here that kibbutzniks would be working in the fields, hear the rockets coming, dive into the field shelters for half an hour, then resume their ploughing or planting.

There are other complications to farming in a much fought-over land. When a kibbutz decided to plant a vineyard at El Rom, the workers had to remove the remains of forty tanks before they could begin planting. It is still impossible to drive for a few miles through the Golan Heights without encountering twisted scraps of weaponry and chassis, resembling dead cockroaches, flung or blasted into the ditches. War memorials have been improvised from old jeeps and rockets. There are bomb shelters every few hundred yards. Half-wrecked Syrian barracks and villages stand abandoned among copses. On the wall of a shattered mosque I saw the jubilant black-letter scrawl: ARIEL SHARON WAS HERE 1967. And everywhere on the Golan ancient stone walls testify that there was a time, stretching back over centuries if not millennia, when this barren landscape was lovingly grazed and tended.

One minor but tangible benefit of Israeli control of the Golan is that the national passion for archaeology is extended to the sites of the region. In Book IV of Josephus's *The Jewish War* you may read of the Roman siege of the Jewish fortress of Gamla in A.D. 66, which ended with half the 10,000 defenders throwing themselves into the ravine and the other half throwing themselves at the mercies of the Roman attackers, with the same wretched results. There were only two survivors. Despite the physical precision of Josephus's account, nobody knew until recently where Gamla was located. But in 1970 Israeli archaeologists tentatively identified the site, and excavated it six years later. One approaches Gamla across a grassy plateau, where there also happen to be the remains of a Byzantine church built of black volcanic rock. On one side of the plateau a cliff tumbles into the wadi below. Birds of prey flap lazily overhead, then plunge into the ravine in search of lunch. In the distance the Sea of Galilee shimmers through the heat haze. A path zigzags down to the base of the spur on which the fortress stands. In March, when I first came to Gamla, the spring flowers were in blossom, providing a palette of tiny irises, scarlet poppies, blue mountain lupins, anemones and hyacinths, all set among a froth of frail ferns. The path descending is steep, as is the further path that ascends the spur to the remains of the fortress, which clings like a limpet to the narrow ridge, with sheer drops into ravines on either side.

From Gamla a road south makes a spectacular descent down a series of hairpin bends to the hot springs resort of Hamat Gader on the Jordanian border. Double fencing marks the border, and the houses of the Jordanian villages on the opposite slope are clearly visible. As the road curls down from the Heights to what I imagine is sea level or below, the temperature warms up, and half an hour later one is among the palm trees and beaches of the Sea of Galilee. It's a short journey from the austere to the luxuriant, from barbed wire to park benches. The two exist side by side, the tense and the pleasure-loving, the vigilant and the easygoing. In Israel such disparities have to be welded together every minute of every day.

# 15 · COOL CHICKS

The kibbutzim are in bad shape, but for the moshavim, things are worse. The explanation is much the same. Encouraged by the boom in the Israeli economy in the 1970s, moshavim borrowed heavily, neglecting to calculate that interest rates might one day rise to their present crippling levels. Moshavim differ from kibbutzim in one crucial respect: each household owns its own property, though such functions as marketing and social services are undertaken communally. Whereas the debt of a kibbutz is borne by the community, the collective debt of a moshav is divided among its members. Since kibbutzniks own no property, they have no personal liability. This is not the case with moshavniks. Of Israel's 430 moshavim, home to 3.5 per cent of the nation's population, only forty are thought to be in sound financial condition. In February 1989 some Galilee moshavim voted to disband themselves in response to the bank's threat to foreclose on their properties.[1] There have been suicides among moshav farmers who can find no way to alleviate their burden of debt.

Another class of settlement, the *mitzpe*, is also in difficulties. *Mitzpim*, most of which were founded about fifteen years ago, are settlements in rural areas that have no agricultural economic base; their members work outside the community, often in towns. Those who came to live in *mitzpim* tended to be escapees from moshavim or families who wanted to get away from city life without committing themselves to kibbutz or moshav membership.

As in the case of the kibbutzim, the plight of the moshavim is an ideological as well as an economic blow. Founded under the aegis of the Jewish Agency along quasi-socialist lines, with each community requiring a degree of co-operation from its members in return for services provided, the moshav movement has lost its viability. Ironically, many moshavim have become victims of their very success. Settlements that thrived felt more secure about borrowing heavily to finance domestic improvements or communal investments or facilities. Less prosperous moshavim were in a weaker position when it came to petitioning the banks for similar loans, and consequently their debt is far lower. Plans have been put forward for restructuring the debt, but the problem goes deeper than that. For even moshavim able to crawl out from under the rock of indebtedness would have to confront the fact that these agricultural communities no longer contribute much to the Israeli economy. Because of overproduction, quotas are applied to poultry, eggs, and fruit, constraints that make it impossible for many moshav members to earn a living. In the early days of the movement there was enough work on each moshav to occupy fifty or seventy families. Now, with technological advances in agriculture, two or three families can often look after the chicken houses, the goats, the fields.

The solution on offer is privatization, a path favoured by the moshavniks as well as the authorities. But this won't be effective unless a solution is also found to the problem of debt, which takes tangible form in the shape of letters from lawyers and banks threatening foreclosure and repossession of properties. Some moshavniks are not unduly worried because they suspect their assets are worth so little that the banks have little to gain by taking such draconian measures.

Avi Marko, who looks more like a record producer than a social work administrator, let me accompany him as he visited some moshavin in the Galilee. The first moshavniks came to Israel in the 1950s from North Africa. The Jewish Agency simply dumped them in the northern Galilee and told them to get on with it, which they duly did, despite the fact that most of the new arrivals had been tradesmen and pedlars and had no agricultural experience whatsoever. They were further hampered by the paucity of suitable agricultural land. Most grazing land and olive groves had long been the property of Arab villagers. The settlers were able to grow apples and pears successfully, but there was little demand for such crops on the crucial export market. Nevertheless, the North Africans turned themselves into excellent farmers, only to discover, once they had mastered their new profession, that it was no longer profitable.

The organization with which Avi is associated is Project Renewal, which brings non-Israeli volunteers to the Galilee. Volunteer organizations are not permitted to tackle the causes of the problems they encounter – it is not up to Project Renewal to solve the debt crisis – but they are free to deal with the social effects, largely in such matters as health and education. Avi often recruits helpers from *ulpans*, which provide a convenient pool of eager young people with sufficient idealism to tolerate the difficult working conditions. They are lent houses on moshavim and *mitzpim*, so that they live among the people they are helping. Avi was then engaged in setting up a pedagogical centre to provide courses in English and teacher retraining, and enrichment programmes in schools.

'Kids who grow up without learning English are at a big disadvantage,' Avi told me. 'Many computer programmes are in English, and university study in many technical fields is just about impossible without a reasonable command of English. Of course we don't want to be seen as imposing our ideas on the schools, so we're trying to develop locally based structures. But often we encounter resistance from permanent teachers, who don't like being told what to do, however tactfully, by a bunch of volunteers. We try to tread carefully.'

In the 1940s a band of Romanian immigrants settled among the Arab villagers of Tarshiha. There was no conflict, but in 1949 the Jews decided to found their own settlement nearby, the moshav of Meona. Here they grew tobacco and fruit and raised chickens. Their numbers were augmented by new arrivals from Morocco, and there are now eighty families at Meona, making it one of the largest moshavim in the Galilee. Ilona, whose husband came here from Romania at the age of three, admitted that Meona had been established for strategic reasons, and that agriculture has never been a going concern here. Many of the moshavniks are teachers and nurses who work outside the community. Meona is responding to its financial crisis by dismantling its communal structures and by increasing the independence of individual members. The post of moshav secretary will be abolished. Once a community based on collectivist principles, Meona will become an ordinary village with minimal economic ties between its inhabitants. Under moshav regulations, only one offspring can take over a family farm. Many moshav families have six children or more, especially on religious moshavim, so the surplus children have to leave and either settle on other moshavim or move to the cities. Thus the moshav offers less continuity and social cohesion than the kibbutz system. Meona in the future will be free of these restrictions.

Before showing me round the moshav, Ilona took me to their local archaeological site. As often happens in Israel, the ruins were discovered by chance, when a bulldozer was clearing a building site. Archaeologists identified the site as that of an ancient Canaanite city, about 5,000 years old. The rubble I peered at through the fence apparently belonged to the foundations of a wall and tower and some houses. The archaeologists suspect that the remains of a Canaanite temple still lie buried further up the slope. But for the moment the temple remains unexcavated, because it lies beneath Arab grazing land, which the Jews are reluctant to take out of circulation, even for the most virtuous of reasons.

Ilona led me from the sublime to the chicken house, which is still collectively owned. The previous summer the heat had killed off many birds, so they had installed a sprinkler system to keep the chicks cool. The smell inside the chicken house was disgusting, and I was disconcerted to find that all the squawking birds were addressing their clamour directly at me, as though I could be of some assistance to them. A third of the stalls are empty, because of the egg quota. The eggs are marketed by Tnuva, the state agricultural processing organization, so the moshav is concerned only with their production. 'With this kind of set-up,' Ilona said, 'it's impossible to make a profit. In the early days we had to have a collective system. Now it no longer makes sense.'

We tramped down to a neighbouring shed to inspect the goats, raised for their milk, which Tnuva transforms into cheese. Ilona told me how good their milk was, and I sipped some of the stuff while under observation from a mouse that sat twitching on a counter. The milk was indeed delicious. The goat raising has already been privatized: Ilona's family is solely responsible for the maintenance of the herd and buildings, and they will receive the revenue it generates. To hedge her bets, Ilona also has a small jewellery studio in her house, and is trying to market her products in the United States.

The farm buildings at Meona are unattractive: walls, as well as roofs, are usually made of corrugated iron. But the moshav's houses are large, even luxurious. It's not unusual for a family to occupy a six-bedroom house. Many of the newer houses have been built by the children of moshavniks, who work outside the community but continue to live within it. The landscaping was haphazard: attractive low stone walls around the houses were cut into by ugly concrete steps leading up to the entrance. There are gardens, but also dry ditches and untended slopes.

We were invited to supper with Mimi, a Moroccan woman whose husband came to Meona when he was eight. She is a teacher, her husband a gardener. We were clearly her guests rather than his, for the husband was watching television in a distant corner when we arrived, and stayed put; an hour later he left the house without a word. Mimi came to Israel without her parents at the age of fourteen, married at seventeen, and gave birth to five children. Her sister had married at fifteen. A woman of great warmth, Mimi looks older than her years, but carries matriarchy with charm and dignity. As soon as we arrived, we were ushered towards the most comfortable chairs and plates of food flowed in from the kitchen. To accompany our Arab coffee, we nibbled crêpes rolled with honey, which were so delicious that my appetite was almost exhausted by the time we sat down to dinner.

Mimi and her family are in the same plight as most other moshavniks. They are saddled with a share of the huge debts run up by others. When one looks at the grand house in which she has lived since 1973, one has some idea of how those debts were incurred. Mimi told me she wouldn't exchange her house for the grandest mansion in Tel Aviv. I decided not to tell her that you won't find many houses as grand as hers in Tel Aviv.

Although Israelis tend to deny individual responsibility for misadventures, the moshavim were also victims of circumstance. In 1977 the new Likud government overreacted to thirty years of state controls and unleashed the mechanisms of the market economy. Unfortunately many of those who wished to exploit the new economic freedom had limited experience of financial management. Banks, unfettered, acted without much sense of social responsibility and allowed, even encouraged, the centralized purchasing organizations of kibbutzim and moshavim to take out loans that became burdensome as interest rates rose threefold. Some Israelis made fortunes out of lending money to organizations that they must have known would be unable to afford the repayments if the economy sagged. Other financial institutions behaved as cavalierly as the banks. Ilona told me that her family had been badly burnt by an insurance company.

'It's very difficult to get dispassionate advice on financial matters,' commented Avi, 'and when things go wrong, no one takes responsibility. Financial management has become a juggling act. You invest sensibly in a savings scheme, but that ties up your money for a few years. So when a week later your car unexpectedly dies on you, you have to go to the bank and borrow at 40 per cent to get a new one.'

There is much bitterness among the moshavim at what appears to be the preferential treatment given to the kibbutzim. Both movements are in difficulties, but the plight of the moshavim is worse; yet it is the kibbutzim who have already been bailed out, while the moshavim are still awaiting a solution. The suicides are the most terrible indicators of the despair of some moshavniks, especially those in remote areas where there is no other way to earn a living. The colourful mix of cultures evident on many moshavim makes for good brochure design, but it can also lead to fragmentation. Feuds have developed between groups of families on some moshavim, and if they are North African, the culture makes it very difficult to resolve such antagonism. Sometimes this conflict is taken to absurd lengths, as at Moshav Goren, which has split into two, Goren Aleph and Goren Bet. Many families are desperate to leave divided moshavim, but they have nowhere to go.

Transportation complicates life on the moshavim. The primary school between Tarshiha and Meona caters for 300 children, drawn from twenty-four moshavim and *mitzpim*. Some of them have to travel forty minutes each way from border settlements. According to Avi, there are 181 different bus routes required to ensure that all these children can get to school. Air raid shelters are used as classrooms, not only because of a shortage of space, but to accustom the kids not to regard shelters as threatening areas. Sometimes the children are put through a chemical warfare drill with gas masks. When Avi and I arrived at the school late one morning, the pupils were engaged in less fearful tasks. Under his arm Avi was clutching a video of *Sesame Street*, which he handed to Monique, the English teacher. She pushed it into the video player, and a few seconds later the bouncy noisy ten-year-olds were entranced into happy silence.

I asked Monique how she would characterize these children.

'Culturally deprived, I guess,' she said, resignedly. 'Kids from moshavim often have no cultural exposure at all. It's not just that they don't know who Yitzhak Perlman is, they don't even know what a violin is. They rarely leave the area, and to go to Tel Aviv is a big treat for them. Many of these children are from North African or Iraqi backgrounds, and they're rambunctious.'

'But I've always been told that Jews value education above all else. Why not here?'

'That doesn't apply so much to third-generation Israelis. They're less focused on education, more materialistic. Some parents from a European background, they do push their kids, but it's hard to generalize. I try to explain to the parents the importance of learning English, but it's an uphill struggle. Let's face it, some of them don't even speak good Hebrew and they can't spell. It's because in most cases the parents don't speak Hebrew as a first language.'

'Up near the border,' Avi explained, 'there are Jewish teenagers who don't speak Hebrew either. They speak Moroccan or Tunisian Arabic, just like their parents. But even for the motivated kids the problems are daunting. The libraries are pitiful, additional classes or programmes are often in places the kids can't get to, and the resources available are incredibly meagre.'

After lunch Avi took me to another school at Betzet. Israeli primary schools usually close at noon or two in the afternoon, but Betzet functions as a community centre after school hours. It was a hot day and I appreciated the sensible provision of arcades alongside the buildings, which sported railings and doors painted a vivid and decadent lilac. Supplementary classes were on offer this afternoon for moshav children. 'It's a nice idea in theory,' said Avi, 'but not many kids want to stay on after school. So the numbers are dropping.'

'What happens to the children who don't come to these afternoon classes?'

'They go home, they watch videos, they hang a cat, they do all the other things kids usually do.'

The children were absorbed in draughts, assembling jigsaws, playing pickup sticks, moulding coloured plasticene. Older children were working with computers, using English as well as Hebrew programmes. The teacher had failed to show up for this class, but it didn't seem to make much difference, as the children were managing perfectly well on their own. Down in the air-raid shelter smaller children were painting and making pictures out of tiny beads. In the gymnasium about ten children were learning to fence. Their Yemeni instructor told me that activities such as fencing counteracted the isolation of these rural communities. As a competitive sport, it can be played against teams from other areas, thus encouraging contact between children from different regions and different backgrounds.

Everybody complains about Israeli schools, but Avi took the view that despite the problem of attracting top-quality teachers, the general standard of education in Israel was quite good. Unfortunately, the curriculum was fairly staid, with regular testing and very little lateral teaching. Although the school day is short by European standards, it is common for children to be given homework from the age of six onwards. Bible studies are compulsory, while music or sport hardly feature at all on the regular curriculum. The gaps are filled either through participation in one of the numerous youth movements, religious and secular, that expose children to sports and other activities, or through 'grey education'. This refers to any projects that supplement basic education, and such supplements, whether school outings or music or art coaching, have to be paid for by the parents. Parents must also buy textbooks, and in some communities participate in school supervision. In other words, the supposedly free educational system is underwritten by parents. Now that parents find themselves paying for certain elements of their children's education, it has become easier for the government to cut the education budget, since they know that parents will take up the slack.

The educational structure is complicated by the fact that there is no uniform school system. Indeed, there are four: secular, Orthodox, ultra-Orthodox, and Arab. Many of the most committed teachers and gifted students are creamed off by the kibbutz school system, and under-financed urban schools suffer from large classes, inadequate teachers, and increasing instances of violence.[2] Fragmentation and inequality are increased by the inability of some parents to pay for 'grey education', which means that their children are excluded from the extracurricular activities that flesh out the rudimentary education they are offered. It has been estimated that the cost of 'grey education' for each child amounts to NIS 800 each year, which for many families is a hefty sum.[3]

Avi took me next to Geranot, a remote *mitzpe*. An American volunteer who lives there told me about the community: 'It's nothing like Meona. The land at Geranot is leased from the Jewish Agency, and people live in the same temporary housing that the JA put in when the community was founded. Because nothing is owned by the people who live there, nothing can be upgraded. We've been trying to bring some cultural life into the area, but it's hard to get people to participate. They won't come out of their houses. There are forty-five families at Geranot, and the *mitzpe* is only nine years old, but already the community has severe financial problems. Ideas haven't worked out, and people won't co-operate with other communities in the area. We need manpower, we need money, and both are lacking. The biggest problem is lack of transportation. Many people can't afford cars, and the bus system is atrocious. I spend hours every day just waiting for buses. You can't even hitch, because there are so few cars on the road.'

Boaz came to Israel from the Caucasus as a boy, and has curiously Polynesian features. He lives in one of the uniform boxy houses of which Geranot consists. In the living room a hamster frolicked in a cage; there was an upright piano, a few shelves of books, and back numbers of *Gun Digest*. Boaz was wearing a loud check shirt, and his shock of hair looked as though it had been trimmed with garden shears. His manner was extremely forceful, and, although lacking in formal education, he struck me as shrewd and intelligent. His three children sat curled up on the sofa watching television while we talked. I felt cold, even though it was springtime. Cold winds lash the hilltop settlement, and the houses have no central heating.

'Our major problems,' Boaz told me, jabbing in my direction with a cigarette, 'are economic and cultural. It's no longer security, though I have three guns in the house – just in case. Today our problems are different. Most of the people here are from Arab countries, and most of them are not well educated. A very few of us came from kibbutzim and moshavim. But life is very hard for all of us. We need to persuade the government to revise the whole settlement system and change the centralization of the economy. I would like to work the land, but around here the land is tied up and I'm not allowed to. But we should be encouraged to do what we're good at. This is good land for sheep and cattle. The cheese industry needs sheep's milk. But we import it in dried form from Europe instead of producing our own. And because of all the restrictions placed on us, the *mitzpim* are dying.'

Avi interrupted him. 'But are you prepared to be responsible for your failures as well as your successes?'

'Yes.'

Unlike Elaine Levitt and the disciples of Stef Wertheimer, Boaz saw no future in industrial development of the Galilee. 'In 1988, 4,000 factories closed in Israel. And if you start up a factory in the Galilee, your costs are higher because of transportation. Tefen is subsidized by the government and many of the employees are Arabs who are prepared to accept low wages. I don't work at Tefen. I work in Haifa. So do many of my neighbours. But in the evenings we're stuck in Geranot. That wouldn't matter if the quality of life here was good. But it's not. Nor am I satisfied with the education my children are getting. We want our children to have the best, to be more successful than we have been. We don't earn much, but we bought the eldest the piano. I won't let them play with the neighbouring children. Why not? Because I know their parents, and I feel those kids are going to end up as burdens to us all. But I don't want my children to become like that. I've tried to set up other activities here – classes in welding, photography, painting – but nothing worked out.' I asked Boaz why, if he was so dissatisfied here, he didn't move to a moshav.

'That's exactly what I would love to do, but it's a great risk, and my wife is unwilling. For me it would be a dream to farm some land, which my children could at least inherit, even if they didn't want to farm it themselves.'

As we were leaving, I shook Boaz's hand and said: 'The next time I see you, I hope you'll have your farm.'

He beamed, and looked heavenwards, clasping his hands. 'I hope, I hope.' And added, 'You're always invited.'

In the evening we returned to the school near Meona, which at night becomes a community centre. People were gathering for choir practice in the main hall, while out in the lobby a short, dark-skinned woman with sprightly eyes and a cigarette glued to her fingers paced up and down. Avi introduced us.

'I'm Tova,' she said. 'I run the community centre without a centre. That's why we're meeting at the school.'

'At least you have a community.'

Tova, wishing to encourage more social life in the Galilee, had persuaded a well-known songwriter, Nahum Eman, to fuse members of local moshavim and *mitzpim* into a choir. He held auditions and selected the singers, who were told they had to be prepared to attend weekly rehearsals. The choir has been wildly successful. 'See that woman in the second row? She had a Caesarian a week ago, and she was given three weeks off to recover. But she refuses to miss the rehearsal. Within three years this will be the best folk-song choir in Israel.'

Nahum Eman is writing new songs for the choir about the region in which they live. From what I heard at the rehearsal, the singing was technically accomplished, but I couldn't get to grips with these 'folk songs' composed the day before yesterday. For Israelis it's a way to amalgamate the different cultures that pervade in the country.

Driving back to Karmiel with Avi, I spoke of the impermanence of so much Israeli construction. The depressing Jewish Agency houses of Geranot, the half-hearted landscaping, the neglect of exteriors in order to lavish money and attention on interiors, this all added to a sense of transience, as though within ten minutes entire communities could be uprooted and transferred elsewhere. Was this, I wondered, an architectural reflection of some deeper lack of confidence?

'You do,' he agreed, 'get the impression here that everything's an experiment. In many respects we've built an artificial society. On the moshavim there are all kinds of restrictions that distance those communities from life as it's lived in the rest of the world. They won't accept single people or old people. There are reasons for that, but it prevents moshavim from reflecting all kinds of social realities.

'Privatization may help, if only because among other consequences it means you can sell your house to anyone you like. It's curious that you mention the outward appearance of these places, because we're conscious of that too. We are trying to improve the landscaping at these settlements. The government isn't going to do it, so we're encouraging people to take more pride in their surroundings. But getting people to co-operate round here is very difficult. Tova's choir is very much the exception. For the most part people up here just aren't interested in each other. It makes the ideals of Zionism seem very remote indeed.'

I had not been in Israel for very long before I realized how easy it is to live here without having any contact with the Arab population. In Tel Aviv, Arabs are employed to sweep the streets and work in the kitchens of restaurants. In West Jerusalem they are encountered more frequently, riding the buses or walking down the Jaffa Road; but of course they live in one of the suburbs of East Jerusalem, where Jews are unlikely to make social calls. On Kibbutz Hazorea, where the members hold idealistic left-wing views, regular contacts with the Israeli Arabs who live nearby were infrequent, not out of fear or contempt, but because kibbutzniks tend to keep to themselves. The Arab construction workers at Hazorea ate at their own table. Not that the kibbutz had any greater degree of contact with Jewish Yokne'am just a mile from its gates.

However much Israeli Arabs protest their loyalty to the state, they still tend to be regarded as a kind of fifth column. That there should be tension between Jew and Arab within Israel is hardly surprising. Vladimir Jabotinsky, the arch-nationalist Zionist politician who still inspires right-wing politicians today, wrote in 1923: 'The Arabs loved their country as much as the Jews did. Instinctively they understood Zionist aspirations very well, and their decision to resist them was only natural . . . There was no misunderstanding between Jew and Arab, but a natural conflict.'[1]

Such a view, later mirrored in demagogic form by the likes of Meir Kahane, has the merit of honesty, although Jabotinsky had no intention of making any concessions to Arab sensibilities and suggested they should be seen in much the same way as American Indians or Australian aborigines. Other Zionist leaders were less hard-headed. Theodor Herzl seemed to believe that the Arabs of Palestine would be more than happy to share in the benefits the Zionists would be bringing with them from Europe, and such paternalistic views were widely shared, if not so explicitly stated, by the socialist leaders of the newly independent state. After all, the nascent nation had just fought a war in which 1 per cent of its population had died fending off attacks from neighbouring Arab states, so they were hardly disposed, whatever their political persuasion, to regard Arabs remaining within Israel's borders as bosom friends. Indeed, in 1948 areas with large Arab populations, such as the Galilee, were placed under military government which continued until 1966. During that period severe restrictions were imposed on the freedom of movement of Arabs outside their immediate areas of residence; military governors had draconian powers at their disposal, including detention without trial.

If the Jews were wary of the Arabs in their midst, the Arabs had no reason to feel any great warmth for their new masters after 1948. Many Arabs had fled the country in 1948 and some of their lands were seized. 'Security' also dictated the seizure of Arab lands in border areas and other parts of the country where the military authorities wished to dilute the Arab population. Compensation was often paid to the owners of the land, but not always. Some seizures were justified with legalistic explanations based on the confused situation that existed when title had to be proved through a series of regimes, Ottoman, British Mandate, and now Israeli. Some questionable seizures were subsequently made legal retroactively by the Land Acquisition Law of 1953. There was not much the Israeli Arabs could do about all this, for they were a small minority. Of the 900,000 Arabs living within Palestine in 1947, only 150,000 remained after the establishment of the state. Most of the Arab leaders had fled, urging other Arabs to follow suit since they could return to their villages after the Israelis had been vanquished; the remaining population were left in a state of confusion, ill-equipped to hold their own against the Israeli authorities.

Although severely constricted by their new rulers, the Arabs undoubtedly benefited materially from the Israeli state. Villages were granted a degree of autonomy at local level, and over the years political structures did develop. There was never much direct participation by Israeli Arabs in mainstream Zionist political parties, though in the late 1950s they were admitted to full membership of Histadrut and some Arabs have been active in Mapam and to a lesser extent in the Labour Party. They were free to form their own political parties and to be represented by them in the Knesset, but their influence on national politics remained marginal.

The sense of grievance from which most Israeli Arabs suffer is kept alive by the refugee problem, for forty years a thorn in the side of the state. Most of the rocks I dodged when travelling through the West Bank were launched from refugee camps, and it seemed ludicrous that decades after the War of Independence hundreds of thousands of refugees should still be housed in appalling conditions a few miles beyond the frontiers of Israel. Arab nationalists argue that it was the creation of the State of Israel that caused the problem, but this is a simplistic view. On the other hand the Israeli argument that the Arabs who fled in 1948 did so of their own accord and had been welcome to stay put is equally simplistic, especially given the conditions of war and terror in which rapid decisions had to be made. Nor have the Israelis ever wasted much sympathy on the hundreds of thousands of Arab families which, swept up in events over which they had no direct control, lost their homes. Israel's efforts to improve conditions in the camps were ruled contrary to United Nations regulations. The Israelis also maintain, with considerable justification, that the Arab states have refused to make any serious effort to absorb the refugees, which they could easily have done. Instead they have allowed the camps to remain as a blot on the moral landscape, a pawn in the long battle to secure a homeland for the Palestinians. The pious protestations of solidarity with the Palestinian cause from the countries which waged war against Israel are hard to reconcile with their own expansionist ambitions in 1948 to occupy as much as they could of the land the British had so conveniently vacated. After all this time, and after so much human misery now passed on to future generations, the arguments seem increasingly futile.

Right-wing Israelis never tire of pointing out that Palestinian nationalism is a relatively recent phenomenon, that until the past few decades the local Arab population didn't even think of itself as Palestinian. This may well be true, but it has become, like so many of the historical arguments that bedevil Israeli politics, irrelevant. The Jews were driven by a longing for a homeland of their own so extreme, and so understandable, that they neglected to consider that similar aspirations might be felt by others occupying the same territory. Palestinian nationalism, indeed, captured the Arab and later the international imagination as a reaction to the triumph of a rival nationalism. The only surprising thing about this is that many Israelis still find it perplexing. Of course the Israelis are at the receiving end of the more extreme manifestations of this nationalism in the form of terrorist attacks and refusals to recognize Israel's right to exist; thus they have little patience with the rhetoric of Palestinian nationalism and profoundly distrust even the more moderate elements in the Palestinian leadership.

It is one of the many ironies of the situation that not only was Palestinian nationalism born out of a reaction to Zionism, from which it has borrowed many strategies, but that Zionism in its modern form owes much of its vibrancy to its response to the threat of Palestinian nationalism. The two nationalisms feed off each other. Curiously, the Arabs living within Israeli borders have been consistently moderate in their attitude; the greatest militancy in support of the Palestinian cause is to be found well outside Israel's borders. Yet, as Amos Elon has written, 'There is an unexpected element of irony in the fact that the Israeli Jews, who owe their existence as a nation to their extraordinary memory of past history, should now be forced to rely on the Arabs forgetting theirs.'[2]

The Holocaust factor also comes into play. There is an unfortunate tendency for Jews to be dismissive of the sufferings of other peoples on the grounds that they have been less atrocious than their own. Not surprisingly, when Israel's more fanatical opponents liken Israeli actions to those of the Nazis and liken Palestinian sufferings to those endured by the Jews, the citizens become very impatient. Because Jewish history is not taught to non-Israeli Arabs – the Holocaust isn't even mentioned in Jordanian schools[3] – Arab opponents of Israel are unaware or dismissive of Israeli sensitivity on this particular score, and underestimate the doggedness with which the Israelis intend to ensure their survival. On the other hand, some Israeli politicians exploit the terrible fact of the Holocaust in order to excuse the inexcusable.

Nothing can disguise the fact that in many respects Israeli Arabs are second-class citizens. Because Israel is by definition a Jewish state, its other citizens cannot share in every manifestation of that citizenship. Certain professions are closed to Arabs, especially those linked to security matters. Although Israeli Arabs are not excluded from military service, and groups such as the Druze serve as a matter of course, it is inconceivable that a Jewish unit guarding a border area could be under the command of an Israeli Moslem Arab. The education offered Israeli Arabs may compare favourably with that available to their fellow Arabs in South Yemen, but it still lags behind the standard of Jewish education. Classes are larger and many of the schools are physically in poor condition. One Arab teacher told me: 'I have taught Jewish students for twelve years, and they get worked up when the air-conditioning breaks down for a day or two. In Arab schools we are more concerned about whether we have doors and windows.'

Relatively few Israeli Arabs go to university or enter the professions. The majority either eke out a living on their farms or, increasingly, remain dependent on the Israeli economy for employment. The many Arab doctors in Israel are almost all trained outside the country. Because Jews are unwilling to take jobs as manual labourers, such employment has become an exclusively Arab preserve, even at left-wing kibbutzim. Even a hardline sociologist such as Dr Rafi Israeli admits: 'The fact that Arabs enjoy civil rights, such as the right to vote and to be elected, does not alleviate in the least their frustration at their inability to obtain full acceptance into the Israeli bureaucratic and political elites.'[4]

Marriages between different religions are against the law, although this applies to Jews wishing to marry Christians as well as to Jews wishing to marry Moslems, or any other permutation. Inter-religious marriages do occur, very infrequently, but either one of the partners converts, or the wedding takes place outside Israel.

The standard of living among Israeli Arabs has undoubtedly risen in recent decades, just as it has in the Occupied Territories, but Arabs still lag behind the Jews when it comes to material benefits. David Shipler quotes the following statistics from 1983: 'Only 16.8 per cent of the Arab households had telephones, compared with 75.8 per cent of the Jewish households. Private cars were owned by 46.4 per cent of all Jewish families and only 25.9 per cent of Arab families; 92.5 per cent of the Jewish households and 66 per cent of the Arab households had television sets. The proportion of Arabs in the population is about one in six, but it is only one in sixty in senior government posts, one in 300 in university academic positions ... As of the early 1980s, there was not a single Arab among the 625 senior officials of the prime minister's office, the Bank of Israel, the state comptroller's office, or the ministries of Finance, Housing, Health, Industry, and Communications.'[5]

Of the 980 senior posts in the Ministry of Education, just forty are devoted to Arab education and of those only thirty-two are filled by Arabs.[6] There is one Arab, Mohammed Massarwa, in the Israeli consular service. Menachem Begin promised to appoint an Arab to the Supreme Court, but never did so, and neither have his successors. Israeli Arabs earn half as much as the Jews but must tolerate an infant mortality rate twice that of the Jews.[7] Nor are Arab villages immune from the general decline of agriculture in Israel. Whereas in 1950 half of all working Israeli Arabs were dependent on agriculture, by the late 1970s that figure had dropped to 16 per cent. This decline in manpower had no effect on their prosperity, which matched and often exceeded that of Jewish immigrants from North Africa.[8] Until a few years ago an average-sized family landholding provided enough income to ensure a reasonable standard of living. This is no longer the case, and in some villages cottage industries have been set up to generate additional revenue.[9]

The undoubted improvements in the standard of living among Israeli Arabs – invariably presented as the outcome of Israeli magnanimity rather than as a result of the Arabs' own hard work – have only served to increase expectations which cannot be fulfilled. It is among the younger educated Arabs, not their peasant parents and grandparents, that the greatest radicalization has taken place.

From an early age Jews and Arabs are kept apart. Their schools are separate. This is not a form of apartheid, for Arabs no more wish to attend Jewish schools than Jews would wish to enroll in Arab ones. The separate schools were conceived as a liberal recognition that different cultures and heritages require different educational approaches. Yet it seems peculiar that even in a city such as Haifa, where Jews and Arabs coexist with little friction, separate education is maintained. Arab schools are not free to teach what they please, nor do they have any control over expenditure on Arab education. School principals are appointed by the ministry of education rather than by local councils, and Israeli Arabs suspect that the ministry is more interested in candidates' political respectability than in their ability as teachers or administrators. The curriculum, devised by the ministry, stipulates, for example, that from the third grade Arab children must study the Bible and Israeli history and literature. About 20 per cent of the school week is devoted to Jewish history and culture. In the words of the State Education Law of 1953, the object of state education, for Jew or non-Jew, was 'to base elementary education . . . on the values of Jewish culture and the achievements of science, on love of the homeland and loyalty to the State and the Jewish people.'

Contemporary Palestinian literature and culture are ignored. Anton Shammas, the Israeli Arab novelist, described this aspect of his education as follows: 'The system of Arab education in Israel, at least in my time, produced tongueless people, more at home with seventh-century Arab poetry than with that of the twentieth century.'[10]

An Arab politician elaborated this theme for me: 'Our education doesn't give us a sense of identity. At school I knew a huge amount about the Old Testament and Jewish history and the Holocaust – but I felt ashamed when a Jew asked me about Palestine and the Koran. Nowadays it's better and Arab children do learn about the Koran. In high school I learnt so much Jewish literature that I could have lectured about it all night long, but I was taught nothing about Palestinian poetry, for instance. It was only later, when I went to Tel Aviv University, that I studied Arabic as well as Jewish literature. The fact is that the materials in our schools are often unrelated to who *we* are. When the school principal brought Jewish guests into the classroom when I was a boy, all the Arab children had to sing "Hatikvah". It wasn't for years that I realized that we were singing a Zionist hymn. We learnt the anthem parrot-fashion. Do you recall the words? "So long as still within our breasts, the Jewish heart beats true . . . So long as our hopes are not yet lost – Two thousand years we cherished them." This is what Arab children were required to sing.'

There is no reciprocity. Jewish pupils are not expected to study Arab history and culture. Arabic language teaching has now been introduced into Jewish schools, but is as yet far from universal. As the sociologist Dr Majid Al-Hajj told me: 'Arabs are considered to be a cultural and religious minority within Israel, but not a national minority. In contrast, the Jews think of themselves in national terms and hence national issues are at the centre of their curriculum. Israel makes policy in such matters as though oblivious to the fact that it is a minority within the region.'

The ministry has been persuaded, by Dr Al-Hajj among others, to introduce into the Arab curriculum elements that deal with the Arabs' role within Israel. 'The programme will be introduced at the eleventh grade and above. It'll deal with political, demographic, and socio-economic issues, all of which have been ignored up till now. It's in Israel's own interest to give the Arabs here greater confidence in their own culture. If they don't acquire a sense of national identity in school, then they will acquire it from parents or politicians who may well be hostile to Israel. By ignoring these subjects in the past, the ministry was reinforcing our feeling of alienation within Israeli society. There's certainly greater flexibility than there was before the intifada, but everything remains tightly under the ministry's control, and many teachers are afraid to deal with these issues. Ten years ago teachers raising such matters with their students were putting their careers in danger, and it's going to be difficult to persuade some of them that this is no longer the case.'

The most profound grievance among Israeli Arabs concerns the question of land, or rather the lack of it. Long ago B. Z. Dinur, Israel's first education minister, declared with breathtaking arrogance: 'For the Arabs of Israel – all rights, but to the Land of Israel – no right.' One can follow, with dismay, the ideological trail, despite its whiff of contradiction, but the awesome insensitivity, a common characteristic among some early Zionists, is memorable. Such sentiments encouraged Israelis to regard the Arabs as second-class citizens. There is no shortage of official justifications for the confiscation of Arab lands, many of which had indeed been abandoned in 1948. In the Negev it's the army that requires huge tracts of land used for grazing by Bedouin tribes; in the Galilee the reason may be recreation or development. But the net result of the whole process is that it has become increasingly difficult for Arabs to cultivate their farms or build their homes in security. Within two years of independence, the Israeli government had confiscated 2,500,000 dunams of Arab land, with legislation after the fact to put the expropriation on a legal basis. (There are four dunams to the acre.) Although the Arab population in Israel has grown from about 150,000 to 750,000 since 1948, Arab land ownership amounts to no more than 550,000 dunams. Nor are the losses confined to rural areas. Municipalities such as Nazareth and Umm el-Fahm have lost up to 90 per cent of their landholdings. Consequently these crowded towns lack room for expansion, and many residents resort to building that could be, and often is, ruled illegal, opening residents to the risk of seeing their homes demolished.[11] On March 30, 1976, Israeli Arabs declared a Land Day to protest against the expropriation of 20,000 dunams of farmland. By the end of the day six Arabs were dead, seventy injured, and 260 arrested. The anniversary of Land Day has been marked by mostly peaceful demonstrations in the years that followed, and has kept the issue of land confiscations alive among the Arab population.

Israeli fear and distrust of its indigenous Arab population feeds off the illusion that this population is monolithic in its culture and politics. Nothing could be further from the truth. The Arabs are divided between those who believe that, however justified their grievances against the state, their future lies as a minority within Israel, and those who espouse, however discreetly, the Palestinian nationalist view, which in its extreme form is profoundly hostile to Israel. The semi-nomadic Bedouin of the Negev are quite different in their culture from the settled villagers of the Galilee or the Druze of the Golan. Christian Arabs have no sympathy with the Islamic fundamentalism that is becoming more and more pronounced in Israel, and tend to be more moderate in their political views. Israeli-Arab politics is fragmented, just as the numerous Zionist parties reflect competing interests and beliefs.

Although physically Jews and Arabs can be so alike that it is sometimes impossible to distinguish one from the other, both peoples harbour wretched stereotypes of the other. The Israelis do their utmost to ensure that Arab textbooks and publications, which often portray Jews as murderous thugs, don't find their way into Israel or the Territories. Yet the stereotype of the 'dirty Arab' has become self-perpetuating. Employed as a labouring class to do all the jobs that Israelis have become too fastidious to perform, Arabs find themselves unwittingly conforming to such overtly racist perceptions. Both stereotypes underestimate the moderation of the opponents, and numerous surveys have shown that the majority of Israeli Arabs, despite their grievances and their notional support for a Palestinian homeland, wish to continue to live peaceably within Israeli borders. After all, three-quarters of all Israeli Arabs are Israeli-born, even if circumstances conspire to make them feel like aliens.

In March 1989 the Speaker of the Knesset, Dov Shilansky, was asked whether Israel was also the homeland of a fellow MK who was an Arab. He replied: 'It is his country, the land of his birth, but not his homeland, just as Lithuania was our country, the land where we were born, but never our homeland. Rights, the full rights of citizenship, those I want to give him. But this cannot be his homeland. The Arabs have twenty-one countries ... Which country he sees as his homeland is not my problem.'[12]

Mr Shilansky is wrong. It is his problem. Israeli Arabs, unlike most of their Jewish fellow citizens, have become bicultural and bilingual. Whatever their dissatisfaction, they are free to participate in Israeli life and culture. They may have every sympathy with their fellow Palestinians in their intifada, but they have no intention of packing their bags and joining them. Dr Al-Hajj told me: 'Arabs feel increasingly on the periphery, outside the national consensus. They do support the intifada, but only within the confines of the law. They are perceived as a hostile minority, yet if there were a Palestinian state, Israeli Arabs wouldn't move to it. But this situation can't continue indefinitely. Israeli Arabs are very dynamic, very politicized. Which way they'll move in the future will depend on such issues as citizenship rights – education, budgets for Arab areas, employment – and the peace process.'

The Israelis have adopted the curious policy of trying to isolate the Arab population from access to views that, in Israeli eyes, subvert the status quo. Many publications from other Arab countries are banned; some of these are grossly antisemitic, but many are merely supporting a nationalist line that the Israelis find unpalatable. The Israeli authorities control the use of textbooks in the Territories as well as within the Green Line to ensure that no 'propaganda' is taught. All Arab publications within the area under Israeli control, such as the newspapers of East Jerusalem, are scrutinized by Israeli censors. Nevertheless the English-language Arab newspaper *Al-Fajr* manages to publish articles highly critical of Israeli policy. Such restrictive measures can of course enjoy only a partial success. Textbooks and newspapers are not the only means of communication in the late twentieth century. If Israeli Arabs thirst for the incitement the Israeli authorities are so anxious to discourage, all they need do is turn on the radio and be harangued from Syria or Iraq or the Arab nation of their choice. (Jordanian television is easily picked up within Israel, and offers, indeed, the only English-language television news in the region. These excruciatingly boring broadcasts are dominated by the doings of King Hussein, who is shown nightly shaking hands with interchangeable dignitaries or chairing identikit committees on salt production.) Palestinian expression of nationalist views is even more strictly curtailed by the Israelis. It is illegal to fly the PLO flag or to voice support for that organization, and the government has, and uses, powers of arrest and detention to deal with unco-operative Arabs.

The widespread ignorance of Israeli Jews leads to the worst kind of stereotyping of Arabs not only as dirty and backward, but as feckless and unreliable. The radicalized Arabs of the Gaza Strip, for instance, are not distinguished from the more pacific Israeli Arabs of the Galilee. Even liberal-minded Jews responded uneasily when I talked to them about the Arabs. Avi told me: 'I'm on good terms with some Arabs. I know an Arab who has invited me to his house, and he's been over to mine, once. But there's always this sense of distrust. People are reluctant to invite Arabs to their homes because of crime. After all, most crime in the Galilee is Arab crime.'

Dr Al-Hajj remarked to me: 'Arabs do have stereotyped views of Jews as well, but not to the same degree that Jews have stereotyped views of Arabs. This is a function of minority/majority relations, which are asymmetric here as elsewhere. The minority is more willing than the majority to bridge the gap and integrate. Jews are afraid of Arabs, and that makes them unwilling to share their greater resources and power. There is a lack of connection, there is ignorance, and the continual conflict between the two sides just makes matters worse. Jews tend not to know Arabs and think of them only as potential enemies.'

It would be misleading to suggest that all is discord and strife between Arab and Jew. There are numerous attempts at co-operation. The best known, but least successful, is Neve Shalom, established in 1970 as an interfaith community near Latroun. After fifteen years all the community had to show for its efforts was a population of eighty, of which 60 per cent is Jewish. Neve Shalom also organized workshops for a total of 10,000 Arab and Jewish high school students, which must have had more lasting benefits than the experiment in communal living. The founder was Father Bruno Hussar, a perfect exemplar of the racial and cultural and religious confusion that is so typical of Israeli life. A Jewish convert to Catholicism who has lived in Israel since 1953, he was born in Egypt but is an Israeli citizen.

Arabs and Jews meet at university level, especially at Haifa University, but also at Hebrew University in Jerusalem, where organizations such as Beit Hillel encourage discussions between Arab and Jewish students about the most intractable political problems facing both sides. Other organizations, such as Haifa's Beit Hagefen, confine themselves to cultural activities. An organization called Nitzanei Shalom arranges for Jews to live among Arabs in their villages. In the Jezreel Valley, 'Youth Who Sing a Different Song' was founded in 1985 after two Jewish teachers were killed by Arab extremists, prompting reprisals against local Arabs. The organization seeks to improve Jewish-Arab relations by setting up workshops for high school students. These worthy attempts to build and strengthen ties between the two communities are all private initiatives. Successive Israeli governments have done virtually nothing to encourage such efforts, however tentative, at greater integration.

Givat Haviva, the Institute for Arabic Studies established by the Artzi kibbutz movement, is overtly political in its efforts to bridge the gap. The founders came from Kibbutz Hazorea, where some of the early settlers, who had learnt Arabic before emigrating to Israel, made deliberate attempts to establish good relations with the local Arab population. Mapam, the political party to which the Artzi kibbutzim are attached, has been the only Zionist party to have included Arabs not only in its ranks but among its leadership. (Arab participation in the Labour Party has been relatively insignificant. The National Religious Party used to attract support from Arab voters, because until 1984 the NRP controlled the Interior Ministry and thus the purse strings of municipal budgets.) At Givat Haviva Arabic culture is taught as a whole: not just the language, but the customs and the history. There are also courses for Arabs on education and Jewish–Arab relations, and workshops that bring together Jews and Arabs for a few days.

Yoram Meron of Hazorea, who helps to run Givat Haviva, told me that the strength and persistence of the intifada have baffled and puzzled many Jews, some of whom respond by wishing to meet more Arabs and learn their language so as better to understand the situation. Father Hussar also notes a side benefit of the intifada: 'Today, meetings between Arabs and Jews are truer. Arabs no longer come to meet with Jews from a position of inferiority, as the intifada made them more proud and more equal.'[13] The deleterious effect of the intifada on these co-operative ventures is that some Israeli Arabs who were hitherto happy to participate have come under pressure to be less hospitable to the Jews. More significant than these admirable efforts at co-operation is the broad indifference, both at official level and among ordinary Israelis, to such aims. The Jews seem to render their Arab neighbours invisible, as though they could dream them into absence. That will not happen. Unless the nightmarish political programmes of Moledet's Rehavam Zeevi and Kach's Meir Kahane are brought to fruition and the Arabs of Israel are kicked out of the country, Arab and Jew are going to have to live together.

Welcome to Umm el-Fahm, the second largest Arab town in Israel. You turn off the main road from Hadera to Megiddo and crawl up a badly potholed road that winds up the slope. From the road, if you dare take your eyes off it, you have an admirable view of a not yet completed domed five-storey structure, the community centre donated by Islamic organizations. This grandeur in waiting is in stark contrast with the road-level landscape, which consists of junked cars, half-junked cars on blocks, stagnant puddles, piles of rubble forming a kind of solid effluent from abandoned house construction, and garbage everywhere, piles of it, strewn bouquets of it. There are a few villas on the outskirts of town, and a couple of banks with gleaming modern façades, but with those exceptions Umm el-Fahm is a dump. Until a year ago there was no library and no sports or recreational facilities. Any kibbutz with a hundred members enjoys better facilities than this town of 27,000 inhabitants.

From the early 1970s until 1989 Umm el-Fahm was governed by elected officials of the Democratic Front for Peace and Equality, which has incorporated the Communist Hadash movement. In the 1989 municipal elections the Hadash mayor, Hashem Mahamid, was trounced by a candidate of the Islamic Bloc. The people of Umm el-Fahm had tired of Hadash's inability to improve their quality of life. Mayor Mahamid claimed, with some justification, that the resources were not available for such improvements. With the inadequate budget at his disposal, he had done his best. The voters thought otherwise. Still, the mayor was correct. Israeli Arabs constitute 17 per cent of the population, but only 2.3 per cent of the budget comes their way. Despite the budgetary restraints, Mayor Mahamid had, in five years, increased the number of homes connected to the sewage system from 10 per cent to 60 per cent, and those connected to the telephone system from 200 to 2,000. Other improvements had been made, in classroom construction and water pipe renewal, but Umm el-Fahm was still a dump. Municipal workers often do not receive their salaries on time, and withdraw their labour, which makes the situation even more miserable.

Not only are Arab municipal budgets paltry in comparison with those allotted to Jewish towns and settlements, but elected Arab officials carry no weight with the central government. Resources in Israel are limited, and are more likely to be doled out to those with political clout, whether they are the directors of prestigious kibbutz movements or the strident settlers of the West Bank. Arab mayors wait at the end of the queue. Because most of them belong to non-Zionist parties, ministers in Jerusalem gain little political advantage by acceding to their requests. Those ministers, moreover, have considerable discretionary powers. Elected councils can be dismissed by ministerial fiat and replaced with appointed councils, though this rarely happens, as the government prefers to avoid direct interference in municipal affairs. However, when certain Arab councils began to make pro-intifada noises, they received warnings that

Jerusalem might interfere if they didn't lower their voices. Just two months before the 1989 elections, the interior minister, Arye Der'i, almost replaced Mahamid with an appointed commission because of the town's financial disarray.[14]

Mayor Mahamid was doing his best within the severe constraints in which he had to operate, but he received only 23 per cent of the vote. (Nevertheless he was rewarded for his efforts in January 1990, when he replaced the retiring left-wing veteran MK Meir Wilner in the Knesset.) The new mayor is Sheikh Mahajneh, who ran on an Islamic platform. In Nazareth, Islamic movement candidates picked up six out of nineteen council seats, and even won two seats in Lod, where only 15 per cent of the population is Arab. Although some Israelis have taken mild fright at this result, interpreting it as the advance guard of a fundamentalist army, the sheikh's success was a simple recognition that Islamic organizations have done more for Umm el-Fahm in a few years than municipal councils had been able to do in decades. The municipality has its hands tied, but Islamic groups have access to volunteer labour and private donations. The five-storey community centre at the top of the town will house a medical centre and library as well as a mosque. The Islamic Association, which raised the money for the centre entirely from private sources, had already opened a bookshop and clinic, inaugurated a sports league, operated day-care centres, and provided textbooks to poor school-children. For all this the people of Umm el-Fahm have said thank you, and if the Islamic fundamentalists are indeed the main beneficiaries, successive Israeli governments have only themselves to blame for discriminating against Arab towns and villages.

The discrimination is seen even more clearly in Nazareth, where the Arab town exists alongside, or more precisely below, a newer Jewish town, Upper Nazareth. There are 4,000 Arabs living in Upper Nazareth, which has a total population of 28,000. The experiment in peaceful coexistence has not been an overwhelming success, for a local Jewish organization has been pressuring residents not to sell their houses to Arabs and has been agitating for the removal of the Arab residents. It is hard to see what the Jews have to complain about, for it is the Arabs whose houses have not been connected to the sewage system and whose rubbish is rarely collected. Arab and Jew pay the same taxes to the municipality but receive different qualities of service.

Yet Upper Nazareth as a whole is in a privileged position when compared with its large Arab neighbour. Nazareth, with a population of 55,000, is spread over only 8,000 dunams, whereas Upper Nazareth, which is half the size, enjoys 28,000 dunams. In 1984 the municipal

206 · WINNER TAKES ALL

budget for Nazareth was NIS 355,000, while for the far smaller Upper Nazareth it was NIS 432,000; Nazareth received government subsidies to the tune of NIS 58,000, while Upper Nazareth received NIS 122,000. Upper Nazareth has been designated a development town, giving it access to all manner of rebates and subsidies, while Nazareth itself, along with every other Arab municipality in the country, has not.[15] Towns get more money from the central government than villages do. Jewish communities become towns once they have a population of five to seven thousand. There are Arab communities with ten or fifteen thousand inhabitants which are still classified as villages. In fact there are only three Arab towns in the whole of Israel: Nazareth, Umm el-Fahm, and Shfaram. Given such discrepancies, it is not surprising that Arab voters are rewarding the munificence of the Islamic Bloc.

Arab voters are beginning to drift away from the Arab parties, at least at the municipal level, and remain disenchanted with the Zionist parties. I found different opinions as to whether Labour governments had served the Israeli Arabs better than Likud regimes. Some thought this was so; others felt that Likud, while more overtly hostile to Israeli Arabs, at least made its position clear, whereas Labour politicians spouted fine sentiments but delivered little. Dr Al-Hajj is one of those who believes that from 1977 to 1982 the Likud government did much to improve the plight of Israeli Arabs. Nevertheless about 40 per cent of Israeli Arabs do vote for Zionist parties such as Ratz or Labour, even Shas. There are only seven Arab MKs, but if the 320,000 enfranchised Israeli Arabs were to vote exclusively for their own parties they would have up to twenty seats in the Knesset, which would make them a powerful bloc, unless they were too busy fighting among themselves. Nevertheless, given the pro-PLO views of two of the principal parties, Hadash and the Progressive List for Peace, it is inconceivable that, in the present political climate, either Labour or Likud would form a coalition with their aid. There were two Labour MKs, but after the intifada began one of them, Abdel Wahab Darousha, left the party, since he couldn't stomach being a colleague of Yitzhak Rabin, the hard-line minister of defence. Before the 1988 elections Darousha formed his own Arab Democratic Party, and was elected. An Arab politician said to me: 'When Darousha was returned to the Knesset in 1988 he was entitled to serve on a Knesset committee, but his appointment was blocked. If one Arab MK can't function properly, what do we need fourteen for?'

In November 1988 Hadash and the Progressive List for Peace attracted 34 and 15 per cent of the Israeli Arab vote respectively. Both parties recognize the PLO as the sole representative of the Palestinian people but also pledge their loyalty to the state of Israel. The Islamic fundamentalists support the former but not the latter. The movement within Israel is led by Sheikh Abdullah Nimr Darwish, who insists he is no extremist, but if a talk he gave at Hebrew University is anything to go by, he means business. According to a report in the *Jerusalem Post* he declared that 'the ultimate goal of the Islamic movement is to place the entire world under the dominion of the Prophet Mohammed . . . Once in power, the Islamic movement would institute Islamic law and reject any traces of "Western or Eastern" constitutions.'[16] The electoral successes of the fundamentalists are too recent for any final judgments to be made regarding the threat they pose, at least potentially, to the stability of Israel's body politic.

In the view of Dr Al-Hajj, the rise of Islamic parties is the consequence of frustration and alienation. 'People have begun to return to religion in a search for a framework that will give them greater social confidence. On election day at Umm el-Fahm there were green flags of Islam everywhere, but I'd bet that most people flying the flags never go near a mosque.' The power of local families and clans remains strong in local elections, especially in the villages. 'Israeli Arabs didn't experience urbanization in the way Arabs did in other lands, so the old social structure has in many ways been reinforced. One third of all Arab marriages take place within these kinship groups, these clans. There is very little mobility for Arabs within Israel, so people tend to stay put, and the old structures are maintained.'

How a head of a family votes determines exactly how his wives and children and their wives and children will vote. This clan loyalty also means that leadership is localized. Together with the fragmentation of Arab political parties – the seven Arab MKs represent five different parties – this makes the Arabs far less politically potent than they would be if united under a charismatic leader.

In Kafr Bara, an Arab village east of Tel Aviv in the area known as the Triangle, I was looking for a local leader called Kamal. It was Friday afternoon, a rest day for Moslems, so Kafr Bara had its shutters down. But I found a grocery that was open, and when I asked for Kamal, I was surrounded by jabbering kids. The grocer was happy to give me directions but first he wanted me to step into his shop and have something to drink. I declined on the grounds that I was late for my appointment, as indeed I was. So he sent a boy to show me the way. I parked the car in Kamal's driveway and was led into the house. I removed my shoes and found myself in a long room with enough seats, in the form of armchairs and banquettes, for twenty people at least, ranged along either side of three low tables. Although it was a sunny afternoon, the curtains were drawn and the lights switched on. Some of the light penetrating the curtains was greenish, presumably because of tinted windows, which are common in Arab houses. Kamal greeted me warmly. He is a good-looking man of thirty, with squarish features and a dark well-trimmed beard. He remained barefoot throughout my visit. The other four men in the room were, like Kamal, in Western dress, but there was one imposing figure, tall and stately and with piercing black eyes, who wore the regalia – full-length robe and a long black cloak, *keffiyeh* on his head and a stout walking stick on his lap – of an Arab dignitary. He was the Sheikh of Tulkarm, and he had been the guest preacher at the local mosque during Friday prayers. We talked books. What did I think of *Hamlet*, *A Tale of Two Cities* and *Wuthering Heights*? After a frank exchange of views on nineteenth-century British novels, he rose and took his leave.

When all the other visitors had gone, Kamal took me into another room, again with a multiplicity of sofas and curtains drawn. As in the Druze house at Daliyat, one wall was filled with a huge coloured photograph, this one depicting an Alpine torrent and bridge. The other walls and ceiling were pine-panelled, shiny with polish. Artificial flowers dangled from hanging baskets. A traditionally dressed woman wearing a headscarf entered the room with a tray containing small cups of very sweet Arabic coffee. This was, I assumed, Kamal's wife, and she often reappeared, bearing trays of tea and orange soda, in the course of the afternoon. Kamal had clearly decided to devote the rest of the day to my visit, and adopted a leisurely approach to our talk, padding it out with refreshments and digressions. He had just been elected to the local council on a list supporting the Islamic line, though he admitted to me that he was not religious. In Kafr Bara the Islamic movement candidates had won 70 per cent of the vote. It took him half an hour to answer my first question. Sometimes he would ignore my question with a polite wave – body language for a parenthesis – and launch into a lecture on the subject of his choice. The calls of the muezzin from the local mosque punctuated his speeches, and indeed obliterated parts of them. The first thing he wanted me to understand was his sense of identity. This he described to me, rather mystically, as a series of circles. That was nice to know, I said politely, but I was more interested in his personal sense of identity.

He leaned back on the sofa. 'I am Israeli.' He paused. 'But my behaviour, my customs, are Palestinian. I derive my identity from my village and my language. So I have a conflict. I am Israeli, but I identify with the Palestinians. If I identify with them too closely, I risk imprisonment. So Israel is pushing me and other Arabs to the margins. Yet I can't be an Israeli because I am not equal with the Jews. After all,' he added, in a formulation that I was to hear repeatedly from Arabs and which expressed a genuine and almost intractable perplexity, 'my country, Israel, is still at war with my people.'

He told me the story of Kafr Bara. According to property deeds, this village of 1,200 souls is over five hundred years old. Before 1948 the villagers, who were farmers and shepherds, owned 8,000 dunams (2,000 acres). After the War of Independence some villagers fled to Jordan or other Arab countries. Some left because they were afraid of the triumphant Jews; others thought they were leaving temporarily and intended to return to reclaim their land. But after 1948 the landholdings were reduced to 2,600 dunams. Why? I asked him.

'The reasons are complex. Under Turkish and British rule, villagers tried to lessen their tax burdens by saying they owned less land than they in fact farmed. The Israelis based their assessment of land ownership on those old tax returns. In 1953 the Knesset passed the absentee property law, which led to the confiscation of land owned by Arabs who had fled in 1948. Next fallow land was confiscated. My father used to graze sheep on fallow land, so the land was in use. But when the Israelis took aerial photographs, they concluded that the land was unused. We are still in dispute with the authorities about some of my family's land.

'Listen. The young people in our village want peaceful relations with the Israelis. But it's difficult to have peaceful relations when after forty years we're still arguing about who owns the land. We don't even feel secure in our houses. When I explained this situation to the Israeli authorities, they called me a fanatic! With less land there is also less work for the villagers, and many people here work in Tel Aviv or Petah Tikvah. There they see how the Jews live, and they want to be equal with them.'

He told me how nervous and suspicious some of the older villagers in particular had become. 'They believe the Jewish settlements on the West Bank were built as places to which Israeli Arabs would one day be transferred. All this politicians' talk of "transfer" upsets them.'

'But the Jews are nervous and suspicious of *you*.'

Kamal sighed. 'For generations Israeli Arabs have tried to prove their loyalty to the state. During the wars there were broadcasts from neighbouring countries calling on Israeli Arabs to stay in their houses and thus cripple Israeli industry, since the Jews had all been called up. But we ignored them. Some of us contributed our trucks and vehicles to the army. In 1973 my father, who always took his holiday during Ramadan, sacrificed his vacation and continued working, and worked twice as hard as usual. The Jewish owners of the ceramics factory where I was working at the time had been called up, so I kept the place open in their absence, and my brother worked as a volunteer bus driver in Jewish areas. These are not isolated examples. We expected that the government would regard us as citizens with full rights. We want equality, but we don't believe it will come to pass. The Jews say we're not equal because we don't serve in the army, but I'm not ready to fight my cousins and neighbours in Jordan or Syria. The Jews were sensitive to the Druze, who serve in the army but weren't mobilized to fight in Lebanon against other Druze. Druze serve in the army but they're still not equal to the Jews. There is no law that says we Arabs can't serve in the army, and there is no law that says we *must* serve. Ultra-Orthodox Jews don't serve. The solution I propose is a period of compulsory national service consisting of community work within our villages to help raise their standards to those of Jewish communities. At the moment we pay the same taxes but get poorer services – on the grounds that we don't serve in the army.

'Let me tell you about our village school. We have 300 children but only four toilets, one for the male teachers, one for the female teachers, one for the male pupils, and one for the female pupils. The smell used to be so bad the whole village stank, and I was embarrassed to bring Jewish groups here. Of course a foul smell in the village only reinforces the view some Jews have of "dirty Arabs". So the Islamic movement put in twenty new stalls. They also gave us six bus stops. Before they did that people waiting for the bus had to shelter from the sun and the cold in their houses, and would often miss the bus. These may sound like small matters to you, but they affect our quality of life.'

It seemed to me that what Kamal was telling me was that Arab villagers were slowly emerging from a period of inertia. A spot of self-help in Umm el-Fahm would soon dispose of the garbage in the streets, even if it couldn't improve the sewage system. Arab dependency is nothing new. From Turkish times onwards, they grew to expect that their affairs would be managed by remote governing authorities. The wider political context was such that there was no point in boldly taking the initiative. What puzzled me was that since the discrepancies between Jewish and Arab facilities were so great, it was odd that the intifada had not crossed the Green Line.

Kamal replied: 'The intifada hasn't spread to Israeli villages because we are loyal. Also life is less difficult here than in the Territories. We aren't under military rule. But when I hear stories from my relatives of the days before 1966 when we *were* under military government, I feel intifada in my heart. Perhaps also we are a bit spoilt. We're used to a certain standard of living and don't want to share the privations being endured in the Territories.'

Kamal, like Jewish politicians, was probably playing down the extent to which the intifada has spread inside the Green Line, for there have been hundreds of reported incidents of the throwing of stones and petrol bombs, though on nothing like the scale experienced in the Territories.

With the hospitality that is almost inescapable in Arab households, Kamal urged me to stay to dinner, but I had an appointment in Tel Aviv and left the village as I had entered it, serenaded by dozens of piping children.

Both hard-line Israelis and sophisticated Israeli Arabs believe that true equality between Jew and Arab in Israel is unattainable. The political scientist Rafi Israeli has written: 'The wishful thinking which accompanies the vision of a liberal democratic Israel where the Arab minority can achieve parity with the Jewish majority, simply runs counter to the fact that most Arabs in Israel cannot be true Israelis.'[17] By 'true Israelis' he means that they cannot be Jews in a Jewish state. Dr Majid Al-Hajj agrees that Israeli Arabs can never achieve total equality with their Jewish neighbours, but he does believe that the situation can be improved. 'There are specific problems that need to be and can be solved. I'm talking about education, resources for Arab communities, helping graduates to find jobs. We have a dangerous situation; 40 per cent of graduates are unemployed or in blue-collar jobs. We have an alienated elite in our community. Nor is it easy for us to emigrate. What we want is integration. We want to operate within existing institutions. But if this is refused us, then the only alternative is some form of autonomy. The government has to realize that they have to relate to Israeli Arabs as well as to Jews, and they have to provide a model of coexistence. If they can't even live harmoniously with their own citizens, how can they form a bridge to the Arab world around them?'

Herod, two thousand years ago, picked a wonderful spot for his new city of Caesarea. Sea breezes flicker across the dunes and the salt air of the Mediterranean moderates the Levantine heat. Dedicated to Augustus Caesar, Caesarea was the principal port of Judea and the residence of Pontius Pilate. In 640 it passed from Byzantine into Arab hands, from which it was wrenched by the Crusaders in 1107. By 1265 the city was back in the hands of Moslems, who destroyed most of it. Five hundred years later the Ottomans plundered what was left of Caesarea in order to embellish their own buildings. The ruins might have been left to sink gradually beneath the dunes had it not been for the kibbutzniks from Sdot Yam nearby, who began to excavate them.

The principal Roman relic is the steeply pitched amphitheatre, but this has been largely rebuilt. Scattered across the open space between the stage and the sea are broken columns lying on their sides like fallen trees. Only the security fence around the site – like the power station at Hadera just down the coast, an eyesore one has no choice but to accept – mars the exhilarating view.

The bulk of the site consists of the Crusader city. The elegantly vaulted gatehouse is mostly intact, and one of the most stirring Gothic buildings in Israel. The Crusaders reused the Roman remains, so their city is graced with recycled capitals, columns, and paving. The interior of the city is now little more than an expanse of stone and sand with only a few foundations protruding. But there are more substantial ruins closer to the sea: a Roman warehouse, and the never completed Crusader church with its three rounded apses. From the fishing jetty one can gaze northwards up the jagged coastline, with the ruined walls of the city blending into the rocky shore.

The present century's contribution to Caesarea takes the form of crass conversions of some buildings along the shore into shops and restaurants. Have coffee at Herod's Palace Café, and buy trash souvenirs at the Glass Centre Factory Showroom. These buildings are identified by large signs made of crude black lettering on orange backgrounds, which from a distance resemble discarded orange peel. These emporia were failing to rake in the cash on this bright March morning. Apart from forty male soldiers being given a conducted tour by an attractive female soldier, the only tourists were a few Japanese who were introducing shorts-clad Israelis to the sartorial charms of the blue suit and the 1978 Bucharest-style plastic hat. The Japanese were confounded by the *embarras de richesse* in the souvenir shops. Should they take the fake antique glassware with silver appliqué or lash out on the ill-proportioned smoky-glass goblets, or economize on one of the candles that resembles lethal tropical fruit?

There's a more compact and far more ancient site at Megiddo, about fifteen miles inland from Caesarea. The ruins cap a large mound that rises above the edge of the Jezreel Valley. The Canaanites got here first, almost 5,000 years ago, and left behind a temple with a round altar. In the tenth century B.C. King Solomon built a palace at Megiddo, and in the following century King Ahab stabled his chariots here. It was still a military site in the twentieth century; Field Marshal Allenby used the fortress as a base for fighting the Turks in 1917, and it was from here that, during the War of Independence, the Israelis launched successful attacks on Arab forces.

Megiddo is of course none other than Armageddon, so there are more battles to come. When I tramped around the site, Israeli jets flying low overhead to and from the large air base in the valley contributed suitably cataclysmic sound effects. I found the ruins hard to read, despite the many explanatory signs and charts. However well documented, a hole in the ground is still a hole in the ground. Looking at the fragment of a score is not the same as listening to music.

Everywhere else in the world it was International Women's Day, and in West Bank towns Israeli troops and border police were busy breaking up marches by Palestinian women, but here on Megiddo it was National Centipede Day. I have never seen so many of the horrid creatures in one place, and their frolicking almost put me off visiting the main attraction of Megiddo, the sinister subterranean tunnel built 2,000 years ago as part of the city's water supply system. But I gritted my teeth, said farewell to the sunshine, and trotted along the tunnel and out the other end.

I was meandering in a circuitous way, down from Galilee towards the fleshpots of Tel Aviv. I had spent my first night in Israel in Tel Aviv and was in no hurry to return. Founded in the early years of this century, Tel Aviv does not charm visitors with its architectural distinction. In its early years, to judge from the sepia photographs on display at the historical museum, it resembled Dodge City without the guns. The town was a cluster of humble houses and shacks, populated by men in hats who spent their days standing about aimlessly in the streets, attending minor civic occasions, such as the inauguration of a new extension ladder for a fire engine.

This early stage of urban development seemed to have been exhausted quite rapidly, and the houses on the dunes soon transformed themselves into the blank-faced city by the sea. A. B. Yehoshua, who wisely lives in Haifa, has left a vivid description of 'Tel Aviv in winter – a town without drainage, no outlets, spawning lakes. And the sea beyond, murky and unclean, rumbling as though in retreat from the sprawling town.'[1]

And that's in winter. Try it in summer, when the hot desert wind, the *chamsin*, drives urban Israelis to desperation as they fail to keep cool. Amos Oz summed up the appeal of Tel Aviv in July in his story 'Late Love':

'Before we built a city on this spot the sand dunes stretched right down to the beach. The desert touched the sea. In other words, we came here and forced these two furious elements asunder. As if we poked our heads into the jaws of the sea and the desert. There are moments on hot summer days when I have a sudden feeling that the jaws are trying to snap shut again.'[2]

Tel Aviv is little more than a grid of streets lined with peeling stucco houses and small business blocks of stained concrete and crooked lintels, with signs askew. Even its fans admit it has no personality. Tel Aviv has that hot-climate look of cities where the humidity marks all surfaces with smears like sweat patches on a shirt. Many of the apartment blocks are on stilts, with overhanging balconies, most of which are fronted with shutters and sliding blinds that offer permutations of extra rooms, cool caverns or washing-line space, according to the demands of the season. On pedestrianized Nachlat Binyamin, some balconied stucco houses have been freshly painted in bright pastels, lilac and beige, showing what could be done if anyone could be bothered; though most of the concrete apartment blocks are incapable of being brightened up. There are a few zippy but anonymous modern hotels and offices. The airlines usually manage to erect a building that doesn't droop with fatigue within two days of completion, and the beachside hotels are solid enough. Some of the inhabitants seem to be peeling along with the buildings. Along Hayarkon, the coastal road that follows the shore from the Yarkon River all the way to Jaffa some three miles to the south, you see not only Scandinavian beach bums looking for winter sunshine, but elderly Moroccans stumbling along in army fatigues, and old couples sitting on benches watching the buses emit exhaust, just as they did on Broadway when they lived on the Upper West Side.

Of course it doesn't matter what Tel Aviv looks like. It's a city of street life, not of vistas or façades or palaces. It's where Israeli secularism runs riot. Women can wear their shortest skirts, and you won't find a howling mob of porridge-faced *haredim* outside your front door if you keep your café open on Shabbat. You'd be more likely to find a howling mob of frustrated *kibitzers* clutching chess boards outside your front door if you decided *not* to open on Shabbat. A *kippa* is a rare sight outside the ultra-Orthodox stronghold of Bnei Brak, which unlike Mea Shearim, is far from the town centre. There are a few missionary outposts of the Orthodox in downtown Tel Aviv, but they are pleasantly inconspicuous.

All of Israel is cosmopolitan, but nowhere more so than Tel Aviv. There are Hungarian and Polish and Russian bookshops, as well as Yemeni restaurants where you can actually eat well. In Tel Aviv you don't have to look like a kibbutznik to blend in, and elderly people in particular seem content to live as though they were still in Vilna or Prague. The Germans are fairly easy to spot, especially the women, who wear sturdy shoes and blouses adorned with a brooch. The Hungarians dye their hair and dress in stronger colours. Some of the Russians still wear cheap leather or mock-leather blousons and flat peaked caps, while Russian women take great pains to coif their hair so that it becomes indistinguishable from a wig. There are indications that many older people find it difficult to make ends meet on small pensions in cramped apartments in an inflationary economy. They wear mismatched clothes, for clothing is expensive in Israel and taste has to be a secondary consideration.

There is no clear boundary between shop and street. Façades fold away so that shoppers can wander in to flick through the racks of oversized spangled sweaters or whatever other merchandise, usually in execrable taste, is on offer. The celebrated Jewish appetite is well catered for; every ten yards you will find a snack bar, a juice stand, an ice cream parlour. Next to a bus stop on Allenby, a shop selling cassettes blares Israeli rock music, which vies for hideousness with Hindi rock music, onto the street. Nobody notices, as the clamour blends in with the other street noises, bus-roar and car-hoot and the hoarse yells of lottery ticket vendors. Along Hayarkon and among the food and drink complexes near the big hotels, there are pubs, but they cater mostly to the tourists. In Tel Aviv, as elsewhere in Israel, you encounter hardly any native drunks. Men throwing up in the street are invariably imports from northern Europe.

Perhaps because there are one or two Jews in Hollywood, Israelis have access to all the latest movies. For months after my return I was able to dazzle friends with lucid critiques of movies just opening in London that I had seen months earlier in Israel. My first experience of Israeli movie-going was perplexing. In Jerusalem I had gone to see *The Unbearable Lightness of Being*. After two hours the film came to an abrupt end with the amorous reunion of the protagonists, and the lights went up. I left. It was only later that night, when recalling the plot of the book, that I realized I had probably mistaken the interval for the conclusion. So the next night I returned to the cinema at the same time that I had left it the night before and explained to an unconvinced manager that I had made a mistake because of my unfamiliarity with local customs and should therefore be allowed to see the second half of the film gratis. At first he said no, but I persisted and, since there were only five people in the cinema anyway, he let me in.

In Tel Aviv I aimed higher, by attending the Israeli premiere of the controversial film about gang rape, *The Accused*. This was the hottest show in town, so I turned up at the cinema well in time, but was amazed to find the place deserted. Had I made a mistake? I asked one of the five other people in the auditorium. No, no, they assured me; in fact the showing is sold out. The lights dimmed, and the ads flashed onto the screen. Some were American advertisements with an Ivrit soundtrack, others were Israeli originals, all of which featured a bunch of cute smiling kids singing a jingle. People trickled in for fifteen minutes after the film began, but settled down soon enough. It was midnight by the time I left the cinema, but I could see enormous queues waiting for the next screening, and the streets were blocked with traffic. Friday night in Tel Aviv. While Jerusalem prays, Tel Aviv plays. Hayarkon was jammed with cars and you couldn't get a table at the restaurants. On Dizengoff, the street in Israel the *haredim* would disapprove of most, the pavements and snack bars were packed with teenyboppers, many of whom commute into Tel Aviv on Friday nights. Ten new night clubs have opened in the past year, and all are thriving. Down in south Tel Aviv, a drab commercial area, garages and workshops are transformed at night into dance halls for weddings and other celebrations. Down here you can make as much noise as you like, as there are no neighbours apart from rats and beetles, and they don't phone the police to complain.

Nevertheless, everybody was up bright and early on Saturday and heading for the beach. The sands are separated from the bustle of Hayarkon and the promenades along the street by raised areas with stone benches and ramps that lead down to cafés, at which old women knitted while their husbands read the newspapers. The beach, though large, is noisy. Israelis are not self-effacing by temperament and the younger specimens are addicted to batting balls around with wooden paddles, which produces a thwacking noise about as restful as hammering fence-posts into the ground.

Set back from the beach on Hayarkon, between the Hilton and the Carlton, is a weird Gaudi-esque house. It was put up a few years ago by an Israeli builder who always longed to have the house of his dreams, and very strange dreams they must be. The building is a basic Tel Aviv apartment block on stilts, but it has been encrusted with white plaster on its sea-facing side; this swathes the balconies and functional units such as water towers, stabbing jagged white fingers into the air, their random pointing suggesting the whole building has been involved in a motorway pile-up. More white plaster is moulded over the sides of the house, with the edges seemingly pulled or torn out so as to allow views from the windows. On the street side a wild rural landscape has been painted in rather flat colours on a panel extending the full height of the building; large holes have been punched into the panel like chaotic origami. Other surfaces are rendered in sculpted, sand-blasted concrete or the most shallow bas-relief. The metal railings by the entrance are a grotesque parody of Art Nouveau. The atrium of the interior is supported on columns, each of a different design, while just outside the house is a sculpture of a bench with two people sitting on it gazing at the building. There were long wrangles with the municipality when the house was in the planning stages, but eventually permission was granted. There are undoubtedly people who loathe the house, but nobody is indifferent to it and I often saw small knots of passersby stopping to take a closer look. In a city as architecturally blank as Tel Aviv, that is worth having.

On Saturdays the cafés are busy, but not as busy as on Fridays, when the weekend begins. At noon on Friday a megavolt sound system is installed on Nachlat Binyamin and lets rip. There is dancing in the streets. Complaints from the neighbours too, I dare say, but the weekly festival has municipal blessing and attracts hundreds of revellers. A similar scheme operates in northern Tel Aviv, but there the programme is more classical. On Friday afternoons old-timers gather at the Bonanza café on Trumpeldor, near the cemetery, and there they sing the old songs from the pioneering days and the War of Independence. Everybody knows that certain people gather, week in, week out, at the same café; there they have the same conversations with the same circle of friends, sip the same coffee and nibble on the same cakes.

Since Tel Aviv is the country's major centre of publishing and journalistic life, a great deal of activity whirls around the Writers' House and the

Journalists' House on Kaplan Street. Both clubs contain restaurants which serve the same function as the intellectuals' cafés. Everyone discusses politics, which in Israel are so gloriously volatile. In the evenings there are lectures and literary evenings, just in case a Tel Aviv resident is short of something to do. My evenings were usually spent in one of the Yemeni restaurants near the market. I was tempted to eat at one of the hole-in-the-wall places, just a few tables under an awning over the pavement, but that was to risk being served lung on a stick. Instead I went to one of the more formal restaurants such as Gamliel or Meganda, where the food was good and the henna-haired waitresses, slender of build and high of cheekbone, even better. Perhaps the grilled meats at the Meganda weren't quite as tasty as I thought at the time. It's just that when I recall dives like the Romanesc near City Hall, which featured Steak Antricot and Spinal Chord, I can't help thinking fondly of the Yemeni places.

One would expect Tel Aviv to be chaotic, but it isn't, even though parking is almost impossible. Everybody wants a parking place outside their apartment block, and that cannot be arranged. This is a major talking point in which I could take no interest. The answer to the problem is to have fewer cars, but that's not the answer anybody wants to hear. The city can also become dirty, for after the winter months it is unlikely to rain for eight months and the grime doesn't get washed away. The street sweepers mostly come from the Gaza Strip, and if there is trouble down there and they can't get to the city for a few mornings, the streets remain dirty and the garbage isn't collected. Most residents seem to think that the mayor, Shlomo Lahat, does a good job. He is a Likudnik, but doesn't act like it, and in 1990 was urging the government to begin official talks with the PLO. He is admirably dismissive of pressure from the Orthodox to close the city down on Shabbat. With his slender, almost pinched face, and white hair, he resembles Johnny Carson. Mayor Lahat is given to grand cultural gestures the city can't really afford, but nobody seems to mind.

There's a street in Tel Aviv, near the lower end of Dizengoff, that looks much like any other downtown residential street. Until you look upwards, and see that one of the roofs is forested with radio masts, not to mention two enormous satellite dishes. This is the home of Mickey Gurdus. I went to see him after my afternoon in Kafr Bara, and found him at home, an easy-going man with receding greying hair and a beaming smile. He is usually at home, and never takes holidays, for his profession is to monitor broadcasts from all over the world. It's a job Gurdus inherited from his father, a Polish-born journalist who worked in Berlin and Warsaw until 1939, when he made his escape to Romania and thence to Palestine. Confined to a wheelchair, Gurdus senior decided to monitor radio broadcasts and pass the information on to European newspapers. Mickey Gurdus does much the same, only his clients tend to be major American television networks.

We sat in his office, a small room lined with vast banks of electronic equipment. There are stacks of tuning and receiving equipment, four televisions, full-sized and miniature, a globe, a fax machine, a world clock, numerous small lamps, and a chaos of wires beneath the desks and tables. The non-electronic universe is represented by bundles of newspapers and files, a squadron of model airplanes suspended from the ceiling and, on one wall, stickers advertising the countless news stations and networks which he supplies with information. While we talked the television flickered. He hit some buttons, and, one after the other, we watched, late on a Saturday afternoon, the CBS Morning News, a cabaret from Chile, a Libyan soccer match at which there were no spectators, and a concert from Moscow – 'second channel,' Gurdus remarked, as though apologizing for the dullness of the programme – as well as European satellite broadcasts. With more effort he could have pulled from the sky television stations from China and central Africa. To assist him in his work, he has acquired a working knowledge of Arabic, English, French, German, Russian, and Polish. I asked him whether this endless listening and watching doesn't induce rapid fatigue.

'Fatigue?' he wondered. 'On the contrary. I get restless when it's quiet out there. If I go out in the evening, I take a short wave radio with me, to make sure I don't miss anything, and I also video any programmes I need to watch.'

Gurdus comes into his own when a hijacking is taking place. He calls in interpreters when he is monitoring, for example, broadcasts from Iran, and he has the edge over his competitors at the BBC and other networks because he knows where to look for relevant information, though he occasionally comes across news items by pure chance. Some of the information he picks up is sensitive, especially from Israeli military sources, so he has to check with the military censor before passing it on to his clients.

'The possibility of missing something must be a nightmare for you. How do you sleep at night?'

'I sleep beautifully, and I do miss things. I was tipped off about the Israeli raid on Entebbe, but I was ill in bed and ignored it. For me this is a good way to make a living, and it's getting easier all the time, as the technology keeps improving. I do monitor aircraft and military communications, but it's not all hijackings and politics. Everybody knows that

I get worldwide sports results quicker than anybody else, so in Israel I've become a one-man sports centre. The Israeli football coach comes here to watch overseas matches so he can assess the opposition before an important international.'

Gurdus is at the centre of a vast electronic hub, but there are times when Tel Aviv seems cut off from the rest of Israel. There's a strike on the West Bank tomorrow? Who cares? My favourite café will still be open. Some crazed children in Mea Shearim have stoned a tourist carrying a camera on Shabbat? So what? My wife is still going to put on her bikini and lie on the beach all day. Occasionally the harsher realities of Israeli life do impinge on this serious but hedonistic city. Walking down Dizengoff one morning, I found King George Street cordoned off by the police, who had found a suspicious object on the pavement and had called in the bomb disposal squad.

And there is an underside to life in Tel Aviv. Everybody knows that Arabs are brought into town each day to do the jobs nobody else wants to do: street cleaner, kitchen slave, construction worker. Arabs from the Territories may not stay overnight within the Green Line without permission and are supposed to return each evening to their homes. Many do not, for it is simply impractical, especially if one is working in a restaurant that stays open until midnight. Employers provide basic overnight accommodation for their Arab workers, and the authorities usually turn a blind eye. This has provided an opening for that unsavoury political party, Moledet, which has made something of a stunt out of running to ground Arabs staying illegally in the city and turning them over to the police, with the sanctimonious justification that they are only making a citizen's arrest and requesting the authorities to uphold the law. At the same time the Shas-dominated United Religious Front was distributing leaflets calling for an Arab-free Tel Aviv on the grounds that the Arabs 'steal municipal resources'. Fortunately the citizens at large seem impervious to these more vicious expressions of right-wing zeal.

Tel Aviv is not a city for nature lovers. Greenery is scarce. There's a patch at the park along the banks of the polluted Yarkon, and another in Ramat Gan. The main attraction, the sole attraction of Ramat Gan, is the safari park, which was opened in 1974. There used to be a zoo near the municipal buildings in Tel Aviv, but nobody cared for the smell and, besides, the land was too valuable to be squandered on a bunch of animals. So the authorities moved the zoo out to Ramat Gan. This, in the words of the safari park's curator, Amelia Terkel, 'was an unusually sensible decision for this crazy country to have made'. The park has been a success, and now the municipality of Ramat Gan wants to acquire it from Tel Aviv. Naturally they can't agree on the price, and have been wrangling for two years. Consequently, the zoo has been without a director for two years, and no decisions on major new projects can be taken.

The 225-acre park replicates an African terrain, complete with water holes. Visitors may drive through the park and inspect the wildlife from the safety of their vehicles. The first beast I saw from Mrs Terkel's car was a chicken. Then I spotted a pile of impressive droppings, deposited by some of the thousand animals in the park. We turned a bend and I saw them all: the hippos, the thirteen white rhinos, the eland and gnu, Thomson's gazelle and the foul-tempered zebras. Had I come two days earlier I would have seen an additional zebra, but one of them had been attacked, fatally, by a cross rhino.

The park is especially proud of its white rhinos which, thanks to horn-craving poachers, are fast becoming extinct. Not only is the horn reputed to have aphrodisiac qualities, but it is a status symbol in places like Saudi Arabia, where a sword handle made from rhino horn wins the envy of princes. When Mrs Terkel told me that the zoo had recently sold one of its rhinos to another zoo for $5,000, I thought of a friend in England who was fascinated by rhinos. For $5,000 she would almost certainly want to buy one for her garden. 'Ah,' said Mrs Terkel, 'the purchase price seems low, but wait till you hear about the transportation costs.' Not to mention the British quarantine fees. I abandoned the idea.

While we were admiring the beasts, a truck came by laden with crates of fruit and vegetables. These, Mrs Terkel told me, come from the *souks* of Tel Aviv and Bnei Brak, where religious law obliges Orthodox traders to put aside a tithe of produce that may not be consumed by humans; instead they donate it to the zoo.

The zoo draws Israelis of every shape and kind. I watched a *haredi* family making its way slowly past the cages. (I calculated that they had paid in entrance fees NIS 68, or £23.) The ultra-Orthodox flock here during Passover, when religious Jews are encouraged to put themselves in touch with nature. During the Purim holiday the zoo organizes a parade of baby chimps and lion cubs, watched by an excited crowd of children in fancy dress and Purim masks. Educational programmes are important, and high school students are invited to work as volunteers. The administration employs an Arab guide and encourages contact between Jews and Arabs by taking kindergarten groups from both communities round at the same time. Many of the staff are Arabs from the Territories, and they are authorized to spend the night at or near the zoo, which means they may not see their families for weeks or months at a time.

At Ramat Gan there are capuchin monkeys intelligent enough to be trained to assist paraplegics with pressing buttons and opening doors. There is a white baboon called Einstein, and a camel called Hans. It is a fantastical world, only marginally more sane than the rest of Israel.

Those who live in Tel Aviv adore the place, even if its attractions are not obvious to visitors who do not wish to sit on the beach all day. Dan Bavly put it this way: 'I was driving to the airport the other day and got caught in a traffic jam. Nothing unusual about that, except it was one in the morning. It was annoying, but it was also impressive. It tells you something about the pace of this city. People work hard here, they're in their offices at seven-thirty or eight each morning, there's no siesta, and they're still in the cafés or driving around at one in the morning. The next day they'll be at work by eight as usual. Look at the amount of theatre you have in this small city. Most of it may be fairly awful, but at least it's there. People here have insatiable appetites, for culture and for food. Tel Aviv is a city of manic exuberance. It's a good city to live in, and fairly well run. It has its problems, of course, but the municipality does seem to respond to pressure. This may not be the cleanest city in the world, but it compares favourably with most other Mediterranean cities. The only drawback is that it's expensive.'

Another fan of the city is Yael Dayan, daughter of the famous general and a well-known polemicist of the left. She lives in Ramat Aviv, the suburb north of the Yarkon River where the university is located. Ramat Aviv blends suburban streets and luxurious tower blocks. Yael Dayan's father was a fanatical amateur archaeologist, and in her spacious flat near the top of a tower block many relics of civilizations past are on display, together with Oriental carpets, laden bookshelves, and plump cushions stifling every chair and sofa.

'What's good about Tel Aviv,' she told me, 'is that it represents normalcy within Israel. Jerusalem is atypical, it's a laboratory with all its different strands, like molecules that keep bashing into each other. It's a wonderful laboratory, but I wouldn't want to live in it. Israelis are Mediterranean and outgoing, they love the beaches and cafés, and that's why this is such a splendid city. It's informal, you need never be alone here, and it keeps going twenty-four hours a day. It's no accident that it's such a lively centre for the arts and the media. If a theatre isn't being used for a performance one evening, you can be sure there's a seminar or a reading of protest poetry taking place there instead. This is the place where petitions are organized and where people hold huge demonstrations against the government. Tel Aviv is a live-in newspaper.'

Jerusalem has no shortage of cultural activity when you consider that half the population won't touch the stuff for fear of being contaminated with beauty or truth or a fresh idea. But Tel Aviv is awash with it – concerts by the Israel Philharmonic Orchestra are wildly oversubscribed – and lesser cities such as Haifa and Beersheva also sustain excellent orchestras. Gordon Street in Tel Aviv is stiff with art galleries, and there are half a dozen museums in the city. Few other cities of 300,000 people can match this kind of vitality, although Tel Aviv also draws in the residents of neighbouring towns such as Herzliya and Netanya and Petah Tikvah.

When I went to the Tel Aviv Museum at six-thirty one evening, the place was still humming. Art appreciation classes were in full swing, with young and old Israelis seated on the floor in front of Picasso sculptures or Romney portraits. The museum is well stocked with lush Renoirs, dull Pissarros and Boudins, a good group of Ensors, a cheerful Matisse, two blood-warming Bonnards, striking Max Liebermanns, and an outstanding collection of early Soviet graphic art. The Israeli art section was closed that evening, so instead I looked in on a superb visiting show of modern sculpture from Dallas. Israelis don't appreciate their art in thoughtful silence. Around every piece, especially the more outlandish ones by Stella or Oldenburg or Lichtenstein, they were volubly expressing their opinion, damning and praising, snorting with derision or nodding with approval. The audience participation was as interesting as the art.

This lavish museum doesn't come cheap. In fact, it's broke. So broke that the administration, having deducted taxes from employees' salaries, neglected to pass the money on to the authorities. In July 1989 the taxmen pounced, and bailiffs ransacked the museum, carting off computers, television sets, and other office equipment as an inducement to the administration to pay some, if not all, of the NIS 5 million it owes the government. But this is a minor drawback: the whole country is living beyond its means, so why shouldn't the Tel Aviv Museum?

The visual arts flourish at a more modest level too. If many of the small galleries in Jerusalem are filled with kitsch projected at sentimental American Jews, this is less true of Tel Aviv, though an Israeli arts administrator assured me that it was difficult for the small galleries to survive.

'There are very few buyers of contemporary art in Israel,' she told me, 'so many galleries, after one or two successful shows, have to close down. Others are run by dedicated owners who aren't primarily interested in making money. The only major buyers here are the museums. The economic boom of the late seventies benefited the arts too, and it wasn't hard to find purchasers for Israeli art. Unfortunately, people who bought as a form of speculation were disappointed to discover that their purchases didn't increase in value. So they stopped buying.'

The Jerusalem Foundation set up the Artists Studio in Talpiot in 1980; this is both a gallery and a network of twenty studios for which individual artists pay only token rent. Many of these artists had previously used their kitchens as studios, and being provided with proper facilities allowed them to be far more ambitious. Quite a few have achieved international recognition, but only rarely can Israeli artists live off the proceeds of their work. Some do, such as Danny Karavan, the inventive sculptor who specializes in environmentalist work. Some teach. Others, such as Menashe Kadishman, adopt such strategies as working in Israel but selling in New York. In order to establish a reputation, Israeli artists have to show their work abroad as well as in Israel itself, where they must fight for attention from the handful of serious collectors. Many artists, such as Ya'acov Agam and Avigdor Arikha, are based in Paris.

'Another problem,' said the administrator, 'is that Israeli prices are too low in relation to the British and American markets. How can a Manhattan gallery make any money from a low-priced Israeli artist who lives in Jerusalem? That's why so many of our best artists live abroad.'

Most of the art I looked at along Gordon Street was of mediocre quality. Many painters have adopted a sub-Chagall style; others affect an attenuation of line reminiscent of El Greco at his most woeful. Gauguin, Fantin-Latour, and Cézanne are also popular models. I stared at dozens of thickly-daubed still lifes, appalling landscapes with a faint watercolour wash obscuring the lack of talent and precision, winsome headscapes, and calligraphic assemblages like mussels piled on a rock. Views of Old Jerusalem are popular even in Tel Aviv. There were some attempts at originality: Jack Jano's jumping tin men assembled from old soda tins, and wood men made of planks and splinters savagely nailed together. Unfortunately it was not a formula one cared to see repeated too often. Tin cans also featured, along with clothes brushes and cups and saucers, in the lively, engagingly pointless floor constructs of Simcha Speizer, displayed at the Marbat Gallery, next door to the Carnit Institut of Contact Lenses. Noemi Givon's gallery offered a show of accomplished calligraphic watercolours by Fima, a Jewish artist born in China in 1916, but resident in Paris since 1961. All these galleries are evidence of Israelis' passionate and widespread interest in the visual arts. Almost every home I visited in the country was a museum of sorts, with landscapes, calligraphic designs, bas reliefs – all 'original' though often in a rather dreary and commercial style – on every wall. Israelis may lack taste, but not enthusiasm.

Among the performing arts, modern dance has an enthusiastic following. At the Jerusalem Theatre I had seen two dancers, Liat Dror and Nir Ben-Gal, perform a curious work called 'Donkeys' in front of an audience that included many teenage girls as well as the Swedish ambassador. The performers lugged heavy blankets across the stage, presumably signifying pointless labour, and then whichever dancer was doing the lugging would break into a high-pitched whingeing diatribe about how awful it was to work so hard unaided. The dancers then swopped clothes and roles and repeated the whole thing. It was quite entertaining, given the slenderness of the material, and the dancing was fluid enough, despite much arm-flailing reminiscent of the willowy girls in the Feiffer cartoons.

In Tel Aviv I called on Michael Zukerman, a management consultant who also acts as impresario and business manager of the Tmu-Na Dance Theatre. Since its foundation in 1982, the company has performed both at the Israel Festival and at theatres in the United States and Europe. Tmu-Na has a regular core of performers and a recognizable style and dance language, but only survives with the help of grants from various foundations. I asked Zukerman why Israeli dance companies have acquired a fine international reputation.

'I'm not sure, but I suspect it's because dance is language-free. Tmu-Na, like some other companies, does use dialogue, but it's more a matter of signals than narrative. I find theatre more typical of Israeli society than dance, but it doesn't travel as well, with rare exceptions such as Sobol's *Ghetto*. Dance can be intensely Israeli in the sense that artistic expression is connected to the origins of the artists, but at the same time the success of the work isn't dependent on the audience grasping that national content. This only applies to companies like ours. Larger companies work with choreographers from all over the world, so their style is obviously more international.'

The performing arts are thriving. According to Zukerman, the percentage of tickets bought per capita is higher in Israel than anywhere else in the world. Theatrical companies can survive perfectly well by staying at home, and those that travel usually do so for the prestige it brings rather than because the fees are enticing. For dance companies, on the other hand, the audiences are much smaller, which is why it is tempting to look abroad to gain a larger following. Zukerman suspects that one reason why the performing arts are so popular in Israel is that there is a strong tradition of children's theatre, regularly attended by hundreds of thousands of children. This establishes the habit of theatre-going, to which Israelis remain addicted as they grow older. Despite the Israelis' passionate enthusiasm for the arts, the level of state support is extremely low. Public funding of orchestras, theatre companies, and dance groups, and of museums and libraries, amounted in 1988 to no more than NIS 40 million.

About half the plays performed in Israel are native products. Israeli theatre sprang from the Russian tradition, and this retarded the development of specifically Israeli dramaturgy. But that has all changed. Successful local festivals, such as the Acre Festival, have brought more Israeli works to the stage. 'Young Israelis actively want to develop their own culture,' said Zukerman. 'Their parents, many of whom came from Europe, weren't greatly interested in creating an Israeli culture. They were content with the culture they knew. But now the pendulum is swinging again and Israelis are taking a fresh interest in what's happening artistically in Europe. American influence was much stronger twenty years ago than it is now, and European works have filled that gap. After all, the vast majority of Israelis come from Europe or North Africa, not from America.'

Other culture freaks suggested to me that Israeli theatre was losing its sense of direction, if only because events move so fast in the Middle East that it is increasingly difficult for dramatists to reflect current preoccupations in their work. Opera has been moribund in Israel in recent years, though a private developer has renovated an opera house in Jaffa, where the first production, *La Traviata*, opened during my last visit to Israel.

The largest purchaser of the arts, according to Zukerman, is an organization called Culture to the People. Its artistic committee auditions productions as well as individual artists, and, if pleased with what they see and hear, will agree to distribute these productions or programmes to communities all over Israel. Out of about fifty performances that Tmu-Na will mount in any year within Israel, about thirty-five will be away from the cities. About 350 kibbutzim and other organizations can purchase productions or art shows or concerts from the organization. The purchase cost is always subsidized by Culture to the People, though the subsidy will vary. A high-quality but impoverished company may receive a 50 per cent subsidy, whereas a well-established troupe might only receive 25 per cent. The company receives its full fee, while the purchaser acquires high-quality performances for far less than the commercial rate. The organization also offers less formal events, such as talks by actors, which are cheap to present but can engage the interest of hundreds of people.

Until 1989 theatrical performances were subject to censorship, but in March 1989 the interior minister, Arye Der'i, announced that censorship would be suspended for two years, although film censorship would remain. This came as quite a surprise, since Der'i belongs to the ultra-Orthodox Shas party. The sting in the tail was that the minister also intended to strengthen the laws that would permit prosecution of those who give offence to individuals or groups. Since at any time in Israel dozens of groups claim to be offended by ideological or religious opponents, it will be interesting to see how Der'i puts this proposal into practice. The former journalist Amnon Ahi-Nomi was unimpressed by this outburst of open-mindedness: 'Abolishing censorship can't do Der'i any damage among *haredim* because they never set foot in a theatre anyway. At the same time it gives him a reputation for great liberalism among the wider Israeli public.'

Israelis are avid consumers of books, despite their high cost. Half the adult population reads at least one book each month.[1] The 120 Israeli publishers issue a phenomenal 4,500 new titles each year. In 1988 Hebrew Book Week organized book fairs in 32 small communities as well as the major cities. The annual Jerusalem Book Fair is not only a useful venue for publishers and literary agents, but a festival for Israelis from all over the country, anxious for a glimpse of the latest publications and guest writers. In 1989, for good measure, the organizers threw in an international conference on Spinoza to which the public was invited. Although the fair is an international forum, Israel has no shortage of fine poets and writers of its own, and rewards them with high status. Israeli writers are widely translated, which gives them an international presence few writers from other countries of comparable size, such as Norway or Hungary, can match.

'Israelis may be no more intelligent than any other people,' a friend remarked, 'but they are more involved. If a group of intellectuals publish a manifesto in the Friday newspaper supplements, the whole country not only knows about it, but discusses it. Friday's statement becomes Sunday's talking point in offices and taxis. Even a poem can generate this kind of controversy.'

I went to see the novelist A. B. Yehoshua, who also relishes his subsidiary role as controversialist. He was lured from Jerusalem to Haifa about twenty years ago and has no regrets. Admiring the view over the sea from his spacious flat on the slopes of Mount Carmel, I could quite see why. Although much translated, Yehoshua is wary of international fame.

'If you get too much of a reputation outside Israel, people become suspicious of you. Take, for example, Amos Oz. He's been attacked a great deal recently, and I think some of that has happened because he has acquired such a fine reputation outside the country. On the other hand, there are writers such as Elie Wiesel who have an international reputation – and a Nobel Prize – whereas most Israeli intellectuals don't think highly of him at all. It's very easy to acquire a good reputation in Israel. Write two or three good short stories and people will immediately know about it, because this is a small country. The literary community is very intensive and we all consume culture very heavily. When I was starting to write in the late fifties, every Friday six newspapers had literary supplements, all waiting for people to send in stories. And there were also four or five literary magazines. Now we have fewer. But on the other hand, publishing is becoming easier as the cost is lower than it was ten or fifteen years ago.'

I asked him whether he felt comfortable being both an acclaimed writer and a public figure.

'Zionism was founded by writers,' he replied. 'Herzl was a writer, a frustrated playwright. Most of the other early Zionists were intellectuals. From the very beginning Hebrew writers joined the Zionist movement and this is why they were so important to the movement. There was also the whole question of the renewal of the language. Unlike other nationalist movements, in the beginning we didn't have territory and we didn't have language. So writers had to provide the language. At the beginning of the thirties there were about 200,000 Jews here. In Poland alone there were three million. But by then the majority of Hebrew writers – Bialik, Tchernikovsky – were already here, working with the language, even though the great public for Jewish writing was in eastern Europe. And there has always been this tradition of the intellectual as a speaker, as a prophet.'

'I think of the early days here, the 1920s, the 1930s, as the time of the pioneers. How did they get on,' I asked, 'with the intellectuals sitting in Tel Aviv writing their poems and pamphlets?'

'The two were very much connected. The workers had a lot of respect for the intellectuals, who were really an integral part of the labour movement. So there was no tension. Even the right-wing writers, though there were very few of them, came out of the labour movement.'

Israel had changed enormously since those first stirrings of an indigenous literary culture. Today most Israelis are of North African and Middle Eastern descent. What kind of impact had that had on Israeli literature?

Yehoshua didn't hesitate. 'We increased our readership! The first generation that came from Arab countries, they didn't know anything about us, but their children are great readers, and the fact that there are such high sales of books here – it's unbelievable, far higher than in any other country – some of this is explained by the great boom of new readers. Some of the Oriental Jews were also beginning to write. If you try to describe the typical writer of the 1950s and 1960s sociologically, you would find an upper middle class Ashkenazi, left of centre, Labour-oriented, urban. Now there are writers coming from other layers of society.'

As Yehoshua described it, Israeli writers during the Zionist period and the early years of nationhood were at one with the aims of Israel's political leaders. But that was no longer the case, and I wondered when the ties had been loosened.

'From 1967 we began to quarrel over such matters as Palestinian rights. In 1977 we found ourselves with a right-wing government, but that for us was just another wave crashing over us. There was a whole group of writers, including Oz and myself, who were all the time entering into a very deep antagonism to the Establishment. Nowadays there are many people who think as we do and we feel less isolated than we did at the end of the sixties.'

'Did you feel alienated?'

'Never. We were in opposition but not alienated. I am free to say whatever I want, every newspaper is open to me, I often have to put off television and radio reporters who are asking for my views, I'm even invited to speak to the army. I can name another ten writers and artists in the same position. I have the same channels to the Israeli people as the prime minister. It's a wonderful position to be in, but very complicated in other ways – and not so wonderful. I gave an interview to *Newsweek* and before it was even published in America, Israeli reporters had taken one sentence from it – where I say I can understand how, without comparisons of course, how the Germans could say in the Second World War that they didn't know what was happening around them, as I can already feel the Israelis beginning to shut their eyes – and this sentence was on the news every hour and all the country started screaming at me. This happens all the time. We are in a constant fight. The problem for me is that too much attention is focused on us.'

'How do Arab writers fit in to the Israeli scene? Anton Shammas is quite well known outside Israel, but I can't think of any others.'

'Shammas is not an Arab writer. He is an Arab writing in Hebrew. But he is a special case, he's very integrated. Shammas is popular here and often writes in the newspapers. But most Arab poets are known only to an Arab public. There's an inflation among Arab poets. There are six or seven hundred of them. It's unbelievable how many there are just within Israel. We know their names, four or five of them, but the level of their literature is quite different. Theirs is a kind of ideological writing. The refreshing thing about Shammas is that he was putting the Arab–Israeli conflict into a wider and far more human context than the usual one. In most Arab writings about the discrimination against them we cannot recognize ourselves. They are so exaggerated. But the public for these writers is outside Israel, and there they cannot describe a Jew as a regular human being.'

Israeli writers used to be influenced by Russian literature, because that was the culture they grew up with. Nowadays, according to Yehoshua, the intelligentsia everywhere reads the same writers. 'Previous generations of Israelis spoke Russian or German better than they spoke Hebrew, but that's a thing of the past. So now we're reading translations of Kundera, Eco, Marquez, just like everybody else. Faulkner was extremely important to me, and indirectly to people who were influenced by my writing. Jewish-American literature was important at a certain time, Bellow especially, but less so now.'

'And how would you rate Israeli literature in a world context?'

'I would say we have not produced enormously great writers, but still . . .'

A poet widely regarded as Israel's finest, Yehuda Amichai, agreed to see me in his cool cave of a house in Yemin Moshe in Jerusalem, but it was not a comfortable talk. Perhaps his public reticence complemented the private poignancy and intimacy of his poems. He seemed supremely uninterested in the questions I was putting to him, and perhaps he was justified. He did note the lack of public support systems – such as Britain's Arts Council or the American network of writers in residence – for poets in Israel, but this was compensated for by the multiplicity of outlets for poetry, such as the Friday literary supplements. For someone who has written so brilliantly about Jerusalem, he had remarkably little to say about its special qualities, which he seemed to shrug off. Poets, of course, are not performing animals, and Amichai was under no obligation to be articulate outside his chosen medium of poetry.

I had hoped to learn something from him about the suppleness or inflexibility of Ivrit as a literary language. Earlier generations of Hebrew poets, such as Bialik, had been acutely interested in the problem of how to incorporate new terms into an ancient language, but this was not something that interested Amichai as a poet. He told me he was content to work with the language as he finds it. Ivrit, in his experience, is as receptive to rhyme or to formal structures or to free verse as most other languages.

Ivrit is based on ancient Hebrew, but was founded as a modern language by a Lithuanian immigrant named Eliezer Perlmann, who changed his name to Ben Yehuda. Hebrew in the 1880s was a literary language only, but he revived it as a spoken language, bringing it back, in Amichai's phrase, 'from a two-thousand-year vacation'. Ben Yehuda brought up his son to speak only Hebrew; at the time he must have been a unique child. Later immigrants were encouraged to trade in their German or Russian names for Hebrew ones. They often selected names that carried desirable biblical allusions or were taken from the towns and mountains of Israel or suggested prestigious attributes: thus Oz means 'strength', Lahat means 'blaze', and Amichai means 'my people lives'. In this way the programme of Zionism extended even into the names that newcomers adopted. Amos Elon has observed: 'In other countries, mountains are sometimes called after great men; in Israel men more often call themselves after great mountains.'[2]

The founders of Ivrit had to devise ways to incorporate new terms into what was essentially a biblical language. It was easy enough to give words such as 'television' a Hebrew lilt and transform them into *televizia*, but the guardians of Ivrit at the Van Leer Institute in Jerusalem, performing a linguistic policing not unlike that of the Académie Française, tried whenever possible to invent new words that would be unique to the language. Thus Ivrit has come up with its own words for Israel's flora and fauna and even for computer jargon, though such terms tend to exist side by side with the international ones. Nevertheless certain words slip under the net: the Ivrit for 'tights' is *tightsim*.

One drawback of modern Ivrit is that it is a lousy language for cursing, unless you wish to sound archaic and use biblical words such as 'harlot'. Even Yiddish is better for congratulations than for curses. So Israelis are obliged to borrow English, Arabic, and Russian swear words. My ear couldn't differentiate between curses and blessings, since Ivrit has always struck me as a remarkably ugly language. The sound of classical Hebrew is very beautiful, musical and intensely rhythmic. Not so Ivrit, which is harsh and abrupt. In Italy I am greeted with the seductive welcome of *buongiorno*. In Israel I was hailed each morning with *boker tov*. The nurse in a kibbutz is a *metapelet*. But gather two or more nurses together, and you have *metaplot*. A friend in Jerusalem, who herself spoke an exceptionally abrasive form of Ivrit, didn't disagree.

'Sometimes,' she told me, 'I wonder, I even worry, about the effect of our language on Israeli ways of thinking. Ivrit is short, it's laconic, and perhaps this conditions the ways in which we think.'

I asked A. B. Yehoshua whether Ivrit was a difficult language to use as a literary medium.

'The language is hard,' he agreed, 'but the way in which it functions is not without stylistic movement. The style is very short and condensed. But in terms of vocabulary we can't even try to compare Hebrew with the richness of English. Many words have entered the language, many words were invented, but still we are in a certain way limited in our vocabulary. On the one hand, the ancient, biblical part of the language can give you an immediate kind of evocation, something that you can't get in other languages. You can touch a word and a whole box of echoes emerges. But as a writer you have to be very careful not to drag in things that you don't want to take. The words are not clean, they are full of associations, but part of the language has such strength in its associations that you can play with these words as long as you do it carefully. At the beginning of the century, when Ivrit was invented, this play was done very openly. Then it was used so much that it became ridiculous. There was a period when people had to refrain from all words with rich religious and historical associations.

'I find the language is becoming a bit staid because we aren't receiving fresh injections from newcomers to Israel in the way we used to. One of the enjoyments of reading Shammas is that he is coming from outside, bringing the colour of an Israeli Arab to the language, and this was a completely new thing. He wanted to demonstrate how much Hebrew he knows, and there was one page where I found four words I didn't even know the meaning of. We also have a linguistic problem in that the country is so small. You can't retain the language of an area, a locality. In English you can listen to someone speak and characterize his region, his class. Not here.'

Einstein Road in Ramat Aviv leads to the gates of the university, a sprawl of low-slung departmental buildings separated by lawns and gardens, among which immense sculptures are strategically placed for maximum aesthetic impact. The architecture and the palm trees are reminiscent of southern California campuses, but not the promenades lined with Roman and Byzantine milestones and other antiquities. The buildings themselves present the usual roll call of benefaction found in almost all Israeli institutions, an outpouring of endowment. In the middle of the campus stands the Diaspora Museum. The museum, which was opened in 1978, only takes the story of the diaspora up to the nineteenth century, but a new wing under construction will bring the chronicle up to date. There has been tremendous wrangling over the content of the new wing. Should, to give just one contentious example, space be allocated to the large *Israeli* communities in the United States?

This immensely popular museum was intended to be an educational tool, to remind young Israelis that there are vital Jewish communities in the diaspora too. Its youth department seeks to ensure that every Israeli child is taken here at least once. The museum's founders felt strongly that after 1967, when Israel entered its macho phase, it was tempting, especially for Jewish youth, to forget that there had been such a thing as Jewish history between Bar Kochba's revolt of A.D. 132 and the Six Day War.

There are no original objects in the museum; models and replicas have been used throughout. If you want artefacts, you can go to the Israel Museum in Jerusalem. The Diaspora Museum is a slow walk through Jewish consciousness, examining in turn such aspects of Jewish life as the family, the community, the culture. Exhibits are supplemented with short films on such topics as life in eastern Europe, in Salonika, in Fez. Study areas allow visitors to explore family names and origins and Jewish music. Rather than lecture visitors, the museum tries to embrace them within specific environments. Jewish life is put into the context of the various cultures in which it was couched: Babylonian, Byzantine, Ottoman,

Yemeni. The final section, called Return, chronicles by means of rapidly changing audiovisual slides the various stages of *aliyah*, accompanied by stirring Zionist songs and overlooked by a large *menorah*. I found this concluding section vulgar in its triumphalism. Indeed, I didn't much care for the whole museum, which, while reasonably informative, also seemed manipulative. The conscious decision to keep texts to the minimum also seemed a curiously inappropriate one for so literate a people as the Jews, since it reduces the experience of visiting the museum to a succession of fleeting images. Adverse reactions such as mine do not trouble the museum authorities, who are content to offer visitors a multitude of messages; we are at liberty to select those we find sympathetic and to ignore the rest. The very diversity of reactions to the museum gratifies its designers, for some visitors accuse the museum of preaching Zionism, others of glorifying the diaspora.

Between 1919 and 1975 two million immigrants came to Israel: 55 per cent from Europe, 21 per cent from Africa, 19 per cent from Asia, and 4 per cent from the Americas. In the late 1980s there was much concern that the rate of emigration to Israel, of *aliyah*, was dropping sharply. The great waves of immigration from Moslem countries had more or less ended. Some Soviet refuseniks had come to Israel, but the majority of Jews leaving the Soviet Union headed for the United States. The same was true of the Jews leaving Argentina in droves. Idealistic teenagers and retired couples came to Israel from Britain or the United States, but the numbers were small, and most American immigrants tended to be the newly Orthodox who settled in suburbs such as Har Nof in Jerusalem.

It was not hard to explain why so few new immigrants were arriving. Political tension, the intifada, inflation, military service into middle age, terrorist attacks — these were sufficient to dissuade all but the most dedicated from starting a new life in Israel. Only the sudden increase in Soviet immigration in 1990, for which Israel seemed ill-prepared, began to reverse the trend.

Bringing the diaspora to Israel has always been the primary task of the Jewish Agency. After the establishment of the state, the Agency, which had been a kind of surrogate government before independence, should really have ridden into the sunset. But, in the manner of bureaucracies, it stayed put. It defines its role as the establishment of rural settlements; social amelioration and the development of vocational schools; investment in certain industries; the running of Youth Aliyah, which offers schools and other youth camps for socially deprived children; and the running of absorption centres for new immigrants, though this function will be handed over to the government in 1990. Since this will save the Jewish

Agency about $50 million, it has agreed to take over various matters now handled by the government: agricultural research and development, and running the Diaspora Museum and Yad Vashem, which almost went bankrupt in 1988.

Although the Agency claims not to duplicate any activities of the government, there does seem to be considerable overlap. The Agency is financed by diaspora fund-raisers, such as the United Jewish Appeal in the United States. About half the $800 million raised for Israel in the diaspora each year comes to the Agency, and some of that money is passed on to the World Zionist Organization, which also establishes, with the help of the government, rural settlements, including some in the Occupied Territories. There seems to be little difference in role between the Agency and WZO, and David Angel of the Jewish Agency expressed the difference as follows: the Jewish Agency 'plans for the Jewish future' and WZO deals with Jewish and Zionist education.

Both the Jewish Agency and WZO are strongly criticized for their top-heavy structures. The Agency's parliament, the Jewish Agency Assembly, is composed of representatives of all the fund-raising organizations and Zionist parties. The Assembly then elects and appoints a Board of Governors, a blend of seventy-five major donors and politicians. Every five years WZO convenes the World Zionist Congress, which consists of 400 delegates from Zionist parties and organizations, half of them from the diaspora. This Congress elects the seventeen members of the Zionist executive, but five of those seats are occupied by Agency dignitaries. The powers of patronage that go with a top position in either organization are immense; for posts that influence educational policies there is also jockeying between Orthodox and Reform. Both organizations appear to be composed entirely of officers, with only a paltry rank and file. The structure is being reformed, gradually. The Zionist organizations employ hundreds of *shlichim*, emissaries who spend a few years in diaspora countries supposedly recruiting new immigrants. The reforms will abolish eighty-five of those posts, which are costly to run and of dubious efficacy. The pressure for reform has come from the major donors, who are fed up with seeing their millions disappear into the great maw of the bureaucracies. Many fundraising organizations in the diaspora have set up their own offices in Israel, both to monitor the political situation and to keep an eye on the way their money is being spent.

Those who emigrate to Israel are often appalled by the complex bureaucratic procedures which await them. The government has a special ministry of absorption to deal with immigrants, but nothing is that simple in Israel. If you need help with housing, you must apply to the ministry of housing; but if you are applying for assistance with the mortgage, you must hurry along to the ministry of finance. To attend an *ulpan* to perfect your Ivrit, you must consult the ministry of education. To an Ethiopian who has just walked halfway across Africa the process may seem impossibly baffling. Nor is the situation improved by the constant infighting between government ministers, Jewish Agency officials, and lobbyists for special interest groups such as Soviet Jewry. Resources, as always in Israel, are limited, and there is no agreement as to whether money is better spent on new arrivals or in ensuring that families that have already been in the country for a few years are provided with the flats and jobs for which they have long been waiting.

Immigrants may spend three years as temporary residents before making a final commitment by taking up citizenship, though there is nothing to stop you applying for citizenship the day after you step off the plane. Once a citizen, you may vote, but if you are male and under forty-five you must also register for military service. To become an Israeli is not necessarily a process of trading an old identity for a new one. That was certainly the goal of the pioneers, who discarded their bourgeois ways, threw away their neckties, and absorbed themselves in physical labour on the kibbutzim. Not so the Yekkes, as the German immigrants are still known. Just because they were now living, often through force of circumstance, in a former malarial swamp in the Middle East, they were not going to abandon their *Kultur*. Perhaps they didn't click their heels, but in every other respect they remained thoroughly German, preserving such values as punctuality – not a word that appears in Israeli lexicons – and wearing the 'correct' clothes in all weathers.

New immigrants usually gravitate towards their former compatriots. If you are looking for British *olim* (immigrants, but the word is literally if somewhat mystically translated as 'those who ascend') you should head for the towns north of Tel Aviv, to Netanya or Ra'anana. Netanya, indeed, is sometimes referred to as Brighton on the Mediterranean. There is more mixing between national groups in development towns such as Karmiel, but it is often only the children of immigrants who are able to make a complete and effortless identification with Israel. One British immigrant said to me: 'My neighbours are from Morocco, from Brooklyn, from Iraq, from France. I may not choose to spend my evening at Iraqi folklore concerts, but our kids don't care about the ethnic origins of their playmates. That's as it should be, of course, even if my own kids sometimes strike me as foreign.'

Between 1965 and 1987 90,000 'Anglo-Saxons' made *aliyah*. Not all of them stayed. At present there are about 60,000 North Americans, 40,000

Britons, 15,000 South Africans, and 7,000 Australians.[1] There is some wry amusement about the all-purpose name given to them. Dr Amiel Ungar at Tekoa noted: 'They call us Anglo-Saxons, as though we had to come to Israel in order to discover that we could claim King Harold as an ancestor.' On arrival the Anglo-Saxons are assisted by organizations such as the British Olim Society, which helps new immigrants snip through the bureaucratic tangles and find jobs. The average rate of *aliyah* from Britain is 700 per year. Before 1967 the figure was closer to 400; it shot up to 2,000 after the Six Day War, and then dwindled. About one fifth of them returned to Britain. I asked Yigal Levine, who runs the society, what makes immigrants change their mind.

'I suspect it has more to do with financial factors than with social problems. About half the *olim* are in their late teens or twenties. They're starting their lives here in a strange environment. It's not always easy. Some go to kibbutzim, a very few to new settlements or development towns. In 1988 only 5 per cent of immigrants were over sixty-five, so it simply isn't true that most people who come on *aliyah* are looking for a place to spend their old age in the sun. Adaptation is rarely a major problem, especially for Brits, who are famously adaptable. And most *olim* are well acquainted with Israel before they move here. We Britons make good settlers, and tend to keep a low profile. Very few of us are prominent in politics, which I regret, as politics is about the only way one can make things happen in this country. The more liberal and left-wing parties think the Anglo-Saxon vote is important to them, but we don't really know how our *olim* vote. There are social difficulties, as the pace of life is more frenetic than in England, and Israelis don't share the British sense of reserve. They can seem horribly inquisitive, but they just enjoy getting involved with other people. The other shock for the men, even though they know all about it theoretically, is having to spend forty or fifty days each year on reserve duty.'

Alex Berlyne, a Mancunian who was literary editor of the *Jerusalem Post* and a professional observer of the Israeli scene, reminisces: 'I've been here forty years and I'm still confused about this place. But it's not as bad as Manchester. Manchester was full of grotesques. They had feuds at certain synagogues that went on for thirty years. In other respects life is quite hard here, and diaspora Jews have no idea how we live. When I'm in England I stay with an old school friend. He's made a lot of money and he's semi-retired. Last time I saw him he said to me: "I'm going to devote the rest of my life to finding the perfect sausage." Here in Israel if you can get two square meals a day and not get your throat cut you're doing quite well. It's just a different world. My friend in England has a luxury yacht, permanently crewed. Here we're just out of the orange-crate furniture stage.'

The immigrants who changed Israeli society more profoundly than any others were the so-called Sephardi or Oriental Jews. They came from such countries as Morocco, Tunisia, Egypt, Yemen, Iraq, and Iran, sometimes for economic reasons, sometimes because life had become too uncomfortable in increasingly militant Moslem countries. By the 1980s the Oriental Jews had become a majority within Israel. Their values, their culture, their customs, differ markedly from those of the Ashkenazim who had hitherto dominated Israeli life. Other than their specifically religious belief and culture, the two groups had little in common. The early Zionists thought of themselves as pioneers, building a nation from scratch. The country they fashioned was based on European models; its values were those of European social democracy. None of this meant much to peoples who had lived under a variety of authoritarian Moslem regimes and did not share the fundamental Zionist sense of mission. The new immigrants, pouring into Israel in their tens and hundreds of thousands, had to learn not only a new language but a new ideology, a new value system.

All Jews are equal, but some are more civilized, more tractable, than others, and the Israeli Establishment couldn't avoid patronizing the new-comers. David Ben-Gurion, in the late 1960s, could still be heard remark-ing: 'Those from Morocco had no education ... Maybe in the third generation something will appear from the oriental Jew that is a little different. But I don't see it yet. The Moroccan Jew took a lot from the Moroccan Arabs. The culture of Morocco I would not like to have here. And I don't see what contribution present Persians have to make.'[2] As recently as 1983 the left-wing politician Shulamith Aloni described Orien-tal supporters of Menachem Begin as 'barbarous trivial forces ... driven like a flock with tom-toms'.[3]

Such contempt was to prove extremely damaging. Some of the Ash-kenazim clearly believed that the Oriental Jews were tainted because of their exposure to Arab culture, an exposure that had turned many of them into fanatical Arab-haters. The Ashkenazi Zionists also mishandled the process of integrating these strange people into Israeli society. Young people from Morocco or Yemen were encouraged to shed their cultures, with their distinctive folklore and music and dress. Everything that had been familiar to these people was taken from them, and in its place they had to assume the styles and values of an essentially secular Zionism that bore little relation to the way they had been raised. Israeli officialdom paid no heed

COMING AND GOING · 239

to the different cultures of these immigrants. Moroccan families straight off the boat were deposited in towns where there was no work to be had and told to build themselves a new life. For many Oriental Jews the problems of adaptation proved too great. Slums developed in the new towns and in the old cities. Without a proper job, heads of family lost both their self-respect and the respect of their children, and the entire family structure began to fall apart. Children, unanchored, often turned to crime.

At the same time the government was seen to be welcoming European and American immigrants with the most generous benefits. Militant Sephardim reacted by forming an organization known as the Black Panthers, though it was less violent in aims and rhetoric than its American model. The great mass of Oriental Jews made their political strength felt in another, far more effective way: by denying support to the ruling Labour Party. Menachem Begin, who was as staunchly Ashkenazi in his background and culture as any other Israeli leader of the 1970s, skilfully exploited the situation. The Orientals, who dominated the development towns, made their political power felt at municipal levels especially. By 1984 Likud had won the electoral support of two-thirds of the Oriental Jews, who also form the backbone of the religious party Shas. The swing to the populist right within Israel is a direct result of the political power of the Orientals. There are still hundreds of thousands of Sephardim who have neither forgiven nor forgotten the disdainful attitude of Labour's old guard, and they would not dream of supporting that party, even though it could be argued that it was in their economic interest to do so.

Most Israelis believe the friction between the Western and the Oriental Jews is diminishing, and for one simple reason: intermarriage. The children of the Oriental immigrants have now grown up. Many marry within their own community, but an increasing number do not. These young people are Israelis before they are Iraqis or Tunisians. Moreover, many of their grievances are being resolved. They are still insufficiently represented at a ministerial level, but they dominate the development towns. One is less likely to find national neighbourhoods in the cities. Half the population of Tel Aviv is of Oriental origin, but that no longer determines where you live to nearly the same extent that it did twenty years ago. Yet despite the mixing of the cultures and the consequent diminution of antagonism between them, the Oriental Jews have tasted power and are not likely to relinquish it.

A Christian Israeli told me he still regards the influence of the Orientals as a time bomb within the body politic. 'This is gradually becoming a Levantine country,' he told me. 'It's a question of demography. Almost all the recent immigration has been from African and Oriental communities, with the exception of the Soviet Jews. The Ashkenazim are outnumbered, and the Sephardi majority do not share their values. The rich American Jews who give their money are funding Western-style institutions that will be less and less important in a Levantine Israel. The academics, the intellectuals, the people interested in art and symphony orchestras – they are Westerners, but they are now in a minority. The Orientals are resourceful and many of them are clever. The quarter of a million Iraqis tend to be hard-working and productive, the Yemenis are obedient and ask for little. But they just aren't interested in Western culture. And the Holocaust, which is so important for the consciousness of Western Israelis, means little to them.

'Menachem Begin promised the Orientals 10,000 jobs, and at the end of the day he gave them 20,000. They now fill almost all the lower civil service posts, and the police force. No Western Jew wants to be a cop for $450 a month. But for the Orientals, it means access to power, and once they've achieved it they use it to bolster their own community. A head of department who is a Moroccan Jew will only appoint other Orientals. They bear a grudge against the Ashkenazim who patronized them, and this is their revenge. Of course the Sephardim still need the expertise of the Western Jews. What worries me most is that as the Sephardim gain more power, peace becomes more remote. The Westerners, they want an accommodation with the Arabs. The Orientals, they don't care about the Arabs, and want nothing to do with them.'

This analysis seemed too schematic to me, as though the values of both Ashkenazim and Sephardim were frozen in time, whereas both have become modified by exposure to the realities of Israeli life. When I put these views to Yael Dayan, she was particularly critical of the conspiratorial tone. 'The Sephardi community has *not* achieved power, and those individuals who have done so are usually aligned to Western culture. The rise of Sephardi influence is not a political development but merely the effect of the passage of time. There's no objective there, no programme. These days the choice of culture is no longer so determined by one's background. You'll find Orientals at the Israel Philharmonic. And so-called Oriental folk music attracts lovely Israeli blond girls too. Look at popular music. Is it Sephardi? Is it Ashkenazi? There's no real clash of cultures. Think of it as an extension of pluralism. The cultures are blending.'

And that view seemed too balmy, too incompatible with the Israel of the development towns. I raised the issue with the educationalist Dr Moshe Dror, who put it into his own peculiar, even operatic perspective:

'People say that Zionism is a product of persecution, but it's really the product of a nationalist world view. In Christian Europe the Jews were the only non-players. In Moslem countries Jews were *dhimmis*, and while they may not have been first-class citizens, they were not persecuted because they were Jews. But in Europe the only non-Christians were the Jews. The Moors were around for a while, but in the fifteenth century they were pushed out for good. Until recently, most Israeli leaders have come from the old nationalist Zionist tradition of eastern Europe. They still focus on a post-Holocaust environment, and see the whole world as being against us. In the Moslem world Jews were allowed to flourish, though with constraints. Arab feeling against Israel is political, not racial, and the crisis in this country is that Israelis from Moslem countries are becoming Europeanized, and learning to share the European paranoia, the conviction that everybody hates us.'

If Oriental immigration has long been a *fait accompli*, this is not true of Soviet immigration. At least the Israeli government and the Jewish Agency hope it isn't true. Although the swimming pools of Los Angeles seemed a more alluring prospect to most Russian Jews with exit visas, a steady trickle – 10 per cent in 1988 – did make its way to Israel, although many of them later left for other countries. By 1989 the Soviet-Jewish population of Israel was estimated at 200,000. That the Soviet authorities placed obstacles in the way of Jewish emigration was not surprising when you reflect that those emigrants included 15,000 engineers and technicians, 3,500 scientists, and 10,000 doctors and nurses. The Israelis themselves estimated that it would have cost the country about $3 billion to train a professional corps of that scale and quality, so the arrival of these Soviet Jews was not just a boost to the country's morale but a major national resource.

At Ben-Gurion University in Beersheva, over 7 per cent of the faculty consists of Soviet Jews. Alex Yakhod's story is typical. His father was a diligent Communist and a professor of Marxist philosophy in Moscow. Alex's brother applied for an exit visa in 1971, whereupon their father was fired. The brother came to Israel in 1973; Alex and his parents followed two years later, to be joined in 1977 by other members of the family. Although Alex had learnt Hebrew underground in Moscow, he found it of little use when he came to Israel. Nevertheless he managed to complete his doctorate here and was offered a job at the university. To obtain their visas and face the pressure put on them and their families by the Soviet authorities, refuseniks such as Dr Yakhod needed huge reserves of tenacity and endurance. Some spent months or years in prison. Once in

Israel, it was hard for that pugnacity to dissipate. Most refuseniks have strong, hard personalities, and they find it difficult to adopt a new and more conciliatory role once they are settled in Israel. Their expectations of life in the land of milk and honey are often inflated, and they are ill prepared for the practical difficulties of Israeli life: housing, inflation, communication. Some of them, through no fault of their own, had not worked for years before receiving their exit visas, and when they arrived in Israel it came as a shock to realize that their professional qualifications had become rusty.

In the Soviet Union refuseniks were regarded as heroes within their own community, and given similar adulation by their supporters in the West. Once in Israel, they must cease to dwell on their sufferings, however genuine and however nobly borne, for there is no shortage of Israelis – camp survivors, torture victims, Ethiopian orphans – who have tales every bit as terrible as their own. Moreover, in the Soviet Union they were regarded as leaders within the community, but once they had reached the safety of Israel they no longer had such a role. Even their sense of Jewishness was jeopardized after emigration. Dr Yakhod elaborated: 'To be a Jew and to be an Israeli are as different as day and night. For years the refuseniks have been identified as Jews, and then overnight they had to become Israelis. Soviets who live in the United States are still Jews and like to identify with Jews. They remain conscious of antisemitism because of their constant humiliation in Russia, and as a result they feel overwhelmingly Jewish. For me, as an Israeli, this talk, which I hear all the time when I visit the United States, is meaningless.'

I visited a Russian family, now living in a Jerusalem suburb, who had been in Israel for only four months. Uri, who had been a refusenik for ten years, is a physicist and a tennis player of nearly professional standard; Natasha an immunologist. Her parents had left the Soviet Union at the same time as them, but Uri's elderly father had been refused an exit visa. Their flat was bare of all but the most rudimentary furniture, though one of the rooms was stacked high with boxes, which had just arrived from Moscow and contained much of their furniture, their favourite records, their books, their china. Their piano and motorbikes were still on the way. Natasha removed some dishes from one of the boxes and proudly set them on the table. As she poured coffee and handed round the cake, I realized that the family was using their china for the first time in their new home. They clearly had a deep need to maintain some kind of continuity with their life in Russia, despite the harshness and frustration they had experienced. Scarcely aware of these upheavals, emotional as well as territorial, was their two-year-old daughter, a vivacious little thing who still spoke only Russian. Indeed her parents had been reluctant to send her to kindergarten, where she would pick up Ivrit rapidly, but might, they feared, forget her mother tongue. Uri and Natasha were receiving free instruction at an *ulpan* for five months, but were finding it very difficult to learn the new language, and Natasha's elderly mother wasn't even bothering to try. Each of the two families receives a stipend from the government of NIS 700 monthly, plus an electricity allowance of NIS 100, and they may live rent-free for one year. After that, they are on their own.

Their response was clearly a complex one. The family displayed a mixture of warmth and reserve, gratitude and wariness. Profoundly relieved that their worst troubles were over, they also felt uncomfortable that they were so dependent on the generosity of the government and those Israelis who have befriended them. For them the greatest stumbling block seemed to be the realization that they were no longer Russians, and to be an Israeli was an unknown quantity. Uri in particular was taking evasive action, spending too much time on the tennis court and neglecting his studies of Hebrew. He was reluctant to face the fact that a physicist, however gifted, who hasn't worked in ten years is of little use. The family was toying with the idea of moving to a development town, where the cost of living would be lower, the environment more welcoming to a two-year-old, housing more easily available and jobs easier to find. A few months later they moved to the Golan, one more immigrant family making the painful transition to new identities and new lives, while unable to shake off their old memories.

In 1989 over 7,000 Soviet immigrants came to Israel, marking the beginning of what was expected to be a dramatic increase. Forecasts that about 100,000 more would be arriving each year during the early 1990s were greeted with joy – at least Israel will have a large-scale influx of fresh *olim* – but also with alarm. The absorption centres and housing facilities for immigrants are already stretched and inadequate; the volunteer groups who aid new *olim* will find it difficult to cope. It will cost, it has been estimated, about $3 billion to absorb the Russians, and this prediction has been met with alarm and indignation by some urban leaders, who observe that for years Israel's poor have experienced cutbacks in welfare and education, and rising unemployment. Now, all of a sudden, because Soviet Jews are to be the beneficiaries, huge sums of money, denied to the poor, will be made available. Within Israel, arguments rage as to the extent of the nation's preparedness for such a huge new wave of *aliyah*, and over how the absorption will be financed. Of course much of that money will be raised in the diaspora. For decades diaspora organizations have campaigned on behalf of refuseniks. Their goal of persuading the Soviet regime to permit Jewish emigration is being achieved, and now the activists, and all Israelis, must deal with the consequences.

Walking to synagogue with Dr Reuven Feuerstein, we passed a group of Ethiopian teenage girls. They were dressed in their Shabbat finery and looked very pretty indeed.

'To me this is astonishing,' said Feuerstein. 'Ninety per cent of the Ethiopians who came here were illiterate. There is no written Ethiopian history. Everything is preserved by means of the oral tradition. Their society could hardly have been more different from ours, yet see how well the Ethiopians have integrated! But they needed help to ensure they could function in our culture. People think that if you have a strong native culture it is more difficult to integrate into a strange society, but the opposite is true. The very strength of Ethiopian culture and tradition made it possible for them to integrate *without* losing their cultural identity.'

Rachamim El-Azar, an Ethiopian who came to Israel in 1972 and now works for Kol Yisrael, broadcasting in Amharic to his community in Israel, agreed that young Ethiopians have adapted rapidly to Israeli life. They are fashion-conscious and less interested than their parents in family closeness. Unattached to the main branches of Jewish heritage, they can blend easily into either Ashkenazi or Sephardi groups, whose rivalries and tensions mean nothing to Israel's 17,000 Ethiopians. Indeed, Israel as a whole must have struck Ethiopian Jews on arrival as utterly mysterious. The Ethiopians are unacquainted with the Gemara, the Talmud, the immense codes and commentaries that dominate Jewish theology. Their version of Jewish law was written down in Ge'ez, and consequently Ethiopians had no knowledge whatever of Hebrew, in any form. Festivals such as Chanukah meant nothing to the Ethiopians, isolated in their remote villages from the rededication of the Temple by Judas Maccabeus in 165 B.C. that is celebrated by the festival. Religious Jews from any other part of the world could follow a synagogue service, but not the Ethiopians. Zionism to Ethiopian Jews was a religious, not a political, doctrine; Zion was the land of milk and honey, not a bustling semi-Westernized nation state. On arrival they found that everything about Israel differed from their expectations: language, skin colour, food, the most basic customs.

Their arrival in the mid-1980s was laced with trauma. For many, the journey north across the Sudan was strenuous in the extreme; some died, and others came close to starvation. By the time they reached Israel, 80 per cent of them were ill. They were placed in absorption centres and given medical checkups, Hebrew lessons, and introduced to the mysteries of banks and government agencies, of domestic appliances such as the telephone, the refrigerator, the stove. Their efforts at integration into Israeli society were assisted by Ethiopians already settled in the country. Yet six years later 3,000 Ethiopians are still living in absorption centres, even though the government had intended to house them all within a year. About 1,800 children still live in youth villages. The Israeli government was vociferously opposed to racism, but some Ethiopians encountered it all the same, especially when they had to deal with private landlords. 'As far as I am concerned,' El-Azar said, 'anybody who harbours racist feelings is the person with the problem. I'm not bothered when somebody calls me a black.' More difficult to deal with than rare instances of overt racism was the paternalism of the authorities, who failed to appreciate how different the Ethiopian Jews were, and thus made many mistakes.'

Predictably, the older people found the adaptation most trying. Their societal structure was patriarchal. In Israel that structure was undermined. All of a sudden proud heads of families, who felt they were too old to master a new language, found themselves dependent on others for survival in an alien society, and this dependency gnawed at their dignity and pride. The older people had no function in life, and rapidly lost their zest for living. Traditional observances were impossible to maintain in an essentially urban culture. During menstruation, an Ethiopian Jewess would go to live in a separate hut from her family; and after giving birth to a daughter she would remain in isolation for up to eighty days. Such customs can't be respected when you are living in a two-room flat in Ashkelon. Despite the Ethiopians' commitment to Jewish rites and customs, pedantic Israeli rabbis cast doubt on the authenticity of their Judaism. Isolated from mainstream Judaism for 2,500 years, the Ethiopian brand is certainly distinctive, but these people are undoubtedly Jews and they resented the implication that they were not sufficiently kosher. The Chief Rabbinate argued that Ethiopian Jews should undergo 'symbolic' ritual conversions, so that there could be no doubts about their Jewishness. The Ethiopians found such suggestions offensive, and bitterly resented the rabbis' insistence, until December 1988, that Ethiopian Jews could not marry without a certificate of symbolic conversion. There was no such thing as a secular Ethiopian Jew, so to cast doubt on the validity of their religion was to question their entire cultural identity.

That identity is endangered in, of all places, Zion. Ethiopian Jews rarely attend synagogues; since their liturgical language is Ge'ez, they cannot follow the services. Some of them are losing contact with Judaism. Because the culture is orally transmitted, it becomes especially fragile in a new environment. The children of the Ethiopians, thrown into a world of popular music, examinations, and zany clothes, may not show much interest in their tradition, and their parents in turn may be reluctant to impart it to their restless offspring. According to Rachamim El-Azar, some of the younger generation are keen to prevent the loss of their culture: they are recording the oral tradition and preserving old costumes and artefacts. The fifteen-minute Amharic broadcasts every evening also help to keep the community together, though El-Azar has to fight for even this sparse amount of air time. Yet it may be a losing battle. There is no nostalgia for village life among young Ethiopians; they enjoy urban life and modern appliances, and wish to be part of Israeli society in general, not a freak show on its fringes. Nor is there any unity of purpose among the sixteen Ethiopian community groups. Instead they are at loggerheads, indulging in the infighting endemic to Israeli life but so wasteful of energies that ought to be focused on the problems of the community itself.

Most Ethiopians who have managed to come to grips with the whole notion of parliamentary democracy feel that Likud has been more responsive to their problems than Labour. It was Begin who made the deal with the Ethiopian government that began the exodus from the farms, and Likud that masterminded Operation Moses, which rescued thousands of Ethiopian Jews until the glare of publicity made it necessary to halt the operation before it was completed. Israeli Ethiopians believe that the government should be doing much more to help the Jews who remain in Ethiopia to leave. They contrast the well-publicized campaigns for Soviet Jewry with the hushed and ineffective diplomatic efforts apparently being made by the government on behalf of Ethiopian Jews. No one knows exactly how many are left behind: estimates vary from 8,000 to 20,000. Community leaders are constantly organizing petitions and demonstrations to keep the issue in the public eye and on the political agenda. The heart-rending issue is one of divided families: 1,800 Ethiopians now in Israel came here as children without their parents; a third of Ethiopian adults came here without their spouses. Moreover, old people left behind in the famine-stricken villages of Ethiopia now have no one to support them, and as their children, now in Israel, reach adulthood, they feel increasingly guilty about this. Nor is it possible to send money home, for there are no banking facilities in rural Ethiopia. The community leaders, while keeping up the pressure on the government to negotiate for the reunification of families, also realize that excessive criticism of the beleaguered Ethiopian government could easily be counterproductive.

★

The opposite of *aliyah* is *yerida*, and the opposite of *olim* are *yordim*. For in addition to the sharp decline in the numbers of diaspora Jews making *aliyah* – more than 8,000 in 1986 and 1987 – there is a startling rise in the number of Israelis spending long periods abroad. In 1987 120,000 Israelis left the country. Some are young people touring the world before settling down, some get married to foreigners, others may be postdoctoral students completing research at an American university. Nevertheless, many who leave do not return. Of those who left in 1986, some 35,000 stayed away. Some may eventually return, but I wouldn't bet on it. Nobody has accurate figures concerning people whose status is deliberately kept muddied, but according to Jewish Agency figures 375,000 Israelis live permanently abroad. In North America alone there are said to be 200,000 Israelis, including 32,000 graduates and 8,000 engineers, a resource Israel can ill afford to lose.[4] If Rina Bar-Tal, who heads an association for the prevention of *yerida*, is to be believed, a million Israelis have left since 1948: 600,000 live in North America, 200,000 in Europe, and 200,000 live elsewhere.[5] These figures are probably exaggerated.

There is a stigma attached to leaving the country, though as the journalist Tommy Lapid slyly observed, 'Of course, no one ever *emigrates* from Israel. They are always going to pursue further studies. Some years ago one wouldn't even speak to *yordim* if one encountered them when abroad. That's changed, partly because of the numbers involved, and also because attitudes have become less rigid. These days potential *yordim* speak of wanting to see the world, and this makes the decision, when they slide into it, much easier.' Other Israelis remarked to me that the astonishing thing was that the great majority of Israelis stayed put, despite the physical insecurity and the low salaries for professional people. Dan Bavly added: 'Israelis who live abroad tend to maintain their identity. They don't join local Jewish communities, they keep to themselves. Israelis aren't joiners. Because Israelis are so loath to immerse themselves within another society, it's very hard to say at what point they cease to be Israelis. It's their kids who become the emigrants. When Israelis who left twenty years ago come back for a visit, I find they speak the same colloquial Ivrit I do. I hardly notice they've been gone. But their kids! There's the difference.'

Most Israelis understand that the educational system produces many highly qualified people for whom there are no jobs. There is also a shortage of funds for research. Ambitious academics, especially scientists, have little opportunity to pursue complex research projects within Israel. According to Dr Alex Yakhod of Ben-Gurion University, Israel lacks the very costly super-computers now common in the United States.

Consequently, the foundations that hand out research grants are reluctant to give money to Israeli institutions, so scientists have little choice, if they wish to pursue their careers, other than to leave for American universities. Artists too, whether the painters already mentioned or musicians such as Yitzhak Perlman, Daniel Barenboim or Pinchas Zukerman, find that Israel offers them too small a canvas, too confined an auditorium. Many of the distinguished Israelis living abroad maintain links with their native country, either by making frequent return appearances or by investing in Israel. This is something that Israelis are prepared to live with, and it is arguable that a constant coming and going from Europe and America can do no harm to Israel's international image. Some people simply want to get out, and there are helpers awaiting them, as this blunt advertisement in the *Jerusalem Post* demonstrates: 'American male willing to enter into fictive marriage with woman interested in American citizenship.'

On the other hand, Israeli attitudes towards the diaspora are ambivalent. Israelis are educated in the Zionist belief that all Jews belong in Israel. So many of them feel that although it's good of diaspora Jews to keep writing cheques, they'd rather have the flesh than the money. Abba Eban, that most urbane of Israeli politicians, has written: 'Diaspora Jewry is the architect of our strength, but by withholding its human resources it is also the author of our weakness.'[6] Criticism of Israeli policies from diaspora Jews is often resented on the grounds that it's easy to attack from the sidelines. Dr David Clayman, who directs the American Jewish Congress office in Jerusalem, summarized the attitude of some Israelis as follows: 'Thanks for the money, but we can't get too excited about it, as it only represents a tiny percentage of the Israeli budget. We know that you need Israel to establish your own Jewish identity. After all, most diaspora Jews are not religious, and your identity as Jews is bound up with Zionism. In a way we're doing you a favour by taking your money.'

Amnon Ahi-Nomi observed: 'Israelis tend to see other Jews as cousins. There's a big debate right now about whether we are Israelis first or Jews first. People argue about it deeply, but it's entirely theoretical. It's not something we feel in our hearts. When Israelis go to live abroad, they remain Israelis. They speak Ivrit and move in Israeli circles rather than Jewish ones. Israelis don't feel they have to go to synagogue twice a year to feel Jewish. We pay Israeli taxes – we know who we are. We simply don't understand the diaspora's preoccupation with Jewish identity.'

However, of the $24 billion Israeli budget, about 25 per cent is spent on defence, and 40 per cent on servicing the national debt, which leaves only about $8 billion for administration, investment, and services. As a proportion of this latter sum, the diaspora's annual contribution of $800 million is far more significant, and the same goes for American military and economic aid, which amounts to $3 billion. Some of the most celebrated institutions in Israel – the Hadassah hospitals, the Jerusalem Foundation, Hebrew University, many museums, Youth Aliyah, and ORT training schools – would collapse without the generosity of diaspora Jewry. The political establishment recognizes this. When the Henry Ronson ORT school in Ashkelon was opened in October 1988 by the British businessman Gerald Ronson, who had contributed $6 million, the prime minister himself turned up to grace the occasion. The intifada has had little impact on contributions. Dr Clayman explained: 'Americans will never sell out mother. Whatever mistakes Israel may make, the wrongs against Israel are much greater. What's more, most of the big givers are politically on the right, and they believe the media are biased and they aren't swayed by news reports. They share the neurosis of being Jewish, that everybody is against us. The problems arise with younger Jews, who have different memories, and have only grown up with an image of Israel as a military occupier. This is a failure of Jewish education.'

Israel maintains good relations with the diaspora, not only because the money comes in handy, but because the diaspora, given the extent of *yerida*, is still seen as a potential supplier of manpower. Even though *aliyah* from the United States mostly consists of a handful of newly religious Jews, the Israeli government devotes much energy to keeping American Jews happy. It's probably more a question of public relations than money, but the money is important too. Perhaps the main reason why Shamir refused to go into coalition with the *haredi* parties rather than Labour in 1988 was that he would have been obliged to support amending the Law of Return, which would have enraged American Jews, most of whom belong to Reform or Conservative congregations. Shamir, for perfectly sensible pragmatic reasons, was not prepared to jettison this vast reservoir of support.

The Israelis are skilled at wooing the leaders of diaspora Jewry. American representatives, such as Dr Clayman, are accorded near ambassadorial status, an indication of how highly Israeli officials rate their importance. Dr Clayman, among other duties, organizes visits to Israel for American dignitaries, and gives them access to ministers and generals and other important Israelis. The visitors are then able, on returning home, to pepper their speeches with remarks such as 'As Shimon Peres was saying to me the other day in Jerusalem . . .', so the strategy does wonders for the ego of diaspora leaders. Clayman also publishes an impressive newsletter, *Congress Monthly*, that reports on a whole variety of issues relating to life in Israel and, unlike many Israeli publications, makes no attempt to gloss over the stresses and strains of Israeli life.

'Israel probably overestimates the importance of American-Jewish organizations,' he told me, 'just as antisemites do. Our organizations have the appearance of power, and AJC missions are received by heads of state. There are 420 national American-Jewish organizations, and one tenth of them belong to the major umbrella body, the President's Conference. In fact the AJC has only 50,000 members, yet we act, as do all the other organizations, as though we speak for six million American Jews. Perhaps we are taken more seriously than we deserve.'

The Israeli government is quite happy to squeeze the arm of the diaspora when it serves its purposes. The most blatant exploitation of diaspora loyalty took place in March 1989, during the worst phase of the intifada, when Yitzhak Shamir invited prominent diaspora Jews to the Prime Minister's Conference on Jewish Solidarity just two weeks before he was due to leave for Washington to present his nebulous peace proposals to President Bush. He cleverly enlisted the support of Shimon Peres, so that this propaganda exercise would not be viewed as an extravaganza for the sole benefit of Likud, even though that is largely what it was. Some of the guests did give speeches critical of government policies, or lack of them, but the conference did what it was supposed to do, which was to issue a vote of confidence in the government. There was fierce debate about the way in which the invitations had been issued. Some prominent critics of the government were not invited at all; others refused the invitation, on the grounds that they did not intend to be manipulated by Shamir. Although the position of those who refused to attend was entirely defensible, they also played into Shamir's hands by reducing the voices of opponents at the conference. Robert Maxwell, who for many years had not even admitted to being Jewish but has now reasserted his identity and written lots of cheques, and the immensely rich Vivien Duffield-Clore, who lives as a tax exile but keeps the money rolling in, were among the British delegates, while other far more distinguished British Jews were not invited at all.

Although Shamir permitted his critics to voice their views, he made it clear on the eve of the conference that in general he expected diaspora Jewry to toe his line. When asked whether public criticism of Israel was in order among diaspora Jewry, he replied: 'They should restrain themselves. Each one has his own opinion, and we will not prevent anyone from expressing his opinion at the conference, but after the state of Israel consolidates its own attitude, they should not fight against it, because this hampers Israel ... I am not asking total identification with all of my positions, with everything I say. I expect identification with the main things.' [7] There was no shortage of support for this line. The Swiss film producer Arthur Cohn was as blunt as any: 'Irresponsible criticism is counterproductive. It indirectly supports all those who put Israel's existence into question. It weakens the force of the memory of the Holocaust and strengthens, indirectly and unwittingly, anti-Israel and antisemitic circles.'[8]

Of course there has always been a debate about the extent to which Jews who choose to remain in the diaspora are entitled to voice criticisms of Israel. Since the arguments on both sides have been set out in my book about British Jewry, *The Club*, I shan't reiterate them here. Let me give instead an Israeli view, that of Amos Oz, which I suspect would accurately reflect what many Israelis think about this matter: 'It is your duty to state, Buddy, you are on the wrong side of the road. But whenever you say this I think there are two preconditions. First, to state the fact that you say whatever you say from the point of gut solidarity with Israel. Secondly, it would perhaps be a helpful thing to talk *to* the Israelis rather than *about* the Israelis.'[9]

Tel Aviv looks at its best when you're leaving it. From the edge of the promontory at Jaffa, a couple of miles to the south, you can look onto the curving bay, with the thumbs of the luxury hotels and apartment towers lining the shore. I spent a good deal of time in Jaffa, or, to be more precise, at its Arab bakeries. I developed an addiction for the miniature pizzas and hot pita breads smeared with olive oil and a dusting of piquant herbs. I would carry the food up the road that climbs the promontory, find a bench with a view, and munch away. Most of Jaffa is a sprawling slum, but not this corner. Some of the old houses along Yefet, with their thick stone walls and graceful pointed arches, lurk behind grim, character-less façades or high walls. A Church of Scotland school is painted a fitting blue and white, and opposite it dozes the lovely courtyard and garden of the former French hospital. Gardens and walls, old and secure, form a quasi-monastic retreat from the vibrant street life of the modern city just to the north.

After much of the predominantly Arab population fled in 1948, families from Bulgaria and Romania, followed by Oriental Jews, moved in. Attempts by Arab families to return to Jaffa and renovate the buildings where they had once lived were rebuffed.[1] The restoration and rebuilding of the old quarter on the promontory was undertaken by and for Jews. It is much applauded and much visited by tourists. To be sure, the whole area has been skilfully designed, with roads that take traffic through the area without disturbing it; the plazas rarely seemed crowded, and the restaurants that occupy the majestic stone houses offer many styles of cuisine and soothing views of the coastline and the shimmering sea. Yet the whole quarter is a lifeless re-creation of a neighbourhood that had died. It projects the same skilful revivalism as the Jewish Quarter of Jerusalem's Old City, but none of the haphazard liveliness of Arab Akko. The winding alleys seem sanitized, with ceramic house numbers suggesting a quaintness that is entirely bogus, and wrought-iron signs over the entrances to jewellery workshops, art galleries, and studios. The scrubbed stonework reveals the architectural simplicities of the old houses, an arch here, a corbel there, but also modern globe lamps and humming air-conditioning units. The old quarter forms a mock-picturesque backdrop to what is essentially a tourist trap in the form of such establishments as the Show-Biz Italian Experience and the Pubousel pub.

Israel has more artists' quarters than any other country I can think of. The quarters are plentiful, the artists less so. I visited Frank Meisler's gallery here, the home base for an international operation with branches in Jerusalem and London's Burlington Arcade. Meisler specializes in deftly executed silver- and gold-plated sculptures calculated to make visiting American Jews reach for their travellers' cheques. The vitrines are filled with Chasidic fiddlers and elaborate *mezuzot*, as well as more original pieces depicting Sigmund Freud and women with immense globular breasts. Meisler's style is distinctive, but it's driven home with hammer blows. For a few hundred dollars you can adorn your mantelpiece with a chunky reminder of your Jewish past, religious or secular, according to taste. Meisler is obviously onto a good thing, but it does seem a waste of a formidable talent. Behind every design there appears to be a marketing strategy. His weighty Jerusalem Sphere, a globe depicting the Old City on its surfaces, is inventive, but it comes as no surprise to learn, since Mr Meisler is at pains to inform us of the fact, that it occupies a prominent spot in the Downing Street drawing room of Mrs Margaret Thatcher.

On my gluttonous visits to Jaffa, I would walk after my lunch to the main plaza, which is dominated by the mustard and pink neo-baroque St Peter's Church and the luxuriant gardens just opposite. From the plaza there is a view not only onto Tel Aviv, a view that prompted feelings of gratitude that one was not actually there, but onto the slender minaret rising from the port below, a reminder of a different culture, now displaced. Far more appealing than the panorama of the city was the view in the opposite direction, over rock and surf and minaret and out to an open sea flecked with the confetti of bobbing gulls. I would walk into commercial Jaffa to the flea market, its small, darkened, high-ceilinged shops crammed with clothes, brass and copper, lamps, bangles, carpets, and furniture. A few tourists might be nosing around, but the owners are slack in their salesmanship and prefer to play backgammon and sip coffee with their neighbours. The commercial centre of Jaffa is tawdry, grubby, with rutted streets and the funky smells of oil and sesame seed from the bakeries blending with the saltier whiffs from the fishmongers. I liked these sombre streets with their decrepit warehouses and neglected mansions. One long-time Tel Aviv resident was fairly dismissive of Jaffa: 'In general you don't live there if you don't have to. It's quite druggy, and drug-dealing is, together with prostitution, one of the few areas where Jews and Arabs work well together.'

Driving from Tel Aviv down to the south, I was pursued by dark rainclouds that dumped torrential waters onto the streets. The main roads through Jaffa had been transformed into lakes; cars had stalled in the water, causing minor traffic jams. The frightful conditions did nothing to lessen the aggression of other drivers, who leaned on their horns and screamed at each other through the cascades. The rain turned into hail, which whitened the windscreen to such an extent I had to stop the car and wait till it was over. The signs to Beersheva played tricks on me. One informed me the city was 70 kilometres away, and a few kilometres further on Beersheva had receded, for it was now 74 kilometres away. The high winds persisted as I drove south, and eucalyptus trees, bowed in the wind, painted their leafy brushstrokes more rapturously than usual. I lunched at a petrol station. At the next table sat three truckers, all eating in silence as they read their newspapers. One of them finished his meal, took a tiny pamphlet from his pocket, and raced, *sotto voce*, through his prayers. I drove on. The landscape was uneventful, a succession of immense fields stretching to the horizon.

Beersheva sprawls. The largest town in the south, it is a modern city of apartment blocks surrounding an older town that still contains stately Turkish houses and a mosque, now converted into a museum. Modern Beersheva is dominated by the bold towers of the university and hospital. I decided to stay at the youth hostel, which is conveniently situated close to the old town. The hostel has a guest house, indistinguishable from a hotel, with clean and well equipped rooms. But it was March and still cold, especially at night. I went down to the reception desk. The woman behind the counter ignored me. This is standard practice in Israel, where no official will acknowledge your presence until addressed directly. I spoke, and eventually she looked up and gazed blankly towards me. Was there any heat in the guest house? No, she said, returning to her crossword puzzle. I pointed out that there were radiators in the room, and was there any chance of the heat being turned on? She shrugged, which is body language for 'tough shit'. I could have tolerated her indifference, and even the lack of heat in a room where at night I would have to work wrapped in a blanket, had I not noticed that her fat bum was being warmed by a two-bar electric fire.

Nor was the management any more accommodating when in the morning I asked for my passport. Why did I want it back? they asked, suspiciously.

'I'm going to the bank,' I replied, 'and, in any case, I've paid in advance for the room.'

'You can leave your education card instead.'

A flattering suggestion, since twenty years have elapsed since my student days, but impractical, since I didn't possess the document in question. Instead, they settled for my visa card.

I returned to the youth hostel a week later, but there was no sign of recognition from the sour woman behind the counter. I paid, and took my luggage up to the room. No towel. Back down to the desk to ask, politely, for a towel. That will be three shekels, I was told. Since I was already paying 60 shekels for the room, I objected to being asked to pay additionally for the privilege of drying myself after a shower, especially since during previous stays I had not been charged. Those were the rules, I was told. I called for the manager. If I didn't want the towel, he said, I needn't pay for it. It was optional. This was not a hotel, he reminded me. A purpose-built establishment that rents rooms by the night to tourists seemed a fair definition of a hotel to me, but this was not going to be a fruitful argument. I handed over the shekels.

I was reminded, while all this was going on, of remarks made a few days earlier by Israel's tourism minister, Gideon Patt, at Shamir's Solidarity Conference. 'Don't do us a favour by coming here,' he had told delegates. 'We won't beg for people to visit Israel.' If that is the attitude of the minister, then it is hardly surprising that the same dismissive condescension is found lower down the chain of command.

Tourism is not a rewarding activity in Beersheva. There's the museum, and that's about it. The day after I arrived in town was Friday, and at lunchtime I took a walk into the old town centre. A haze of white sand was obscuring the end of the main street, the fallout from sandstorms down in the desert. Along the pedestrian precinct, which is cluttered with food stalls, I bought some pizza and joined the teenagers seated on the low stone benches that encircle the silvery trees. An old tramp limped up to the nearest pizza stand. A waitress not only handed him a slice but wished him 'Shabbat Shalom' as he shuffled off again. He was evidently a regular visitor to the stand, where I saw Jewish charity in action at its most unobtrusive. Pop music was blaring from somewhere. The *tefillin* brigade had set up a stall, and a black coat moved purposefully towards me. I snarled engagingly, and he made a rapid retreat. A few hours later it was Shabbat and I retreated to my room to shiver and read, emerging at eight with a keen appetite.

Even in Jerusalem you can get a meal on Friday nights at the YMCA or the Cinematheque, but Beersheva makes no concessions to tourists or visitors. The old town was dead. Every single falafel and pizza stand, and during the day there are dozens to choose from, had shut down. I drove to the university, but the campus gates were closed and there was not a soul to be seen. Perhaps the students were in their hostels, eating. The hospital was nearby: perhaps there would be a cafeteria to accommodate expectant fathers and anxious relatives? No, there wasn't. I drove back into the town centre, parked, and consulted the map. I looked up and was astonished to see three little boys, with pale *payot* and the stiff peaked caps and white stockings of the Belzer Chasidim, standing in a doorway staring at me. Had they been airlifted from Jerusalem? 'Shabbos, Shabbos,' they hissed at me.

This was the last straw, not only to be forced by rabbis to go without dinner but to be upbraided by children for searching for food. So I gave the pre-teen angels some of their own medicine. 'Piss off, you creepy little buggers,' I yelled, and they scampered off, presumably to seek out another transgressor to fuel their self-righteousness. It was at this point that I dimly recalled reading about a Chinese restaurant. There seemed a faint chance that these fine enterprising people would want to satisfy the hunger of the secular and the non-Jew. It took me a while to find the place, but it did exist, and it was open. I fell into the warm lantern glow of the restaurant, showering blessings on the indifferent waiter, and ate amply and well. Beersheva, I should add, is a predominantly secular town. Marked by the large contingent of Soviet immigrants at the university, it has spawned a whole generation of excellent chess players and hosts an international tournament.

A few days later it was Purim, the festival that marks the deliverance of the Jews from the evil machinations of Haman, vizier to King Ahasuerus of Persia, in the fifth century B.C. The event is celebrated by throwing parties, especially for children. Downtown Beersheva was packed with children dressed as princesses and cowboys; the few children not in costume had daubed their faces with war paint. People of indeterminate age were dressed as clowns, and one of them, mysteriously, was pregnant. Along the pavements stood clusters of balloon sellers and vendors with trolleys loaded with sweets and toffee apples. You can't say no to a child during Purim. Their parents were no better at saying no, and the pizza stands were doing a roaring trade at ten thirty in the morning. Four-foot-high Princess Esthers in tall conical hats and pink crepe frocks took over the streets, but in more sophisticated towns one of the more popular costumes was, I read, the Salman Rushdie outfit. Rushdie had recently been condemned by the Ayatollah Khomeini, and whether the students' decision to incorporate him into the festivities was a supportive tribute or mere insensitivity, I do not know. That evening I had to go to Ben-Gurion Airport to meet someone, and here too the concourse was filled with princesses and Batmen perched on the shoulders of bearded fathers and well-structured mothers. Passengers arriving from London on that balmy March evening must have been pleasantly surprised to find that Israel, far from being strife-torn and jeep-patrolled, was instead a giant fancy dress party.

Tourists stranded in Beersheva on a Thursday are in luck, for there is something to do, at least during the morning. A few acres of wasteland south of the town act as a magnet to hundreds of Bedouin, whose encampments encircle Beersheva and penetrate the dunes and scrub of the desert. Thursday is market day, and Arabs come from the Territories as well as from Bedouin towns to shop and trade. The main part of the market sells the usual tat found in any Middle Eastern bazaar: cheap copper jugs, toys, household gadgets, jeans and sweaters, shoes, a few rugs, bolts of gaudy cloth. More alluring were the stalls selling spices and ten kinds of olives and peppers and dates. Germans and Scandinavians with complexions that ranged through all conceivable shades of boiled prawn tiptoed among the rubbish, cameras at the ready. Among the shoppers were Bedouin women in traditional robes, long and heavily embroidered, black velveteen shawls over their heads, their faces half concealed behind white veils. At the sheep market, more spacious than the one in Jerusalem, ill-shaven traders amuse Arab onlookers with the vociferousness of their haggling, while the animals moisturize the already soggy ground. Ninety per cent of Bedouin drive Peugeot pickup trucks and from the back of one of them an Arab was doing a roaring trade in medicines and unguents.

My main reason for coming to Beersheva, other than to buy a camel, was to visit the university, which represents the intellectual powerhouse behind the local attempt to throw mankind into an inhospitable environment and make the most of it. The original title of the establishment set up in 1956 says it all: the Negev Institute for Arid Zone Research. In 1973 the institute was incorporated within Ben-Gurion University, and renamed in 1982 as the Applied Research Institutes. The Institutes preserve the letter David Ben-Gurion wrote announcing their establishment. It ends, characteristically: 'Set to work and succeed.' It has done both. Perhaps the notion of taming the desert, of squeezing from it every thrust of agricultural productivity, is arrogant in conception, but the Israelis felt they had little choice. Tourists come to the Negev desert to admire its landscape and wild life, but that is an insufficient economic base for the region. Ben-Gurion wished to extend the agricultural wizardry perfected by the kibbutzim to the problems of cultivation in the desert, as though the arid wastes were merely one more obstacle in the way of the fulfilment of the Jewish people. Development of the desert was undertaken under pressure and at speed, and planning authorities were none too scrupulous when it came to respecting the fragility of the environment. Few Israelis believe the desert is valuable in itself and for itself. It is an excellent place for military camps, but its unproductive vastness is still regarded by many as one of the few flaws in God's plans for the Jewish people.

Water is, by definition, in short supply in arid zones. The National Water Conduit I had seen carrying water down to the farmlands from the Sea of Galilee ends close to Beersheva, and gives no benefit to the Negev. Sixty per cent of Israel's land surface is desert, much of that land mountainous and unsuitable for cultivation. The Jordan Valley, from the Dead Sea down to Eilat on the Red Sea, receives hardly any rainfall at all. Drinking water is supplied by sinking artesian wells and passing the water through a very costly desalinization process. One project the Institutes have been working on is developing the agricultural uses of salt water. Agronomists at the Boyko Institute for Saline Water Irrigation have established that certain crops, notably melons and tomatoes, thrive with salt water irrigation, which is obviously far cheaper than desalinization; under the stress of salt water, it appears, the plants produce more sugar. The drawback is that at the germination stage, the plants need pure water, and so it is necessary to have two systems of irrigation available in the same fields. (Much of this research has been conducted jointly with Egyptian scientists, one example of many such co-operative ventures since the two countries made peace.) Researchers and farmers feel that although this kind of investment is unavoidably high, it is worthwhile, as it enables Israel to export winter fruits at high prices.

The scientists are also working on the processing of sand and stone in order to produce substitutes for metal and wood, although this technique is not yet applied on an industrial scale. They have succeeded in transforming sand into a dustless chalk, though its benefits, other than for schoolmasters, escape me. Up on the Institutes' roofs stand tanks in which various kinds of algae are grown; from them chemicals are extracted for use in natural food colouring and cosmetics. Unsightly tropical plants from Africa are brought to Beersheva from the wild and then domesticated so as to regularize the yield and quality of their fruit. Soon the greengrocers of the world will be peddling the nut of the yerib and the fruit of the foul-scented carella. One shrub was imported from some distant savannah and cultivated with the intention of offering it to hungry sheep as a tasty fodder. Unfortunately the product met with resistance from the consumer.

The research could have been a costly mistake, but some bright spark decided to try rearing the shrub as an ornamental plant. It now generates $3 million annually in export income. Professor Mizrachi has developed a seedless tomato which has a shelf life of four weeks. This development benefits not only the consumer but the farmer, who need not rush to pick his entire crop at the optimal moment. The same professor, whose genius flourishes most opulently in the tomato house, has also worked wonders with the slow-ripening Andean tomato, which he has crossed with other species to produce some miracle of succulence. In greenhouses I saw other plants being kept under observation: the monkey orange and the mongongo, the oil-laden jojoba and the bountiful Botswanan marula tree. Edward Lear would have loved it.

The next day I drove south into the desert to the kibbutz of Sede Boqer to look at another aspect of Israeli inventiveness at the solar energy station that was built here in 1985. Almost every Israeli household makes use of solar energy, if only to heat water. By law, all new houses must use solar water heating, although homes also need an electricity supply as backup on cloudy days. Even bus stops in the desert, which are not connected to the electricity grid, have small solar panels above them; batteries store the energy generated by the panels, which provide lighting at night. Sede Boqer is the only place in Israel where all solar energy systems can be tested in identical conditions. The station conducts no research, but simply tests commercial installations and measures their performance. In Britain there would be armed guards at the gate of any such establishment, but the Israelis, much more sensibly, have turned it into a tourist attraction that employs three full-time guides.

Solar energy is not a new technology. In 1515 Leonardo da Vinci thought of using large mirrors for heating purposes, but never pursued the idea. It became feasible to use the sun to generate energy a century ago, but the abundance of oil meant that there was no incentive to develop this technology. Since the 1950s the Israelis have been working on the commercial development of the available systems. Each system has its disadvantages. The largest installation consists of parabolic mirrors that direct the sun's rays onto a focal point through which an oil-filled tube passes; the oil heats up, and flows into a water supply, which turns into steam which drives a turbine. A computer enables the mirrors to track the rays of the sun as it moves through the sky. The drawback, however, is a serious one: the system only works on sunny days. There is an alternative: an all-weather system that operates by the action of the rays on silicon layers that have different chemical compositions with different numbers of electrons; sunlight stimulates a reaction that gets those electrons moving, which generates the current. And the drawback? Twofold: the system is both costly and inefficient. The scientists here hope that by the year 2000, 8 per cent of all Israel's energy needs will be met from sources other than coal or oil, and half of those alternative sources will be solar.

Sede Boqer is also the home of the Institute for Desert Research, a branch of Ben-Gurion University. The institute, which has no undergraduates, has fifteen departments, including meteorology, hydrology, and architecture. I was shown more agricultural marvels, including the prickly pear that has no prickles, a godsend to harvesters. The architectural department has constructed on the campus an adobe house, which is not only pleasant to live in but remarkably energy-efficient. It contains such devices as a 'kinetic wall', which during the winter months faces outward during the day to absorb the warmth of the sun and is then swivelled at night to warm the room. I was taken to lunch in the cafeteria by the public relations manager, but within two minutes we were joined by her entire family. So instead of quizzing her about the institute, I had to listen to the burblings of her three-year-old, who also kept kicking me under the table. Israeli tolerance for children and their misbehaviour is boundless; my own threshold, however, is scarcely measurable.

My main reason for visiting the institute was to track down Zvi Lovenstein, an expert in run-off farming, which intrigued me. Eventually I found him, and encountered not a wild-eyed Israeli but a tall cheerful Dutchman with startling blue eyes. His research all started, he told me, with the Nabateans, who lived in the northern Negev 2,000 years ago. There have been extensive excavations of their cities, and among the objects unearthed were wine presses and other artefacts that proved that there was large-scale cultivation in the desert. 'We can work out the methods the Nabateans used,' says Lovenstein, 'but that's not to say that we can simply copy those methods and restore a flourishing agriculture to the Negev. The Nabateans grew crops to feed themselves. We are more spoilt. We grow crops to convert them into cash. To grow these cash crops we need to use irrigated water, but irrigation is given a 90 per cent government subsidy. It's artificially sustained. I'm looking at something completely different, at three categories, all of which are problematic in Third World countries as a whole, not just in the Negev. We're looking at food, at firewood, at fodder. Our project is examining the natural water supply that's available in desert conditions, and then seeing which plants and what kind of cropping system are best adapted to these conditions. We can't alter the environment, so we play with the plants and the cropping.'

The Nabateans made the desert bloom by trapping the run-off water after heavy rains, and then using it for cultivation. Skilful engineers, they built channels to divert rainwater to their fields, and cleared stones from those channels so as not to impede the flow. 'What's important is not the amount of rain, but its intensity. The soil is important too. If the soil can't absorb the rain, the water will be wasted. What we're doing is building dykes that will keep the water where we need it most. This is a strange thing for me to be doing as a Dutchman, coming from a society where we are so anxious to keep the water out. If we get four inches of intense rainfall, we can trap four or five times as much within our dykes. Twelve inches of water will take two days to infiltrate the soil. That's sufficient moisture to support plant life here for a whole year, but only if you crop it correctly. In the southern Negev, though, you need much more moisture to grow a crop successfully. The soil down there is more sandy, and less suitable for agriculture. Up here the soil responds to rain by swelling and forming a crust, which slows the rate of absorption.

'You'll find similar soil in the southern part of the Sahel, in parts of Mali, Senegal, Ethiopia, and Nigeria. We're not developing this method of cultivation for kibbutzim, but for smallholdings such as one finds everywhere in the Third World. Kibbutzim use drip irrigation, which is dependent on back-up pumps and fairly sophisticated equipment and training, which are beyond the means of most peasant economies. We have a number of graduate students from Third World countries at Sede Boqer, and I keep telling them: don't copy us, adapt from us. The conditions in other countries aren't identical to those here. I'll give you an example. We suggest to some of these students that they encourage villagers who use run-off farming to cut frequently the trees they grow. This stimulates their rate of growth. People object that the logs from frequently cut trees are small, but that makes them easier to transport, especially if they have to be carried. One drawback of using run-off farming to grow trees is that it seems wasteful because of the space you need to leave between trees. But we encourage the planting of annuals among the trees, so the farmer can utilize the rest of the space and take advantage of different water levels. With run-off farming, it's possible to construct a whole ecological system.'

At the institute's experimental farm near Avdat, Lovenstein and his team grow grapes and sunflowers, as well as plantations of eucalyptus and acacia and other trees, some of which give plentiful firewood and foliage that provides fodder that camels and goats and cattle find appetizing. 'We can construct a whole chain, so that it becomes meaningful to ask the following kind of question: How much rain do you need to produce a glass of milk?' As Lovenstein intimated, the main purpose of this kind of research is political. By helping Third World countries to adopt such techniques that will support peasant economies without enormous expenditure, Israel can earn goodwill. Thus the government supports this kind of research and subsidizes research students from Third World countries.

Driving back to Beersheva from Sede Boqer, I passed the turnoff to Ramat Hovav, a reminder that the desert has other, and less desirable, uses. Ramat Hovav is a huge complex of chemicals factories. It can be identified nasally from afar by the aroma of lavatory fresheners. Just beyond the factories is Israel's toxic waste dump. I drove close to the perimeter fence, but seemed to be attracting too much attention from the guards, and drove off again. Prevailing winds and water tables are such that Beersheva gets the worst of the water pollution, while the air pollution drifts south towards Sede Boqer.

A woman named Bilha heads the Beersheva branch of the Society for the Protection of Nature. Her skill lies in making the authorities believe she has more power than is probably the case. She insists on involving the society in discussions as to whether planning permission should be granted for new industrial projects in the region. Her greatest weapon, which she does not hesitate to use, is ready access to the media. If some aspect of the development of the Negev worries her, she only has to make a few phone calls and the entire region will know what's bothering her. Her responsibilities are vast: she has to monitor not only the desert but the more northerly region that stretches from Ashdod, the port south of Tel Aviv, to the Dead Sea. The society is best known for its field schools, where thousands of students and ordinary citizens come each year to study the geology and wild life of various regions, but those schools also function as the eyes and ears of the society.

Bilha has plenty to worry about. 'Ours is a small country, and so there is great demand for land for houses and highways and factories. Soon we will need to build local substations to deal with the energy that will be produced at the major power stations at Hadera and Ashkelon. There are plans for a train line to Eilat, and for more factories in the Negev. There are proposals for a wind power project, which sounds a good idea, but that will mean putting up disfiguring installations on hilltops and mountains. The society isn't opposed to development – that would be foolish – but we want it to take place with the least possible environmental damage. Israel has so many other problems that environmental issues tend to be shoved to one side.'

Another of Ben-Gurion's enterprises in the Negev was the establishment
of development towns, a wilful attempt to show that industries could
flourish even in the most inhospitable of environments. Dimona was
founded in 1955 about twenty miles south-east of Beersheva, when thirty-
six newly-arrived North African families were dumped here in the desert
with a pile of Jewish Agency tents and huts. The immigrants made the
best of it, and Dimona thrived. By the late 1970s it had a population of
31,000. Its economic base consisted of two textile factories, the Dead Sea
Works to the north, to which Dimonans commuted, and a chemical
factory. There was also an establishment referred to as the chocolate
factory, a joke name for Israel's leading nuclear research station. In the
1980s things began to go wrong. The factories began to lay off staff: the
workforce at the Kitan textile plant shrank from 1,700 workers to only
500. The children of the original settlers, now adults, began to realize that
the real opportunities for personal prosperity and gracious living lay not
in the northern Negev, but in the megalopolis around Tel Aviv. Many of
the best educated moved away from Dimona, leaving a vacuum as their
parents reached retirement age.

The challenge for the government is to persuade businesses and individuals in other parts of Israel that an exciting future awaits them in
Dimona and the other ailing development towns. Incentives offered to
stimulate investment in the Negev – a 40 per cent reduction in taxes, and
a reduction in or even exemption from local taxes for a few years – are no
different from those offered to people who wish to invest in Kiryat Gat, a
town halfway between Beersheva and Tel Aviv, and far lower than those
offered, for political reasons, to West Bank settlers. Other factors discourage potential investors from sinking their money into the sands at
Dimona. The town is far from the major ports and transportation costs
are high. Such factors seemed of secondary importance in the 1950s and
1960s, when investors knew the government was determined that the
development towns should succeed. Thirty years later, the population is

disenchanted and the government seemingly more interested in defending
every inch of Eretz Yisrael than in ensuring that the inches it already
controls function efficiently. Liberal Dimonans blame Likud for neglecting
the development towns over the past decade, but that doesn't prevent the
local electorate from favouring Likud candidates, though by 1988 their
share of the vote had dropped from 60 to 50 per cent. One Dimonan
commented: 'It's amazing. Likud screws these people, and then they turn
around and vote for Likud. It's because they have simplistic attitudes.
They're anti-Arab and Likud defends their position. The rest of the
policies they don't even think about.' Shas also appeals to the Dimonans,
for they are mostly Sephardim, and the party won 17 per cent of the vote
in 1988, even though few Dimonans are ultra-Orthodox.

I drove to Dimona on a clear March morning along a featureless road,
passing Bedouin camps and signs warning travellers to stay well away
from army firing ranges. Dimona is a well laid out town at what seems to
be a spot chosen at random in the middle of the desert. Many of its small
apartment blocks near the town centre are showing their age, and some
are boarded up, but there is new building on the fringes, where Dimonans
prefer houses to flats. There's a selection of 'British cottages', small two-
storey houses, and whole blocks of 'patios', the Israeli term for small
bungalows with gardens. Dimona used to have the largest cinema in
Israel, but it had hard wooden seats and neither heat nor air conditioning,
and it is being replaced by a small cinema in a complex that will include a
disco and a banqueting hall. Dimona is a strangely colourless town.
Although the new suburban houses sport cheerful red roofs, the older
buildings are faced with stucco or pebble-dash scarcely distinguishable
from the sand of the desert.

I called on Mike Diamond, the local co-ordinator of Project Renewal,
engaged here in setting up a business enterprise agency; they also provide
assistance with management training. 'We do our best to cut through
Israeli bureaucracy,' Diamond told me. 'Any would-be investor has to
stand in four hundred queues at various offices for anything from five
minutes to five hours. We want to make sure that when the businessman
arrives in Dimona, we can hand him the keys to his office and let him get
on with his work.' In the months that followed, the scheme met with
considerable success.

When I walked into Diamond's office in the municipal buildings, he
was talking earnestly to colleagues sprawled around the conference table,
clutching their mugs of coffee.

'I'm terribly sorry about this,' Diamond said to me in a firm Glasgow
accent, 'but you couldn't have come on a worse day.' He obviously didn't

understand that the worse the day the happier I am. I have more use for despair than for contentment.

'What's the matter?'

'Half the town is in a state of shock. It's the election results.' He sat down again, glumly. In the middle of the night it had become clear that the incumbent mayor, a progressive ex-diplomat called Eli Allali, had lost the run-off election to the Likud candidate, Gabi Lalouche. In the first round Allali had been 150 votes short of outright victory, but last night he had lost by a surprising 500. The obvious explanation for this slump in support is that the Labour candidate, eliminated in the first round, had not subsequently been supporting Allali.

'So you have a new mayor,' I said. 'Is that the end of the world?'

Diamond explained that Allali had been an outstanding mayor who had brought culture and greenery to Dimona, where both amenities had previously been in short supply, and had replaced slummy apartment blocks with better housing. The new mayor, he suspected, would be less committed to maintaining this level of development, and might cut municipal support for Project Renewal itself. Diamond had experienced some difficulties in establishing Project Renewal, as the municipality, understandably, didn't fancy the idea of outsiders looking over its collective shoulder. Allali had, however, been on his side, and now the future seemed less certain.

'And on top of all that, the authorities chose election night to change all the phone numbers in Dimona, so everything is chaotic.'

Diamond finds he must be a diplomat as well as an administrator. 'You have to know how to play the game round here. We've set up a dental clinic, as the standard of dental and health care here is wretched. The truth is that our clinic is fairly mediocre at present, but it would be fatal for us to express criticisms that might undermine it altogether. So suggestions for improvement have to be made in a roundabout way. The last thing we want to do is tell the people of Dimona how to run their town. We're trying to give the residents the power to make their own choices, and all we want to do is advise them on the options. Unfortunately politics keeps getting in the way. If the amount of energy and dedication that's gone into these local elections had been directed towards improving this town, Dimona would be a tremendous place. The town's affairs have been neglected for months, and now everyone is too burnt out to get on with the main business of improving Dimona. It's the same story in almost every other development town. With the best of intentions the government and the Jewish Agency have always looked after Dimona, and the people here are no longer accustomed to do things for themselves.'

During the previous year, Project Renewal had set up a volunteer programme, and the eleven participants had been adopted by local families, who invited them for meals and gave them a place where they could put their feet up. Some of the volunteers work in schools and help with English teaching, which, in Diamond's view, is appallingly taught. 'The headmasters are delighted to have volunteers and assign them to the weakest students, but we see the volunteers' role as being to give additional assistance to the bright students. It's just another example of teachers fleeing from responsibility. In Israel this phenomenon is called "small heads". The reason why people behind counters in banks and offices are so unhelpful is that no one wants to be responsible for solving your problem.'

A few doors down the corridor is the office of a young American woman, Tracy Amar, who runs a programme aimed at persuading Anglo-Saxons to settle in Dimona. Tracy lived for some years in Jerusalem, where she met her husband, a Moroccan-born Dimonan working in the capital as a choreographer.

'Two years ago we moved back to Dimona.'

'Why?'

'It seemed a good Zionist thing to do.'

At present about 60 per cent of the population of Dimona is of North African origin, and there is also a sizable community of Indian Jews. Tracy put together a proposal to bring to Dimona Westerners who could bring a freshness of approach to the town. The municipality accepted her proposal, which she believes is unique of its kind in Israel. She has had some success, and a few of the volunteers recruited from the *ulpans* have now moved permanently to Dimona. Her total score is ten. 'It would be higher, only I won't let anyone move to Dimona until I have found them a job. It's hard to place certain highly qualified people. There's no call here for accountants or computer technicians. What we need are teachers and people involved in social services. Many *olim* find it hard to get established in Israel. They give up and leave. We have to make sure they feel welcome in Israel, and I want people to realize that in communities like Dimona they can enjoy a good standard of living. Taxes are low, and you can rent an apartment for eighty dollars a month. For $60,000 you can buy a small villa, and for $100,000 you can get a large house. Ground plots cost from four to ten thousand. It's hard to match those prices anywhere else in Israel. And food is cheaper here too. Dimona was awful five years ago, I admit. But in the last few years the municipality has built new parks and cultural centres. Of course there's more going on in Tel Aviv or Jerusalem, but when we lived there we couldn't afford to do all 'those things. Here cultural activities are subsidized. Ra'anana used to be a dump, and now it's a great place. I can see Dimona going the same way.'

While Tracy was giving me her animated pep talk, a bearded man came crashing into her office without knocking, exchanged a few hasty words with her, picked up the phone on another desk, and held a rapid conversation before crashing out again. I found the interruption disturbing but Tracy didn't bat an eyelid, so presumably such scenes are commonplace. Despite her success in attracting qualified immigrants to Dimona, she found it harder, despite the incentives, to persuade them to stay.

I left the municipal buildings and drove to a spartan block on the edge of the town to visit the former principal of the largest junior school. Heavily pregnant, she was taking a two-year leave of absence. Her English was minimal, so we communicated hesitantly, but she managed to paint a fairly depressing picture. Forty per cent of her pupils came from poor homes, where their parents were more preoccupied with daily survival than with such luxuries as educational standards. She described the one high school in Dimona as mediocre. The students were average at best, and it was very hard to attract good teachers. There are few inspectors to monitor standards in the Negev, and only a handful of parents were pushing for educational improvements. If a teacher is useless, there is little point in complaining, since it may prove impossible to find a replacement. If they can afford it, it's not uncommon for parents to send their children to school elsewhere by boarding them with grandparents or relatives in a major city.

The principal had come to Dimona from Beersheva twelve years ago, and she still misses it. 'In Beersheva there are places to sit with my husband and have coffee, but there's nowhere pleasant to go in Dimona. It didn't use to be like that.'

'Will the new mayor make any difference?'

'Allali was a good mayor and tried to help the schools. Now he's gone, we may go back to Beersheva. It's not just that we don't want Lalouche, but Allali's defeat is the last straw.' Her husband, also a teacher, comes from the Jezreel Valley, and would like to return there; she would rather go to central Israel. She expects they'll compromise by moving to Beersheva, where they can both find work as teachers.

I told Mike Diamond later that I found my talk with the principal very depressing. She gave the impression that difficulties and obstacles, which are not unusual in the teaching profession, were insuperable.

'The situation in the schools is pretty bad,' he said. 'The supply of local teachers is dwindling. If you talk to the teachers, they'll all tell you that Dimona's problems derive from a lack of funding at all levels and poor administration. No teacher will ever accept that they may have *some* responsibility of their own for this state of affairs.'

To ensure that my view of Dimona was not entirely gloomy, Diamond sent me off to the conservatory in Shivat Hanimim, once the grubbiest neighbourhood in town. The Geneva branch of Project Renewal took the district under its wing and it has become positively fashionable. Older houses, built of stone, are being renovated, and I saw some sumptuous villas in the final stages of construction. The Genevans also renovated and expanded the conservatory, which is built around a sunken area in which a pool and fountain splash gently. The fountain is not there solely for aesthetic reasons; it also provides a neutral background of constant burble to drown out other sounds such as conversation that could interfere with music-making. Window grilles are required for security reasons, but the designers didn't want the conservatory to look like a prison, so the thirty grilles were fashioned in the form of a musical score. Wander round the exterior with a recorder, and you can toot excerpts from Bach's Art of Fugue.

The 460 students attend the conservatory after school. There is no entrance test and any child can begin to learn an instrument from the age of six. After a few months their progress is assessed, and those with no aptitude are politely shown the door. The more able can study until they are eighteen. The fees have been heavily subsidized by the municipality, so nobody can claim that they cannot afford to attend classes here. I told the director, Yossi Hartman, that since most Dimonans came from non-Western backgrounds, I was surprised that they were able to develop a keen interest in classical music.

'It's true,' said Hartman. 'We have many North African children who have never heard a note of Western classical music, but they pick it up fast and within a few months they can discuss Mozart and Beethoven as if they've been listening to them all their lives. These kids are open-minded. If they're enjoying what they're doing, they don't care about which culture it comes from.'

'And where do the teachers come from?'

'They're Russians. Of the twenty-two teachers here, nineteen are from Russia. It's the same at all the conservatories.'

I told Hartman that I was astonished to find an expanding music conservatory in a small town with grave economic problems, a town without a hospital or first-rate schools. He was surprised by my surprise.

'Hospitals need staff and equipment. A conservatory can start, as we did, with a small nucleus. Today we have special equipment, such as computers for teaching music theory. The child sings or plays to the computer, which then corrects the mistakes. We also find that through the children we can reach the parents, who practise alongside their children. Most of the piano students have pianos at home.'

'Do you teach too?'

'My instrument is the double bass, but I regret to say that there are no students for me. We don't have voice training either. Unless you have a first-rate voice teacher, you can damage the vocal chords.'

I returned to Mike Diamond's office, to find him in conversation with a tall bearded gentleman with spectacles and greying hair wearing – an unlikely costume in the desert – a dark three-piece suit. Inside this heavy woollen splendour was, of course, a rabbi, the splendidly named Rabbi Yitzhak Elephant. He and his wife had come to Israel from New York and he became a rabbi in Beersheva before moving to Dimona. Four years ago he was elected its chief rabbi. Although of Ashkenazi background himself, Rabbi Elephant has no difficulty officiating at Sephardi ceremonies and knows the different melodies of each congregation. He estimated that about 20 per cent of the population was Orthodox, and a further 30 per cent went to synagogue and kept kosher homes. There is no conflict between the religious and the secular; indeed, many of the secular Jews come from traditional backgrounds, and may still observe certain Jewish customs and festivals, even if they don't believe in them intellectually. The *haredi* population is negligible, though there is a *kolel* in Dimona with about thirty students. The rabbi was not in an expansive mood; his answers were clipped and brusque. Mike Diamond attributed this not to self-importance but to gloom at Mayor Allali's defeat.

After lunch with Diamond's Swiss assistant Lisa – it took longer to find a snack bar that met her hygienic requirements than it did to eat the sandwich – she introduced me to Chesi, one of the thousands of Indian Jews in Dimona. He had come to Israel from Bombay with his parents as a child of eight. Once in Israel, the disoriented family, none of whom spoke Ivrit, was happy enough to be pointed in the direction of Dimona. His parents came to Israel because they believed it was the promised land, that their children and grandchildren would have a better life than in India. Chesi's father was a clerical worker, and his mother had been a teacher until her children were born. The family arrived in Dimona and found the Moroccans firmly in control of the town. His father was fifty-five and could only find work as a gardener; his mother also went out to work. This devastated his father, since it meant he had to share control of the household, which was psychologically difficult for someone from his background. At the age of thirteen, Chesi moved to Kibbutz Ein Gedi, an oasis on the shores of the Dead Sea. Chesi has a hard military look, short black hair flattened onto his head, no trace of fat, no soft furrows, a face that looked as if every pore had been scrubbed clean, and it came as no surprise to learn that he had been a major in the air force. He now wants to return to Ein Gedi, but his wife wants to remain in Dimona. So small a country, and so many couples seem tugged to different parts of it.

The Indian community, although dispersed throughout the town, still retains many of its traditions, such as liturgical melodies and wedding dances. Chesi did not believe there was any discrimination against the Indian population, 'But sometimes we find ourselves at the end of the queue, especially when it comes to finding work.' Widespread dissatisfaction among the Indians prompted some of them to form their own political faction, Or (which means 'light'); it had won two out of the seventeen council seats. Another cultural tradition maintained by the Indians is, of all things, cricket, and their team is one of fourteen in Israel. Chesi is the vice-captain, and very proud of it.

'Just the other week we played against the British Embassy.'

'Did you win?'

'No. But then we had to lose out of courtesy to the visiting team.'

Was he joking? I couldn't tell, for Chesi too was deeply depressed by the mayoral election results. As we were saying goodbye, the clouds that had been gathering all afternoon opened and it began to pour. 'You see,' said Chesi, pointing upwards, 'Allali lost last night, and the heavens are crying.'

'Why is everyone so upset? Politicians are not irreplaceable.'

'Allali made a dream come true. He turned Dimona into a flower in the desert. He brought us trees and culture and sport. His defeat is a terrible blow to the town.'

Tracy Amar had told me about the 'Westerners' who had come to live in Dimona, and I went to visit one of them. Dr Moshe Dror is the founder of the town's English Centre. A New Yorker, Dror was ordained as a rabbi in 1959. Just for good measure he also has a doctorate in communications. He was president of the New York branch of an organization called the World Future Society and ran a council for the promotion of art in Jewish life. He then moved to Switzerland and worked on humanistic psychology. 'Then one of my associates in Switzerland went off to start a college in a town near here called Yerocham. Yerocham is notorious for being a development town that failed to develop. I had a choice: I could either accept a well-paid job in Brussels and earn a fortune, or I could join my former colleague. Yerocham was the asshole of Israel, but I went there anyway. I became the dean of the college, and a short while later it folded. While I was there two things happened to me. I met a wonderful Tunisian woman who is now my wife, and I became aware of how magical the desert is. When the college closed, most of my colleagues left the Negev, and some left Israel altogether. But I decided to stay in the desert, and Dimona was the nearest town where I thought I could earn a living. There's something in me that still is sufficiently convinced by the madness of Zionism to want to try to contribute by staying here. So I founded the English Centre.'

The Centre opened in October 1988, and within one week 250 students, including adults, had enrolled. The fees are heavily subsidized by the town, and there was some doubt about whether that generosity would continue under the new regime. A large, ebullient, and highly articulate man, Dror is an ardent proponent of electronic communications. He has been developing an electronic networking programme, so that children can contact other children from all over the world. 'But to take advantage of this, they need a common language, which has to be English. I'm trying to think ahead to the skills these kids are going to need in 2000. I can't be sure what they are, but I can be fairly certain that they won't be linear. We're teaching English not so that kids can pass exams but so that they can use the language after they've left school. We're also training English teachers to use computers. Since teachers are not flocking down to the Negev, we'll have to develop programmes that are not people-dependent. The idea is to develop the programmes at the Centre and then get them into the schools.

'Before long the whole concept of the school will change radically. At present we talk of ratios of students to teachers. These will become reversed once students have the facilities to plug into numerous networks, each with electronic access to a large number of teachers. Books are getting more costly each year, but computers are becoming cheaper. It's far less expensive to move information electronically. I'm hoping we can make Dimona a future-oriented town. I'm always trying to push at the edges. The revolutions of the past have all aimed at bringing more people into the circle of humanity. The French Revolution showed that peasants were human too. The abolition of slavery showed that blacks were human too. In this century we've discovered that women are human. The question now raised by Artificial Intelligence is: Who is in the club of humans? Electronic and optical systems are rapidly becoming akin to nervous systems.'

'I'm not sure I want to go on a date with a robot, though.'

'How can you be so sure?'

'Fix me up, and we'll see.' I then asked Dr Dror how this electronic revolution, a worldwide phenomenon, would affect Israel in particular.

'Israel at present is defending an anachronism, the nation state, and it has to defend its obsolescent world view with the blood of its youth. Today power is wielded not by nations but by multinational corporations, and they do it with information. Geography is interesting but irrelevant. Now information, unlike pure science, is value-laden. It has to be organized because there is so much of it. Fortunately processing information is what Jews excel at. We've been doing it for 2,000 years. Look at a page of the Talmud. You have the text in the centre, and commentaries surrounding it. Read an ordinary text, and the movement is uni-dimensional. What you hope to get from the process is answers to questions. Read the Talmud, and the movement is multi-directional to the commentaries, and what you get is not answers but questions. Go in to any yeshiva and you'll see people rarely study alone. They gather round a table with their books and argue. The Talmud builds social systems. It's directly comparable to windows on computers – you can summon up information from a variety of sources. Judaism is the only culture that does this. That's why Jews win Nobel prizes. It's all to do with the way they approach information systems. It also explains why Orthodox Jews are often superb computer technicians and programmers. Israel is full of first-rate software inventors.'

'Jews win Nobel prizes by the bucketful,' I interrupted, 'but Israelis haven't won any in forty years.'

'That's because people's creativity decreases after the age of thirty-five. Israelis spend three years in the army, and then weeks each year on reserve duty. The country has never been at peace. What's amazing is what has been achieved given the conditions we live under. We have no shortage of creative talent. The problem is that it has had to be misdirected.'

I couldn't help wondering whether Dr Dror's own energy was misplaced in a town such as Dimona. It was nice of the mayor to plant a new park and import dance companies for a week, but that didn't deal with the economic problems of Dimona, the exodus of its brightest scions, and growing unemployment. Nor were Tracy Amar's dozen Westerners, however fresh in ideas, likely to turn the place around. Local politicians, with a nice turn of irony, had asked the government in Jerusalem whether they would consider 'annexing' the Negev. Dr Dror's gloomy analysis would appear well founded. 'People talk of getting industry to come to this part of Israel, but it's not going to happen. In any case the industrial culture is collapsing worldwide. Twenty years ago this was the frontier, but now the frontier is in the Territories, and huge amounts of money are being poured into the settlements. The politicians come out with all kinds of crap about incentives for the Negev, but the fact remains that this region is starved by the government, whatever the politicians say.'

By January 1990 18 per cent of Dimona's workforce remained unemployed. The town needs a huge number of small businesses to make a dent in that statistic. Dror's idealism was to founder on managerial reefs, and in late 1989 his centre closed. The worst fears about Mayor Lalouche would turn out to have been exaggerated, but at the local political level the infighting was to be as ferocious as ever.

# 22 · DOORKEEPERS AND TENTDWELLERS

My forays into the Negev often took me past the Bedouin camps scattered along the slopes overlooking the main roads. There would be a tent; a long black oilcloth or other waterproof substance stretched over a frame, providing enough space for sleeping and living areas. A donkey or camel, or very occasionally a battered white or grey pickup truck, might be parked nearby, alongside the pen for sheep or goats. Unwieldy household items, such as tyres, old stoves, pumps, or water tanks, might be dotted haphazardly within the enclosure. These belong to semi-nomadic Bedouin, who do not wander from place to place in search of pasture, but move from one regular camp to another according to the season. Of the 311,000 inhabitants of the Negev, 70,000 are Bedouin, 10 per cent of whom live in tents with their flocks; the remainder live in Bedouin towns such as Rahat or in illegal settlements. Before 1948 the Bedouin tribes were dispersed throughout the Negev, but two factors obliged them to move into a more confined area. First, kibbutzim were established close to grazing lands that had been used by the Bedouin; and secondly, after Israel withdrew from the Sinai following the peace agreement with Egypt, the IDF requisitioned huge tracts of the Negev, building three airports, establishing firing ranges, and taking over hundreds of square miles for military manoeuvres. Nature reserves have also removed grazing land from use.

Today almost all the Bedouin live just to the east and south of Beersheva. This displacement of the Bedouin is not unique to Israel. The same thing happened in Syria, Egypt, and Jordan. But in the Arab countries it was possible for some of those Bedouin to farm in a more conventional way. This possibility was closed to them in Israel, where almost all farming is undertaken on Jewish kibbutzim and moshavim. They are a poor community, with an infant mortality rate double that of the Jews; almost half the Bedouin have no running water. Deprived of land for their flocks, many Bedouin had little choice other than to move into urban settlements and become unskilled wage labourers, forming a local proletariat. There are very few Bedouin teachers or lawyers. Each family unit belongs to a clan which in turn is part of a large tribe. Marriages usually take place within the clan, so that marriages between second and third cousins are commonplace. A fifth of male Bedouin have two wives, and each wife and her children must have their own tent. The birthrate is high, though birth control is not unknown. In 1981 over half the Bedouin population was under fourteen, compared to 30 per cent of the Jews. Since there is no rubbish collection and no sewage facilities, the Bedouin observe strict rules of hygiene. They move their tent every few weeks, and maintain personal cleanliness by washing their hands before and after meals despite the shortage of water. Dust rather than dirt is the main irritant. Nevertheless encampments are often troubled by huge rats, ferocious enough to devour chicks and baby turkeys. All storerooms must be sealed with cement and food is never left out in the open.

Some desert land is cultivable, especially near the bottom of wadis that receive an occasional soaking. The Bedouin plough the stony soil with camels or tractors, and the women harvest the crop by hand. Those who work in the fields rise very early and stop before the heat becomes too oppressive. During the rest of the day, the women remain deliberately idle so as to conserve energy and water. While the women work in the fields or tend the flocks, the men may be seeking new pastures for their sheep or going to market or sitting around with their friends, drinking coffee and talking politics. When guests arrive at a Bedouin tent, the etiquette is formal indeed. Visitors are offered both sweet tea and bitter coffee. Women and children retreat to their part of the tent while guests are being entertained, though the children are sent in with plates of food and drink and expected to report back on the conversation among the menfolk.

Some of the difficulties of the nomadic way of life are inherent to it. Others are imposed on it by unsympathetic Israeli authorities, who would prefer the Bedouin to pack up their tents for good and troop off to the planned settlements the Israelis have been constructing for them. There are repeated reports of harassment by the Green Patrol, the special police units attached to the ministry of agriculture to ensure that no Bedouin cultivation or grazing takes place in an unauthorized zone. Flocks that stray are often confiscated. Repeated Bedouin requests to set up their own equivalent of moshavim have been refused by the government, and virtually all irrigation water flows to Jewish agricultural settlements at the expense of Arab farming.

In October 1987, 500 police and soldiers cordoned off the unplanned Bedouin settlement of Laqiya and uprooted 2,000 olive trees and 500 dunams of planted land. A Bedouin clan claimed to have owned the land since 1905, but the Israeli authorities did not recognize that claim.[1] In March 1989, 900 dunams of wheat and barley planted by Bedouin near Tel Arad were sprayed with poison and destroyed. The only explanation I could discover for this act of destruction was that once crops sown on public land had been reaped, the land would have become the property of those who planted the crop; consequently, such plantings have to be nipped in the bud. Israelis also complain that the Bedouin overgraze their flocks.

Gideon Kressel, an anthropologist at Sede Boqer, explains that 'the phenomenon of Bedouin overgrazing is a result of grabbing as much land as you can, because who knows where you will be forced to move next year. Instead, the authorities should give Bedouin rights to the land – as they do to Jewish settlements – for forty-nine years. Once you "own" it and you are responsible for the enrichment of the flora, you will be careful not to overgraze.'[2]

Despite the traditional way of life that prevails among the semi-nomadic Bedouin, they do not shun the modern world. Almost all Bedouin babies are now born at Beersheva hospital, which has extremely high standards of care. No Bedouin lives more than twenty-five miles from Beersheva. It was at the hospital that I met Gillian Hundt, an English anthropologist who had been invited to spend a year and a half living with two Bedouin families. They had been welcoming and unfailingly friendly, but the other side of that coin was that privacy was nonexistent. 'There is no social role for unmarried women among the Bedouin,' she told me, 'so I was treated as a girl but allowed the freedom of a man.'

I sat in on a lecture she gave to a group of visiting American women, rich and, if you hit them at the right time, generous. It was Gillian's turn to be nice to the donors, and she gave a succinct talk about Bedouin life. She then introduced the audience to Sayyid, a former truck driver who now operates the hospital's mobile medical unit, visiting Arabs unable to get to the hospital. There are no addresses in the desert, but Sayyid knows how to find people. Gillian had spoken about how over the decades the Bedouin had been losing more and more of their land, and one of the visitors wanted to know how Sayyid felt about that. He shrugged, and said that they were resigned to it.

Later, in Gillian's office, she recalled the American's question, which she clearly considered very stupid. Sayyid smiled, and gave the un-diplomatic answer he had not dared to give in the auditorium: 'The Arabs have a saying: somebody who doesn't have land has to shit in his hand.'

Land, indeed, is the great unresolved issue among the Bedouin of both the Negev and the Galilee. All land in Israel is leased from the government. However, some Bedouin tribesmen possessed documents issued under the Ottomans which established at least their right of usage, if not their direct ownership. Right of usage is recognized under Israeli law, so the government agreed to compensate those Bedouin for the loss of their land. Between the promise and the cheque stretched years of procrastination, and some Bedouin, apparently, are still waiting. Two years ago, 1.5 million dunams of Negev land were still in dispute. The 8,000 Bedouin displaced when one of the Negev airports was built were offered compensation but no right of appeal, which, according to Gillian, is unprecedented in law. Ironically, Bedouin sharecroppers, who had nothing to lose, moved swiftly to the planned settlements that the Israelis were building, while landowners, clutching what they thought were title deeds, took their cases to court and invariably lost, since their title was hardly ever based on firm written contracts that the courts could recognize as binding. Bedouin who have land claims pending before the courts are reluctant to move to the new settlements, even if they would like to, fearing that to do so could prejudice their claim.

The government, in any case, preferred to encourage the Bedouin to move into these settlements, where they were offered cheap building plots and mortgages. New towns such as Rahat, from which the inhabitants commute to Beersheva and Arad, were equipped with medical clinics and schools. Despite the provision of modern facilities in the new Bedouin towns, they lack a realistic economic base. Industrial zones were designated close to the settlements, but no industrial development has taken place. Without a steady income, many Bedouin are reluctant to take on the responsibilities of home building and mortgages. Many families now living in settlements, planned or unplanned, maintain ties with their nomadic past by keeping flocks, but no provision is made for agricultural activity, despite repeated pleas from Bedouin leaders to the government.

For some reason Rahat, a Bedouin planned settlement with over 10,000 inhabitants, is omitted from my road map of Israel, but it was not hard to find. It is not so much a town as a collection of villages, each sprawling across a hillside or two in a jumble of stone and stucco houses, while in the dells and valleys between the different parts of town are tents and shacks and flocks. Many houses are built on stilts, allowing for additional construction if the space is needed later by children who marry. The roads are reasonable and Rahat has little in common with, say, the slumminess of Umm el-Fahm.

The nomadic past of the people of Rahat is on display at Kibbutz Lahav, north of Beersheva, where there is an interesting Bedouin museum. I inspected embroideries and musical instruments and photographs of Bedouin holy places, but I learnt little about how the Bedouin live today. The customs recorded in the museum are close to extinction in Israel. The exhibits showed how the Bedouin were pioneers of recycling. Nothing is discarded. Horns and hooves of goats and camels and sheep are fashioned into toys; skins are turned not only into clothing but into sandals, water canteens, and storage utensils. The date tree provides not only fruit but roof supports. Despite the good intentions of the kibbutzniks at Lahav, and they do much to bring Jewish and Bedouin children together, this kind of display unavoidably reduces the people it celebrates to the condition of the picturesque and thereby consigns them to the history books. Two minutes in Rahat is all it takes to realize that the life recorded so affectionately at Lahav and the realities of Bedouin life in modern Israel are worlds apart.

One lunchtime I called on Gillian Hundt at her office. I was rapidly introduced to a tall man with wire-framed spectacles, who was on the phone explaining how exhausted he was. I realized that he was none other than the leading Israeli authority on the Bedouin, Dr Clinton Bailey. I suspected that his expressions of weariness were being directed at me just as much as to his interlocutor. I had a choice: I could either torment Dr Bailey by attempting a swift interview, or I could leave him alone. I took pity. He had come to the hospital to visit Swalim, a dark-skinned Bedouin in robes and *keffiyeh*, whose son had fallen off a camel with disastrous consequences. Swalim was so worried about his son's plight that he had slept beside his hospital bed for two weeks, and the nurses were becoming more worried about his undernourished condition than they were about his son the patient. Dr Bailey and Gillian plotted ways to fetch Swalim his favourite foods and to induce him to defer his anxiety long enough for him to eat them. The plot was hatched and executed, successfully.

Gillian had to take a young Bedouin and his wife to a clinic near an unplanned settlement. After she had deposited them, she would introduce me to some of the tribesmen. The Bedouin wife had failed to become pregnant, and since her husband had already divorced one wife who had failed to conceive, Gillian feared that a similar fate could await wife number two if she failed to swell with his child. Hence the appointment at the gynaecological clinic. Gillian, although she grumbled constantly at how busy she was, seemed to devote a great deal of time to good works, while irritably denying that she was doing anything of the kind.

The Village, which will have no other name here, is inhabited by a few thousand members of a Bedouin tribe that had lived here until 1948, when they moved east towards Arad. The tribe moved back to its original land when the Israelis promised to build them a settlement, but a flurry of court cases involving land and access roads meant that the ministry had to renege on this undertaking. The shanty town that is the Village developed instead. There is no paving, and I feared for the springs of my car as it lurched from rut to trench. The Village is not connected to the electricity grid, so the only electricity supply comes from their own generator.

Gillian took me to the house of a friend. Most of the interior consisted of a large room painted blue and green. There were mats on the floor, and low mattresses around the walls; a similar layout to the other Arab houses I had visited, but far more rudimentary. A man was asleep on one of the mattresses. He stirred briefly to greet the visitors, then lapsed back into sleep. The only decoration consisted of posters of soccer teams.

Gillian introduced me to Suleiman, a bearded young man who had agreed to talk to me. First, however, he wanted to know my 'line'. What did I think of the treatment of Arabs within Israel? What did I think of the intifada? I said I was an observer rather than a political activist, at least when I was working on a book, but Gillian reacted impatiently to this, supporting Suleiman's wish to know where I stood on issues close to his heart before he confided his own views. So I answered his questions, and Suleiman seemed satisfied.

He took me up to the highest point of the Village, close to his own small house. He told me the story of the Village, which differed slightly from Gillian's account. He confirmed that his ancestors had lived here before the move to Arad, and he showed me the ruined stone houses on the slopes above the Village where his relatives had once lived. By 1975, when the government agreed to build a settlement for his tribe, half the tribe had moved to Jordan. His family had been tailors and were not nomadic, though other members of the tribe moved around the country with their flocks. When Likud came to power, the promises made in 1975 were broken, according to Suleiman. (Not as simple as that, glosses Gillian. After the return of Sinai to Egypt, other projects, notably those connected with the airports in the Negev, assumed greater urgency than the new Village.) So now the tribe has to be content with this shanty town. The generator is expensive to run, and it is also costly to transport water in tanks from the supply centre down near the main road. 'On either side of my village are two Jewish settlements,' said Suleiman. 'At night their lights go on, while we stay in the dark.

'The land around here used to belong to us. Now some of it is rented, and the rest has been given to the kibbutzim and moshavim, which also have irrigation. Before 1975 most of our tribe lived off the land, usually with our flocks. Now most of us are working for low wages in the towns, and we're luckier than many other tribes. Even those of us like me with proper qualifications find it almost impossible to get suitable jobs. There are a few Bedouin who get some university education and become lawyers, but most of us find it very hard to get jobs because we don't serve in the army. Four hundred dollars a month, that's a good salary for a Bedouin. There are a few flocks belonging to our village, but we have so little grazing land that we have to buy fodder for our animals. We can use the land on the hills behind our village, but it's too poor for grazing. Owning sheep is a form of independence, so the government is against it. Look down there. That's unused agricultural land between us and the road, but the government refuses to lease it to us so we can plant crops.'

'Why hasn't the kibbutz across the road taken that land?'

'Because it's right next to a Bedouin encampment and they want to keep their distance.' We walked along the slope towards Suleiman's house. 'The house where we met belongs to my father. Actually, it's not a house, it's a shack.' I had to agree. 'He is still waiting for a plot on which he could build a proper house. When I got married I wanted my own house, so I built this one in forty-eight hours. I built it really fast so that the soldiers wouldn't destroy it. Yes, it's illegal, and I've been lucky. A neighbour of mine built a house and he was fined $8,000. Sometimes these fines cost us more than the house – we only use breeze blocks. Come. I'll show you what's left of his house.' We walked down to a pile of rubble. I asked Suleiman where his neighbour lives now. 'He lives with his six children in a tin shack. He was also sentenced to six months in jail. He appealed, and instead he is working for six months in the hospital – but he gets no salary. They tear down our houses because they don't want us to have any roots, because they want to keep us preoccupied with our daily problems. The Jewish settlers are given fortunes by the government. We're not asking for fortunes. All we want is to be able to live and to have a home.'

The conditions in the Village were the worst I encountered anywhere in Israel. No Jew would tolerate them for five minutes. Yet it took some time to pry from Suleiman the admission that some communal facilities did exist. There is the gynaecological clinic as well as a clinic run by Histadrut, and a modern school. The clubhouse and children's playground were constructed by the villagers, though Suleiman grumbled that these facilities were far inferior to those found in Jewish settlements.

'If life is so difficult for you here, why don't you move to one of the planned settlements? Like Rahat?'

'We could, but our tribe would lose its identity. Here we all know each other. We are all kin. All that would be lost if we went to a large town.'

Suleiman invited me to enter his house. The word WELCOME is scrawled in Hebrew, Arabic, and English on the door. His wife, a tall woman swathed from head to toe in black cotton, was seated on the ground in the hallway playing with their son. She smiled, and then rose to fetch some tea for us, while Suleiman disappeared into another room to pray. I understand your dissatisfaction, I said to Suleiman when he returned, but how do you see your future and that of your son?

'It's impossible to have dreams in Israel,' he replied, with that touch of rhetoric that came easily to him. 'Before I went to college I had the same dreams as any Zionist, but after college my vision became much darker. In order to hold down a job here you have to be deaf, dumb, blind – the police are always checking on you, and if you open your mouth you risk losing your job. That is why I have asked you not to write down my name.

'The difference between animals and human beings is that human beings hope. We Bedouin want to show that we are not "dirty Arabs". We have fewer drug and drink problems than the Jewish community. The Jews must accept that we are not in opposition to them despite our grievances. We know we have to live with Israel. We have no choice. I have many Jewish friends, and feel no hatred for Jews.

'But as for the government, for Zionism . . . The government forces us to think only of the most basic problems, of bread and tea. They want us to be dependent on the state. You can't get sweetness when you apply such pressure. We don't want to teach hatred to our children, but how can we teach our children to love Israeli soldiers? Late at night they come to our village, and the children want to know why. They are here to practise the techniques they use in the Territories, because the conditions of our villages are so similar. I used to work in a supermarket, and the owner, a Tunisian, spoke Arabic. One day we were talking, and a customer said to me: "Don't speak Arabic. My dog doesn't like it." If my child had been with me, what do I tell him when he asks me to explain these things?

'The government is trying to isolate the Bedouin, just like they've done with the Druze. They try to maintain that we aren't Palestinians. But the Jews have double standards. It's fine for them to be a community, but not for Arabs. But of course we are Palestinians. It's impossible for us to be like the Jews. How can we hate the Arabs of Gaza and love the Soviet Jews?'

His wife came in with a tray, which she set down in front of us. This prompted Suleiman to change the subject.

'Tell me, my friend, what do you think about Salman Rushdie?'

Here we go again. I spoke about the importance of freedom of speech and defended Rushdie, but had to take care not to sound combative, especially since I happened to have in my shoulder bag a copy of Rushdie's book on Nicaragua. He then asked me about my family, and when he heard that my wife would be visiting Israel the following week, he urged me to bring her to the Village. We would be welcome to stay at his house, and our safety would be assured. Although we did not stay the night, I did take my wife to visit Suleiman and his family. Our arrival in the Village produced a gratifyingly large contingent of children to escort us to Suleiman's house. When we left an hour later, I thanked him for his time, and, shaking my hand, he said: 'I didn't help you. I help myself.'

A few days later I was talking to an Israeli doctor reputed to be knowledgeable about the Bedouin, so I asked him how the Israelis could tolerate its citizens living in such deplorable conditions. I described these to him, but he couldn't see what the fuss was about. Probably, his wife suggested, they like living that way.

'You and I wouldn't put up with it. No Jews live in tin shacks.'

'Well,' she said, 'there has to be a good reason for it, because we Israelis are very good to our minorities. Perhaps the land they are occupying is needed for other purposes. You can't have people settling down wherever they choose.'

I told them about the destroyed houses I had seen in the Village and elsewhere. What justification could there be for bulldozing homes in a peaceful village?

'The trend these days is away from houses, isn't it?'

'What do you mean?'

'Oh, people are always wandering off with a tent and being close to nature.'

'Yes, but usually when they have a comfortable house to go back to.' The doctor couldn't seem to distinguish between going for a ramble and being made homeless by ministry *diktat*.

'I'll tell you what really used to annoy me,' he said. 'When I was in charge of the medical services in this town, I kept trying to get the ministry to give us up-to-date equipment, but they never had the budget for it. But when I went to Arab clinics in the Triangle I could hardly believe what I saw. They had all the top equipment, far better than anything we had. So it's nonsense to say that the Israelis discriminate against the Arabs.'

What troubled me about the doctor and his wife is that they clearly refused to think about the issue at all. That there might be a yawning gap between how Israelis are supposed to behave and how many of them did behave was not to be contemplated.

On my return to Jerusalem I went to see the political scientist Dr Rafi Israeli, who has a special interest in the subject. Land confiscations were, he said, inevitable, 'but when Bedouin land is taken by the army, compensation is offered to them. The situation is not much different from that in North America, where native populations were also displaced.'

'Displacement isn't exactly the *mot juste* for what happened to the Indians, is it?'

'I'm not saying the situation is identical. In Israel there has been emigration by many Arabs, and that's another reason for confiscation. Sometimes land is needed for public use, such as reservoirs. Reservoirs make irrigation possible, and this also benefits the Arabs, but they never speak of that. It happens that the Arabs live in the least populated areas of Israel, which also happen to be the areas where the army needs land. You can't practise tank manoeuvres in Rehovot or Netanya. I'm not denying that there is also a political element. Jewish settlements are founded in areas within the Green Line where there's a high density of Arab population. That was necessary for security reasons and to offset any possibility of secessionist demands. Those demands are a reality, as we hear every year on Land Day, when demonstrating Arabs shout about "liberating" the Galilee.'

'This may all be so, but it doesn't explain the vast difference in living standards between Arab and Jew.'

'Of course there are disparities, but there are also disparities within the Jewish community. There are Jewish slums not far from areas of great wealth. And remember that among the Bedouin, for example, standards of health, life expectancy, and education are far higher than among Bedouin in Arab countries.'

'But why should the Bedouin compare their living conditions with their relatives in Jordan? Why not with their Jewish neighbours in comfortable, well-equipped settlements just down the road? Why should Arab municipalities receive a third of the aid that central government gives to Jewish ones?'

'There are these discrepancies, I agree. But when these people openly say that they support the PLO and they speak of liberating the Galilee, why should we pour more and more money into enemy hands? I spend forty days on reserve duty, and my two sons are in the army right now. We *deserve* more than the Arabs. Arabs have the right not to identify with Israel, but then they can't claim that they are discriminated against.'

'Do they not also have the right not to see their houses demolished?'

'They are demolished when they build illegally. Since 1948 the Arab population has increased sixfold and the vast majority of them have found housing. Demolitions can only take place with a court order, and thank God we still have an independent judiciary. In my view the courts are often *too* lenient. Jews can't build illegally either. We don't want shanty towns in our midst. That's why planned settlements were built. There are alternatives to living in unplanned settlements.'

Dr Israeli had touched upon most of the arguments that justify the treatment of Israeli Arabs as second-class citizens: some are not loyal to the state, very few are prepared to perform military service. On the other hand, discrimination, whether intentional or fortuitous, against Israeli Arabs is not only questionable in terms of natural justice, it is also imprudent. People with grievances seek redress; discrimination hardly reinforces loyalty to the state responsible for it. Only those on the far right advocate deporting the Arab population. Kahane argues that it is stupid even to expect Israeli Arabs to be good Israeli citizens, so the honest and sensible thing to do is ship them out to countries such as Jordan where these conflicts won't arise. When Kamal in Kafr Bara told me he was an Israeli by birth yet did not have the same rights as Jewish Israelis, he was stating something undeniable. Given that Kahane's proposal for dealing with the dilemma is unacceptable, how is it to be resolved? I put this question to Dr Israeli.

'I would be more sympathetic if I didn't always hear the Arabs clamouring for their rights, but never speaking of the responsibilities they owe the state in return. They are not obliged to serve in the army, and most of them don't. Those who do serve, like the Druze and the Bedouin trackers, receive benefits.'

'The ultra-Orthodox don't serve in the army, and they aren't denied benefits. Why the double standards?'

'That is perfectly true, and I think we should be consistent about this. Those who do not share the values of the Jewish state, be they Arabs or Orthodox Jews, should be denied citizenship.'

'Some Arabs have told me they are willing to undertake voluntary service as an alternative to military service, but this option is not made available to them. Wouldn't that be a satisfactory way of letting them discharge their responsibilities?'

'Frankly, I am sceptical. They may talk of being prepared to do voluntary service, but even in noncontroversial ways they fail to make their contribution. They won't participate in the night watches at the universities, for example. What it comes down to is this. Israeli Arabs must decide whether they wish to give allegiance to our state, and that means allegiance to the flag, willingness to perform military service, and to learn fluent Hebrew. If they aren't prepared to do this, they should be deprived of citizenship and given the status of residents. And exactly the same should apply to the ultra-Orthodox.'

'Should an Arab prepared to give that kind of allegiance be allowed to become a high-ranking military officer in the IDF?'

'He should be eligible to become chief of staff, if it comes to that. I want to stress that I don't blame the Arabs for the present state of affairs. Successive Israeli governments are responsible. For instance, we have two separate educational systems, so how can we expect to have one citizenry?'

'But both sides seem content with the system.'

'That doesn't mean we should perpetuate it. Separate school systems widen the dichotomy. But in the end everyone must make their own choices. We can't have Arabs identifying with the intifada within Israel. Jews may criticize the government fiercely, but with very few exceptions they remain within the system. How many Jews, other than *haredim*, refuse to serve in the army? What we have among the Arabs is a fifth column, which is unacceptable. Israeli Arabs constitute one fifth of the Palestinian "nation". They claim to be a national minority, and the consequence of that is that we are living with them in a binational state. That in turn means that Israel is no longer a Jewish state. Demography reinforces this. It's suicidal for Israel to accept this state of affairs.

'In my view there should be three choices. The Arabs can be full Israelis with all rights in return for full participation in the system. Or they can move to a Palestinian state to the east. Or – and I believe 80 per cent of Israeli Arabs would choose this third option – they can take Palestinian citizenship to achieve the national identity they seek, while at the same time they can remain within Israel as tax-paying residents. Jordan could be the basis for such a Palestinian state, but where the exact boundaries are drawn would be a matter for negotiation. With such a solution, demography becomes unimportant, because the Palestinians will have their separate citizenship.'

'That solution only becomes feasible if the Israeli government is willing to concede the eventual possibility of a Palestinian state, which it shows no sign of doing. In the meantime militancy among the Arabs is growing.'

'Indeed, and that's why we need to find a solution quickly. I find the rise of the Islamic movement, for instance, very worrying.'

'Some say that it is less a movement of religious fundamentalism than a self-help organization.'

'The theory that Islamic candidates are winning votes because of Arab gratitude for services rendered doesn't conflict with a belief that the Islamic movement is a militant one. The movement has been able to show that it is more "pure" than the Communists, who have been shown up as incompetent. But we must see the movement in a wider context than Israeli municipal politics. Their tactics are identical to those of the Islamic Brotherhood in Egypt. They have decided not to rebel against the system but to build their own infrastructure. The fundamentalists in the Territories – the Hamas – and their disciples within Israel such as Darwish, make no secret of wanting Islamic dominion over all of Israel. Many of their leaders were released from jail in the late 1970s on the condition that they remained nonpolitical. Hence their policy of setting up an infrastructure that could be regarded as the foundations of a parallel state. At present the political content of the movement is only latent, but it is certainly there, and the fundamentalists beyond the Green Line make no secret of it. Islam has become a rallying point. It doesn't matter whether the supporters are religious or not: if they gain increasing power, the end result will be the same.

'Hence the urgency of resolving the Arab issue within Israel in *national* terms. It is true that Arabs are not treated equally here, and we must expose this myth of equality. Politicians such as Ehud Olmert want a quiet life, so they work to lessen the inequalities. But in my view they are merely perpetuating the problem. But I accept that, politically, this is a hot potato.'

Dr Israeli's proposed solution is shared by quite a few of his countrymen. It has the merits of logic and clarity, and seems to perpetrate no injustice on the Israeli Arabs. But are his proposals practical? What, precisely, are the rights that the Arabs who do not pledge allegiance to the Israeli state will forfeit? According to an article by Dr Israeli, 'Arab residents will not be required to serve in the military or to enrol in the Israeli public educational system, but will not enjoy civil rights such as the right to vote, and will have to provide for their own private education.'[3]

Others, such as Dr Israeli's colleague at the Hebrew University, Yehoshuah Porath, suspect the motives of those who espouse this kind of solution: 'Those who demand that military service be immediately made obligatory for the Arabs of Israel, and who make Israeli citizenship conditional on the fulfilment of that obligation, are fully aware that the obligation will not be met and are actually looking for a way to deprive the Arabs of Israel of their Israeli citizenship.'[4]

The Likud MK Michael Eitan endorses the proposal of making Israeli Arabs choose between Palestinian identity and limited Israeli citizenship, or full Israeli citizenship with full rights and full duties, but accepts that such a solution can only be offered once a Palestinian state has come into existence.[5] Since that outcome remains in doubt, it seems likely that Israeli Arabs, like it or not, will have to continue to live with the status quo, as expressed by the Likud minister of minority affairs, Ehud Olmert: 'Israeli Arabs should neither be compelled to serve in the army nor be treated as second-class citizens because they don't . . . It bears on the relationship we have with them. They identify with the purposes of the Palestinian revolution, as they call it. Right or wrong, good or bad, we have to see this as reality.'[6] But realities alter, and how long this status quo will persist in the face of pressures exerted by the intifada, by discrimination, and by the growing power of the Islamic movement, is anyone's guess.

I hadn't wanted to go to Eilat: just a string of luxury hotels along a beach. But after a week in dusty Beersheva, a few days in a beach resort sounded more tempting. I set off for Sede Boqer and the road to the south. For fifteen miles I passed between army firing ranges. Notices warn travellers to keep off the ranges, but this doesn't seem to deter the Bedouin from pitching their tents and tethering their donkeys and camels on these slopes and dells. Ben-Gurion, after his retirement from politics, had lived at Sede Boqer, and he and his wife are buried there. A low stone amphitheatre embraces the two simple tombs on a terrace in the corner of the kibbutz where they lived. The inscriptions make no reference to Ben-Gurion's status or achievements, and the text simply informs the reader of the year in which he and his wife made *aliyah*, implying that this had been the most important event in their lives.

Driving south from Beersheva, you cross a landscape of thin scrub over parched rolling hills. This is desert, but not the dramatic desert of dune and rock, mountain and wadi, which is first revealed from this terrace at Sede Boqer. The terrace is on a clifftop that overlooks, hundreds of feet below, the dry riverbed of the Zin. It was here that Moses faced an incipient revolt of the Children of Israel: 'Why have ye brought up the congregation of the Lord into this wilderness, that we and our cattle should die there? And wherefore have ye made us to come up out of Egypt, to bring us in unto this evil place?'[1] Looking down into the wilderness, it's hard not to side with the discontented. It's a most spectacular view, and the distant mountains glow in constantly shifting shades of beige and buff depending on the time of day and the angle of the sun. Some of the more sheltered slopes are kissed with dabs of springtime greenery, while down in the wadi, which only contains water after very heavy rain, the light shrubbery indicates the course of the Zin. Ibex live in this wilderness, and in very hot weather they come up to the kibbutz in search of greenery. This is no place for human habitation, as the Israelis of 3,000 years ago discovered in five minutes flat.

Continuing south from Sede Boqer, I turned off the road along the dirt track that leads towards En Avdat. I parked the car and wandered into the desert. It was March and the desert, for a few brief weeks, was in bloom. The loveliest of the flowering plants is the wild tulip, a bright scarlet flower on a very small stem. It does not bloom every year, but I was in luck, and these bursts of scarlet rising from the arid soil were ravishing in their solitary beauty. Two purple plants were splashed along the relatively moist roadsides: the ubiquitous muricandia, and the furry-stemmed salvia lanigera. There were two common yellow plants, senecio and diplotaxis, and carpets of white riboudea. Crawling along the ground were the big lilac flowers of malva and the little purple tubes of erodium, a plant that only flowers before noon. Set back from the road were a few tiny wheat and barley fields of the Bedouin, often planted in the same sites chosen 2,000 years ago by the Nabateans. There is, of course, no irrigation, and the success of the crop depends on winter rains and run-off water. By late May the crop is ready to be harvested.

I have to come clean. Plant identification is not my strongest suit, and when I gave a hitch-hiker a lift in this direction, I made a deal with him. He was a botanist from Sede Boqer, and in exchange for the ride, he would tell me everything he knew about the local flora.

One of the roads from Beersheva leads to remote Nizzana, which is nothing more than a border crossing into Egypt. This part of the desert is sandier than the more easterly regions, and I found the air dimmed by distant sandstorms. Out of the immense milky cloud loomed enormous white airships, tethered at an army base. Close to the border is the Nizzana project, a cluster of buildings housing delinquent children sent here to learn trades and farming. The border post consists of a few huts and a barrier. I approached, then stopped and turned around, as I didn't want to take the car into Egypt.

At that moment a tall soldier came running towards me from the barrier. Either I had committed some violation and was to be reprimanded, or he wanted a lift. It was the latter. Was I going to Jerusalem? No, but I could take him to the nearest bus station. It was Friday and he was desperate to get home in time for Shabbat. He spoke good English, for the simple reason that he had grown up in Golders Green. A doctor, he was stationed at Nizzana on reserve duty. It was not the most enthralling posting: on a busy day, two cars might cross the border. Two of the other reserve soldiers there at Nizzana also happened to be doctors, so this God-forsaken spot probably had that week the highest density of doctors to population of any place in the world.

About twenty miles south of Sede Boqer the modern town of Mitzpe

Ramon is spread over two hilltops in a cluster of tightly packed four-storey apartment blocks and so-called patio houses. The newer clifftop section of town overlooks the magnificent Ramon Crater, a broad brown canyon braided with dry wadis, with tramlines of shrubbery on either bank. On this northern side of the crater, radio masts and an observatory jut into the air, and there are some embryonic industrial parks on the road to Beersheva. The government hopes to attract new investment to Mitzpe Ramon, which is certainly a more attractive new community than towns such as Yerocham and Dimona.

I spent a night at the field school, one of many in Israel run by the Society for the Protection of Nature, along the cliffs to the west of town. The school, which was built in 1982 and can sleep 140, is used mostly by students on field trips, but also by families of experienced hikers who come at weekends. The school specializes in overnight trips, and a few weeks earlier guides had taken ten groups of twenty-five children on a four-day trek. The field schools combine educational and informational roles: Mitzpe Ramon has a centre for ornithological information, issues weather and road reports, and maintains a good library. Because the army controls so much of the desert, the field school cultivates good relations with the IDF, and often acts as guides to soldiers. Indeed, according to the school's director, Rami, the best guides are women who take on the job as part of their military service. In return the army consults the field school before planning military exercises, so as to minimize any damage that could be done to rare species or unique features in the desert.

'This is the only place in Israel,' Rami told me, 'where you can hike in terrain where there are no trails. It's quite possible to find yourself in a wadi where no one has walked for 2,000 years. We keep stumbling across Nabatean remains, and the other day I came across one of their panther or tiger traps.'

But of course by exploring virgin territory it ceases to be virgin. 'Hikers can't avoid leaving marks on the land, whether in the form of burnt-out fires or footprints. It's so dry here that these marks, not to mention tank tracks in the military zones, can stay for decades before they disappear. The guides we use are extremely careful about leaving the fewest possible traces, but we can't prevent people coming back on their own or with less scrupulous guides.'

If mere use of the wilderness, however reverential, can pose a threat to its survival, so too does modern tourism. 'There are plans to build a five-star hotel in Mitzpe Ramon. I've no objection to that, but they want to build it as a seven-storey tower on the clifftop. If they go ahead, it will be visible from all over this part of the Negev, and it would wreck the landscape.'

At dusk a soft sapphire light fell over the canyon, and later, under the light of a full moon, the expanses of rock and desert and valley took on a deep blue radiance, blurring on the horizons into a strange and distant haze. Far off to the east I could see lights, either from a Jewish settlement in the Jordan valley or from a village in Jordan itself. In the morning I walked part of the way down into the canyon. As I descended I looked up to see the striations of the bare rock of the cliff walls, offering a geological chart I was too ignorant to read. The trail was strewn with succulents with deep green leaves, unexpected in a desert, and with highly coloured droplets of flowers. White snail shells were scattered along the paths and packed under rock overhangs. The trail deteriorated, and as I was ill equipped for serious hiking, I clambered back up the path, collected my belongings from the cabin where I had spent the night, and pointed the car southwards.

For a long while the road crosses ridged flatlands framed in all directions by hills. Although it had rained the week before, the sandy soil was fissured with thirst; but it was also bursting with flowering shrubs, now in their week of greatest vigour. Walking into the desert from the road I was conscious not only of the greater heat, for by now I was a thousand feet below Mitzpe Ramon, but of a blanketing stillness broken only by sudden descents of whirring insects that swooped and vanished.

Continuing southwards I crossed a few low passes, and coming over the last of them I saw the Jordan valley below me, flesh-pink in colour, with the grim wrinkled brows of the Jordanian mountains beyond. Kibbutzim have planted large neat fields and orchards on the valley floor, and I drove into one of them, Samar. I had tried to arrange to visit this very left-wing kibbutz, but had been told I would not be welcome, a response that only made me the more eager to see it. At two in the afternoon it was deserted. The houses, sand-coloured cubes, were lifeless; shrubs were flowering around an empty pool. I spotted a young woman doing some repairs near a work shed, and she turned out to be English. She told me that almost all the kibbutzniks here were Israeli, and they survived by cultivating winter vegetables and date plantations; they also shared a date processing plant and fish farms near Eilat. This kind of economic base is typical of the kibbutzim and moshavim in the Jordan valley.

Shortly before Eilat, I turned right, and back into the mountains, to visit Timna Park, a wilderness of granite and sandstone. It's a remarkable place, filled with strange rock formations that resemble mille-feuille pastry; here and there the rock had taken on the fluid shapes of Dali's dripping watch. I wandered into a narrow and shady canyon – a welcome shelter from a relentless sun – to look at the crude Midianite rock engravings of chariots. At the top of the canyon a boulder is wedged between the walls, and behind it, blazing in the full sunlight, are immense yellow cliffs. The sheer variety of colourings at Timna is astonishing. There were no birds, and hardly any insects. Just stillness, amid awesome cliffs and bare granite rocks too impermeable for any plant life to get a grip.

I arrived in Eilat in the late afternoon. To the left was the beach hotel district and just beyond it the border and the Jordanian town of Aqaba that shares the head of the Gulf of Aqaba with Eilat. To the right the more residential areas of the town scurry up a steep hillside onto a kind of plateau. Straight ahead is the straggling port area, with its warehouses, docks, new car depots, and unsightly plants of the Dead Sea Works. Beyond the port is the North Beach with its pretty marina and another batch of hotels. Nearby is the town's most famous tourist attraction, the underwater observatory at Coral Beach, but I was deterred by the curiously worded sign: THE REEF TANK IS CLOSED FOR YOUR FUTURE ENJOYMENT.

It's not hard to see why Eilat is popular, especially with Israelis, for it is devoted to hedonism. None of the conflicts, and little of the aggression, that marks most Israeli life impinges on pleasure-loving Eilat. This has much to do with its location, over a hundred miles south of any other town of comparable size. This has engendered a kind of psychological isolation, and Eilat feels more like an island than a shoreline resort. The intifada has not diminished trade. It's as though Eilat were somehow detached from Israel itself. The town is packed with small cafés, Lebanese grills, cake shops, and at the tawdry multi-level tourist centre at the foot of the hill, a plethora of fast food hovels, each playing a different and clashing cassette of rock music, and dubious Oriental restaurants, one of which was presided over by the absurd Shlomo, who pads around in a white sheet and fez. Tourism is so important to Eilat that it can be studied at the local high schools. The course is effective, as I didn't encounter any of the usual Israeli brusqueness in Eilat. The inhabitants as well as the tourists can enjoy Eilat's special tax status, for VAT is not charged here, which means that food and petrol and even the *Jerusalem Post* are considerably cheaper than anywhere else in Israel.

There happens to be a British honorary consul in Eilat, and I decided to pay my respects. Since my hotel happened to be opposite the consulate – how had I missed the fluttering Union Jack across the street? – she insisted I come right over for a cup of tea. The consul, Fay Morris, and her husband Reginald, remain thoroughly British in manners, even though they have lived in Eilat for thirty years. Reginald, a tall taciturn doctor, must be the only man in Eilat who wears a tie. It took a while to defrost him. Fay, who resembles a younger Mary Whitehouse, is garrulous but, unlike her husband, great fun. We took tea on the terrace while she told me about all the splendid parties they had thrown. I asked to see their pet crocodile, but I had come at the wrong time of the year, since it was hibernating inside something that looked suspiciously like a coffin. When the Morrises came to Eilat it was, according to Fay, rather like a Wild West town. There were only 2,000 inhabitants, but after 1956 the little town expanded as immigrants began to settle there. I had fancied that this motley assortment of Moroccans, Dutch, and Romanians had somehow landed up in Eilat and then found they couldn't get out again, so they stayed put. This is what happens to many British tourists, who then appeal to the honorary consul for help. 'It's very nice to have you here for tea,' Fay reminded me, 'but there's more to being consul than giving tea parties. Rescuing those impoverished students and getting some of the more unruly ones out of jail takes up an awful lot of my time. And money.'

Fay suggested that I return later in the evening and join her on an outing to the mayor's reception in honour of Eilat's fortieth birthday.

'Will the mayor mind if I gate-crash?'

'I doubt it. The whole town is invited.'

We were joined by a friend of Fay's who was taking a week's holiday in Eilat. A woman of little humour, Rona's sole topic of conversation was herself, and she told me at great length about her personal preferences in food and music. When she discovered that I was a writer, she asked me to send her a copy of my latest book. I thought about this hard, trying to think of a single reason why I should. While I pondered, she offered in exchange to send me one of her books. That helped me to reach a firm decision, and I told her the answer was no.

At eight I set off with the two ladies to the plaza opposite the municipality buildings. Fay had not been exaggerating: the entire population had been invited. The old-timers were gossiping in little groups, the teenagers were dancing to the rhythmic wailings of a Moroccan *chanteuse*, and tinies in shorts and frocks were stuffing their faces with sandwiches and cakes from the buffet. It was clearly Fay's mission to introduce me to everyone in Eilat. No sooner had I struck up a conversation with one celebrity than she was dragging me off to meet the next. 'Now here's a good person for you to meet,' she would say, hauling me off to meet, in succession, the German (or was it the Swedish?) consul, the Egyptian consul, half a dozen teachers at the school where she teaches, a local agency reporter, the mayor's mother, the Sephardi rabbi, and the Sephardi rabbi's wife, a delightful woman wearing a dapper little white sailor's cap instead of the usual dreary snood. Fay forced the bemused mayor, Rafi Hochmann, to shake my hand. A handsome man in his early thirties, Hochmann had triumphed at the local elections and was clearly combining his personal celebrations with those of the town. In his powder-blue suit, he looked like the heart-throb of southern Israel. He effortlessly conquered Rona, who told us repeatedly how dishy he was. For my part, I was bewitched by the mayor's wife, who came from the same glamorous mould, and I was not surprised to learn that she was the star of the local theatre.

Once the reception was coming off the boil, Fay suggested we go off to dinner. Rona wanted to take a look at Jet, Eilat's newest night spot. So we drove down to the beach area, and parked outside a discreet little complex of bars and restaurants surrounded by a low floodlit wall. We entered a patio focused around a pool. A fish restaurant and bar led off from the patio – Fay darted off to greet the people in the bar, all of whom she knew – but the centre of the complex was occupied by an elegant restaurant, with swish geometrical décor coloured a half-dozen shades of dusty blue. Its tall darkened windows were covered with black blinds, a pleasingly *de trop* touch, and the walls were mirrored so that you can keep an eye on other tables without it being too obvious. The lampshades were made of metal, and the name of this game was Cool. I was put off by the silent movies being screened onto a blank wall behind the stage, and repelled by the elderly singer crooning Beatles songs in a strong Israeli accent. I also didn't fancy having to deal with the bill at the end of the evening.

But Rona was so entranced by Jet that she announced that dinner would be on her. Done. I was content, and Fay deliriously happy, since this week in Eilat the *crème de la crème* were trying out the new restaurant. Here they all were, the manager of the Sonesta Hotel in Taba across the border in Egypt, the manager of the Dead Sea Works, the dentist who co-owned Jet, and a leading *belletriste*. While we were inspecting the menu, the crooner was pensioned off and the band launched into 'Roll Out the Barrel' and other ghastly tunes. A group of bald Swedes rushed to the dance floor with their overdressed wives. They were an ugly lot, but they danced with all the precision of a Prussian regiment, and when the band switched to a Latin American medley they expertly ducked and pulled and swerved all over the dance floor. Meanwhile Rona kept telling me how good the band was, which it wasn't. Fortunately the food was acceptable, and the waitress had the modesty and charm of someone who hadn't been doing the job for more than a week.

By eleven thirty I was flagging, but a jazz band was installing itself on the platform and Fay was becoming agitated. The drummer was Arale Kaminsky, said to be the best percussionist in Israel. His co-musicians consisted of a brisk and proficient pianist, a hard-working bass player and an excellent saxophonist, who looked like a mathematics teacher. The group was good, very good, and as the midnight hour came and went, they got even better. Fay, transfixed, thrummed her fingers on the table. 'I can't tell one tune from another,' she confided to me, 'but I love rhythm.' Rona took an opposite line. 'I only enjoy jazz when I can recognize the tune,' she explained, thus missing the entire point of improvisation. Rona was clearly hating every minute of it, and whenever the music reached a new pitch of excitement she would pluck my sleeve and drone, 'I must tell you . . .' before embarking on some tedious anecdote about her children. She began these interventions whenever she mislaid the tune, which was, of course, the very moment when the performance became interesting.

Rona, to be fair, was suffering from a rheum as well as from boredom, so after an hour Fay suggested we leave.

'Please, we can stay,' said Rona, 'I'd be very happy to stay. I like the music very much, especially when I can follow the tune, though I think the singer we heard earlier was better. Let me tell you something . . .' And she sneezed.

Fay rose to her feet, and we followed her as she threaded her way through the crowded restaurant. The *crème de la crème* looked up in astonishment, since they had come here specially to listen to the hottest entertainment south of Tel Aviv. Fay drove us to Rona's hotel.

'Why don't you come in and have some coffee?' urged Rona, not wishing to be a damp squib.

This was too much for Fay. 'Your hotel will be completely dead now,' she said dismissively, 'and in any case sitting in the lounge having coffee would be a bit of an anticlimax after what we've just been listening to, I must say.'

Rona was embarrassed. 'We could have stayed at Jet. I was enjoying the music very much, especially when I could hear the tune.'

Fay was having none of it, and Rona was decanted from the car into the hotel lobby with instructions to get a good night's sleep. Fay was twitchy with ill-concealed irritation, and as she swung the car out of the driveway, I said quietly: 'We could go back.'

The honorary consul braked, and turned to me, her eyes wide open. 'Really?'

'Why not? It's not that late. Just for half an hour?'

'What a wonderful idea! I'd never have suggested it! Yes, why not? Just because I have to teach at eight tomorrow morning – never mind – just half an hour.'

So back we went to Jet, and the face she had lost by creeping out earlier was regained as she swept back in, making a triumphant re-entry into social space. We ordered some beers and stayed for an hour.

'You'll probably think this is a terrible idea,' she said, as she was driving back to the consulate, 'but my school is having a fancy dress party tomorrow, and you're very welcome to come along.'

And at nine the following evening I rang the doorbell. The gate was opened by a creature wearing a printed Punjabi suit, a Saudi headdress, tinsel from Christmas tree decorations in her hair, and a dozen necklaces, including one of Turkish meerschaum. It was the honorary consul. 'This one is from Tibet,' she explained, poking at her necklaces, 'and this little box that swings about is for carrying jewels or drugs. But what are you going to wear?' She stared at me, horrified by my attire of shirt and trousers. She opened a trunk and began rummaging. She fished out a leather Crocodile Dundee hat, and pushed it down onto my head. 'Good. It fits.' More rummaging. 'Here we are. This is a feather headdress from Paraguay. We'll curl it round the hat and it'll look very splendid.' Was Reginald coming too? No, he wasn't, and I could quite understand why.

We looked like idiots, but so did everybody else at the party. The teachers came dressed as beggars, as Arabs, as monkeys. The headmaster, a bearded gentleman with granny specs, wore a short skirt and green tights, and another teacher also came in drag, in a worryingly convincing impersonation of a French whore. Every party needs an organizer, and ours was a slender and very pretty Moroccan woman dressed in a ravishing black and gold shift with a similarly embroidered robe over it, and on her head a half-spherical white cap, also embroidered. There was dancing, of course, and here the Moroccans, including the Bible teacher who was built like a boulder, excelled. There were games too, and we were divided into teams. My team had to put on a fashion show, which meant drag for me, but our show was something of a flop, since the clothes we were parading were no more outrageous than the clothes we had worn to start with. Another group did a ballet, another a cancan, but the best performance came from the group who improvised a Moroccan wedding complete with ululations. I left early, as I didn't want to cramp their style. The honorary consul, I have no doubt, danced till dawn.

It is not only Europe that is studded with freak territories, marooned pseudo-principalities such as San Marino, nations like Monaco that are all trappings and no substance, and fortresses of the church such as the Vatican, all of which appear to exist for the sole benefit of stamp collectors. Israel has, or had, Taba, a tiny corner of the Sinai that had not been returned to Egypt after the peace agreement. For a decade Taba remained a disputed patch of sand, but during that period it prospered under a more neutral regime: the Sonesta, the most luxurious hotel on the Gulf of Aqaba. Early in 1989 Israel, after putting the dispute to arbitration, agreed to return Taba to Egypt. Except among ardent super-nationalists, this was no cause for tears. Nobody had ever claimed that Taba was intrinsic to Eretz Yisrael; and the owners of the Sonesta were well satisfied with the $40 million that the Egyptians paid for the hotel, together with the assurance that it would remain under Israeli management for twenty years. Even the small bar and beach resort once operated by the late one-eyed Rafi Nelson next door to the hotel had been sold for $1.5 million.

The week before I arrived in Eilat Taba had been formally returned to Egypt, so every resident of Eilat was crossing the border to see whether the change of sovereignty had made any difference. I followed the crowd to the border. The Egyptian authorities were there in strength, to judge by the number of officials, all in dazzling uniforms. This was a big day for Taba, as President Mubarak was due to arrive there for a ceremony involving long speeches and flag-raisings and guards of honour. I tried to park at the Sonesta, but footmen – perhaps they were policemen – with whistles indicated that I should park further along the main road. This I tried to do, but was met by finger-wagging heavies, presumably security men keeping the place clear for Mubarak. Back to the Sonesta. This time I didn't ask; I just parked, and wandered back to the parade ground.

There, behind the spacious beach area a band was rehearsing, pounding out Wagner. In the bay a small warship stood at anchor, while smaller craft plied the waters and a schooner glided by. The hills of the Sinai took on a rich sandy colour in the morning light, while those on the other side of the bay towards Saudi Arabia were still gauzed with haze. After an hour of wandering about, I grew bored. Nobody would tell me when Mubarak would arrive, and even if he turned up in five minutes, the chances of a personal interview were slight. I strolled back towards the Sonesta and paused by a group of hotel staff who were looking at the preparations. They were talking to an American immigrant, who was arguing that Israel should not have returned Taba to the Egyptians. One of the Israeli women from the hotel turned on him: 'More of our soldiers should die for this little beach? This was never part of Israel in the first place. Didn't enough die in Lebanon in 1982? And for what? Perhaps we will have some more peace rather than this endless killing.' That shut him up.

Re-entry into Israel proved more difficult. The Egyptians had installed six immigration officers to deal with arrivals, and another six to handle departures. The Israelis, however, had only one official on duty, and insisted on a security check of luggage and person. To cross into Egypt had taken five minutes; to return to Israel took forty, and would have taken much longer had I not been unencumbered by luggage and thus able to jump one of the queues. The Egyptians, it was thought, were deliberately upstaging the Israelis by showing how well they could handle such matters. They had constructed a new customs shed in seventy-two hours and were doing their ostentatious best to ensure that delays were kept to a minimum. There was also speculation that the Israelis, prompted by foolish remarks made by the tourism minister Gideon Patt to the effect that only 'masochists' would want to go to Taba after it was returned to Egypt, were out to make life as uncomfortable as possible for those determined to make the attempt. The previous day a bus containing 170 tourists from Eilat had set off at six in the morning on a day trip to St Catharine's monastery in the Sinai. There had been a three-hour delay at the border, and when they finally reached the monastery it was closed. On the return trip there was a two-hour delay at Israeli immigration, so the culture-starved tourists were additionally starved of their dinner when they eventually got back to their hotels. The tourists were fed up, and so were the tour organizers, who had to refund the cost of the wasted journey. If the delayed border crossings were indeed an Israeli exercise in spite, they were remarkably counterproductive.

I decided to drive back north along the almost deserted road that follows the Egyptian border. It took me through the mountain reserve adjoining the Sinai Desert. The landscape was unremittingly arid. The mountains, stark and sharply defined in the dry air, were coloured contiguous shades of buff and granitic red, with occasional moss-green bands coursing through the exposed rock. Near the military airport at Uvda, I picked up a hitch-hiking soldier.

In slow cautious English he told me about his plans. 'I have been in the army for two and a half years, and in five months I will be out. When I leave the army, I will work and then travel for two years. At eighteen I stopped having fun. Now I want to have fun. So I will go to America and the Far East and Australia. Then I will come back and find a job.'

'How's it been in the army?'

'It is a good thing to serve my country, otherwise I wouldn't do it.' Quite. He asked me about my travels. I told him where I had been, and then he said: 'Will you stay in Israel?'

'To settle?'

'Yes. To settle.'
'No.'
'Very understandable.'

I wanted to visit a development town that wasn't beset with problems, wracked with unemployment, plagued with drugs or depressed by election results. So I polled my friends and they said with one voice: Arad. This is a town of 15,000 inhabitants set, like most development towns, in the middle of nowhere; in this case, east of Beersheva and about ten miles short of the Dead Sea. The site was chosen by Arye Eliav and the other founders because of its proximity to the Green Line – it's only a few miles north to the West Bank from Arad. Instead of sitting in Jerusalem and mapping out a town for other shmucks to live in, Eliav and his associates moved here themselves in 1962, living first in tents and then in asbestos huts during the construction phase. The philosophy behind the town was unashamedly elitist. A committee vetted would-be settlers, from whom references were required to suggest that they were, potentially, good citizens. There was a clear preference for settlers who already enjoyed a measure of professional success and were therefore likely to continue that way and to inspire others to follow. This system of selection was pursued for about ten years, by which time the tone of Arad had been established, and later arrivals adapted themselves to it. It also became a model for other more recent development towns; Karmiel, for example, is known, flatteringly, as the Arad of the north.

In the early 1970s, when Morris Roth came here to practise dentistry, it was a social paradise, with virtually no crime, no unemployment, no social problems. Now there are all three, but still only to a trivial extent. When I suggested to Roth that Arad had been founded on elitist principles that made it *sui generis*, he replied: 'I don't think the principles on which the other Negev towns were founded, namely of busing immigrants from Haifa by night to the desert and dumping them there, were preferable. Those who planned towns such as Dimona never lived in them. The opposite is true of Arad.'

Morris Roth arrived at the same time as hundreds of Russian and Romanian immigrants, and the ethnic variety of the town is best gauged, as so often, in its cemetery. The Russians have done well. One supermarket is almost entirely staffed by them, and they are also prominent in the municipal administration. There are no ethnic ghettoes in Arad, and the various national groups live jumbled up together. Only the *haredi* community, made up of Gerer Chasidim, keeps to itself. The black-coated, black-hatted gentlemen scurrying about seem out of place in this bright modern town, but they came to Arad for the same reason as many other residents. The air is exceptionally pure, and the dust and pollen count very low. This makes Arad attractive to asthma sufferers, such as the Gerer *Rebbe*. He built a summer residence here, and naturally his court accompanied him and set up a yeshiva. The *Rebbe* is now too frail to travel to Arad, but about 200 families of Gerer Chasidim have remained. The municipality makes a conscious effort to maintain the purity of the town's climate: plants and trees that produce troublesome pollen are banned, and prevailing winds prevent the outpourings of nearby factories from moving towards Arad. It is estimated that a fifth of those living in Arad are asthmatics. Many came from Haifa, with its notorious air pollution problems. Ironically, the very industries that caused that pollution are those in which many Arad residents work, namely, the chemical industries near the Dead Sea.

Arad is well run: the municipality comes close to balancing its books. Prompt local tax payments are insisted upon, and in return the town provides a good level of services. This is in sharp contrast to towns such as Dimona, where the municipality is in arrears and the town in a state of physical decay, which in turn diminishes any pride the inhabitants may have had. Although Arad's infrastructure would enable it to support a population of 75,000, that kind of growth is unlikely to occur, if only because the region offers insufficient employment. Nor are the tax incentives generous, since people have been content to move to Arad in the past without them. The economic woes of the nation have made their impact on Arad, however. Hundreds of workers once employed in the chemical factories at Dimona now have to commute to jobs in Tel Aviv. Younger people are leaving Arad, which they find soporific, and settling in the cities.

Arad is a Labour Party town. The mayor from 1967 until 1988, Avraham Shochat, known universally as Baiga, came to Arad as part of Arye Eliav's planning team. He also made the useful move of marrying the daughter of Levi Eshkol, who later became prime minister. Baiga was repeatedly re-elected with the largest popular vote of any mayor in Israel, and in 1984 was still mopping up 89 per cent. After his departure for the Knesset in 1988, his successor received only a miserable 65 per cent. In that election, an independent candidate performed better than the Likud candidate. Arad is also a secular town. The cinema is open on Friday evening, and buses run on Shabbat. The presence of the Gerer Chasidim hasn't affected this, even though one of them is a member of the town council. The *haredi* community refrains from putting pressure on their fellow citizens, because they know perfectly well what the reaction would be.

Arad is brilliantly designed on the premise that the site should allow for growth but never become congested. Dozens of blocks of flats are built along pedestrian precincts in long strips, with inlets from a perimeter road providing convenient parking while leaving the precincts free of traffic. Because of this layout, there is never any need to cross more than two streets to reach any point in Arad. Children can walk to school, and their parents to the shops, without ever crossing a road. Moreover, each precinct is provided with ample gardens and playgrounds. The commercial centre, the Merkaz, is also pedestrianized, with car parks all around. If the town wishes to expand, all it needs to do is build additional strips of housing parallel to those existing at present. There is also a villa district on the periphery of Arad. The original settlers were rewarded by being offered free land on which to build houses, and most took advantage of it. Houses must be built at least partially of local stone, and must have gardens. Here too a lesson was learnt from the mistakes of Dimona, where instant luxury slums were created when plot purchasers built their new villas right up to the edges of their lots.

Arad is crawling with culture. Many of the world's greatest violinists have performed here in recent years. The Habimah Theatre is a regular visitor, and many travelling exhibitions also pause in Arad. Morris Roth took me to see the local cultural centre, where even the cafeteria is decorated with original prints. The centre caters for all interpretations of culture: there are rooms for adult education and ballet classes, and down in the basement rehearsal rooms for rock groups. The library is immense. An archaeological museum will exhibit finds from the nearby site at Tel Arad. There are two theatres. The asbestos huts in which the original settlers lived have been converted into an artists' colony – no town is complete without one – though the municipality intends to redevelop that whole area. The sports facilities include two gymnasia, two football grounds, a pool and tennis centre, and a roller-skating rink – unlike Umm el-Fahm. The only drawback to living in Arad is that every summer an Arab-Hebrew folk festival is held here. Half an hour of guitar strumming and choral whooping is just about tolerable, but this festival goes on for three days – day and night.

I asked Roth about relations with local Arabs. He told me that many of the town's policemen are in fact Bedouin, and that in Arad not only are many construction workers Arab, but so are the contractors who employ them. He has noticed some changes recently: an occasional road block erected by demonstrating Arabs, and minarets rising above Bedouin settlements not previously known for their piety. The intifada has had little impact, except that travellers to Jerusalem no longer take the direct road via Hebron.

If relations with the Arab population are good, the same cannot be said for Arad's most bizarre inhabitants, the Black Hebrews. Thirty-nine of these Americans came to Dimona in 1969 claiming to be Ethiopian Jews. At first their story was believed and they were made welcome; by 1971 there were three hundred Black Hebrews in Dimona. However, a bus driver living in Arad happened to be one of the few Ethiopians who came to Israel before the 1980s, and he exposed the Black Hebrews as fraudulent. Some were sent back to the United States, but many have remained. By 1986 their numbers were estimated at between two and three thousand. Led by Ben-Ami Carter, they propound a most peculiar set of beliefs. They are, they claim, the 'real Jews' and intend to reclaim Israel for themselves by getting rid of the so-called Jews who presently live there. As for the Arabs, the Black Hebrews consider them to be the descendants of European Crusaders, and thus intruders in Israel just as much as the Jews. It has proved difficult to keep track of the Black Hebrews, since they shun conventional medicine, including immunization, and neither births nor deaths are registered. Women are kept in a subservient role, and there have been many reports of brainwashing and whipping within Black Hebrew families, all of which have been denied. Despite their unsavoury and even sinister programme, the people of Arad clearly consider them marginal and do not seem agitated by their presence.

The genuine Ethiopian community of Arad is mostly housed in absorption centres. According to Morris Roth, their problems continue to be severe, largely because family structures have broken down. The children behave badly at school, and receive no parental support with homework or encouragement to go on school outings, either because the parents are too poor or because they simply don't grasp the complexities of modern education.

I enjoyed Arad. Its location is alluring, set on a plateau between the rolling northern Negev and the wilder, more barren hills of the Judean desert. Its cleanliness and orderliness are a physical manifestation of the healthiness of the climate. The streets, like those of a capital city in which only the Party elite own cars, seem far too broad for the traffic. Around the Merkaz are restaurants and snack bars, the cinema and numerous shops. That the Romanian restaurant, La Marcel, featured on its menu a dish called Caviar Crap did not inspire confidence; but it was reassuring that nobody ever ate there, not even the owner and his wife, who sat at a table reading newspapers and knitting. Rapid research established that the only acceptable place to eat was the smart and clean Tokio pizzeria. It was run by South Americans, the only Israelis I ever encountered who served pizza and wished me 'Bon appétit'.

My choice of hotel was less astute. The smart hotels are on the edge of town, near the villa district, but I opted instead for the older Hotel Arad in the town centre. The hotel was originally the dining room of the founders' settlement, and the motel-style cabins seemed as ancient as any of the structures in Arad. As he was walking me back to the hotel, Morris Roth observed: 'Oh dear, you may be in for a rough night. I've seen some buses pulling up outside, and if they are full of kids on an outing, there could be some noise.' There was. All night long the kids played football, tuned their transistors to maximum volume, slammed doors, screamed at each other, tortured domestic animals, frolicked with witches. Their teachers made no attempt to discipline them, but then the whole notion of disciplining children is alien to the Israeli way of life. They were still at it at six thirty, when, I deduced, they finally collapsed with exhaustion. I dozed off for an hour and rose at eight, determined to exact vengeance. I planned to thump on the doors and wake the little angels up and wreck their morning, just as they had wrecked my night. They'd had their fun, and now it was time for them to be at the receiving end of a little creative hooliganism. I stalked over to the next block only to find that all the doors were open. The rooms looked as though a party of English lager louts had spent a week in them, but they were empty. The tinies had fled. Instead of retiring to bed at six thirty, they had simply headed for the dining room to inhale some breakfast before boarding their buses.

I told the sweet ditzy manageress that I had never spent a worse night in any hotel. She apologized, but said that they were 'just' children, and seemed genuinely surprised that I hadn't enjoyed their company. So was a sabra friend in Jerusalem, who had told me that Israel was 'paradise' for children. Nor, she added, do Israelis emulate the British custom of beating their offspring. Point taken, but their paradise was at the expense of my repose. She also remarked that Israeli children had become much more individualistic in recent years.

'Like you,' she told me, 'I grew up in the sixties, when in America and Europe young people were rebels. In Israel this didn't happen, as there was less for us to rebel against. Our parents were pioneers or refugees. We knew the price our parents had paid, not only in their earlier lives but in the War of Independence, and that spirit wasn't something we wished to challenge. We felt it was important to pull together, but now young people feel more free to express themselves. And good luck to them. It was different when I was growing up. My parents came from Germany and Poland, and I was growing up in a place completely different to what they had known. I had a sense of disconnectedness. Everything smelt of new paint. There were no grandparents, no family heirlooms. The past that mattered to me was not our past in Europe, but the past of 2,000 years ago. That's why Israelis are so passionate about archaeology. There's a direct link between our past and our future. My parents' personal past was so terrible, but I was alive in the same country and speaking the same language as my ancestors over 2,000 years ago.'

The road from Arad to the Dead Sea passes through barren hills so taut in their undulations that one loses all sense of height and direction. A group of camels motionless on the crest of a hill looked like an advertising agency's dream. From the observation point over Metzad Zohar I had a splendid view onto the Roman fortress far below. The fortress itself is barely distinguishable from the pale chocolate slopes and wadis among which it lies. Behind one of these ridges rusts a collection of junked cars, like bugs that have received their final squirt. On this hot day I could scarcely see the Dead Sea, and the haze resembled the gauze to which old-fashioned opera producers are addicted. The road descends to a small coastal plain that separates the Dead Sea from the cliffs that shield the mountains, and from the cliff walls knobbly protrusions stick out like toes.

The Dead Sea itself is repulsive. A slick of salt grips the beach like petrified scum, forming a glistening cappuccino crust over the mudflats. Dust storms or haze obscured the horizon, and the pale green of the water modulated into what I took for sky. The water itself was warm and soft to the touch, clammy in its oily caress. I did paddle in the stuff, and this prompted Israeli drivers hurtling past to hoot and wave, but then Israeli drivers will hoot and wave at anything, out of sheer merriment as well as impatience. Further south the flats are crossed by pylons and rusting pipes; there's a pumping station, a wrecked works area, and the vast complexes of the Dead Sea Works, which profitably extracts chlorides and potash and sulfides and other chemicals from water that is only 75 per cent liquid. Jetties reach out into the inland sea, and along the shore is scattered the detritus of construction work: old piping, concrete slabs, dumped machinery. Not even the water has a sparkle to it, only a glassy matted sheen as lifeless as the sea itself. The Dead Sea is dropping by thirty-two inches every year because of evaporation and the diversion of waters from the Sea of Galilee into irrigation systems. Looking inland, the view is little better. The brown cliffs bristle with strange piranha-teeth rock formations, and around Sedom, the landscape is heavily eroded, with bulbous pillars and protrusions as lumpish as the toes further north.

With fiendish cleverness, the Israelis have persuaded tourists from all over the world that this nightmarish landscape is a thing of beauty. Ein Boqeq, a row of slab-like hotels, is the main tourist centre. Along the beaches the tourists float on their back reading newspapers, a case of life imitating postcards. Entertainment consists of sampling overpriced hotel food and drink and the obligatory excursion to Masada, which does at least live up to its reputation. The story of Masada is well known, but worth encapsulating, since it plays so important a part in Israeli national mythology. The mountaintop site was the domain of King Herod, who built yet another of his palaces here. He picked a hypnotically beautiful and seemingly impregnable site. During the Jewish revolt against the Romans, the imperialists laid siege to the fortress with vigour and brutality; sheer force of numbers ensured that eventually they would subdue the 960 Jews. In A.D. 72, realizing the end was imminent, the Jews committed mass suicide rather than fall into Roman hands. Although this story is told in gripping detail in Josephus's *The Jewish War*, nobody knew where the site was located. Today it seems an obvious site for a great fortress, but it was only in 1963 that excavations confirmed that the mountain was indeed the ancient Masada.

Two paths (plus a cable car, which seems against the spirit of the place) ascend Masada: the arduous Snake Path from the Dead Sea side, and the Battery Path on the inland side. I ascended the Battery Path to the flat mountaintop. At one end, the prow of the mountain, the terraces of the Herodian palace look out over the coastal plain, while behind it are the fortifications and the innumerable structures adapted or built by the Jewish Zealots: the storehouses, the synagogue, the cisterns, the houses. Today the only inhabitants of Masada are small gerbil-like creatures with plump bodies and very short tails. They know no fear.

Among the ruins the prudent Israeli authorities have erected shades where visitors can shelter from the sun while their guides brief them on what they are about to see. Some guides adopt the proprietorial 'we' when speaking of the Jewish occupants. They love to tell how the Jews filled their storehouses with grain and oil and other provisions before their suicide, so that when the Romans entered the fortress, they would realize that the Jews had not died from starvation but with their pride intact. When the storehouses were uncovered by Professor Yigael Yadin and his colleagues, it was discovered that many of the contents of the earthenware jars – dates, figs, walnuts – were still edible. What brings Masada's brief history to life is the view, especially from the Herodian palace, down onto the plain, where the siege walls and camps built by the Romans are clearly visible, as in an aerial photograph, and the sense of encirclement is acute.

The synagogue here is labelled as the oldest synagogue yet found in Israel, but I recalled seeing a synagogue at the far more ancient site at Tel Arad. I took this problem to a Jerusalem tour guide, who explained that the 'synagogue' at Tel Arad was not a true synagogue, but a temple, a place of sacrifice rather than communal prayer. The structure at Masada was definitely a synagogue, though its claim to be the oldest in Israel is no longer correct, since older ones have been found in the Golan. When I took the same problem to Alex Berlyne, he had an instant explanation: 'Probably one is Orthodox and the other's Reform.'

Returning down the Battery Path, I was looking forward to a cold drink at the buffet below. I could see a coach disgorging a party of Israeli kids – quite possibly the same little horrors who had stolen my sleep – and by the time I reached the buffet it was under siege, as eighty small children held out their coins and shrieked their first-person-singular war cry 'Ani, ani, ani!' as they competed for the vendor's attention. I then saw two more coaches, with similar cargo, pulling into the car park, and I abandoned the attempt.

It is an Israeli rite of passage that all schoolchildren must make at least one ascent of Masada, not only because it is the most dramatic archaeological site in Israel, but because it has acquired a peculiar symbolic value. Patriotic ceremonies take place on the mountaintop in a strange marriage of archaeology and triumphalism. Like the Alamo in San Antonio, Texas, it has become a symbol of heroic resistance rather than a reminder of catastrophic defeat. Perhaps Masada derives its power as an Israeli symbol because its inhabitants retained control over their lives until the very end. The shaming aspect of so much of the most horrific Jewish experiences of the past century – the pogroms, the extermination camps – was that the Jews were helpless in the hands of their murderers. Masada, it seems, has become a symbol of Jewish freedom, even if it means the freedom to die. In the martyrology of Jewish history, it is the defenders of Masada and Gamla who were able to choose the heroic death denied to the six million Jews of Europe forty-five years ago. Heroic their death may have been, but, it seems worth reminding oneself, they were self-inflicted, and such deaths are the worst waste of all.

# 25 · UNRAVELLING

When I first arrived in Israel, I had called on the former journalist Amnon Ahi-Nomi, who had not been slow to offer me advice.

'How long will you be staying?'

'I'm not sure. About four weeks in Jerusalem, then I'll return to Israel for a longer visit in a few months' time.'

'I wouldn't come back if I were you. Spend your four weeks here, and then go away and write your book. The longer you stay the more confused you'll become. Whatever you do, don't linger.'

I'd ignored his advice. Now, my travels almost at an end, I spoke to him again.

'So how did it go?'

'I've travelled a lot, spoken to many people, seen the sights. But of course you were right all along. I don't feel any closer to "understanding" Israel than I did before I arrived. Detached observers lose their detachment in the process of observing. My notebooks resemble the pieces of a jigsaw puzzle that won't join up.'

'Yes,' he said, happily, 'and it'll probably stay that way. Israel's diffuseness is part of its character. It pulls in different directions. The country is like a cumbersome and badly oiled machine, except in times of crisis when, almost inexplicably, it all pulls together and works.'

On my penultimate evening in Israel I went out to dinner with Amnon and his wife Daniela at Kamin, a small restaurant in West Jerusalem to which they had introduced me and which had become a favourite haunt of mine. Amnon said he wouldn't have anything to drink. 'I have gout, brought on by almost fifty years of eating and drinking too much. If you live that kind of life, you have to pay the price. But let me tell you it's been worth it. How can we help you?'

'I'm puzzled by the Israeli working day. Some people start work at seven, others at nine. Some offices close at two, others at four. Other people I've been trying to contact for months are never in their offices at all.'

'This is simple to explain. In certain offices and departments there are regulated working hours, usually from seven thirty to two thirty. You clock in and you clock out. But during that time you also have to fit in your shopping, your trip to the bank, and other important matters such as your second job. That's why when you phone an Israeli in his office, he's never there. As a result, the average office worker or clerk puts in about two hours' work a day. In two hours, he can do relatively little harm. Just imagine if Israeli clerks worked a full eight hours each day – there's no saying what terrible shape we would be in. Next.'

'Queuing. Israelis don't seem very good at it. I was in the post office the other day, and everybody who came up behind me had some story about why they ought to be ahead of me. They all sounded plausible, but if I'd paid any attention, I'd still be in that queue.'

'Of course, that's because Israelis hate to queue. If you go into a bank or any other institution and you see three queues, the first thing you must do is evaluate the queue. You'll go to each in turn and tell the person in front of you that this is your place. After you've studied each queue, you'll decide which one you're actually going to stand in. Better still, you'll find a relative or neighbour near the front of one of them and get them to buy your stamps or hand in a form. Another strategy is to start panting and say you are in a terrible rush because your sick grandmother is waiting outside –'

'Yes, that's one of the lines someone tried to feed me yesterday.'

'– or if not a grandmother, then a baby in a car. If somebody objects to this, you can have a row. Everyone enjoys a row. The worst thing you can do is protest to a queue-jumper that you've been waiting for an hour and don't intend to relinquish your place. If you've really been waiting an hour, that means you *have* to be a shmuck.'

When I put the same question to Alex Berlyne, his explanation was more philosophical. 'You queue for a bus when you know one will be along in a few minutes and you have a chance of getting on it. If you don't know whether the bus will come along and whether if it does you will be able to get on it and get home in time for dinner, then there's no point queuing. You just make a dash for the bus when it pulls up. This principle applies to all aspects of Israeli life.'

This lucid exposition was a revelation. At last I understood the source of a grudge I had been nursing for over twenty years. Hitchhiking on a lonely road in Calabria, I had been joined, after a three-hour wait, by a burly Israeli student. When half an hour later a car did stop, the Israeli pushed me aside and leapt in, explaining, 'I'm in a hurry.' It wasn't, as I had been supposing, despicable rudeness, but a practical application of the principle that you don't stand in line for something that may not arrive. Of course, it's also true that Israelis have no manners. None. The standard explanation is that the pioneers were socialists eager to shake off the totems of bourgeois respectability and class distinction. When you've spent all day draining a swamp, the niceties of table manners or saying good evening to everybody in the room are pointless trivialities. Fair enough, but the youngest living pioneers must be well into their fifties, which leaves the rest of the population to account for. Another explanation claims that Jews, having struggled for their homeland, now find that they have to do all the jobs – selling stamps, waiting on table – that they always assumed other people did, so if they must perform menial tasks, at least they should enjoy in compensation the right to be grudging and unpleasant. Punctuality is also regarded as demeaning. Avi told me: 'I had to see the mayor of a small town and I was twenty minutes late for our appointment. So I apologized as I walked into his office. The mayor shrugged. "If you're an hour late," he said, "you might think of apologizing."'

My sabra friend in Jerusalem took it amiss when I told her how rude Israelis were. 'We're not rude, we're nervous. Ours is a society in stress. But at least we're democratic. Everybody here expects their opinions to be given equal weight whatever their educational background or profession. We may not have the exquisite manners of you British, but we have more respect for each other.'

Amnon's view was straightforward: 'Israel has culture but not civilization. It's not that we're bad-mannered, but that we have no manners. The reason, as you know, is that the pioneers derided the whole notion. To them manners were associated with insincerity, with not being honest and forthright. Anyway, what makes you think that the Jews of Europe were ever noted for their table manners?'

'You say you have no manners because Jews are so forthright, such incorrigible individualists. Yet you also have these absurd bureaucratic structures.'

'Bureaucracies are part of the Israeli experience. They were our way of coping with waves of immigration, an alternative to putting them on the dole. So we have hundreds of thousands of civil servants, most of whom have no real job.'

Avi offered a more historical explanation: 'Many of those who built up the country came from eastern Europe, where people tend to be ill-mannered and they expect bureaucrats to be rude and obstructive. There's no tradition in Israel of public service. We also have a clash of many cultures in Israel. Some people come from countries where it's normal to shout and scream at each other. You have to remember that everybody has to struggle in Israel, that constant reserve duty doesn't help either. Everyone is trained in violence, and there's always aggression in the air.'

Elaine Levitt, who has to deal constantly with bureaucracies, added: 'People here accept that there'll be bureaucratic hassles as a matter of course. The only institution that isn't bureaucratic is private industry. Israelis don't think they can change things, perhaps because there's no direct political representation. They've never heard of a boycott. If you complain about something to Israelis, they'll usually reply: "That's how it is." I came to Maalot some years ago. I needed to move in to a house, but was told I couldn't for all sorts of stupid reasons. And there were houses sitting empty, while I was being prevented by bureaucrats from moving into mine. It was ridiculous! So I broke into the house and wrote a letter to the official concerned, told him what I'd done, said that I realized he was a very busy man and he could just send along the papers when he had a moment. I was arrested and spent a night in jail, but I got the system changed. There's lots wrong with Israel, but at least it's never boring.'

In Beersheva, Gillian Hundt, who rapped me on the knuckles every time I offered some generalization about Israeli life, once admonished me: 'In Britain survival is taken for granted. This isn't the case in Israel. Living with that kind of uncertainty leads to completely different cultural assumptions.' She was right, which is why I appealed to Amnon for help in sorting out those cultural differences.

'Let's start with our vices,' he said. 'The great Israeli vice is impatience. We prefer instant coffee to real – it's quicker.' He could have added that it's often more palatable too. Israelis make coffee by adding hot water to ground coffee in a cup. The result is sludge, and is known with typical Israeli candour as *botz*, or mud. It also has no flavour to make amends for its gritty texture. 'We're impatient because we're nervous, always conscious of pressure. Even our generation gap seems to move at a faster pace. In Israel the gap happens every seven years, according to the incidence of our wars. Our humour tends to be black. Because Israel has achieved so much, outsiders often regard us as industrious. But we're not. Our strength lies in our gift for improvisation. We find it hard to work together, which is why our football teams are lousy. We're idealistic but don't like to admit it. We're insecure, so we appear arrogant. Our consciousness of the Holocaust, the Masada complex, the indifference or hostility of the rest of the world, these all compel us to be self-reliant.

'That's why we have our own weapons industry. We have a total population of four and a half million, so we know it's absurd to make our own tanks when we could buy them more cheaply from foreign countries.

But we've never forgotten how in 1967 we bought fifty French tanks. They were sitting on the runway in France when De Gaulle slapped an arms embargo on them. It so happened that we won the Six Day War without them, but they might have been crucial. We felt betrayed. Nowadays we have a fear of being let down by the United States, and this is why we insist on self-reliance, even when it costs us so much. But we're not aloof. When we made peace with Egypt, we longed for closer ties with Egypt, although they didn't want to get too close to us for fear of the reaction of their Arab neighbours. But nevertheless we felt rebuffed. That's because we want a personal relationship with everybody. When you go to the post office to buy stamps, the postmaster will want to know who you've written to and why, and in return you'll want a discount. It never works out that way, but there is this desire to put everything on a personal basis. At work everything has to be personalized. That's why you leave the door of your office open. You want to be able to see who is walking down the corridor, and with whom. It's considered bad form to shut your door and get on with your work. Israelis are poor at manners, at civilities, because they obscure personalization. If somebody bumps into me, he doesn't say sorry, but I'll want to know *why* he bumped into me. And if somebody tells me they have a headache, I won't mutter about how sorry I am. Instead I'll probably say: "You think you have a headache? Let me tell you about the headache *I've* got!"'

Later, when we left the restaurant, Amnon had difficulty extracting his car from the car park. He wouldn't succeed in under an hour unless some other driver allowed him to slip into the main stream of traffic. 'The secret is eye contact. If I can establish a personal contact with another driver, our problems will be over.' And they were. He was also lucky, for Israeli drivers are notoriously loutish. They use the window next to the steering wheel not for looking out of, but for shouting out of. Entire conversations are yelled back and forth in the time it takes for traffic lights to change. Children lean out of buses and yell at strangers. Rules of the road apply only to pedestrians, as I discovered when jaywalking in Jerusalem, while drivers regard the pavement as additional car parking space. Machismo extends to the interior decoration of cars: almost all seat covers have the word TURBO embroidered or stamped onto them. Indeed there is scarcely a car in Israel that isn't marked TURBO. That's a frill, but there are also 500 deaths and 20,000 injuries each year in road accidents in this small country.

Driving on Israeli highways can be a nightmarish experience, not only because of the lousy, needlessly competitive driving, but because the roads are abominably maintained. Yet Israelis spend a fortune for the privilege of risking death every day. Imported cars cost over twice the price charged in their country of manufacture, and the same applies to spare parts. Official statistics conjure up an average driver, who drives 1,000 kilometres a month, spends NIS 1,732 on insurance, NIS 995 on petrol, NIS 1,143 on repairs and tyres; throw in a few more figures for the licence and depreciation, and it costs Mr Average NIS 6,744 each year to drive his car.[1] Since many Israelis earn no more than NIS 12,000 per year, that is a huge sum. You would think that with disbursements on this scale, Israelis would at least try to protect their investment, but they seem incapable of driving with courtesy. The government has launched road safety campaigns, but nobody thinks they will have any effect.

'You're all living in a madhouse, aren't you?' I said to the accountant Dan Bavly. 'Don't you ever yearn for a dose of nice, sedate European orderliness?'

'The normalization of Israel sounds a dull prospect to me,' he replied. 'I don't want Israel to feel like Belgium. If Israel isn't going to be unique, what's going for it? But I don't think there's much danger of this normalization. It's not just a question of this being a national home for the Jews. We have over four million people, and as many political parties and opinions. That's chaotic, but not necessarily bad. On one level, we have the enterprise of all our hi-tech activities, and on the other the vitality of our intellectual life, and it all shows that we want Israel to be different, even if the idealism of the founders is weaker than it used to be. We may not have the pioneering spirit, but we still have constant innovation.'

All this I could admire, and the extraordinary energy of the Israelis. Yet so often that energy seemed misdirected, unfocused, tinged with desperation as much as aspiration. Everywhere I found passion and emotion, but little warmth. The pleasures of Israel included being in a country where almost everyone acts like an intellectual, but I longed for a greater gentleness of spirit. In vain, because Israel is conditioned by the constraints under which it has been forced to exist, and the short time left to me in Israel would be spent trying to see to what extent those constraints could be loosened and the neurosis of the country, simultaneously creative and destructive, assuaged.

Peace. It seemed like a desert mirage, hovering in a constantly receding distance. Everyone longed for it, no one agreed on how it was to be attained. I had heard every conceivable response to the dilemma: Deport the Arabs. Return the Territories in exchange for a peace settlement along guaranteed frontiers. You can't trust the Arabs. The only solution is a Palestinian-Jordanian federation. After what Hussein did to the Palestinians in Jordan a decade ago, there is no way that a Palestinian-Jordanian federation could ever succeed. Not an inch of Eretz Yisrael should be surrendered, ever. And so on. Words, words, and with every day that passed the intifada doggedly continued, bringing more deaths, more curfews, more bitterness, more ugly images on television screens around the world. Western governments, Americans included, were responding to friendlier noises from Yassir Arafat, to the impotent indignation of the Israelis. The heat seemed to be on, yet there was no sense of urgency on the part of the government, and the foreign minister mouthed his platitudes as though nothing had changed.

When I told my friends in Jerusalem that I was going to see Eliakim Haetzni in Kiryat Arba, they groaned. It was typical, they thought, that a European visiting Israel would seek out, not the man on the Petah Tikvah omnibus, but a man who was among the most rabidly assertive of the settlers. It was true that Haetzni spoke, at best, for one wing of Gush Emunim and represented only a tiny segment of Israeli opinion, yet I wanted to be sure that I understood the right-wing case with which I felt instinctively out of sympathy. I'd had countless opportunities to speak to thoughtful liberals in Haifa or Jerusalem, but they told me nothing I did not know, and little that I did not agree with. Haetzni was so virulent in his nationalism that even Yitzhak Shamir had said publicly that he couldn't stand the man. Anyone who can enrage Shamir to that extent had to be worth speaking to, so I headed out to Kiryat Arba. The hour-long bus journey was not uneventful. Just beyond Bethlehem, a boy, his face obscured by his *keffiyeh*, was standing at an intersection hurling stones. None hit the bus, which slowed down, but the boy stood his ground and stayed his hand while he assessed whether we posed any danger to him. Some Arab bystanders were evidently unsympathetic to the boy's belligerence – though whether because they disapproved of throwing stones or whether they feared for his safety after such blatant provocation was unclear.

Kiryat Arba had been established in 1968 on the outskirts of Hebron. The population numbers between four and five thousand, and the 40 per cent who don't commute to Jerusalem work in local light industries that include a stone-cutting machine factory, a printing press, a building materials factory, a winery, and an arms factory. It was difficult for Kiryat Arba to remain out of the news. In 1985 the town had elected a Kach-led coalition to govern its affairs. Attempts were made to fire Arab employees, both from the private and public sector, but the council was forced to withdraw this blatantly discriminatory edict by the Knesset, which blocked its municipal funding until the ruling had been cancelled. Two years later a group of settlers had gone on the rampage at the Palestinian refugee camp of Dehaishe. Frustrated by what they regarded as inadequate protection by the IDF of the roads leading to Kiryat Arba, the settlers took the law into their own hands. According to the *Jerusalem Post* the band of settlers tried to break into homes, fired shots into them, 'sought to block the army's arrival on the scene, assaulted or tried to assault soldiers and officers, and when it was all over flatly denied that they had done anything of the kind'.[1] The settlers were prosecuted, and it was Haetzni who conducted their defence.

Haetzni favours banning all Palestinian institutions such as trade unions and women's groups on the West Bank, on the grounds that they are PLO front organizations. He would even apply the ban to the Moslem equivalent of the Red Cross, the Red Crescent. Flying the PLO flag is already a crime, but Haetzni argues that the appropriate punishment should be deportation.[2] He stood as a Tehiya candidate in the 1988 elections, but since he was only No. 5 on the list, he must have known that his chances of election to the Knesset were negligible. (However, the subsequent resignations of two Tehiya MKs would propel Haetzni into the Knesset in February 1990.) He was born in Germany, and came to Israel in December 1938 and was active in Hagana, the Jewish underground during the years of the Mandate. Although he came from a religious background, he himself is not religious. I could understand the determination of certain Orthodox not to abandon the Occupied Territories, but to find the same strength of feeling among secular Jews was more puzzling. Haetzni is a very excitable man, his voice often rising to a pitch close to the level of a scream and then dropping to a whisper. I have rarely encountered such verbal aggression, but was determined not to rise to the bait. Throughout our talk, it was hard to resist comparing Mr Haetzni with Dr Strangelove, with whom he shares the same mesmeric, barely controlled hysteria glossed over with a fierce logic.

My opening remark proved infelicitous: 'Kiryat Arba hasn't had the best reputation in the past few years.'

He turned his head and drawled: 'On what do you . . . ?'

'Well, there's been quite a lot of trouble at the refugee camps,' I began, alluding to Dehaishe.

Haetzni took the line of greatest perversity. 'This is a good reputation.'

'A good reputation?'

'This is how we earned, with hard toil, our reputation.'

'That's one aspect of it,' I offered. 'There was also something fairly close to hooliganism as well.'

'For example? What do you refer to? You come from England, which is a very hypocritical country, where the BBC says the following: If somebody throws a bomb in Ireland he is a terrorist, but an Arab that throws a bomb in Israel is a guerrilla, or sometimes a commando. If Jews plant a bomb, they are terrorists. So you come from a hypocritical country that has a very bad name —'

It was my turn to interrupt. 'There was an attack in 1987 from Kiryat Arba on a refugee camp.'

'In 1987?' Long pause while Haetzni furrowed his brows. Then his face lit up. 'Ah, on the Dehaishe camp!'

I nodded.

'There was an attack?'

'That's what I have read.'

'I happen to be the lawyer and I know the details very intimately. So you want to know what happened at the Dehaishe camp? This is what interests you?' The note of derision in his voice was wonderful to hear. 'I can tell you. It was in June, five months before the intifada. The Dehaishe camp was already under the control of the Arab Arafat Jugend called Shabiba. So we already had stoning from the camp, for years. It intensified in the summer of 1987, and one Friday a woman on a bus bound for Kiryat Arba got her jaw broken by a stone. Then as a protest ten or fifteen people went in private cars to Dehaishe to protest. They left their cars, they blocked the road, they shouted a few slogans calling for Rabin to resign, and they said Jewish blood is not cheap, or something. After they'd shouted a few slogans, the first stones were thrown at them from the camp. They returned stones, and then there was a fight, stones against stones. Then the Israeli army intervened and there was a scuffle with the army. And then they broke windows in some Arab houses and some Arab cars. *Schluss.*'

Not quite. He continued: 'And they shot in the air. The soldiers shot tear gas and bullets. But nobody was hurt, nobody was hit, and the whole thing is a small joke in comparison with what happens every day now in Judea-Samaria. If Dehaishe was something, you must multiply it by a hundred, and you have it every night. Okay? So if you want action, I can find you better action.'

'I'm quite happy as I am.'

'We are not made of sugar. And if anybody thinks that there are Auschwitz Jews here who will go to the Arab gas chambers, you are mistaken.' His voice was now at maximum pitch, as he let another Western inquirer have it with both barrels. 'And this is how Kiryat Arba gets a bad name. We have had our share of bad press, in which we take pride, because after the balance will be struck, after I don't know how many years, what is bad press will be regarded as good press.'

He rose and led me to look at a painting on the wall that depicted the Hebron synagogue destroyed during the riots of 1929. 'Then came a very illustrious student from Harrow. His name is Mr Hussein, king of Jordan. He has had the best possible British education. He razed the synagogue to the ground and erected on the site a public convenience. Nobody said a word in the whole world. Nobody went to Mr Hussein and asked him if he's had some bad press recently. But we demanded that the Israeli government tear down the public convenience and rebuild the synagogue. The answer of course was *nyet*. So we fought them. There were again clashes with the army and people were wounded. In 1978 there was a year of clashes until the military governor warned that in the next clash somebody would be killed. And then the synagogue was rebuilt and you can go and visit it exactly as it was. Okay. This is another example of how we got our bad press.

'I shall give you a third. One day we discovered that here in Kiryat Arba the authorities put a fence around a plot of land. Why? They said this is your cemetery. We said, thank you very much, but we thought our dead would be buried in the Jewish cemetery in Hebron, which exists from time immemorial. There are graves there of sages from the Middle Ages. It so happened that the small child of a painter who lives here died in Jerusalem. We brought the body here. The army blocked the road, and searched every car to see if it contained the corpse of a Jewish child. They didn't find it. There were hundreds of soldiers and helicopters. They gave in towards the evening and the child was buried in the Jewish cemetery.

We guarded the place for many nights for fear the authorities would take the corpse out. And then the Israeli government discovered a very interesting thing, the greatest discovery after Galileo: that the globe continued to turn around the sun exactly as before in spite of a small Jewish child being buried in this graveyard. And when they discovered this, they opened the graveyard. Today it looks like a graveyard, which it didn't when we liberated Hebron. At that time the bones were washed by sewage and tombstones were stolen. This is what we are fighting for, every step a scandal, and we prosper on this. It doesn't make any impression on us what your press writes about it. For the next two thousand years after Auschwitz everyone should shut up! We remember the British military government here, and the French killed a million Arabs in Morocco, the Americans killed a million Vietnamese, the Russians killed a million Afghans, and everybody sits in judgement on *us*? In one and a half years of intifada we have not reached four hundred Arab dead – and I regret every one who dies, they die for nothing – but nobody has the right to sit in judgement on us. No one says a word about Beirut, not one word!'

He had been striding about as he denounced me for the hypocrisy of the world press, but then he flopped into a chair and shook his head. 'You really made me angry with this "bad press" talk, you know.'

'I haven't said a word,' I shrugged. Perhaps now the paranoid monologue was over, we could discuss the matters I had come to talk about. 'What for you, as a nonreligious Jew, are the ideal borders of the state of Israel?'

'Do you need religious reasons to want Birmingham or London to be English?' Touché. 'The question should be asked quite differently. What brought us to Tel Aviv? In the first place, why did Jews from all over the world come to this corner of the Middle East? The first came in Turkish times, when this was the worst country in the world. Why to this place, if not because of the Bible?'

I free-associated in my mind. The Bible: that sprawling ragbag of poetry and prophecy, cruelty and gore, epic tale and domestic soap opera, injunction and dilemma, battles and more battles. And I responded tentatively: 'Presumably, yes.'

'Not "presumably". Do you have any other explanation? So why "presumably"?'

'Okay.'

'So give me another explanation!'

'Okay. I see that. But I don't want to talk about the history of Zionism.'

'But this *is* Zionism. Nothing else. This is only a continuation of Zionism. You know, we speak a different language. I'm sorry, but I can answer you only in my language.'

'That's fine, that's fine.'

'Okay. Because your question and my answer, the one is Chinese, the other is Japanese. So you must make an effort. Jews came to this country only because of the Bible. Most of the First Aliyah were not religious, they were secular socialists. Why did people like Ben-Gurion come here if not because of the Bible? They went to religious schools when they were children, they drank directly from the spring, the source: the Talmud. They became secular, but that first layer remained. They came here and they raised a new generation devoid of this bedrock. This generation make good soldiers, but when it comes to the motivation to do such a thing as we do, only those who continue to drink from the source join us. Because there is no other reason why we are here. So what is the difference between Tel Aviv and Hebron? There is a difference. Yosef Begun, one of the best known Soviet refuseniks, has just moved to Kiryat Arba. He said, "I spent years in jail in Russia to fulfil my Zionism. Now when I come to Israel I will continue the Zionist way." If he goes to Tel Aviv he has a cheap imitation of Miami. For this he languished in jails? Here he feels that he suffered for something, not the hedonistic, materialistic, rotten parts of north Tel Aviv. I couldn't live there. This is the land of the Bible and Tel Aviv is only the fringes. For me it means a great deal that this is the town of King David. This is the answer. This is Eretz Yisrael. Here.'

'But where does it end? In an ideal world —'

'Ah, this is what you want to know!'

'Yes.'

'You are speaking to a dove. For me it ends with the River Jordan, and you know the answer very well. Our army was in Lebanon in 1982 and but for one crazy voice there was no Gush Emunim demand that we should remain in southern Lebanon because historically parts of it were and are Eretz Yisrael. There was no outcry to remain there or establish settlements, because we are a peaceful people who do not wish to spill blood for more and more territory. It was Eretz Yisrael, but it was not the very heart of Eretz Yisrael. We were in Sinai, and we objected to vacating Sinai, but we declared from the beginning that there would be no bloodletting, no struggle with our brothers in uniform, because we didn't have the feeling that this was Eretz Yisrael.

'Jordan was occupied during many centuries by Jews, yet in Judaism there is a difference between the Land of Canaan, which is from the

River Jordan to the sea, and the land of the two and a half tribes. Moses stood on a mountain in Transjordan and begged God to be allowed into the Land of Canaan. It was denied to him. Then the Bible says God showed him the land from Lebanon to the Dead Sea, and the whole country is described. And the Talmud says that Moses said to God, If I can't enter the Promised Land in the form of a human being, make a beast out of me and let me enter as a beast. And when this was denied to him, he said, Let me enter as a worm, and this was also denied to him. Which shows the feeling towards the Land of Israel, and that the Land of Israel in our genetic code stretches to the River Jordan. Historically, since then, through the First and Second Temple and even after, there were Jews living on the other side.

'Yet if it were for peace, and the Palestinians really wanted a state of their own without destroying Israel, and they would establish that state on the eastern part where they are now a majority, where they would have 76 per cent of Palestine –'

'What is now Jordan.'

'Yes, where they are a clear majority. If this were to happen, 99 per cent of the Israeli population, including what is called the right, would say "Halleluia" and we would be rid of the Palestinian problem. This is the fact. But we shall not forgo *this* land. You want to negotiate with me over Yamit in the Sinai? Take it. But not Hebron.'

'So there is an ideal of Eretz Yisrael, and then there is an accommodation with what is practical, and you suggested one such accommodation –'

'There are friends of mine who say we shall never forgo eastern Palestine, east of the Jordan. They don't agree with me. In theory. But if a Palestinian state were to come into existence there I don't think anyone would make a big row over it. But Judea–Samaria is not negotiable, neither in our hearts nor in practice. It will never be negotiable.'

'But there is such a thing as the Israeli government. A future government may take a different view. What happens then as a practical consequence?'

'I'm not a prophet, I'm not a prophet. Go to Tel Aviv and ask people on Ben Yehuda Street: If Ben Yehuda Street is given to the Arabs for the sake of peace, what will you do? One will say, I shall go to America. Another would commit suicide, a third will shoot at the army, the fourth one will take money, or I don't know what.'

'But not a single person in Israel is suggesting as a practical possibility that –'

'I am only saying that if you want to surmise what would be the reaction of people here, compare it with the reaction of people in Tel

Aviv. It would be quite similar. I don't argue with you. If you want to argue with me –'

'I'm only asking you some questions –'

'– as you are a Jew, make *aliyah*, come here, and then we shall argue.'

'I don't –'

'I only answer your questions.'

'Fine!'

'So this is my answer. You need not agree with me.'

'I only want to hear what you have to say.'

'Because sometimes in your questions there is an implied position. Your position doesn't interest me. You sit in England.'

'That's why I'm not having an argument with you.'

'Serve in the army, send your children to the army, then you will have a personal position. Everybody is teaching us what to do. I never heard an Israeli prime minister teaching Mrs Thatcher what to do in Ireland. But every tourist comes here for an hour and immediately we get a new peace plan.'

'I have every sympathy with you.' And I did. It is exasperating for Israelis to be preached at by visiting tourists and politicians who are ill informed and more interested in flattering their constituencies at home than in helping to solve a complex problem. But Haetzni wasn't going to let me off the hook.

'What do I know about Ireland? If you ask me who is really right in Belfast, I don't know. And I sleep well with not knowing, very well. And for some obscure reason the world cannot sleep until it judges the Jewish case, because it's such a pleasure to judge the Jews.' He clapped his hands loudly. 'Okay?'

'Okay. Now, in an ideal world in which Judea and Samaria remain as part of Israel in a full administrative sense, what would be the position of the Arab population here? Because presumably the adversarial stance would remain. How would it be dealt with? In purely practical terms.'

'You can ask me only about my opinion.'

'That's all I'm doing.'

'Not what will really be. What will really be is very bad, because we have no leaders and no leadership, and what will happen is a war. If this intifada continues for another year there will be a full-scale war.'

'With whom?'

'With all Arab states, headed by Egypt, of course. You must imagine our position as if England during the war with Germany had only Chamberlain. Imagine! And this is what we have today. We don't have any leadership at all. We are orphans. And because of that there will be a war, which is not something inevitable. The intifada is a fuse, and it will detonate the Arab war.'

'Why hasn't it done so in seventeen months?'

'Because it is a long fuse.' Nice one, Haetzni.

'And how is this war to be avoided?'

'By putting down the intifada in two weeks, which is very easy to do. But the Israeli government doesn't do it because of American pressure. But back to your initial question. What I would do, if the intifada were put down, is pass a law that applies Israeli sovereignty in the areas from the Mediterranean to the River Jordan. An hour later the Israeli parliament should legislate personal administrative autonomy for the Arabs of East Jerusalem and Judea-Samaria. Camp David doesn't exist any more. Good riddance. So the Arabs won't get this autonomy from the four-headed monster – Egyptians, Israelis, Jordanians, Palestinians – the monster of Camp David – but it will be legislated by the Israeli government as part and parcel of Israeli sovereignty. There is then no danger that this autonomy will degenerate into a Palestinian state. I want to close the stable door before the horse escapes. So in matters of local government and cultural matters and religion and education and social relief, in anything except security and foreign relations and infrastructures, we could give them autonomy. And tell them this is what you can get in the less than a quarter of Palestine that is in Jewish hands. If you want full sovereignty, in the three-quarters of mandatory Palestine which is east of the Jordan, try to make an intifada on the other side. We'll see what heroes you are. So this is what I would do. Very simple. And now you will ask me: Where will they vote?'

'It had crossed my mind.'

'In my opinion they vote here for the administrative council which governs the autonomy, and once they have a state of their own on the other side, in national matters they can vote there. And as for Israeli Arabs, they will have the option to take up the citizenship of the new Palestinian state. I was very glad to find that this idea already exists in the recommendations of the United Nations. In 1947 the UN passed a resolution to establish two states, a Jewish state and an Arab state. Jerusalem was to be international. The Arab state was to include Beersheva, Acre, Nazareth, and of course Judea-Samaria. The Arabs of course said no, and this is why the war broke out in 1948 and Israel took all those areas. According to the resolution, the 49 per cent of Arabs living in the proposed Jewish state would have the option of taking Palestinian citizenship and voting not in Haifa but in Nablus. This was to spare the Arabs the process of hebraization. I like this idea. Only, after the four wars we have had, I move the voting centre eighty miles to the east, and apply it to the Palestinian state in the east.'

'What if King Hussein says no, I don't like this idea?'

'If King Hussein doesn't like this idea, then we can implement only the first part and wait for better times. We shall not make a war against King Hussein for the Palestinians. This they should do. They are so good at the intifada, let them make a second intifada.' Before I could point out the similarities between his proposed solution, which took as a premise the existence of a Palestinian state east of the Jordan which didn't actually exist, and cloud cuckoo land, he did so himself. 'We have no problem living together with the Arabs. I have many Arab clients, and get along with them very well on a personal basis, no problem at all. The field beyond this fence belongs to Arab neighbours, and when they had the first fruits of the year they brought them to us as a present, and we gave them something too. But to the larger question there is no solution.'

'So you're admitting that the scheme you have just been adumbrating –'

'It will never materialize, because the Arabs don't want *any* Jews in the Land of Israel. Islam does not tolerate any sovereign entity in the Middle East which is not both Arab and Moslem. This is why the Maronites, who are Arabs, can't get a state of their own. That is why the Kurds, who are Moslem but not Arabs, can't get a state of their own. That's why the Copts are persecuted in Egypt. So the Arab intransigence vis-à-vis the Jews and the Jewish state has nothing to do with the so-called Territories. They told the truth until 1967. They said we want to throw you into the sea. In 1967 they learnt this is not good for public relations in the Western world, and now they do it much more diligently. But we are little Red Riding Hood, and we know that this is not a grandmother, this is the wolf, and what the wolf wants is to EAT us. The whole world says, "Go in, don't you see it's such a nice grandmother!" but we refuse to go in, and we have our good reasons. If anybody wants to go in – please, after you.

'So speaking of solutions is brainwashing. The word "solution" suggests in a subtle way that there is in the world a formula which will give a mathematically true answer. There is no formula, the peace process is a lie, all this is sham.' He paused. 'No, there is one solution. Transfer. Kicking the Arabs out, this is a solution, because it puts an end to the problem. Now I do not want to uproot the Arabs here because it is not moral. For me the Palestinian problem is also a moral test for the Jews, that we *can* live together, that we have a place in our hearts and in our land for another people. Looking for a solution sometimes means blood and human suffering. I am looking for a *modus vivendi*. It won't be mathematical, it won't be neat, it won't be logical. But he will live and I will live, which for me is more than enough.

'The fundamental problem we have here is a unique one. It's that if "I was here before you" is an argument, then "before before" is an even better argument. Where in the world do you have a situation of "before" between two nations? If tomorrow you were to discover the ancient Etruscans in the African jungles and an Idi Amin told them to leave, the Italians would have a problem similar to the one we have. For the Italians, the Etruscans belong in a museum and they can make money out of them – but if they were alive and kicking, where would be the international tribunal to judge who is right: the Italians who sit there for who knows how many centuries, or the Etruscans who were there before them?'

Haetzni's realistic assertion that an imperfect *modus vivendi* was preferable to a bloody 'solution' was a weary recognition of the intractability of the problem. With his Etruscan analogy he was again making an important point, highlighting the ultimate futility of nationalist claims. 'Before before', as he put it, gets you nowhere. So, thinking we might be getting somewhere, I said: 'That's what's worrying about arguments from ancient history. Everybody has a prior claim –'

'No!' he said, raising a hand. 'No, not everybody. Excuse me. Nowhere else in the world do you have the phenomenon where a people from 2,000 years ago still exist. Do you say that the ancient Babylonians are demanding Iraq?'

'No, but hypothetically –'

'Hypothetically! But it doesn't exist! And if you want a hypothesis regarding the Indians in America, they were destroyed, like the Aborigines in Australia. We are the *only* non-hypothetical example! If you dig here, any child of seven or eight can immediately read what you dig up. No English child would be able to read what was written by I don't know whom 2,000 years ago. In spite of the fact that we were absent from here for such a long time, this phenomenon is unique because the fate of the Jews is unique. From this stems another thing. Whereas there was never a Palestinian Arab people, which discovered itself in the wake of the British Mandate – there was not even a district in the Turkish empire called Palestine – in the British encyclopedia of 1910 Palestine is defined as the ancient homeland of the ancient Hebrews. Not a word about the Palestinian Arabs, who did not yet know that they were a Palestinian people.'

'That could be seen as a failure of nationalism, not a failure of population.'

'Wait a minute. Why did they become a nation? When they saw that this area, which they designated as southern Syria, when they saw it was called Palestine, they called themselves the Palestinian people. We were lucky the British didn't call the Mandate area Zion – they would then be the Arab Zionist people. So they call themselves Palestinians, and became a nation. Maybe they are a nation, but they are our negative. Wherever there is Eretz Yisrael, they say it's Palestine. If you look at a Jordanian map from 1966, this area is not called Palestine but the West Bank of Jordan. When did this become Palestine? In 1967, when the Israelis took it.' He laughed. 'In other words, when we grew larger, our shadow grew larger! Palestine is our shadow! Show me another dispute between nations where the dispute is not about a border region, like Alsace-Lorraine, but where the dispute is over every identical inch! And where both nations claim the same capital! In other words, the dispute between us and the Arabs is unique and there is no solution for it. As long as Islam is as it is, and it's getting more extreme and more fundamentalist, we can only look for a *modus vivendi*.

'I must make another distinction between the organized Arab political will and the individual. Never, never will you find an organized Arab will to concede a Jewish sovereign entity in the Middle East. But the individual is patient. And you can live off this patience. So in the meantime, we live. With Egypt we have a so-called peace but no normalization. The Egyptians feel that because they have signed a piece of paper with the Zionist enemy, they have to prove to their Arab neighbours that they have remained true Arabs and Moslems. With Jordan we have complete normalization. We have trade, co-operation over secret services – not in spite of having a peace treaty but *because* we have no peace treaty. Hussein has not signed anything. But under the table, everything. In the Middle East, the outer appearance is important. The foolish Israeli quest for a written formalized peace is suicidal. There should be no formalization of any relations at all. Now you see how complex the situation is. We have now in Lebanon an area with an Arab army in Israeli uniforms with Israeli weapons. It is not a chocolate-box army. They fight. They kill and get killed. Why? Because it serves their own interests. Have we signed anything with the Lebanese? Nothing at all. And God beware that we sign anything. It is a *de facto* situation and it serves both sides.'

'On the one hand you are proposing a *modus vivendi*, and on the other hand you are talking about formal annexation and declaring Israeli sovereignty.'

'I was speaking about what we should do unilaterally, without asking anybody, without negotiations, because there is not the slightest hope of finding co-operation on the part of local Arabs as long as there is the slightest doubt as to their future. The Arab knows that if he co-operates with Israel in Judea-Samaria and Israel leaves, and he is then caught by the Arabs, by his brothers, then he will die a very cruel death.'

(Some months after we were speaking, such killings of 'collaborators' had become routine in the Occupied Territories.)

'So there is not the slightest chance of finding an Arab to co-operate, unless he is completely sure that Israel will remain. So the biggest crime we have committed since 1967 is not only that we have left this question mark looming over the future of Israel, but we have made it bigger every year. The only factor which did a little to lessen this question mark has been Jewish settlement. So we have to annex Judea, Samaria, and Gaza, and make it very clear what the future is, if only to give the Arabs a decent environment in which to live. I know of one *mukhtar* in one village who sent one of his sons to work for Hussein, another one to Arafat, and another to Israeli intelligence – as an insurance policy. This illustrates the complexity and tragedy of their position. To have a certain future we must unilaterally make it clear to them that this is Israel and will remain Israel. And then you will find the Arabs to establish this local autonomy. Otherwise you won't find them. No Arab leader can sign an agreement according to which they forgo Jaffa and we forgo Hebron. He will be dubbed a traitor and pay with his life, like Sadat.

'When we were in Lebanon, as long as the army was there, there was no terrorism against Israel there. When it was abundantly clear that we were going to leave Lebanon, the flames of Shiite terrorism against Israel became unbearable. Why? It should have been the other way round. But the real reason is that when they saw that we were going, everybody had to establish an alibi for themselves in order to survive the next regime. So we shall have more and more intifada in the same measure as we show weakness. The settlers are showing the Arabs that we are here to stay, under Israel, without Israel, we shall be here, and anybody who touches us will pay – dearly. The only stabilizing factor which remains in Judea-Samaria and Gaza is the settlers. It is of course the reverse of everything you hear in the media. In the last summer of the intifada 8,000 Jews were added to Judea-Samaria despite the stones and the bottles. Thousands of people have left the Negev and Galilee, and only we have an accretion of people.'

'Still, relatively few Jews are prepared to make that kind of commitment despite all the incentives that are offered.'

'The incentives offered here are not more than in any development area.'

'That's not what they tell me in the Negev and the Galilee.'

'They lie to you. On the border of Lebanon you get more than anywhere in Judea-Samaria, and rightly so because of the danger of terrorists infiltrating over the border. There is nothing like this here. I live here more securely with my Arab neighbour than does someone who lives on the Lebanese border. The 80,000 Jews here live in 140 places. There is not one road junction or Arab town or village, except for Tubas, which is not dominated by Jewish settlements or where the army is not sitting. Those 140 places secure a Jewish future, because we have the superstructure already existing to put in half a million.'

'Maybe I'm doing you an injustice, but it sounds almost as if you thrive on this sense of being beleaguered. It feeds a combative spirit.'

'Why? Why? If one day the Arabs would come here and say let's bury the hatchet of war and live here together, I would be more than happy.'

'But you don't believe it's ever going to happen.'

'I don't say never. I say not in the present state of Islam. I have a choice. Either to go away from here, or to face it. There are peasants living on the slopes of Vesuvius. They know that from time to time Vesuvius erupts, and yet they don't leave. Now Jews know that from time to time there will be antisemitic waves – it has been so for thousands of years – yet they don't leave.'

I felt cast down. Not because of Haetzni's aggression, but because his adherence to the legacy of the Bible, as he saw it, seemed to lead only to a notion of Israel as a kind of fortress enclosed within the walls of its own definitions. If others were prepared to accept them, they were welcome to enter. Otherwise not. I recalled the sad reflections of Rabbi David Hartman: 'Can Judaism stop living in its biblical, self-enclosed language of monotheism and really begin to live in dialogue with the world? The Bible doesn't give me a model for that. The Bible doesn't give me Judaism in interaction: it's Judaism in alienation from the world ... We have no paradigm of the dignity of a powerful nation living in dialogue with the world.'[3]

For Haetzni and his fellow combatants, their hearts are not at ease except beneath the shadow of history, among the tombs and wells and caves of their forefathers. That longing takes priority over all else and justifies all acts. That I sleep safely and calmly in London is, in their eyes, self-delusion.

Haeztni and his wife gave me a lift into Jerusalem. A pistol lay across the dashboard. When we reached Rachel's Tomb and the outskirts of Jerusalem, they clipped on their seat belts. Israeli road law doesn't apply in the Territories. As we approached the city they showed me the bastions just off the road from which Egyptians and Jordanians had fired upon Jerusalem. 'We would be out of our minds to give this away again!'

# 27 · THE LONG FUSE

Those who express astonishment at the failure of Israel and its Arab neighbours to live in peace and friendship clearly have little idea about the depth of suspicion and distrust between the two peoples. In 1947 the Arab states could have had for the asking a Palestinian state alongside the emergent Jewish state, but they rejected the proposal out of hand and attacked Israel the moment it achieved independence. Now, over forty years later, the Palestinian leadership, the PLO, is adopting a stance which could lead to the eventual emergence of a Palestinian state alongside Israel. In the meantime there have been four wars, costly to all the participants in terms of lives and resources, and the cynically perpetuated misery of the refugee camps. It is hardly surprising that the Israelis regard the Arabs as implacable in their hatred of Israel, and treat with the most profound scepticism the newly minted intentions of the PLO to kiss and make up. The forty-two years of Israel's existence have been lived defensively: hardly a year has gone by without either a war, border infiltrations, bloody terrorist attacks, relentless anti-Israeli propaganda over the Arab airwaves, United Nations resolutions equating Zionism with racism, and threats to drive the Israelis into the sea. The Jews of all people are disinclined to take threats to exterminate them with a pinch of salt.

Even among Israelis prepared to see the establishment of a Palestinian state alongside Israel, there are deep worries about the nature of that state. Israel is a democracy, and the flaws of its political system result from, if anything, an excess of democracy. That the democratic freedoms enjoyed by Israelis are not shared to the same extent by the Arabs living within Israel, and to an even lesser extent by those of the Occupied Territories, is perfectly true; but with the exception of Egypt, all the neighbouring powers remain technically at war with Israel. In such circumstances it is not surprising that Israel deals harshly with those who seek to subvert its rule. This is not to excuse Israeli violations of civil rights, but to suggest that these are variations from the democratic norm. That norm does not exist in any Arab state. King Hussein may look like a pussycat, but he stands for no such nonsense as opposition to his rule. Yassir Arafat may sincerely wish to see a future Palestinian state operating on democratic principles, but outside observers, the Israelis in particular, have every reason to be sceptical. Arafat's alleged moderation could easily be displaced in the future by more radical factions, such as the fundamentalist Hamas, the Islamic Resistance Movement. It is perfectly reasonable for the Israelis to be apprehensive.

The bane of the politics of nationalism is tribal memory. It affects the Israelis deeply, and it has blighted Irish politics for three centuries. To hark back to ancient grievances is utterly pointless, but no one is exempt from this folly, it seems. The Arabs too are painfully aware of their repeated humiliations at the hands of the Israelis, who have always managed, through guile as well as might, to beat back vastly superior forces, though usually not without a costly struggle. If many, perhaps most Israelis long to live in peace with their Arab neighbours, there is still scant evidence of a reciprocal willingness from the other side. One consequence of the ferocious rhetoric of the anti-Israeli Arabs is that the genuine grievances and aspirations of Palestinian Arabs have become delegitimized in Israeli eyes. The right to self-determination of the Palestinian people counts for little as long as the Israelis remain convinced that the existence of such a state threatens their own security and even their very existence.

The situation is exacerbated by the mutual lack of understanding. The Israelis, for the most part, ignore their position as a minority nation within the Middle Eastern context: relatively few Israelis speak Arabic. Immigrants from Moslem countries such as Iraq or Iran harbour no fond memories of the people among whom they lived. Similarly, very few Arabs, other than Israeli Arabs, have any inkling about Israel and the realities of Israeli life. As a Christian friend remarked: 'How can Arabs from outside Israel understand the country? They don't *know* any Israelis. They don't travel here. I was with the Egyptian ambassador the other day. He probably understands the Israelis better than most Arabs, but I doubt that even he has much of an idea.' Both Arabs and Israelis are victims of the myths they have evolved of each other.

In the rest of the world, which matters more to Israel than its often arrogant posturing suggests, there used to be considerable sympathy for Israel's evidently beleaguered position. Of course the Arab states and their Moslem allies in Africa, as well as the officially anti-Zionist Soviet Union and the Eastern bloc, espoused consistently anti-Israeli positions. European governments have wavered according to their dependence on Arab oil, and there have indeed been hypocritical denunciations of Israeli actions from one side of the political mouth, while from the other negotiations for some highly lucrative arms deal to a corrupt Arab dictatorship proceed to their conclusion. Nevertheless, the international image of Israel was positive.

That changed during the 1982 war in Lebanon, once the original explanations for the invasion ceased to justify Israel's prolonged and often brutal lingering. The Chinese water torture of the intifada, with stones substituted for drips, compounded Israel's problem. In its response, Israel, trapped within its stance of habitual and perfectly understandable belligerence, has been at a loss. The Palestinians, armed with bottles and stones and occasional petrol bombs, made monkeys of that renowned military machine, the Israel Defence Forces. Petrol bombs can and do kill, and so can rocks, but nonetheless the contest appears to be between unarmed Palestinian teenagers and heavily armed Israeli soldiers. Reporters and television cameramen flooded into the country, and their dispatches and images flashed to all parts of the world. The Israelis could point out that in most countries where such insurrections are in progress, the media are kept well away; even the United States in its battle with mighty Grenada and Britain in the Falklands either controlled news gathering rigorously or excluded the media altogether. Nevertheless, because Israel is a democracy, international press coverage, while subject to restrictions, continued unabated. Thus the intifada has become an overwhelming public relations disaster for Israel, despite the vigilance of its military censors. A cynical soldier to whom I gave a lift one day said: 'There are three ways in which Israelis guarantee that the intifada will continue. The first is the presence of TV cameras. The second is a visit from an American or British minister. The third is a statement from Rabin saying that at long last the intifada is being brought under control. Any of these is guaranteed to bring stone-throwers onto the streets immediately.'

There is a strong tactical argument for crushing the intifada once and for all. The Algerians had no difficulty crushing anti-government demonstrations in 1988. To be sure, a few hundred people were killed, and there was a brief burst of outrage from other countries, but a few weeks later it had all been forgotten. Just two months after the horrific crushing of the Chinese students in Tiananmen Square in June 1989, I was reading articles in the British press about the gradual return of Western tourists to China. In April 1989 Ariel Sharon, Israel's most thuggish politician, proposed deporting the families of stone-throwing children, the demolition of homes close to any attacks on Israeli traffic in the Territories, the mass deportation of the political leaders of the intifada, including journalists, and the establishment of additional Jewish settlements. Such a course of action, and the increased bloodshed that would accompany it, would almost certainly be counterproductive, but there is no doubt that many Israelis favour a stronger response. Amnon Ahi-Nomi was more realistic when he told me: 'There is no switch by which we can turn off the intifada. Most Arabs support it, and the rest are too frightened to oppose it. The intifada has given the Arabs immediate returns. It has given them pride, and persuaded them to bury the hatchet. We know there are divisions among the Arabs, but when we speak to them they present a united front.'

In the meantime the politicians waffle on, interpreting the intifada not as an expression of frustration at Israeli rule and longing for political independence, but as a kind of misdirected machismo. During the 1988 election campaign, I heard Moshe Arens discussing the intifada as an attempt to pressure Israel into making concessions; naturally Israel could not dream of giving ground under such circumstances. Moreover, he regarded the views of Israelis prepared to concede territory for peace as a tacit encouragement of the intifada. Thus, according to Mr Arens, the responsibility for the persistence of the intifada lay at the door of Shimon Peres.

To see the intifada in these terms is a failure to acknowledge that there may be legitimate political aspirations motivating those who participate in it. What appears to be a stout refusal to 'knuckle under' is also an excuse for political inaction, which seems to be the Likud policy. Such inaction is disastrous, if only because the intifada is a brilliantly successful tactical exercise, since it employs the weapons of strikes and demonstrations in place of armed insurrection, thus putting the Israelis in the position whereby any response on the part of the forces of law and order appears excessive. As one of the shrewdest Israeli observers of the intifada, Meron Benvenisti, has put it: 'For the first time in their history [the Palestinians] have succeeded in mobilizing the entire community in a sustained political struggle and in waging a controlled confrontation guided by realistic and not emotional considerations. The leaders of the uprising have permitted no deviation from a quite rigid strategy that makes constant allowances for the population's capacity to endure hardship.' [1]

The intifada is also having a worrying impact on Israel's moral status and international kudos. The Occupied Territories are under military government, and the authorities have almost unlimited powers. Powers of arrest and of detention without trial – doubled in August 1989 from six months to one year – are immense, and verdicts at most trials are not subject to appeal. By December 1989, 1,558 Palestinians were being detained without trial. The authorities' main means of enforcing discipline is to apply the principle that the community is responsible for the acts of individuals within it. Thus, in response to an incident of stone-throwing, a curfew could be imposed on an entire village and houses searched, not because there is any likelihood of apprehending the offenders, but because it does no harm to make life uncomfortable for those who, wittingly or otherwise, shelter the offenders. The rule of law is often subverted by the unilateral actions of the Shin Beth, the Israeli secret police; that there is ample evidence that it has abused its powers is not particularly surprising, since secret police forces are notoriously difficult to monitor. Israelis tend to turn a blind eye to such matters; after all, they argue, if the Palestinians weren't being urged by the PLO to conduct a sustained revolt against Israeli rule, then the problem wouldn't have arisen in the first place. Even at the most trivial level, the Israeli authorities find themselves forced to act with considerable harshness. The tax revolt among Palestinians has prompted such measures as impounding the property of those who have failed to pay their taxes. Although it is possible to find justifications for such actions, even for the rough treatment meted out by the Shin Beth, they can only make the eventual task of reconciliation between Jew and Arab all the more difficult.

When in 1988 television screens around the world showed Israeli soldiers burying Palestinians in the sand on the West Bank, Israel's reputation as a civilized nation plummeted. The Israelis replied that soldiers guilty of needless brutality were court-martialled and punished, which is more than can be said of the soldiers of many other countries, including those most vocal in their criticism of the Israelis. But while one can explain such behaviour, one cannot excuse it, and courts martial usually take place after there has been some public outcry against actions that have, often inadvertently, received publicity. Moreover, double standards operate: compare the sentences meted out to Jewish law-breakers and those handed out to Palestinian offenders. The history of the Jewish 'underground' shows how indulgently Jewish terrorists are treated. And in October 1989 four soldiers convicted of beating an Arab detainee who later died were granted clemency.

To some Israelis brutality against Arabs almost seems second nature. One reserve officer told me: 'The worst thing I ever saw was in Hebron jail, where we had to help move prisoners from one wing to another. This was years before the intifada. There was a flight of fifteen steps, then a sharp turn after a concrete wall, and a further fifteen steps. The prisoners were blindfolded and had their hands bound behind their backs. As each one stood at the top of the steps, one of the border police would kick him until he fell and rolled down the steps, hitting the wall, hard. One of the soldiers tried to stop the brute, who told him, in colourful language, to mind his own business. Eventually it took half a dozen of us to put a stop to it. It was sheer sadism.'

By 1990 the balance had shifted slightly. Four soldiers were jailed in December 1989 for manslaughter or homicide, but no sentence was greater than two years. Thirty-five soldiers had been charged with beating, wounding, assault or brutality, but no officer above the rank of major had been court-martialled, though some have been reprimanded and discharged.[2] In January 1990 the High Court of Justice ruled that a colonel, Yehuda Meir, should be tried for ordering soldiers to break the limbs of Palestinian prisoners, opening up the whole argument over ultimate responsibility for illegal actions. For had not the defence minister himself, Yitzhak Rabin, encouraged officers such as Colonel Meir to give such orders?[3] Other suspensions or prosecutions have taken place because alert American cameramen have produced irrefutable evidence, as in the case of a border policeman who shot dead a masked Palestinian in Bethlehem in December 1989, though whether he will be charged with homicide or merely with lying to his superiors about the circumstances is not yet clear.[4]

It irritates many Israelis that the occupation of the Territories, which some feel was forced upon them by the refusal of their Arab neighbours to negotiate for their return, is perceived entirely in terms of repression. Avi said to me: 'Israelis can understand why we get criticized for what's happening in the Territories, but what irks us is that we are never given credit for the good things we do. Like the vaccination campaign. How many other occupying powers would have done that? Our critics won't acknowledge how much we have improved conditions in the Territories. Occupation is never going to be pleasant, but I'm convinced other countries' armies would have acted far worse. And as for people complaining about our troops going into the *souks* and searching houses, well, we have to do that. We can't have no-go areas under our administration.'

The situation today was summarized for me by Haim Cohn, a highly respected retired chief justice: 'Laws are silent when cannons roar. Israelis take pride in the fact that despite the continual wars we have maintained a highly developed system of law. This still prevails within Israel. But in the Territories Israeli law doesn't apply. Military regulations and Jordanian law prevail. Military government and human rights don't go together. If you deny people self-determination, then no other rights have any bearing. Still, Israeli occupation measures up far better than the Russians or British or French in comparable situations. There have been deportations and demolitions of over 200 houses, but not a single execution. However, elections seem to show that Israelis want the government to use a stronger hand in the Territories. Someone like Sharon would do it by shooting people. Such a policy would pose the greatest danger for us, since it would usher in the demoralization of the Jewish state. So-called realists have contempt for this view. They call me a "beautiful soul" and a town idiot. I am greatly honoured by this. But I am also conscious of a splendid isolation. I have hopes on the one hand, and misgivings on the other. My hopes are that my grandchildren and great-grandchildren will live in peace in the State of Israel.'

While directing the intifada with one hand, the PLO leadership has been playing at diplomacy with the other. Whether or not Arafat is sincere in his stated willingness to renounce violence and to recognize the State of Israel is probably irrelevant at this stage. He has, for whatever reason, been making the kinds of noises the Israelis have been demanding of him for twenty years. Of course the Israelis remain deeply sceptical, but Arafat's volte-face does offer, for the first time, an opportunity to attempt to reach a negotiated peace settlement in the region. Yet a year and a half after Arafat's change of heart it remains a criminal offence for Israelis to have contacts, even outside the country, with representatives of the PLO, and in October 1989 the peace activist Abie Nathan was given a six-month jail sentence for meeting Arafat.

When I began to write this book there was talk of the Schultz plan, which proposed an international conference on the Middle East. This plan was favoured by Shimon Peres, but scuppered by his coalition partner, Prime Minister Yitzhak Shamir. Then we heard mumblings on the part of Likud politicians, including Shamir, about supporting United Nations Resolution 242 (which speaks of exchanging occupied territories for peace, but not, as foreign minister Arens never tired of pointing out, 'the' occupied territories). This came as a great surprise to many Israelis, since Shamir had denounced the resolution at the time of its passage and maintained his opposition to its provisions while the Schultz plan was being assembled, thus dooming it to failure.

Labour tried to resurrect the notion of negotiating with King Hussein, but the monarch decided in July 1988 that he wasn't going to play along. Indeed, he washed his hands of the administrative role Jordan had been playing in the West Bank and let the Israelis handle the hot potato *in toto*. As Abba Eban remarked with his customary acuity, 'We cannot force Jordan to be surrogates for the Palestinian nation.'[5] The unreality of expecting Hussein to ride to Labour's rescue by negotiating some kind of Palestinian-Jordanian federation was pointed out by Jessie Lurie in the *Jerusalem Post*: 'More than half of the residents of his kingdom are former Palestinians. They have given him a guarded loyalty in exchange for economic and political benefits. Why should he risk the precarious stability of his kingdom by adding a million and a half radicalized Palestinian nationalists and Moslem fundamentalists on the West Bank and Gaza? That would be political madness.'[6]

By the time of the 1988 elections there was talk of building on the Camp David agreement, which binds Israel to negotiate with the Palestinians and Jordanians on the basis of Resolution 242, but this also lacked conviction, since Mr Shamir had for years consistently denounced Camp David. It was all very confusing, but hardly mattered, since all the talk appeared to be a smokescreen to persuade the electorate and the world that Likud was committed to some kind of peace process. Likud ministers expressed dismay when the United States, later in 1988, gave the new improved Arafat a sympathetic, if very guarded, reception. Although the Israeli government expressed withering scepticism about Mr Arafat's change of heart, it recognized the need for *some* response. By spring 1989 Mr Shamir was off to Washington, all smiles, and the world suspected he had a plan after all.

Some time later this plan was announced. It involved elections for Arabs in the Territories, but did not specify whether they would be municipal elections or a more general poll. This was a good wheeze, since such elections didn't challenge Israeli control over the Territories. Other potentially contentious aspects of the plan were left open; for example, it was not stated whether or not the 140,000 Arabs of East Jerusalem would participate in these elections. In July 1989 Mr Shamir, without any of the struggles for which he is renowned, allowed himself to be steamrollered by Likud's right wing into attaching so many conditions to his plan that it became even more devoid of real content than it had been when announced. More fireworks, this time from the cabinet, who had voted in favour of Shamir's plan and had no intention of being superseded in their constitutional role by the likes of Ariel Sharon and David Levy. When Peres threatened to pull the Labour Party out of the coalition, Shamir shrugged his shoulders and returned to square one with his peace plan. In September, President Mubarak decided to play honest broker and devised a ten-point proposal, whereby Israel would negotiate with a Palestinian delegation in Cairo. The details need not concern us here, but once again the cabinet split down the middle, with Rabin and Peres giving the proposal a sympathetic hearing while Shamir and Arens rubbished it. The proposal was rejected, and once again, there was talk of Labour withdrawing from the coalition. Early in 1990 the coalition fell apart. In February, after a rowdy public debate with Shamir, Ariel Sharon resigned, stalking off to build a new power base outside the government. As Shamir continued to resist American attempts to facilitate negotiations with the Palestinians, Peres grew increasingly exasperated with the prime minister. In March Shamir fired Peres, and the coalition collapsed. For the first time in Israeli history, a prime minister lost a vote of confidence in the Knesset, and Shamir's ascendency within Likud was threatened. More importantly, just when Israelis had every right to expect some movement in this infinitely protracted peace process, they were saddled instead with a caretaker government and the prospect of more wheeling and dealing as the scattered jigsaw of coalition government was reassembled.

It seems fairly clear that all this talk of autonomy and limited elections was little more than a sideshow. The fundamental issues that would determine whether or not a peace settlement was likely to emerge were whether Israel would concede the principle of trading territory for peace, and whether Israel would negotiate with the only body capable of delivering a peace settlement, the Palestine Liberation Organization; even Meir Kahane admits that the PLO enjoys the overwhelming support of the Palestinians.

On the first issue, Likud said no. 'Not an inch!' was how the prime minister put it. Labour said yes. On the second issue, both Likud and Labour said no. That being the case, they then had to say who they *would* negotiate with. Labour wanted to involve the superpowers in resolving the matter. Likud argued that the only people capable of delivering a peace agreement were the parties actually in dispute; consequently, Likud began its doomed search for opposite numbers who fulfilled the condition of being Palestinian but not supporters of the PLO. Since the few Palestinian leaders who were not PLO supporters were either put out of business by Arafat or commanded no popular support, Shamir had a problem on his hands. The vague proposal for elections in the territories was partially intended to generate a team of 'acceptable' Palestinians.

Abba Eban, foreign minister from 1966 to 1974, pointed to the absurdity of the government's position: 'Diplomacy, like commerce and finance, is not a love feast. It is a conflict between divergent interests disguised as a dialogue on universal ideals. No advantage comes from the prudish flight of Israel and American officials from discourse and, if need be, confrontation with those who, in all circumstances, will be our closest neighbours.'[7] And: 'It is time to come down to earth. There are many things that we cannot do. For example, we cannot select both our negotiating team and that of our adversaries. No one in international history has ever achieved such a thing.'[8]

Other Labour Party politicians nurtured their illusions. In March 1989, one of them told me: 'By the time Shamir goes to Washington there will be a timetable. Shamir doesn't have to worry about the right wing. They're not in the coalition and Sharon is fairly isolated. The plan is likely to involve a re-partition involving some withdrawal.' (Fat chance, if Shamir's subsequent words are to be taken at face value.) 'For the Israelis to sit down with Arafat would be seen as a sign of weakness on our part, so we may have to start with more neutral Palestinians such as the American Palestinians. We can also work through local Palestinians.' At the same time he conceded that most Palestinians support the PLO, and that presumably includes the American Palestinians. If the politicians could get themselves into this kind of muddle, it was hardly surprising that the rest of us were confused.

Of course, Labour's views were not of the slightest interest to Mr Shamir. He had tucked the Labour Party into his pocket by giving the former prime minister Yitzhak Rabin the crucial job of defence minister. So while Peres was talking about peace negotiations, his colleague Mr Rabin was counselling the IDF to use beatings rather than shootings to quell the intifada. No wonder Labour did not flourish in the 1988 elections, since it spoke with an extremely forked tongue. Meanwhile, Shamir was happily painting himself into a corner. In March 1989 he told his supporters: 'The land of Israel belongs to the people of Israel and only to the people of Israel.'[9] He told the *Washington Times* that if Arafat ever came to Israel to discuss peace 'we'd put him in prison'. He urged Mr Arafat to dissolve the PLO, which, if meant seriously, was an impressively stupid remark. He directly compared Arafat to Adolf Hitler, both being 'men who think nothing of killing millions to achieve their objectives'. Millions? As for exchanging territory for peace, Shamir reiterated that this was 'nonsense'.[10] In August 1989 Shamir seemed to be impersonating a deranged ayatollah: 'Peace should and can be attained without forgoing . . . even a sliver of the pupil of our eye, the land of our forefathers, our Holy Land. Peace is not a monopoly of the traitors, those who surrender and yield.'[11]

It is possible that Shamir says one thing to please his domestic audience, especially his troublesome right wing, and another for international audiences, but I doubt it. I do not doubt Shamir's sincerity; at least his intransigence is guileless. He revels in his own obduracy and lack of imagination. As Shlomo Avineri, a former director general of the foreign ministry, wrote: 'Neither Shamir nor Arens nor Sharon is ready, willing or able to [give up control over] Judea, Samaria and Gaza. Their commitment to these areas is deep, honest and unshakeable . . . It is for this reason that they are so dangerous.'[12] Even the annual assessment presented to the cabinet by the intelligence authorities in 1989, and promptly leaked to the press and then denounced by Shamir as 'lies', favoured accepting the PLO as a negotiating partner. Meron Benvenisti sees worrying long-term consequences in Shamir's refusal to have any contact with the PLO: 'Israeli success in breaking up Palestinian unity would force them to confront a local leadership that would be even more formidable than the ageing PLO one, local leaders hardened by Israeli harassment, closely acquainted with the Israeli political system, and capable of manipulating its internal weaknesses and divisions.'[13]

What, then, are the options? One is to maintain the status quo, while offering minor concessions in the name of autonomy within the Territories. This appears to be the Likud line. Another is to pursue the notion of a Palestinian-Jordanian federation. But King Hussein himself shows no enthusiasm for the idea. Another option would be to withdraw from the Territories unilaterally, but this would violate the something-for-nothing rule; there would be no popular support for such action. Yet another option is the annexation of the Territories, as urged by Tehiya and others. This option is not as implausible as it may sound; the Golan Heights have been annexed without any great international fuss, even though the annexation has not been recognized under international law. But as a practical possibility, the intifada, while strengthening the hand of the annexationists, has also weakened it, for there can be little doubt that the Palestinian response to annexation would be far from docile; international opinion, for what it's worth, would also be condemnatory. The advantage of annexation, as Haetzni argued, is that the Palestinians would know where they stood, and all talk of a Palestinian state west of the Jordan would be at an end. Annexation would also increase Israel's Arab population by 1,500,000 souls, and the nightmares of those who fear the eventual demographic extinction of the Jewish state would come much closer to realization. Annexation might also trigger a war with Arab neighbours.

For the moment it seems that the status quo will persist. 'Many Israelis,' one reservist told me, 'support the idea of not returning the Territories. I've stood in Kalkiya on the West Bank and I could see Tel Aviv from there. The sea is only nine miles away. It makes you think that it's better that we stand there than the Palestinians.' Others insist that the PLO has not changed, despite Arafat's protestations, and that the existence of a Palestinian state alongside Israel is simply unthinkable. Such Israelis do not want to hang on to the Territories because they are hungry for more land or anxious to rule over rebellious Arabs, but because they find the alternative even more alarming. Time and again I would hear: 'Israelis are for peace, but we just don't trust the other side. We don't trust the Jordanians or the Syrians. Liberal intellectuals can muster all the arguments they want, but most Israelis don't trust the intellectuals either.' Gillian Hundt thought that 'many, perhaps the majority, of Israelis are intellectually aware that the occupation is wrong, but the psychological fear of giving it up is so great that they feel paralysed.'

On the other hand many Israelis long to see the problem solved and were wildly frustrated by the government's manoeuvres. The novelist A. B. Yehoshua said to me: 'I would never have believed in my life that half of the people are praying that the United States, please, should put more pressure on Israel to negotiate with the Arabs and get rid of the Territories. The Palestinians are ready, Egypt is at peace, but the Americans are so slow!' Even among Israelis prepared to grant Palestinian self-determination there is a further worry: *al awda*, 'the return'. It has not escaped notice that the Palestinian programme is modelled on its Zionist precursor. The Palestinian Declaration of Independence contains entire paragraphs lifted from Israel's Proclamation of Independence. That matters little, but what disturbs Israelis more is the Palestinian adoption of the Zionist principle of the 'Ingathering of the Exiles', namely, that any Jew has the right to come and live in Israel. It does seem anomalous that a Jew who has lived in New York all his life has the right to 'return' to Israel, while a Palestinian whose family actually lived in, say, Jaffa till 1948 has no such right. The consequence of a Palestinian Law of Return in some newly established Palestinian state is the theoretical possibility of that state becoming home not only to the two million Palestinians now under Israel's control, but to the five million Palestinians dispersed worldwide. Now that would be the demographic argument with a vengeance.

Amnon Ahi-Nomi tried to find some order among this chaos of response: 'You can divide both sides into dreamers and realists. Dreamers are people who want the whole cake. Their extreme acts bolster the views of the dreamers on the other side. For realists it's harder. Arab realists have to worry about being regarded as Quislings. Jewish realists have to contend with being patronized as "beautiful souls". Every Israeli has two fundamental fears. The first is physical annihilation. The second is having another million and a half Arabs within our borders, the fear of having to deal with a huge and unfriendly minority. The question then is: which are you more afraid of? Israelis have made their choices, and that is why the country is split fifty-fifty.

'Almost all Israelis desperately want peace. About six hundred songs are written or published in Israel each year. Many are about peace, others are love songs. None are warlike. Our military marches are borrowed from Russian and other sources – we haven't written any of our own. Even Israelis who are warmongers are that way out of a terrible fear: in their hearts they yearn for peace but don't see it as a possibility any longer. Even Sharon hoped for peace in Lebanon by installing a Christian government with which we could make a deal. It didn't work, but he wanted peace as a long-term goal. Once you've chosen between your two fears, you then have to explain the other away. That's why arguments about peace plans take place between Israelis and other Israelis, not between us and the Arabs.'

Amnon was optimistic about the chances of achieving peace. (Truly pessimistic Israelis have long ago taken one-way flights to Europe or Los Angeles.) 'Israel will make peace if an opportunity presents itself. Before Begin and Sadat made peace I was saying – because I'm an incorrigible optimist – that there would be peace between us and Egypt, but it was probably fifty years off. Everyone thought I was nuts, and when Begin and Sadat signed, no one was more astonished than me. Suddenly peace had become a realistic option, and for domestic political reasons Begin and Sadat had to take it. In the process Begin gave away our oil, which we now have to buy back from Egypt. He gave away empty land three times the size of Israel. Sinai was much more important to us than the West Bank is. Israelis loved Sinai, everyone went there. We thirsted for love from Egypt, but for Egypt it was just an arrangement. Of course it wasn't in their interest to become too intimate with us. If they wanted brotherhood, there were more obvious places to look than Israel. But anyway, should another possibility of peace present itself, it will be taken. There are all sorts of scenarios. It could be Hussein who comes to us if he feels his throne is threatened. A worse scenario is another war. Now that Iraq and Iran are no longer fighting each other, we worry that Iraq and Syria might form a military alliance against us. Or perhaps the Palestinians will overthrow Hussein and suggest a treaty with Israel with the West Bank as a DMZ. Who knows? You want fiction? I can give you a library full.'

Dr Moshe Dror took a robust and more idiosyncratic view of Israel's plight: 'Israel has lost its consensus and lost its spirit. That's why people are leaving the country in droves. We've lost our vision. All this argument about more territory in a desert in the Middle East – big deal! All it does is generate tremendous tension, which we take out on the Arabs. Kill an Arab a day! That's the way it's worked out since the intifada began. It's good that we have the Arabs to take things out on. If they weren't around, the focus of all that tension would be other Jews. After 4,000 years of Jewish history, this is what we've come to? Israel used to be the

David battling Goliath. Now it's become the Goliath, and it's not just hostile foreigners who believe that – many Israelis believe it too. Perhaps peace is a chimera. There were very few periods in biblical times when Jews were at peace – why should they be now?'

Echoing Stef Wertheimer's view, he continued: 'The United States should cut off aid to Israel. It would cause great trauma, but we would at least stop being a *shnorrer* state. Those who live off others become infantilized and it's time we grew up and learnt to stand on our own feet. Because of our shortage of resources, everybody feels screwed. It's not only a question of funds, but of good will. People will give their time and their energy if there's a vision, a why – and the vision is dwindling. There's some hope in that the whole system is collapsing,' he said, waxing apocalyptic, 'then it will have to regenerate, reorganize itself, or die. Look at Europe. Two devastating world wars, and now, unbelievably, Europe is more or less united. Perhaps Israel needs the same kind of shock, though not, let's hope, a war. The problem is that Israel has been too successful in its military involvements. But what happens if one day the army should lose, or if, as began to happen in Lebanon in 1982, the price for victory is too high? We have to realize that the gap in military capability between Israel and the Arab nations is shrinking. People do worry about the next war. After all, where I live in Dimona we're in the back yard of the atomic bomb factory. Everyone knew what was going on here before Vanunu spilled the beans. People discuss possible scenarios. What's thrown a spanner in the works is that in the past few years the hero of the world has switched from being Reagan to Gorbachev. This was totally unforeseeable. The whole notion of good guys and bad guys that underpinned the international relations of the entire world has been thrown into confusion.'

The Jewish people are required by their religious belief to be 'a light unto the nations', to set an example in matters ethical and moral. Many secular Jews also accept that injunction as a central element in Jewish culture. For most of their history, Jews have been a peaceable lot, rarely drawn to such authoritarian and potentially violent professions as the army or the police. Once a Jewish state was founded, all that had to change. Jews were obliged, like any other nation state, to take up weapons and police the streets; a succession of wars turned them into brilliant soldiers. A nation of persecuted people finds itself engaged in vigorous trade with a government wedded to racial oppression, that of South Africa. The Israelis can't survive by dispensing with aggression, but there is disquiet that the old requirement to be 'a light unto the nations' seems to have been tossed aside. Many Israelis welcome this. Eliakim Haetzni said: 'Jews are *not* better than other people. It is far better that people think of us as normal people.' Amos Oz, back in 1983, summarized the conflict as follows: 'With one hand we waved very high-flown moral arguments, and with the other we asked for an international licence for savagery and a permit for cruelty and oppression, "like everyone else".'[14] Perhaps the two positions are not irreconcilable. There is no reason why Jews should be especially saintly. Christians, whose religion has as strong an ethical foundation as Judaism, have a sorry record when it comes to tolerance and respect for human life. But while accepting that Jews are as subject to human frailty as any other people, it is still possible to argue that that is no reason to abandon the aim of being 'a light unto the nations', despite the priggish overtones of the injunction.

It is the very normality of Israeli life, even though it comes in an unusually frenzied version, that strikes the visitor. The diaspora Jew will either respond by saying: 'Isn't this wonderful! At last, a place where Jews are not just merchants and lawyers, but where they fill all the social roles, from policemen to farmers and lifeguards. Here, and only here, can the Jew escape from all the stereotypes that centuries of ghettoization and persecution have created.' And the alternative response is: 'In Israel we find Jews performing all the tasks you'd expect in a modern nation. They are not only scholars and violinists and doctors but airline pilots and interrogators for the secret police. Jews have become indistinguishable from any other Mediterranean people. All those decades of Zionism and the splendid egalitarian ideals of the pioneers, and what do they have to show for it? Tel Aviv.' I confess my own response veers towards the second. I do not experience a warming of the heart because I am surrounded by other Jews. Of course I have the good fortune to live in a country that, despite the occasional lapse, is a model of tolerance and acceptance of Jews. Were I a refugee from Iran or Ethiopia I would feel very differently, moving from a society of constraint to one of freedom.

Israel exists because it needed to. Those who question the right of Israel to exist are often the same people who closed or severely narrowed their frontiers to Jews, both during the Nazi persecutions and after the war. The moral imperative for the establishment of a Jewish homeland became overwhelming, and even the Soviet Union supported the founding of Israel. Nevertheless the very notion of a Jewish homeland or Jewish state makes me profoundly uncomfortable. I have no idea what it is that I as a Jew belong to. If it's defined exclusively by its religion, then I'm no Jew. But I don't intend to be dispossessed of my heritage by that kind of argument. It's certainly not a race, and I don't understand in what sense it's a nation. I am a British Jew, and if I wish I can move to Jerusalem and become an Israeli Jew; but that wouldn't make me more Jewish, or alter my sense of Jewish identity.

The Jews are a people, diversified by centuries of dispersal. I do have things in common with some but not all Jews from other lands: similar values and traditions, and a collective memory. Yet when I arrive in Israel, I do not feel that I have come home. It may be deplorable, but I feel more at home, outside my own country, in Avignon or Siena than I do in Haifa. A. B. Yehoshua, who regards the diaspora Jew as a pale shadow of the Jew in Israel – or as he would see it, the Jew in history – would no doubt say that all this puzzlement would cease if I took the simple step of moving to Israel, where I would automatically attain what he calls 'total Jewishness'. I, however, am perfectly content to settle for less and remain where I am.

I am lucky that I do not need Israel, though Eliakim Haetzni and other Israelis seem convinced that new waves of antisemitism could hit countries such as the United States and Britain and shatter the complacency of diaspora Jews such as myself. Iranian and Ethiopian Jews, among many others, however, do need Israel and I am thankful that it exists. But when I speak to Palestinians I am mindful that the state came into existence at a terrible cost. It is very easy to belittle Palestinian nationalism as a Johnny come lately, and Haeztni is right to see it as a kind of mirror image or shadow; for ironically it is 'Israel' that has defined 'Palestine'. Yet there are five million people who can claim that this stretch of the Middle East is just as much their home as it is the home of the Jews, and I find that claim hard to resist. There are Jews who feel a profound rootedness in Israel. After 2,000 years they have returned and, like Theo Siebenberg, they dig in their basements and find inscriptions and ritual objects that could still be used today. This is a unique state of affairs, and one to marvel at.

But the land that Israel fills is not, as many early Zionists wanted to believe, a *tabula rasa*, and the tragic failure to recognize this fact is largely responsible for the desperate position in which Israel finds itself today. The Jews may have been dismissive in their nationalism and arrogant in their triumphs, but the Arabs have much to answer for too. If there were prizes for pig-headedness, the Arab leaders of the first half of this century would be strong contenders. Their refusal to make any accommodation with the Jews of Palestine, many of whom had been living there under mostly Moslem rule for centuries, was disastrous, especially since in 1947 they could have accepted a partition plan that would have given them more land than they can ever expect in the future even under the most generous of peace settlements.

Nevertheless, the establishment of the State of Israel was potentially disastrous, since it left two peoples in dispute over the identical territory. To such a situation there is no definitive solution; there is only submission. Even though one can argue that the establishment of Israel was, despite all the imperatives that lay behind it, an act of injustice towards the Palestinians, Israel is not going to disappear. The more bloodthirsty the threats against Israel from certain corners of the Arab world, the more determined are the Israelis to stay put. An accommodation is essential, not only to restore peace to the region, but to restore peace of mind, peace of soul. The stress of perpetual military alert is tremendous. It shows in relatively trivial matters such as lousy driving and blunt manners, but it also shows in an ugliness of mood that appears to be worsening. The elements of racism in Israeli life – decried by the political establishment but given a new lease of life, a new intensification, every time an Arab terrorist kills an Israeli – are hideous to encounter, if only because the Jews, of all people, know what it means to be at the receiving end of racial hatred. When demonstrators roam the streets shouting 'Kill Arabs!', Jews everywhere are besmirched.

An accommodation must be found because the price of failure is too high. Pictures of Arabs being buried in the sand by Israeli soldiers, however sorely provoked; of Arab children being shot, even by stray bullets; of politicians such as Sharon calling for the assassination of Arafat; of settlers whose grandparents were loaded into cattle trucks on their way to death speaking glibly of 'transferring' Arabs who inconvenience their sense of destiny – none of this has any connection with the Judaism I was taught or with the Jewish culture and tradition from which I still draw nourishment. I can understand why some Jews, in their determination to survive as a nation, act and speak in ways I find utterly alien, but such talk and such actions lessen rather than intensify my sense of Jewish identification. I stand in Hebron and I wonder: how can we have come to this? This is the city of David, and all I see are guns and all I smell, from the *souk* as from the synagogue, is hatred.

Perhaps Eliakim Haeztni is correct when he says that a formal solution is impossible and that a *modus vivendi* is the best that can be hoped for. Amnon Ahi-Nomi, who presumably shares none of Haetzni's views, also told me: 'There is no simple solution. All choices are unsatisfactory. And that is why Israelis are so impatient with foreigners' oversimplifications.' But in the rhetoric of the Israeli right, I not only hear contempt for any peace process but discern no impetus to bring this whole terrible business to an end. The status quo is not the same as a *modus vivendi*. It is not for diaspora Jews to tell the Israelis whether or not they should talk to the PLO, though I believe they should, but if the alternative, as it seems, is to

346 · WINNER TAKES ALL

do nothing, then the alternative is also a formula for disaster, for it is the Palestinians who have taken the initiative. Tear gas and bullets solve nothing. Sadat came to Jerusalem. Why does it seem so hopelessly inconceivable that Arafat should ever do the same?

I read what I am writing as I write it, and I groan as I seem to flounder in a wash of words. The problems seem too great, the will to solve them too feeble, and my own prescriptions altogether inadequate. The scenarios for the future – whether Amnon Ahi-Nomi's library of them, or another friend's prediction that there will be another war 'if the Arabs push us too far' – are all too terrible to contemplate. I came away from Israel with relief. I found the country bewildering but never less than fascinating in its diversity. Encounters with a great variety of Israelis proved stimulating and studded with intellectual surprise. I marvelled at the cultural richness of the country. But in the end the tensions, while providing fuel for my paragraphs, proved too much. Israel, still promoted as a haven for the troubled diaspora, exists in a state of such nail-biting insecurity that most Jews still fleeing from oppression – such as Russian Jews – put Zion on their list as a last resort. No doubt I exposed myself to tensions more than pleasures: you can't write a book about sunbathing in Netanya. The demolished Bedouin houses; the guns on the dashboard; the young father on leave from reserve duty taking his children for a walk with his Uzi slung across his shoulder; murderous soldiers pardoned and walking free just days before Abie Nathan bagan a jail sentence for meeting Arafat; the ugly rhetoric of Kahane and his intellectual bedfellows; the prime minister- ial contempt for those whose only offence was to ache for peace; the realization that for every passionate undoubting Eliakim Haetzni in the hills of Judea there is an equally passionate undoubting Palestinian Arab in the valley below; the bloody-mindedness of the *menorah* raised on a rooftop in the Moslem heart of Jerusalem's Old City; the stones and the anger of those who claim to be the guardians of the Jewish faith – the intensity of it all was too much.

Slowly the great dream seems to be turning into nightmare. The situation is not irretrievable, but time is not on the Israelis' side. With every month that passes the price of survival becomes higher. If at the end of the day Israel becomes indistinguishable in its motivations and cruelties and oppressions from any other hard-pressed nation, so that *realpolitik* becomes the norm and ancient ideals become dispensable, then it is hard to imagine what hold such a nation is going to have on the loyalty not only of the Jews of the diaspora, but of the world at large.

# NOTES

**Abbreviations**
*JP*: *Jerusalem Post.*
*JPI*: *Jerusalem Post International Edition.*

**Chapter 1: Nuns and Knights**
1. David K. Shipler, *Arab and Jew* (London: Penguin, 1987), p. 175.

**Chapter 2: Souk and Wall**
1. A. B. Yehoshua, *The Continuing Silence of a Poet* (London: Peter Halban, 1988), p. 32.
2. *JP*, 16 December 1987.
3. *JP*, 17 December 1987.
4. Quoted in Peter Gay, *Freud: A Life for Our Time* (London: Dent, 1988), p. 598.

**Chapter 6: Torah, Torah, Torah!**
1. *JPI*, 4 February 1989.
2. Abraham Rabinovitch, 'Soul on Fire', *JP*, 22 May 1987.
3. Abraham Rabinovitch, 'Army of the Lord', *JP*, 20 February 1987.
4. Micha Odenheimer, 'A Society in Flux', *JPI*, 14 January 1989.
5. Abraham Rabinovitch, 'Dynasty in Black', *JP*, 27 May 1982.
6. *Jewish Chronicle*, 18 March 1988.
7. Abraham Rabinovitch, 'Soul on Fire'.
8. Dow Marmur, *Beyond Survival* (London: Darton, Longman & Todd, 1982), p. 53.
9. Amos Oz, *In the Land of Israel* (London: Fontana, 1983), p. 136.

**Chapter 7: Among the Patriarchs**
1. *JP*, 30 March 1989.
2. *JPI*, 25 February 1989.
3. Shipler, *Arab and Jew*, p. 103.

## Chapter 8: Facts on the Ground
1. Robert I. Friedman, 'The Settlers', *New York Review of Books*, 15 June 1989.
2. *JPI*, 15 July 1989.


## Chapter 9: Quid Pro Quo
1. *JPI*, 3 December 1988.
2. Charles Richards, *Independent*, 1 October 1989.
3. Benny Morris, 'Laughter in the Dark', *JP*, 24 March 1989.
4. Yoel Cohen, 'Journalists and Soldiers', *IDF Journal*, Vol III, No 2, p. 67.
5. *JPI*, 5 August 1989.
6. *JP*, 2 March 1989.
7. *JP*, 28 March 1989.
8. *JP*, 31 March 1989.
9. *Jewish Chronicle*, 7 April 1989.
10. Amos Elon, *The Israelis* (Tel Aviv: Adam, 1981), p. 295.
11. Michael Yudelman, *JP*, 21 October 1988.
12. Stef Wertheimer, *JP*, 19 January 1987.


## Chapter 10: The Voodoo Factor
1. *JPI*, 17 December 1988.


## Chapter 11: Mozart on the Fish Farm
1. Daniel Gavron, 'Putting the Kibbutz House in Order', *JP*, 10 March 1989.
2. Elon, *The Israelis*, p. 243.
3. Ibid., p. 317.
4. Ibid., pp. 318–19.


## Chapter 12: Which Way to Tubas?
1. *JP*, 6 March 1989.
2. *JP*, 7 March 1989.
3. *Jewish Chronicle*, 24 June 1988.
4. Shlomo Maoz, *JP*, 10 March 1989.


## Chapter 13: Remembering the Names
1. *JPI*, 22 July 1989.
2. Jalal Abu-Ta'ama, in Hareven, *Every Sixth Israeli* (Jerusalem: Van Leer Foundation, 1983), p. 52.

## Chapter 14: Water on Stone

1. Elon, *The Israelis*, pp. 252–3.

## Chapter 15: Cool Chicks

1. Daniel Gavron, *JPI*, 18 February 1989.
2. *JP*, 6 March 1989.
3. *JPI*, 19 August 1989.

## Chapter 16: Sheikspeare

1. Quoted in Conor Cruise O'Brien, *The Siege* (London: Weidenfeld & Nicolson, 1986), p. 175.
2. Elon, *The Israelis*, p. 324.
3. Shipler, *Arab and Jew*, p. 339.
4. Rafi Israeli, in Hareven, *Every Sixth Israeli*, p. 173.
5. Shipler, *Arab and Jew*, p. 439.
6. Majid Al-Hajj, 'The ABC's of Arab Education', *New Outlook*, April 1987.
7. David Arnow, *JP*, 2 April 1989.
8. Rafi Israeli, in Hareven, *Every Sixth Israeli*, p. 172.
9. *JP*, 31 March 1989.
10. Anton Shammas, in Hareven, *Every Sixth Israeli*, p. 43.
11. Marda Dunsky, *JP*, 29 March 1989.
12. *JP*, 10 March 1989.
13. *JP*, 12 March 1989.
14. Oz Frankel, *JP*, 10 March 1989.
15. Marda Dunsky, *JP*, 21 December 1988.
16. *JP*, 31 March 1989.
17. Rafi Israeli, in Hareven, *Every Sixth Israeli*, p. 169.

## Chapter 17: A Camel Called Hans

1. Yehoshua, *The Continuing Silence of a Poet*, p. 1.
2. Amos Oz, *Late Love* (London: Fontana, 1986), p. 119.

## Chapter 18: Three Square Books a Day

1. *JPI*, 9 September 1989.
2. Elon, *The Israelis*, p. 127.

## Chapter 19: Coming and Going

1. Jon Immanuel, *JP*, 21 October 1988.
2. Sammy Smooha, *Israel* (London: Routledge & Kegan Paul, 1978), p. 88.

3. Shipler, *Arab and Jew*, p. 241.
4. *JPI*, 18 February 1989.
5. *JP*, 2 February 1989.
6. *JP*, 3 March 1989.
7. *JP*, 20 March 1989.
8. *JP*, 21 March 1989.
9. *Jewish Quarterly*, Autumn 1988, pp. 45–6.

**Chapter 20: Mongongos for All**
1. Shipler, *Arab and Jew*, p. 432.

**Chapter 22: Doorkeepers and Tentdwellers**
1. *JP*, 19 October 1987.
2. Elaine Ruth Fletcher, *JP*, 9 September 1988.
3. Rafi Israeli, in Hareven, *Every Sixth Israeli*, p. 183.
4. Yehoshuah Porath, in Hareven, *Every Sixth Israeli*, p. 211.
5. *JPI*, 1 July 1989.
6. *JP*, 18 January 1989.

**Chapter 23: The Town That Got Away**
1. Numbers XX: 4–5.

**Chapter 25: Unravelling**
1. *JPI*, 25 February 1989.

**Chapter 26: Little Red Riding Hood**
1. *JP*, 9 June 1987.
2. *JP*, 29 June 1988.
3. Quoted in Shipler, *Arab and Jew*, p. 150.

**Chapter 27: The Long Fuse**
1. Meron Benvenisti, 'The Morning After', *JP*, 22 February 1989.
2. *JPI*, 9 December 1989.
3. *JPI*, 6 January 1990.
4. *JPI*, 27 January 1990.
5. *JP*, 3 March 1989.
6. *JP*, 6 March 1989.
7. Abba Eban, 'The Threats Are From Within', *JPI*, 3 December 1988.
8. Abba Eban, 'Time to Renounce Illusions', *JP*, 3 March 1989.
9. *JP*, 6 March 1989.
10. *JP*, 2 March 1989.

11. *JPI*, 5 August 1989.
12. *JP*, 25 October 1988.
13. *JP*, 22 February 1989.
14. Oz, *In the Land of Israel*, p. 143.

# GLOSSARY

Aliyah: Jewish emigration to Israel

Barmitzvah: religious ceremony by which males take on the responsibilities of Jewish observance

Beth Din: rabbinical court

Daven: the act of prayer, often accompanied by swaying movements

Dunam: a quarter-acre

Haredi (pl. haredim): ultra-Orthodox

Kibbutz: co-operative agricultural settlement in which all property is communally owned

Kippa (pl. kippot): skull-cap

Kolel: religious academy for married Orthodox men

Mechitzah: screen dividing men and women at Orthodox gatherings

Menorah: ritual candelabrum

Mezuzah (pl. mezuzot): small tube containing religious texts attached to a doorpost

Mikveh: ritual bath used by women for purification

Mitnagdim: followers of the anti-Chasidic ultra-Orthodox movement

Mitzvah (pl. mitzvot): religious commandment or obligation

Moshav: co-operative rural settlement which allows for individual enterprise within a communal framework

Mukhtar: Arab village headman

Olim: immigrants

Payot: sidelocks

Rebbe: leader of a Chasidic court

Sabra: native-born Israeli

Sheitel: wig

Shiva: period of mourning

Shul: synagogue

Talmud: cumulative rabbinic commentaries on Scripture and Jewish law

Toraj: teaching; the Pentateuch

Yarmulke: skull-cap

Yerida: emigration from Israel

Yeshiva: academy for rabbinic studies

Yordim: emigrants from Israel

# INDEX